The U.S. Army and Counterinsurgency in the Philippine War, 1899–1902

To James & Kathleen Linn
and
Robert & Shirley Kamins

The U.S. Army and Counterinsurgency in the Philippine War, 1899–1902

Brian McAllister Linn

The University of North Carolina Press
Chapel Hill and London

Library of Congress Cataloging-in-Publication Data

Linn, Brian McAllister.
  The U.S. Army and counterinsurgency in the Philippine war,
1899–1902 / Brian McAllister Linn.
     p. cm.
  Bibliography: p.
  Includes index.
  ISBN 0-8078-1834-8
    1. Philippines—History—Insurrection, 1899–1901. 2. United
States. Army—History. 3. Counterinsurgency—Philippines.
I. Title.
DS682.A2 1989   88-20741
959.9′031—dc19   CIP

The paper in this book meets the guidelines for permanence and durability of the Committee on Production Guidelines for Book Longevity of the Council on Library Resources.

Printed in the United States of America

93 92 91 90 89   5 4 3 2 1

Portions of Chapter 2 appeared in *Military Affairs* 51 (April 1987), and a condensed version of Chapter 3 appeared in *Kansas History* 10 (Spring 1987).

Design by Julianne Mertz Whitling

THIS BOOK WAS DIGITALLY MANUFACTURED.

Contents

A section of photographs can be found following page 86.

Maps

Preface

Historians have traditionally attempted to analyze the U.S. Army's counterinsurgency campaign in the Philippines between 1899 and 1902 through an archipelago-wide perspective. Whether they emphasize benevolence or brutality, Tagalog rebellion or national liberation struggle, scholars have viewed the Army's activities as uniform during the conflict. Despite its general acceptance, there are key weaknesses in this viewpoint. Philippine scholars have already demonstrated that Filipino guerrilla resistance varied from island to island, and even from province to province, in its origins, character, and ideology. Faced with such a disparate foe, an obvious question is whether the Army did not adapt its tactics and methods to the war in the provinces. A further weakness is the assumption that the official Army policies, whether benevolent or repressive, were followed by soldiers in the field. Yet in the Philippines the American combat forces were scattered in some 400 small garrisons, often isolated from each other by terrain or lack of communications facilities. Whereas Army headquarters in Manila could draw up guidelines and issue orders, it lacked the capacity to insure they were followed. Finally, the archipelago-wide perspective leads to a tendency to concentrate upon one or two campaigns or incidents as typifying Army conduct without asking whether these might reflect special circumstances not found in the rest of the islands.

This book will analyze the actual conduct of U.S. Army counterinsurgency operations in the countryside. It focuses on the guerrilla war in four districts on the main island of Luzon and concentrates on both military and nonmilitary aspects of pacification. The book covers the leadership, strength, policies, and tactics of the guerrilla opposition as well as the establishment of civil government, Filipino police forces, Native Scout and auxiliary units, and local intelligence networks. However, it is primarily a military history concerned with U.S. Army operations and policies at the local level. The focus is thus on how American soldiers developed and implemented pacification policies and methods designed to deal with specific conditions in their immediate areas.

Throughout this work I have made decisions on terms and names which require some explanation. Philippine War refers to the period between 4 February 1899 and 4 July 1902 when active military hostilities existed between the U.S. Army and Filipino nationalist forces. This term is chosen because the usually accepted titles such as the Philippine Insurrection, Philippine-American War, and Filipino-American War are unsatisfactory. The Philippine Insurrection suggests a rebellion against a constituted authority when in fact the war broke out before the United States exercised control beyond the city of Manila. The Philippine-American War and Filipino-American War suggest a war between two nations or two peoples, neither of which is applicable. My application of the terms *principalía* and *principales* to the provincial Filipino socioeconomic elite follows that of American soldiers who were there at the time. Although this may cause some uneasiness among Philippine historians, for whom the status and composition of this class is a matter of great controversy, I believe that the definition is adequate for a work that focuses on the U.S. Army. In an effort to avoid confusion I have used, wherever possible, the spelling of Filipino personal and place names used in contemporary American sources, but, on the advice of Philippine scholars, I have removed the accent marks. I have also, again at the urging of my colleagues in Philippine studies, used the term *revolutionary* rather than the contemporary Army term of *insurrecto*, to describe those Filipinos who forcibly resisted American occupation. I have used the terms *partisans* and *regulars* to refer to guerrillas who belonged to permanent military units and devoted the majority of their time to fighting the Americans. Although I would be the first to admit that the distinction between full-time and part-time guerrillas was often negligible, on the whole I believe that it is valid.

Because this book is about the U.S. Army's reaction to the challenge of Filipino guerrilla war, in nearly all cases I have chosen to use the translations of captured revolutionary documents made by American officers serving in the Philippines rather than providing my own. Many of the original revolutionary documents are either lost or, for a variety of reasons ranging from exposure to poor microfilming, virtually unreadable. In those cases where the original documents or microfilms are available in Spanish, I have compared Army translations against my own. Because I do not read any Filipino languages, I was totally dependent on U.S. Army translations for materials in Bicol, Tagalog, or Ilocano. I recognize that relying on documents that have passed through the hands of unsympathetic translators as a basis for an examination of Filipino guerrilla warfare is a hazardous course. However, both my weaknesses as a translator and my emphasis on the U.S. Army's reaction to Filipino resistance leads me to believe that this is the best of several alternatives.

In any issue as controversial as the American occupation of the Philippines, the scholar's own perspective becomes important. Since this work relies heavily on Army operational records and personal papers, it is possible that the views of the officers and men serving in the provinces may have colored my own perceptions. This book should not be taken as a justification for the American annexation of the Philippines or of the Army's conduct. As I have indicated, there were clear instances when Army policies were unnecessarily harsh and when soldiers were guilty of atrocities. At the same time, I have uncovered little evidence to support those who believe that the U.S. occupation of the Philippines was little more than an orgy of racism and atrocities. Rather, the Army responded in a wide variety of ways, both successful and unsuccessful, to the differing challenges it faced. It is this diversity, both in the Filipino resistance and the American response, that makes the Philippine War so fascinating.

Acknowledgments

I wish to express my sincere appreciation to my friend and mentor, Allan R. Millett, who constantly encouraged my research in the Philippine War. Among my many excellent teachers at the Ohio State University, Kenneth J. Andrien and Williamson Murray were outstanding. Research for this book was conducted under the auspices of a U.S. Army Center of Military History Dissertation Year Fellowship and a grant from the U.S. Army Military History Institute. David Trask, Lt. Col. Robert K. Griffith, and Edgar Raines of the Center of Military History and Richard Sommers of the Military History Institute went out of their respective ways to provide support and advice. The majority of my research was conducted at the National Archives and I owe its archivists and staff, particularly those in the Old Military Records Division, a great debt. The Library of Congress, Duke University, the Ohio State University, and University of Michigan library staffs were also of great aid in obtaining documents and suggesting possible sources for study. Jean Klieger provided comfortable surroundings and Anne and Christopher Jay a warm and friendly refuge during the time I was in Washington, D.C. My fellow graduate students at the Ohio State University often served as patient listeners at softball games and watering holes. Carl Boyd and my colleagues at the Old Dominion University offered a collegial atmosphere during the time when this manuscript was going through its final stages. Francis E. Lindsay spent a great deal of time and energy creating readable maps. Particular thanks are due to Larry Yates, Glenn A. May, Norman Owen, and John M. Gates who read portions of this work and improved it greatly by their comments and suggestions. My wife, Diane Linn, my father, James R. Linn, and my mother-in-law, Shirley Kamins, provided honest and supportive editing on the complete manuscript. Lewis Bateman and the staff of the University of North Carolina Press have provided many useful suggestions. Finally, I have a tremendous debt to my family who have had to put up with the Philippine War much longer than the U.S. Army.

The U.S. Army and Counterinsurgency in the Philippine War, 1899–1902

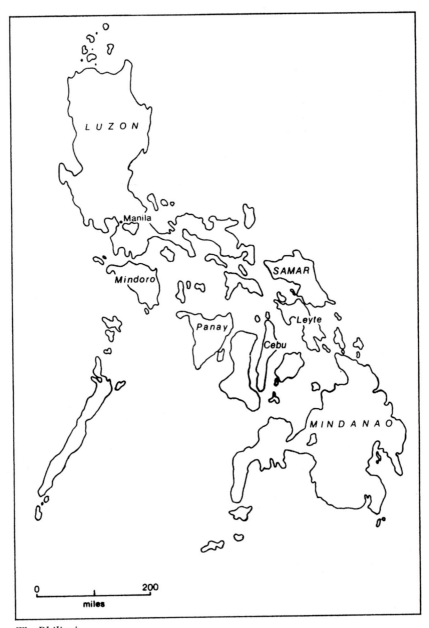

The Philippines

1

The Philippine War

In the early hours of 1 May 1898, a few days after the outbreak of the Spanish-American War, Commodore George Dewey pounded the obsolescent Spanish fleet into submission in Manila Bay. Dewey's triumph touched off a wave of national rejoicing in the United States among a population that would have been hard pressed to locate the Philippines on a map. Although antiexpansionists would have preferred that Dewey should have then turned and sailed away, he instead pondered how best to exploit his victory. The Battle of Manila Bay made the U.S. Navy supreme in the archipelago's waters, but the capital city of Manila was still held by the Spanish. Dewey believed he could force the city to surrender, and he requested a small U.S. Army force to occupy it. His views paralleled the thinking of the administration of President William McKinley, and on 2 May, long before the magnitude of the Spanish defeat was known, McKinley directed that a military expedition be sent to the archipelago.

The decision to send U.S. ground forces to the Philippines entailed commitments that would spread far beyond the simple task of preparing troops for overseas service. The Battle of Manila Bay had opened a number of military and political possibilities, and McKinley hesitated to commit himself irrevocably to one course. In the words of Graham Cosmas, the president believed that war was "an uncontrollable process that, once entered upon, dictated its own course and results. The statesman could do little but ride the whirlwind and cope with the chaos it left behind."[1] Sending ground forces to Manila allowed McKinley the flexibility both to exploit a temporary windfall and to act on future developments. At the least, the capture of Manila would be one more lever to compel Spain to accept peace in Cuba. At the most, the expedition could also serve as the vanguard for the permanent American occupation of the Philippines. To McKinley, the advantages of keeping his future choices open more than outweighed the complaints of the subordinates who had to execute his vague policies. When the commander of the expedition, Maj. Gen. Wesley Merritt, bluntly asked McKinley whether it was his "desire to subdue and hold all of the Spanish territory in the islands, or merely to seize and hold the capital," the president declined to comment.[2]

McKinley's 19 May instructions to Merritt reflect his desire to keep his options open. The president informed Merritt that the expedition had the "twofold purpose of completing the reduction of the Spanish power and of giving order and security to the islands while in the possession of the United States." It is clear that McKinley viewed the latter objective as the more important of the two. He passed briefly over military strategy and devoted most of his attention to effect the "severance of the former political relations on the inhabitants and the establishment of a new political power" in the archipelago. He instructed Merritt to maintain a military occupation and to acquaint the Filipinos with the benefits of American government; the soldiers had come "not to make war upon the people of the Philippines" but to protect them and secure their rights. He insisted that the military occupation "be as free from severity as possible." Yet at the same time, Merritt's powers were "absolute and supreme and immediately [to] operate upon the political condition of the inhabitants." Merritt had the right to levy taxes, seize private property necessary for military purposes, and control the ports. Moreover, only those Filipinos who recognized the authority of the United States were eligible to hold political office. The president's orders thus not only encompassed the immediate goal of defeating the Spanish but also provided the U.S. Army with the future basis for a colonial government in the Philippines.[3]

Whatever its ultimate role, Merritt's expedition assembled in San Francisco with commendable dispatch. One of the Union's "boy-generals" in the Civil War, he had further distinguished himself campaigning against the Indians and as superintendent of the U.S. Military Academy. He assembled a capable and efficient staff, including his second in command, Maj. Gen. Elwell S. Otis. To his displeasure, the majority of his forces consisted of volunteers from the western states, who, although enthusiastic, were undisciplined and lacked much of the equipment they would need for tropical service. Merritt had them camp near San Francisco and turned his considerable administrative talents to providing the necessary training and supplies. Although he was successful in many of his efforts, Merritt was hampered by a War Department ill-prepared for a major war. He was not able to obtain all the U.S. Army regular units he wanted and transportation shortages forced him to dispatch his army piecemeal. His men steamed off to the tropics in heavy wool clothing, equipped largely with obsolete black-powder Spring-field rifles instead of the modern Krag-Jorgensons. Despite these problems, the first brigade of 2,500 men under Brig. Gen. Thomas M. Anderson left San Francisco on 25 May. A month later, when Merritt sailed, 10,600 American soldiers were either en route or had already arrived in the Philippines.[4]

The archipelago that the Americans embarked for consists of some 7,000 islands with a total area of 115,026 square miles. Half of its population, which then stood at over 7 million, lives on Luzon, the largest island, and the site of the capital city of Manila. Luzon's 40,420 square miles are divided by topography into several virtually separate regions with unique terrain, econo-mies, and societies. Within the island are five major linguistic groups includ-ing the Tagalogs, who provided the majority of the Philippine revolutionary leadership against both the Spanish and Americans. The climate is tropical, with a monsoon season that extends from about June to September. During this period common diseases such as malaria, dengue fever, and dysentery become even more prevalent. As the Americans were soon to discover, Luzon's terrain and climate can be greater adversaries than any human enemy.

Luzon had been the site of a Spanish colony since the late sixteenth century, but for many years Spain's attention was turned toward oceanic trade and not the internal development of the island. Manila quickly evolved into a commercial and governmental headquarters, but in the countryside the Spanish ruled through the Roman Catholic regular clergy, commonly re-ferred to as the friars, and the traditional insular elite, who were confirmed in their local power in return for their acceptance of royal authority. This elite, referred to as the *principalía* or *principales*, filled provincial and municipal political offices and served as intermediaries between the faraway govern-ment in Manila and the largely peasant populace. This system fit in well with the already existent stratified social structure which stressed class distinc-tions based on mutual obligation, landownership, patron-client ties, and village agriculture. It was not until the late eighteenth century, when the development of an export economy placed the interests of Filipino *principalía* landowners in increasing conflict with those of the friars and the Spanish government, that it began to break down. As lay and clerical Spanish, or *peninsulares*, flocked to the archipelago to invest in land, sugar, hemp, and tobacco, they clashed with the *principales* also seeking to take advantage of the new prosperity to expand their own control over agriculture. The result was increasing ethnic, religious, and political tensions.

In the mid-nineteenth century, a Filipino reform movement emerged which was determined to secure a more equitable arrangement of both political and economic power. *Ilustrados*, educated Filipinos exposed to European liberal and nationalist ideas, sought to reform the Spanish imperial system. Broadly speaking, they wanted to curb the power of the religious orders, open up official positions to qualified Filipinos, exclude the Chinese, and assume the political authority their education entitled them to. The *ilustrados* were supported by provincial landowners who wanted to consolidate their political and economic power in the countryside without outside interference. These *principales* were receptive to the *ilustrados'* criticism of Spanish and friar abuses and their call for more political and economic opportunities for Filipinos. The *ilustrados* also struck a chord with the Filipino secular clergy competing with the Spanish regular clergy over benefices and appointments. The elitist background of the *ilustrados* made them unwilling to advocate radical social or political change and limited their base of support to wealthy Filipinos. The Spanish government responded to this mild reform movement with enough brutality to supply it with martyrs but not enough to crush it.[5]

In 1892 the center of resistance shifted to Andrés Bonifacio's Manila-based "Highest and Most Honorable Society of the Sons of the Country," or Katipunan society. A blend of revolutionary rhetoric, nationalist ideals, Tagalog ethnocentrism, and secret society rituals, Bonifacio's Katipunan openly sought independence from Spain and sanctioned armed rebellion. The society grew rapidly in the Tagalog region near Manila but in the process became fragmented. Often controlled by local political leaders, most Katipunaneros shared only the most basic common ideology with their fellow members in other areas. While the exact nature, composition, and ideology of the Katipunan remain the subject of lively scholarly debate, it is clear it possessed neither the cellular organization, the rigid discipline, nor the coherent program that have distinguished more recent revolutionary parties.[6]

In August 1896, the Katipunan was compromised when the society's plans were betrayed to government authorities. With the Spanish searching for him, Bonifacio fled Manila, and on 22 August he issued the "Grito de Balintawak," which marks the beginning of the Filipino revolt against Spain. While there were sympathetic outbreaks in the Tagalog regions, Bonifacio's call did not spark a national uprising. The insurgent military forces, which consisted of a "loose formation of municipal militia, each town having its own band of volunteers who served under their own leaders," could seldom unite and were often torn by factional quarrels.[7] In the Ilocano and Bicol regions the inhabitants, fearing Tagalog tyranny, aided the Spanish. Yet with most of their troops deployed against the Moslems in Mindanao, the Spanish could not prevent the rebels from contesting eight provinces in central and southern Luzon. It was not until early 1897 that Spanish regulars and their Filipino auxiliaries could begin to take the offensive. In May the better armed and disciplined Spanish, aided by the rebels' insistence on defending towns, recaptured the most revolutionary province, Cavite, and drove the insurgents into the hills.

The Katipunan response to the Spanish counteroffensive was weakened by internal divisions and personality clashes. The charismatic Bonifacio proved a poor field commander, and other military leaders soon emerged to challenge his authority. One of the most effective of these was Emilio Aguinaldo, a twenty-seven-year-old Tagalog *principal* from Kawit, Cavite. Aguinaldo joined the society in 1895 and used his position as a civic official to recruit and organize a Katipunan faction loyal to himself. When the revolt began, he raised a guerrilla band, assumed the title of general, and soon controlled much of eastern Cavite. Lacking military forces of his own, Bonifacio allied himself with a rival group, but, when the two factions agreed to combine in March 1897, he was deposed as Katipunan leader. Bonifacio refused to accept this demotion, and after an abortive coup, he was arrested, summarily tried, and shot by Aguinaldo's followers. Although this execution left Aguinaldo free to take control of the Katipunan, and later of the Filipino independence movement, it weakened the movement and created a bitter legacy among Filipinos who wanted Bonifacio's social reforms implemented.[8]

Under pressure from the Spanish, Aguinaldo dispersed his forces and, with a small core of dedicated followers, retreated into the mountains of Bulacan province. Despite his defeat in Cavite, he had no intention of surrendering, and on 6 September 1897, he called for the adoption of a new strategy. Arguing that Spain was nearly bankrupt, he ordered his men to avoid occupying towns and instead to follow the example of the Cubans, utilizing guerrilla tactics to fight a protracted war. He followed this with an 11 November 1897 decree, "Regulations for the Organization of Sandahatan Forces," which called for a village militia, or Sandahatan, led by officers appointed by municipal councils. Armed with long knives, or bolos, this militia would hunt down fugitives, gather intelligence about the enemy, and arrest criminals. The creation of this force reflected Aguinaldo's keen understanding of the localistic nature of Filipino society. Manned by peasants and led by their village officials, employers, landlords, or patrons, the Sandahatan would fight on their home terrain and gradually wear the enemy down. If the

Spanish concentrated their forces, the guerrilla militia could scatter to their villages and temporarily assume their civilian identities. As long as such forces kept their firearms and could secure leadership and support from the *principales*, they could continue resistance indefinitely.[9]

Unwilling to launch an expensive and probably futile assault on Aguinaldo's mountain stronghold, the Spanish tried to defuse the revolt by buying off the revolutionaries. Aware of their problems in Cuba, they had no wish to fight another protracted guerrilla war in the tropics. Despite successive defeats, remnants of the Katipunan forces still continued guerrilla resistance in southern Luzon and there was always a danger of new outbreaks. This possibility increased on 5 November when Aguinaldo issued the Constitution of Biac na bato, declaring the independence of the Philippines, and summoned all Filipinos, not just the Tagalogs, to aid the revolution. In such circumstances, the Spanish authorities were willing to pursue a moderate course and negotiate with the rebels. The resulting Pact of Biac na bato was concluded in December 1897. Aguinaldo and some of his followers left for Hong Kong with 400,000 pesos and the belief that the Spanish intended to pay an indemnity to injured Filipinos and were willing to institute reforms.[10]

If the Spanish hoped that the pact would end both Aguinaldo's appeal and the fighting, they were disappointed on both counts. Aguinaldo's ability to negotiate as an equal increased his prestige and made him a symbol of nationalist aspirations throughout the archipelago. While he remained in exile, fighting provoked by Katipuneros, sectional disputes, the brutality of the Spanish reaction, and continuing Filipino resistance racked the islands. The American victory at Manila Bay and Spanish attempts to enlist local support against the United States caused even more unrest. After the return of Aguinaldo from exile on 12 May 1898, the tempo of resistance increased. Suspicious of their Filipino troops, and with much of their manpower besieged by Aguinaldo in Manila, the Spanish garrisons in the provinces were isolated and soon capitulated. By the fall of 1898, military power in much of the archipelago was in the hands of regional Filipino forces, most of whom recognized Aguinaldo's authority in principle if not in practice.[11]

When Dewey brought Aguinaldo from Hong Kong on an American ship, he entangled the heretofore separate American and revolutionary campaigns against the Spanish. In helping Aguinaldo, the admiral followed both prewar U.S. Navy plans to utilize the Filipinos and his own belief that they would be useful allies. It was not until 26 May that he received orders from Secretary of the Navy John D. Long to avoid an alliance with the revolutionaries. By that time Dewey and Aguinaldo had drawn very different conclusions about the nature of their relationship. For both personal and practical reasons, Dewey wished to maintain cordial relations with Aguinaldo. He had no inkling of any future American plans for territorial acquisition and no personal enthusiasm for imperialism. Moreover, he was impressed with the Filipino leader and he sympathized with his struggle against the Spanish. Perhaps inadvertently imitating President McKinley, Dewey took advantage of his temporary military advantage while avoiding any commitment to future action. Like McKinley, he failed to see that his opportunism and ambivalence set the stage for future misunderstanding. For their part, Aguinaldo and his advisors took Dewey's vagueness as evidence of American support. They desperately wanted an alliance with the United States, and, as Leandro Fernandez has noted, it is possible that this desire gradually evolved into the conviction that such an alliance actually existed. Dewey had arranged for Aguinaldo's return, he distributed captured arms to the revolutionaries, and he made no objection to Aguinaldo's 24 May assumption of dictatorial powers, his 12 June proclamation of Philippine independence, or his 24 June arrogation of the presidency of the revolutionary government. To the revolutionaries, Dewey's actions seemed to indicate that the United States recognized Aguinaldo's legitimacy as a national leader. Thus, even before the arrival of Merritt's forces, relations between Americans and Filipinos were fraught with potential dissension.[12]

The arrival of the first U.S. Army ground forces under Anderson on 30 June brought into the open the inevitable conflict between American misunderstanding and Filipino expectations. Anderson met with Aguinaldo and found him less than enthusiastic about the arrival of American ground forces. Anderson's subsequent reports reflected both the delicacy of the situation and the growing tension between the allies. He complained that Aguinaldo planned to capture Manila alone and was interfering with supplies and transport. He also warned McKinley that the president's 19 May orders might have to be reconsidered, for the establishment of a provincial government by U.S. government forces would probably bring conflict with Filipinos. Finally, Anderson argued that the Americans had "underrated the native[s]. They are not ignorant, savage tribes, but have a civilization of their own; and though insignificant in appearance are fierce fighters."[13] He was able to settle the supply problem and arrange for his soldiers to take over a section of trenches before Manila, but, since he was unaware of McKinley's ultimate plans, he was unable to dispel Filipino suspicions. All he could do was refuse to recognize Aguinaldo's government and accept Aguinaldo's refusal to place himself under American authority.

When Merritt landed on 26 July he chose to work virtually independently of the Filipino nationalists. McKinley's orders stated that the powers of the military commander were immediately in effect in the islands, and because of this, Merritt did not think it wise to establish direct relations with Aguinaldo. Indeed, he intended that his attack on Manila be conducted entirely without reference to the Filipinos; he planned to capture Manila solely with his own troops and then to issue a proclamation stating American aims. Having seized the city, Merritt believed he could enforce authority in the event that Aguinaldo's "pretensions" conflicted with future American plans.[14]

The siege of Manila thus became two separate campaigns, with both Americans and Filipinos conducting their own operations while ostensibly cooperating. Aguinaldo's army, a "bush-whacking force of brave and adventurous men, but of very loose organization," was unable to storm the city by itself.[15] The U.S. Army, able to capture Manila by itself, wanted to prevent Aguinaldo's forces from seizing much of the city under cover of the American attack. Determined to avoid joint occupancy, Merritt wondered whether he would have to delay his assault until he had sufficient troops to fight the Filipinos as well as the Spanish. Faced with starvation and fearing a bloodbath if the revolutionaries broke into the city, the Spanish commander resolved this impasse by agreeing to surrender after token resistance if the Americans would keep the Filipinos out. The resulting Battle of Manila on 13 August contained enough gunfire and casualties to satisfy both Spanish and American honor. For the Filipinos, however, it was a stunning revelation of how little they were valued as allies. When the battle began, they joined in the attack and seized control of a few Manila suburbs, but the Americans turned them back from the city. Aguinaldo's forces retreated to their trenches and began a second siege of Manila.[16]

Merritt's capture of Manila marked both the end of active hostilities in the Spanish-American War and the culmination of his career. Shortly after the battle the general was ordered to Paris, but before he left he did much to alleviate tensions. Although insisting there would be no joint occupation of Manila, Merritt did establish contact with Aguinaldo and assured him that if the Americans did not stay they would be sure to "leave him in as good condition as he was found by the Government."[17] At the same time he dealt with Aguinaldo, Merritt also appealed to the Filipino people. On 14 August he issued a proclamation declaring that the Americans had not come to make war on the Filipinos and promising the preservation of personal and religious rights. To give substance to his words, Merritt arranged to relieve much of the civilian distress in Manila: he restored the water supply and arranged for a thorough cleaning of the streets. As a result of his actions, conditions in

Manila improved and the danger of immediate hostilities between his soldiers and Aguinaldo's furious revolutionaries subsided.

The capture of Manila allowed McKinley to take full advantage of his
consistent refusal to place limits on American involvement. Throughout the
war the president had steadfastly kept his options open, taking advantage of
military opportunities but leaving himself uncommitted as to his future plans
for the archipelago. In early May, when he decided to dispatch American
ground forces, it is probable that McKinley viewed the islands primarily as an
area of operations against Spain. As the summer wore on, the successful
embarkation of Merritt's expedition and the weakness of Spanish authority
led to an expansion of his goals. By mid-July, he spoke of acquiring Manila
and Luzon, and by 16 September this had hardened to demanding both from
the Spanish. On a speaking tour of the Midwest and in private conferences,
he tested the waters in early fall and found that the American people and key
Republicans favored annexation. Fortified by the conviction that he was
fulfilling his constituents' desires as well as his own, McKinley instructed his
peace commissioners to acquire the entire archipelago. The military position
of the United States was too strong for the Spanish to do more than engage in
a few perfunctory delays and objections. On 10 December 1898, the Treaty
of Paris formally transferred sovereignty of the Philippines to the United
States. In just seven months, McKinley's opportunistic strategy had led him
from the defeat of the Spanish fleet in Manila Bay to the acquisition of a
colonial empire.[18]

With his territorial intentions finally clear, McKinley also moved to outline
American colonial policy in the Philippines. On 21 December he notified the
secretary of war of his wishes for the administration of the new territory.
From the beginning, he emphasized the high motives behind annexation and
insisted that the United States was to protect and not abuse the Filipinos. In
some detail, he directed that the Army preserve property and individual
rights, open ports to commerce, and collect taxes. Above all, he stressed that
the Army was to "win the confidence, respect, and affection of the inhabitants of the Philippines" and that the "mission of the United States is one of
benevolent assimilation, substituting the mild sway of justice and right for
arbitrary rule." Ignoring the fact that the U.S. forces were confined to
Manila, he claimed that Dewey's victory and the taking of the city "practically
effected the conquest of the Philippine Islands and the suspension of Spanish sovereignty therein." The signing of the peace treaty had simply confirmed this and made it imperative that the military government in Manila
"be extended with all possible dispatch to the whole of the ceded territory."[19]

At the very time McKinley was developing his policy of "benevolent assimulation," events in Manila were moving toward open warfare. Allowed to visit the city if they checked their weapons, Filipino soldiers were accused of robbing civilians and planning an uprising. In the trenches the Americans and Filipinos exchanged insults, blows, and occasional gunfire. Shortly before he left, Merritt urged his men to remember that they came "not as despoilers and oppressors, but simply as the instruments of a strong, free Government whose purposes are beneficent and which has declared itself in this war the champion of those oppressed by Spanish misrule."[20] While some of his soldiers took pride in this noble purpose, others robbed civilians, wrote bad credit vouchers, got drunk, and referred to the Filipinos as "niggers." Their officers, while not as openly contemptuous, were often arrogant: in one incident, a colonel arrested a company of revolutionaries and kept their weapons "as a lesson not to trifle with American troops."[21] Army efforts to clean up Manila's streets, enforce sanitary regulations, or collect taxes were often carried out in a harsh or authoritarian manner with little concern for Filipino traditions and customs.

This inflammatory situation was exacerbated by the poor diplomacy of Maj. Gen. Elwell S. Otis, who succeeded Merritt in late August 1898. Otis inherited a difficult situation. American intentions toward the Philippines were uncertain even after 10 December. The formal annexation of the islands depended on Senate confirmation of the treaty with Spain and that would not occur until Congress met in February 1899. Filipino forces occupied parts of Manila's suburbs and refused to vacate them despite American insistence that there be no joint occupancy. In addition, many of the state volunteers demanded to be sent home, arguing that their military obligation ended with the conclusion of the Spanish-American War. These problems were perhaps insurmountable, but Otis contributed to his difficulties by his own obtuseness and poor judgment. A soldier since 1861, Otis had served with distinction in the Civil War and in several Indian campaigns, and been a prominent reformer in the Army educational system. Legal training and four decades in the small frontier Army had left him with a passion for administrative detail which often became obsessive. He interfered with his subordinates, refused to delegate authority, and tried to control everything from his desk. Isolated in Manila, he obtained most of his information from wealthy Filipinos hostile to any change in the social order. He soon decided that Aguinaldo and the revolutionary forces represented either Tagalog despotism or lower-class anarchy and that a firm policy toward them would secure support from "men of property."[22] In a situation that required tact and flexibility, Otis was pedantic and self-righteous. He compounded these problems with his erratic policies and sudden shifts in mood, which could change within a day from a belief that all conflict could be avoided to the certainty that the revolutionaries were planning an immediate attack. He proved to be a poor representative for McKinley, incapable either of personally handling the situation or of providing accurate information.[23]

By December 1898, the main factor preventing the outbreak of war was that neither Filipino nor American leadership desired it. The revolutionaries were aware that the decision to annex the Philippines was not yet final—the Treaty of Paris still had to be passed by the Senate. They were overly optimistic about the strength of antiimperialist sentiment in the United States and believed a compromise might be worked out which would secure Philippine independence. McKinley also wished to avoid war, informing Otis: "Am most desirous that conflict be avoided. . . . Time given the insurgents can not hurt us and must weaken and discourage them. They will come to see our benevolent purpose and recognize that before we can give their people good government our sovereignty must be complete and unquestioned. Tact and kindness most essential just now."[24] For his part, Otis believed that Aguinaldo's government would soon dissolve from its own internal weaknesses and allow the Americans to make a bloodless conquest.

Otis had some grounds for his optimism; in its short existence Aguinaldo's government was torn by internal disputes. After his assumption of the presidency in June, Aguinaldo called for a constitutional convention for the future Philippine Republic. Meeting in the city of Malolos, Bulacan, this convention eventually produced a constitution which was duly promulgated on 27 January 1899. However, the constitutional convention also revealed deep cleavages between conservatives who favored an accommodation with Americans and a weak presidency, and radicals who wanted complete independence and a strong, centralized government. Composed of wealthy *ilustrados*, military chiefs, and *principales*, the convention failed to institute the political or social reforms that might have gained it the unforced loyalty of the peasantry.[25]

Aguinaldo accomplished far more on the local and provincial level. As a member of the provincial elite he was well acquainted with the ambitions and importance of this group. Soon after his arrival he ordered this elite to institute their own municipal and provincial governments under the auspices of the Philippine Republic. He followed this with a series of rulings that broke up many of the religious estates and others that gave the *principales* title to land. He tried to insure, with erratic success, that his military commanders left these local authorities alone and allowed them a relatively free hand in all their affairs. His policy of conciliating the *principalía* effectively tied them to the revolution and would have important effects on the later guerrilla war.[26]

Despite the efforts of the American and Filipino leadership to avoid war, tensions in Manila defeated all attempts to defuse them. Aguinaldo's control of his army was uncertain and, with or without his collusion, a number of plots developed calling for a popular uprising supported by an attack from the Republican Army. Ever a stickler for legal niceties, Otis repeatedly insisted that all revolutionary forces withdraw from Manila's municipal limits. In some cases this meant that they had to abandon territory they had captured and turn over their trenches to the Americans. This infuriated the Filipinos and caused a number of armed confrontations. As a result, several of Manila's suburbs were disputed areas claimed by both sides. On 4 February 1899, while serving picket duty in one of these areas, Pvt. William Grayson of Nebraska fired on a Filipino patrol that refused to answer his challenge. In a few hours, gunfire had spread up and down the lines, the Americans had gone on the offensive, and the Philippine War had begun.[27]

In the operations following the outbreak of war the U.S. Army quickly established its military superiority over the Filipino nationalist forces. The Americans inflicted terrible casualties on Aguinaldo's soldiers, easily storming entrenchments that were "beautifully made and wretchedly defended."[28] They shattered the revolutionary forces in battle and captured the Republican capital of Malolos on 31 March, driving into the central Luzon provinces in April and May, and sweeping into the southern Tagalog provinces in June. Yet these victories, though carried out with efficiency and exacting heavy casualties on the revolutionaries, proved ineffectual. Numbering only some 26,000 troops, of which less than half could be spared for active operations in Luzon, Otis could not occupy the territory his forces moved through so easily. Time and time again, his soldiers trudged through the rice paddies and hills, fought a few skirmishes with Aguinaldo's forces, occupied a provincial capital or key city, and then withdrew to Manila. The arrival of the monsoon in late May found the Army exhausted, suffering from a 60-percent sickness rate in some units, and with little to show for its brilliant record. Otis was forced to wait for the arrival of a new army in the fall before resuming the offensive.[29]

The American battlefield victories in early 1899 owed a great deal to Aguinaldo's decision to adopt conventional tactics and to rely on regulars instead of guerrillas. Upon his return to the Philippines he had issued a call for the Filipinos to raise Sandahatan and provincial levies. Such forces were enough to drive the demoralized Spanish out of insular towns, but lacked the firepower to assault Manila and the discipline to besiege it. Aguinaldo's *ilustrado* advisors believed that an army, organized, trained, and uniformed along European lines, would demonstrate the high level of civilization of the Filipinos and encourage recognition of their independence. Aguinaldo was less certain. As a veteran guerrilla, he was not enamored with conventional warfare. Moreover, his own experience in 1896, in which he had used his local social and political connections to raise his first troops, made him aware that any Filipino military system must be based on the localistic and personalistic nature of rural society. At the same time, remembering the bloody factional strife of 1896, he realized that only a well-armed and well-disciplined force, completely under the command of the central government, could suppress challenges from other provincial leaders. The military establishment that he gradually developed was an attempt at compromise between a European-style conventional army and rural guerrilla forces. On 30 July 1898, he authorized each Tagalog province to create a battalion of provincial forces which would join three new "Aguinaldo" regiments of federal troops and form the Republican Army. At the same time, he continued to encourage the continued formation of revolutionary Sandahatan, town companies, independent battalions, and other units which drew their strength from local or personal loyalties.[30]

Aguinaldo's plans had much merit, but they failed to create an effective military establishment. Poorly armed and badly disciplined, composed of a melange of volunteers, veterans of the Spanish colonial army, Katipuneros, and provincial forces, the Republican Army resembled a feudal levy more than a modern military organization. By adopting conventional tactics and formations, Aguinaldo canceled the key strength of the revolutionary forces, their capacity for localized guerrilla war. When taken out of their villages and provinces, merged into larger units commanded by outsiders who could not speak their dialect, and required to stand against a better armed and trained enemy, the social cohesion that tied Filipino soldiers to their comrades and officers broke down. It was impractical to expect men who had been successful as guerrillas to abandon their harassing tactics and habit of seeking the shelter of the nearest village and instead to stay in trenches and fight to the last cartridge. It was equally impractical to expect *principales* who formed their own companies out of tenants and clients to obey orders from Aguinaldo's appointees. As Marcelino A. Foronda, Jr., has pointed out, the Republican forces suffered from "intrigues, petty jealousies, and a narrow-minded regionalism which stressed personal loyalties rather than principles and ideas."[31] Every defeat brought forth new accusations of incompetence, treason, insubordination, and lack of support. Although some military leaders were models of probity, others behaved as petty tyrants, allowing their undisciplined troops to loot, rob, and rape. In one instance, the conduct of the local garrison was so bad that the exasperated inhabitants of a town rose up and disarmed them.[32]

The Republican Army also proved politically dangerous. Lt. Gen. Antonio

Luna, an erratic and unstable *ilustrado* much impressed with the French Army, assumed command of the national forces after the fall of Malolos. Luna tried to check regional and personal differences by imposing discipline, removing incompetent or insubordinate officers, and creating a special force of Filipino veterans who had served with the Spanish forces. For a short period he succeeded in rallying the army, but his inability to achieve victory on the battlefield soon left him open to attack by his many enemies. Prone to uncontrollable rages, he quickly alienated his subordinates through his ruthless attempts to impose discipline. They in turn defied his orders and attempted to turn their military units into private armies. Luna's political ambitions soon brought him into conflict with Aguinaldo and contributed to his assassination by the president's bodyguard on 5 June 1899.[33]

The Americans were unable to capitalize on this turmoil because they were in the process of replacing one army with a new one. When it became clear that there would be war with Aguinaldo's forces, the U.S. government had to bring back the troops from the original Manila expedition and recruit new forces designed especially for service in the Philippines. Under the provisions of the Army Bill of 2 March 1899, the regular establishment of the U.S. Army was placed at 65,000 men and its cavalry and infantry regiments were recruited to their full wartime strength. Officered and manned by veterans of the Cuban, Puerto Rican, or Philippine campaigns, these regulars were tough and capable soldiers. In addition, Congress authorized a 35,000-man volunteer force enlisted for two years and designated exclusively for service in the Philippines. Organized into twenty-five regiments of infantry and one of cavalry, the U.S. Volunteers were commanded by regular and state officers who had distinguished themselves in the Spanish-American War. Both regulars and volunteers were subjects to rigorous examination standards and thorough training. The soldiers arrived in the archipelago skilled in the skirmishing tactics, march discipline, and marksmanship necessary to fighting a guerrilla war.[34]

With the arrival of these new forces in November 1899, the Americans went on the offensive in a three-pronged drive directed at the Republican Army in the north. While Maj. Gen. Arthur MacArthur pinned down the Filipinos on the central Luzon plain, Maj. Gen. Henry W. Lawton swept to the northeast and occupied the mountain passes, preventing any retreat to the east. The Filipinos fell back to the north, only to have their retreat cut off by Brig. Gen. Loyd Wheaton's amphibious landing at Lingayen Gulf. Caught between the converging American forces, with their lines of retreat blocked, the Republican Army broke up. The revolutionaries lost their supplies, artil-

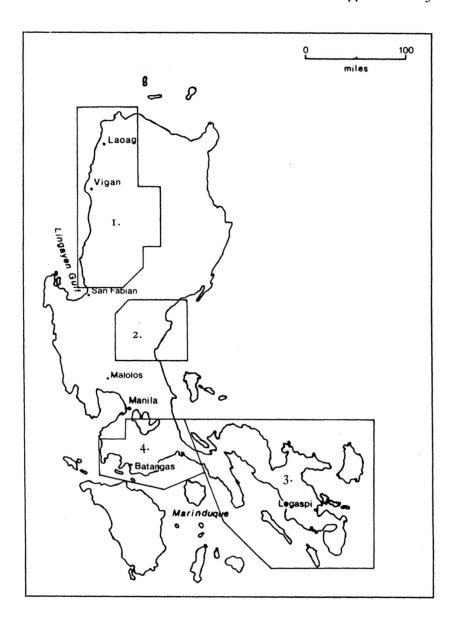

Luzon Island
1. First District, Department of Northern Luzon; 2. Fourth District, Department of Northern Luzon; 3. Third District, Department of Southern Luzon; 4. Second District, Department of Southern Luzon.

lery, and correspondence and some of the most prominent Filipino leaders surrendered or were captured. Aguinaldo himself narrowly escaped, but lost his family, treasury, bodyguard, and much of his staff in the retreat. By December 1899 the U.S. Army occupied most of the populated areas north of Manila.[35]

Otis then turned south. In January 1900, expeditions under Wheaton and Brig. Gen. Theodore Schwan marched into the Tagalog provinces of Batangas, Laguna, and Tayabas. After some early engagements, the revolutionary forces disappeared, and Army units occupied the region with little further resistance.[36] Shortly thereafter, an amphibious force under Brig. Gen. William Kobbé landed in Albay and Sorsogon provinces on the southeastern coast of Luzon. Initially there was stiff opposition, but once the landings were secured the revolutionaries retreated into the mountains with much of the population.[37] The final step in the occupation of Luzon was taken in February, when another amphibious force under Brig. Gen. James M. Bell landed in the neighboring Ambos Camarines province and occupied the area around Nueva Caceres.[38]

The destruction of the Republican Army removed visible resistance and left the cause of Filipino independence apparently defeated. Actually the war had entered a new and far more frustrating phase. On 13 November 1899, as the Americans occupied Tarlac, the last capital of the Republic, Aguinaldo had decided to abandon all pretense at conventional tactics and turned completely to guerrilla warfare. Dividing Luzon up into three politico-military commands, he kept northern Luzon under his own authority and placed Maj. Gen. Mariano Trías and Maj. Gen. Pantaleon García over southern and central Luzon, respectively. He may have envisioned retaining personal control over strategy and operations throughout the island, but such plans were vitiated by his flight from the Americans. Isolated in northeastern Luzon, the president remained a symbol for patriots throughout the archipelago, but distance and the localistic nature of the fighting prevented him from exercising a strong influence on revolutionary military operations.[39]

Aguinaldo's strategy was intended to protract the war until either the U.S. Army broke down from disease and exhaustion or the American public demanded a withdrawal. A conspicuous source of hope was the forthcoming presidential election in the United States: the revolutionaries overestimated the strength of American antiexpansionist sentiment and believed that continued Filipino resistance would secure a Democratic victory in 1900. Instead of placing their faith in conventional forces, Aguinaldo and his lieutenants emphasized the use of small forces which could strike and then disperse, regrouping later at some prearranged rendezvous. Guerrillas were to fight only when they had overwhelming superiority and to rely on skirmishes, raids, and ambushes.[40] In some areas units from the Republican Army simply put on civilian clothing and immediately began to ambush convoys and stragglers. The Sandahatan, virtually untouched by the American offensive, remained in their villages and continued to harass enemy supply lines and communications. In some areas revolutionary leaders established a new Katipunan whose ideology would maintain popular support for independence. By April 1900, U.S. Army garrisons in nearly all areas of the archipelago faced this newly reorganized guerrilla resistance.[41]

Militarily, Luzon was divided into geographical districts and then subdivided into provincial and zone commands. Although Tagalogs dominated the upper revolutionary leadership, combat units were usually raised locally and led by officers from the provincial elites. In most areas these forces were loosely divided into partisans, or full-time guerrillas, and militia. The partisans often were survivors of earlier Republican or provincial regular forces and operated within a zone, usually in one or two small fifty-man bands, having their base camps in isolated *barrios* (hamlets or small villages considered part of a town or municipal jurisdiction) or mountain retreats. It was their job to cut telegraph lines, ambush U.S. Army convoys, and attack towns that had accepted American civil government. The militia operated as part-time guerrillas and otherwise continued their normal civilian pursuits in their native towns. They grew food for the partisans, provided information, and manned the numerous outposts that informed the regulars of any U.S. Army maneuvers. Although poorly armed and disciplined, the militia had more than enough strength to intimidate their fellow villagers into paying taxes and keeping silent. The distinction between the two forces was at best a hazy one, made more unclear by the fact that the militia often provided recruits for partisan units. Neither organization wore uniforms and both often lived in the same villages, posing as harmless peasants and "amigos." There was a great deal of merging back and forth: militia in an area in which the U.S. Army was inactive could become full-time guerrillas, and conversely the partisans would abandon operations and assume civilian identities for months in the face of Army pressure. Exasperated Americans echoed the words of Capt. Delphey T. E. Casteel: "One day we may be fighting with thousands of their people [and] the next day you can't find an enemy, they are all 'amigos.' They have hidden their rifles and may be working for you, for all you know."[42]

The revolutionaries' combat forces were supported by a far larger civilian organization or infrastructure which paid taxes, hid weapons, and provided food. It was staffed by civil-military officers who collected taxes and supervised the supplying of the storehouses, or *cuartels*, through a chain of village appointees. The collectors often operated as political agents by insuring that village leaders conformed to guerrilla policies, by working for the election of sympathetic candidates, and by supervising the operations of the militia. A supportive town government would establish its own militia, send information about American troop movements, hide fugitive guerrillas, and employ the administrative machinery to collect taxes and contributions. The result was a layered guerrilla organization in which partisans, tax collectors, militia, and town governments all operated for mutual support.[43]

As Maj. Gen. Arthur MacArthur noted, the ultimate survival of the guerrilla movement rested on the revolutionaries' ability to control the civilian population. This was achieved primarily by keeping the *principales* firmly committed to the revolution: few peasants, brought up in a society that stressed deference to traditional authority, were able to resist the appeals of their landowning patrons to join guerrilla bands or pay taxes. Moreover, the revolutionaries also used patriotism, secret societies, religious beliefs, propaganda, and appeals to the poor to attract the population. Although often ineffective as either a military or supply organization, the Katipunan provided a clandestine association that appealed to some Filipinos. At times the revolutionaries simply adapted earlier Spanish propaganda and claimed that the Americans wished to impose the Protestant religion or make the Filipinos slaves. They stressed *kalayaan*, or independence, often picturing it in traditional religious folk terms as a sort of mystical paradise on earth. Some guerrillas even stole or constructed religious images to show the peasants that divine blessing attended their cause.[44]

When appeals to patriotism or traditional authority failed, the revolutionaries were willing to use intimidation. William H. Taft, appointed by McKinley to oversee the transfer of government in the Philippines from the U.S. Army to civilian authority, went so far as to declare that guerrilla warfare could not have continued without the revolutionaries' use of terrorism. What Thomas P. Thornton has termed "agitational terrorism" kept an otherwise apathetic population in a state of anxiety, advertised the movement, and eliminated opposition. American records of Filipino atrocities certainly reflect Army efforts to discredit the guerrillas, but captured revolutionary correspondence is indeed full of threats and orders to execute suspected collaborators and to destroy their property. Tragically, terrorism was more easily unleashed than controlled. Some guerrillas could not resist the temptation to strike out at prewar enemies and, in the countryside, terrorism became unregulated violence with Filipinos being mutilated, burned, tortured, or buried alive in a self-perpetuating cycle. The U.S. Army might garrison the towns, but, as the Filipino statesman Felipe Calderon pointed out, "the insurgents, being absolute masters of the fields, impose their will absolutely and despotically."[45]

Compounding the problem of terrorism was the breakdown of public order in many provinces throughout the archipelago. Religious rebels such as the Babaylanes, Dios Dios, and Guardia de Honor flourished from the north of Luzon to the southern Visayan Islands, proclaiming the coming millennium and often fighting both Americans and revolutionaries. Warfare, hunger, and endemic violence spawned hundreds of *ladrones* and *tulisanes*, the brigands who had traditionally terrorized rural society. In some areas *ladrone* gangs numbered in the hundreds and controlled several villages. These outlaws further complicated the issue by convincing some U.S. Army officers that Filipino resistance was nothing more than *ladronism* and that the revolutionary leaders were little better than outlaws motivated by greed. Although the Americans often linked the guerrillas with the *ladrones*, there is little evidence to support this accusation. The guerrilla commanders, overwhelmingly men of wealth, education, and social prominence, kept their distance from the poor outcasts who led the bandit gangs. Some guerrillas summarily executed *ladrones*, and others informed the Americans of the location of bandit hideouts or turned over suspected outlaws to Army justice.[46]

The collapse of Aguinaldo's government, the beginning of guerrilla warfare, the use of terrorism, and the breakdown in social order all contributed to the destruction of central authority and the regionalization of the war. The most famous guerrilla leaders, Juan Cailles and Miguel Malvar in southwestern Luzon, Vicente Lukban on Samar, Ambrosio Moxica in Leyte, and Martin Delgado in Panay, were all essentially regional warlords whose power seldom extended past the boundaries of their provinces. This decentralization was both the guerrillas' strength and their weakness. Local chiefs had a shrewd grasp of the realities of warfare in their own areas and could adapt tactics and policies best suited to their regions. They knew the local population and its leadership, and could draw on patriotism, intimidation, and prewar social connections for supplies, recruits, and information. Virtually autonomous, they could sustain war indefinitely regardless of events in other provinces while any American victory was "only local and had little effect upon general conditions."[47] But the highly insular guerrilla companies were seldom able to combine for a sustained offensive throughout the archipelago, and this failure allowed the U.S. Army to shift troops from theater to theater to meet specific emergencies. Some guerrilla leaders thought of their troops more as private armies or village defense forces than part of a national resistance. Within the guerrilla forces personal rivalries often became dominant, and insubordination, factionalism, and disorganization also existed. Army officers learned to exploit these rivalries and play guerrilla leaders off against each other. Finally, when the Americans were able to construct successful local pacification strategies, the guerrillas could not shift into new areas to resume the war.

To combat Filipino resistance, the Army had to develop counterinsurgency policies and methods while respecting McKinley's insistence that "it should be the earnest and paramount aim of the military administration to win the confidence, respect, and admiration of the inhabitants of the Philippines by assuring them in every possible way that full measure of individual rights and liberties which is the heritage of free peoples, and by proving to them that the mission of the United States is one of benevolent assimilation, substituting the mild sway of justice and right for arbitrary rule."[48] Successive commanders of the Division of the Philippines were often reminded that the U.S. Army had not only a military but a civilizing mission. The Army was not only to suppress terrorism, guerrilla warfare, and brigandage but to prepare the Philippines for colonial government; moreover, this must be accomplished in such a way that the Filipinos would be docile, obedient, and grateful subjects. The Army's emphasis throughout the war on such nonmilitary pacification policies as civil government, education, and municipal police reflects its assigned role as pathfinder for American colonial government. To insure that the Army did not forget its preparatory task, in March 1900 McKinley appointed the Philippine Commission headed by William H. Taft that supervised the transfer of power from the U.S. Army to civilian government. To Taft, the Army's success could be measured by the number of provinces it declared pacified and turned over to the commission's authority. But, ironically, perhaps it was this civilizing mission that inspired much of the viciousness of the war: the Army's mission of making the Filipinos passively accept United States authority ran directly counter to the revolutionaries' determination that the people should actively support independence. The Philippine War became, in many respects, a contest to compel the allegiance of the Filipino people. And so the civilian population, which might otherwise have remained apathetic, was forced again and again to choose sides—and to pay the penalty for misjudgment.

Initially, the revolutionaries' early advantage in this contest of loyalties was greatly aided by the failure of the U.S. Army high command to recognize their very existence. Otis, the Army's commander until mid-1900, never acknowledged that the guerrilla war was a major problem; the destruction of the Republican Army meant that "war in its proper meaning had ceased to exist" and that the persistence of rural violence could be ascribed to remnants of the Tagalog military forces and *ladrones*. Once the majority of Filipinos could live in peace they would see the benefits of American colonial government and join the U.S. Army against the bandit-guerrillas; accordingly, Otis stationed American garrisons in as many towns in the archipelago as possible. To demonstrate the civil character of U.S. occupation, he broke up the former tactical brigades on 7 April 1900 and recombined them into geographical commands. Luzon was divided into northern and southern departments and these were further subdivided into district and provincial commands.[49]

Under the provisions of General Order (G.O.) 43 (1899) and G.O. 40 (1900), Army officers established municipal governments consisting of a local *presidente*, or mayor, a town council, and a police force. These governments were largely oligarchic, for voting was restricted to a small minority qualified by wealth or education. This meant that the Army usually confirmed the local *principales* in their authority, for, in the words of Maj. George T. Langhorne, it was "generally recognized that we can only run these people through their chiefs or leaders."[50] Army garrisons also instituted sanitary reforms, and some cleared roads and built bridges. Soldiers, often equipped with little more than a few pieces of chalk and a poncho for a blackboard, taught Filipino children the rudiments of literacy. In northwestern Luzon alone, within six months of occupation the Army established 203 schools attended by 10,714 children.[51] The American garrisons contributed to the finances of some municipalities by purchasing much of their forage, labor, transportation, and housing from local sources. By mid-1900, when he requested leave from service in the Philippines, Otis believed that his policy was already working and that the situation was "eminently satisfactory."[52]

Maj. Gen. Arthur MacArthur, who succeeded Otis in May, was less sanguine. He recognized that the Army was in the midst of a guerrilla war and he believed that the majority of Filipinos supported the revolutionaries, not the United States. MacArthur was also aware that Otis's strategy had left American forces in Luzon overextended and incapable of offensive action. Moreover, he was dubious about the utility of civil governments; although they might be "useful agencies in the work of pacification," he realized that the revolutionaries controlled many of them, and that their American-appointed officials actually served the guerrillas.[53] Nevertheless, on 21 June 1900 MacArthur declared a ninety-day amnesty during which all guerrillas who surrendered might take the Oath of Allegiance to the United States and return home immediately. MacArthur claimed that this was to give all prominent revolutionaries a chance to surrender, but he was also aware that the summer rainy season would effectively hinder Army operations from June until late August. Whatever the motivation, the amnesty was not a success. Only 5,022 Filipinos surrendered, and many of these were already prisoners of war or lived in areas outside guerrilla influence. MacArthur believed that the upcoming U.S. presidential election explained the "meager result," and recommended that any further development of U.S. counterinsurgency policy await the election.[54]

Throughout 1900, as Otis refused to recognize the existence of the guerrillas and MacArthur attempted to conciliate them with an amnesty, Army officers in the field took the initiative in structuring counterinsurgency programs to deal with conditions in their areas. The dispersal of American ground forces under Otis isolated many soldiers from direct supervision; in some areas orders from Manila took months to arrive and communications from provincial commanders could be delayed for weeks. Garrisoning also gave the troops extensive service in one region and allowed them to develop broad social contacts among the populace. This local knowledge was so important that Brig. Gen. Frederick Funston stated that in the Philippines, "the efficiency of a company depends largely on [its] knowledge of the people in the vicinity, and the country itself, which can be acquired only after some time."[55] Otis's emphasis on civil government left field and company officers with enormous civil-military responsibilities: "It is really a peculiar position in which the Commanding Officers of towns in these islands find themselves these days. In this town and its outlying barrios for instance there are some four thousand people who must go when I say go and come when I say come. . . . It is a big responsibility and sometimes it is awfully hard to decide what is the right thing to do."[56] Thus the very circumstances of service in the provinces forced officers to improvise methods to deal with local problems. As they reported their successes and failures to their superiors, they influenced policies at the next-highest level. Army regional commanders were often able to pacify a municipality or even a province with their own counterinsurgency campaigns long before the rest of the district was free of guerrillas. Indeed, so important was their role that as early as July 1900 William H. Taft informed the secretary of war that "the pacification of the Islands seems to depend largely on the character of the military officer in charge of the particular district."[57]

In the fall of 1900 the revolutionaries in much of Luzon launched an offensive against the U.S. forces in an effort to influence the American presidential elections. Aguinaldo ordered attacks to be made from 15 to 23 September, and in some areas, such as northwestern Luzon, the guerrillas besieged isolated American garrisons. For the first time since the destruction of the Republican Army, there were pitched battles between Filipinos and Americans. On 19 September MacArthur reported "considerable activity throughout Luzon": there were 500 guerrillas in Isabela province, the country north of Manila, including all of Bulacan province was "very much disturbed and [U.S. troops had] numerous contacts with small parties," and there were similar troubled conditions throughout the southern part of the island.[58] That same day, one of the few American military disasters of the war, an ill-conceived assault on guerrilla entrenchments, cost the Americans over one-third of the attacking force. Shortly afterward, an entire American company under Capt. Devereux Shields was surrounded by guerrillas and forced to surrender on Marinduque Island, and in October in northwestern Luzon another patrol was badly mauled when it was ambushed by some 1,400 revolutionaries.[59]

Although the guerrillas scored some tactical successes, their offensive failed to prevent the election of McKinley, and that event insured that there would be no early American military withdrawal from the archipelago. Moreover, the fall offensive had demonstrated even to the most optimistic American civil and military leaders the breadth and intensity of Filipino resistance. Both the high command and the U.S. government were united in their desire for severer measures. To the U.S. Army's adjutant general, Maj. Gen. Henry C. Corbin, "the successes of the Filipinos have conclusively shown that the time has arrived when more aggressive operations would be in order."[60] Secretary of War Elihu Root announced that the Army must resort to the "methods which have proved successful in our Indian campaigns in the West."[61] Accordingly, on 20 December MacArthur instituted a more rigorous policy and placed the Philippines under martial law. Borrowing appropriate passages from General Order 100, the U.S. Army's code of warfare written during the Civil War, MacArthur outlined the rights and obligations that would govern the Army's treatment of civilians and guerrillas from now on. Emphasizing that the Army had an obligation to protect those Filipinos who accepted American authority, MacArthur also asserted that the Army would no longer tolerate guerrilla abuses. In particular, the "amigos," those guerrillas who wore no uniform but peasant dress and shifted from civilian to military status at will, would be held accountable. People who accepted American protection in the occupied towns but who assisted the guerrillas would be punished as "war rebels, or war traitors," as would the secret committees that collected revolutionary taxes. Terrorism would be tolerated no longer; and no one should be misled by the Army's earlier leniency and previous failure to enforce the laws of war.[62]

MacArthur believed that his proclamation marked the beginnings of "an entirely new campaign . . . based upon the central idea of detaching the towns from the immediate support of the guerrillas in the field, and thus also precluding the indirect support which arose from indiscriminate acceptance by the towns of the insurrection in all its devious ramifications."[63] Most historians have accepted MacArthur's view of the importance of his proclamation and John M. Gates believes that the 20 December proclamation "contained the guidelines for the policy that the Americans would follow throughout 1901."[64] But another of MacArthur's explanations seems more plausible: that the document's main purpose was to educate Filipinos on their violations of the laws of war and the punishments that awaited transgressors. As a statement of policy, it provided little guidance and there was much debate and confusion over what punitive measures were sanctioned. Moreover, many of MacArthur's ideas had already been adopted earlier. The sections of G.O. 100 that applied to guerrilla war had been formally issued and enforced throughout much of the Department of Northern Luzon six months before, and the deportation of suspects to Manila had been practiced since 22 September 1900. Probably the proclamation's major contribution was to provide official sanction for some of the more stringent policies either advocated or already applied in the field.[65]

MacArthur's actions were no less vigorous than his words. He assisted the Federal party, a Filipino political party composed of leading *ilustrados*, former guerrillas, and wealthy conservatives who supported American rule. Its members were allowed to travel freely, often with Army escorts, where they negotiated with revolutionary leaders, organized civil governments, and urged the population to aid the Army. Recalcitrant Filipino leaders who continued to work for Philippine independence were deported to Guam. In March, MacArthur instructed post commanders to keep file cards on former guerrillas, suspects, and influential Filipinos in their locales. Finally, he ordered that before they could take the Oath of Allegiance and be eligible for parole, captives henceforth had to demonstrate their commitment to the United States by giving information, surrendering weapons, or acting against their former comrades.[66]

Concurrent with MacArthur's shift in policy, the U.S. Army manpower reached its peak of 70,000, "stronger than it will ever be again" and now ready for "decisive results."[67] By now the Army in the Philippines was composed chiefly of veterans well acquainted with the local geography and population. Moreover, for the first time American military operations were officially directed against the guerrillas and their infrastructure. While the Army continued to organize municipal governments and implement social reform projects such as schools and roads, its primary mission was clearly military. In addition, it could build upon the local successes of the past twelve months. In northwestern Luzon, for example, certain provinces could be left virtually ungarrisoned while troops operated in adjacent ones; and in central Luzon and Bicolandia, newly recruited Filipino auxiliaries either garrisoned the towns or accompanied the Army on its forays into the mountains.

In 1901 the American military placed continual pressure on the revolutionaries on military, social, and economic fronts. The Army's military operations utilized a combination of proven local methods with MacArthur's Philippine-wide policies. While members of the Federal party sought to negotiate the surrender of guerrillas, locally raised native volunteers hunted them in the field. The U.S. Army confiscated the property of prominent revolutionaries and harassed their relatives, a major blow at the elites furnishing the guerrilla leadership. By arresting and deporting or imprisoning many of the *principalía*, the Army struck at their social and economic power and made both the deportees and their supporters realize the consequences of continued warfare. Faced with the loss of their local power and prestige, and aware that the guerrillas were losing in the field, many *principales* swung their influence to the American side. Army units from several provinces or districts combined to block off mountain passes and prevent the guerrillas from escaping over the border. The Army also sanctioned crop destruction and the concentration of the civilian populations of certain villages in camps to cut the guerrillas off from their supplies and shelter. Military commissions tried and occasionally executed captured guerrillas, and Army provost courts, operating in areas still subjected to martial law, were given a free hand to try and punish suspects without evidence. The provost courts could strike at the guerrillas' infrastructure by trying and sentencing Filipinos suspected of paying insurgent taxes, furnishing supplies, or serving in the Katipunan.

While thus demonstrating the perils of continued resistance, the Americans also rewarded the compliant. In some areas, friendly townspeople were allowed to harvest the crops of known revolutionaries. The Army utilized several organizations such as municipal police, Native Scout units, and the Philippine Constabulary which enlisted many Filipinos, giving them an economic stake in American government and sometimes tying entire villages to the American side. Prominent former guerrilla leaders such as Juan Cailles, Mariano Trías, and Juan Villamor secured positions in the American civil government. The rapid institution of civil government in the spring of 1901, often within a month after a province had been declared pacified, made it clear that Filipinos would have some measure of local independence under American colonial rule. Throughout 1901 the U.S. Army successfully alternated both the carrot of benevolence and the stick of military force.

The results of this new Army offensive were apparent almost immediately. Operations yielded far more captured arms while incurring fewer casualties. The capture of Emilio Aguinaldo in March 1901 removed a vital symbol of resistance and Aguinaldo's proclamation acknowledging American sovereignty legitimized the surrender of other guerrilla commanders. By July such prominent revolutionaries as Juan Cailles, Manuel Tinio, Juan and Blas Villamor, Mariano Trías, Urbano Lacuna, José Alejandrino, and Vito Belarmino had surrendered with their arms and men. Only in the Tagalog provinces of Laguna, Tayabas, and Batangas, and the tumultuous island of Samar, was there further resistance.[68]

MacArthur was replaced by Maj. Gen. Adna R. Chaffee on 4 July 1901 at the same time that William H. Taft was appointed civil governor. This division of authority placed civil government in those areas that had been pacified, while continuing military government in the few areas where the guerrillas still maintained a strong resistance. Chaffee, a cavalryman and veteran of the Civil War, Indian campaigns, and Boxer Rebellion, was aware that his present promotion was due in a large measure to MacArthur's inability to work with Taft. Believing that the war was virtually over, Chaffee wanted to concentrate the scattered company garrisons into military camps and turn Army attention back to such military duties as training, drill, and administration. In an effort to replace civil-military organizations with purely military ones, and thus divorce the Army from civil administration, he broke up the old geographical departments and districts and instituted two divisions and seven "Separate Brigades" in October.[69]

Chaffee's attention was abruptly shifted back to the war on 28 September 1901, when a combined attack by townspeople and guerrillas at Balangiga, Samar, killed forty-eight of the seventy-four U.S. soldiers stationed there. He utilized the newly formed Sixth and Third Separate Brigades to crush resistance on Samar and in southern Luzon, but in a manner that shocked people in the United States and provoked a congressional investigation. Infuriated by the "massacre" at Balangiga, frustrated by continued warfare, and outraged at guerrilla terrorism, the Americans ended the Philippine War with vindictive ruthlessness. Brig. Gen. Jacob H. Smith, the commander of the Sixth Separate Brigade, ordered one of his officers to turn Samar into a "howling wilderness" and to shoot any males over age ten. Brig. Gen. J. Franklin Bell, commanding the Third Separate Brigade in southern Luzon, concentrated most of the populace into guarded zones, where many died of malnutrition and sickness. In both Bell's and Smith's campaigns there was great destruction of property, and the civilian population suffered from the loss of crops and animals. As a result of his actions, Smith was court-martialed and retired from the Army, and five other officers were also tried for war crimes. The two campaigns resulted in the surrender of the last revolutionary leaders by June 1902; a month later, President Theodore Roosevelt officially thanked the U.S. Army for the "successful conclusion" of its military services in the Philippines.[70]

These final campaigns, with their harsh measures and the publicizing of Army atrocities, left a dark cloud hanging over the Army's service in the Philippines which has persisted to the present. By 1902, the war had dragged on for three years and the American public, constantly assured by administration and military officials that victory was around the corner, was heartily sick of the continued fighting in the Philippines. From the beginning, anti-imperialist newspapers had published lurid accounts of American cruelties, accusing soldiers of torture, indiscriminate killing, and the butchery of entire villages. There was enough truth to some of these charges to make many of the rest of them stick. The congressional investigation into Army abuses against Filipino civilians and the courts-martial of a few officers did reveal instances of barbaric cruelty. The exposure of Smith's infamous orders and Bell's concentration camps left many Americans with the conviction that these measures had typified the Army's counterinsurgency methods. Ironically, the Army, which had rarely been able to implement a uniform pacification policy in one district, was now accused of pursuing a consistently severe course throughout the archipelago. Although, as Richard E. Welch, Jr., has pointed out, public apathy would gradually weaken the atrocity issue in 1902, the perception of a racist and brutal American soldiery terrorizing Filipino civilians gradually became accepted in university textbooks, popular histories, and even within the Army itself. When the United States once again involved itself in guerrilla warfare in Southeast Asia, the lessons and experiences it had so painfully gained in the Philippines were virtually ignored.[71]

2

Guerrillas and Guardias
The First District, Department of Northern Luzon

In 1900 Maj. Gen. Elwell S. Otis wrote:

> A review of the telegraphic dispatches . . . shows the difficulties experienced by General [Samuel B. M.] Young's troops increased greatly after they entered these northwestern provinces, because of the efforts of the Tagalo[g] chiefs to incite the inhabitants to active hostility by every possible artifice, appealing to their creed, superstitions and race prejudices, and by ruthlessly enforcing the demands which they made upon them through robbery and murder. The dispatches show that our men were gladly received by the mass of the people upon entering the provinces, that later, a portion of the people under insurgent impressment contributed in men and money to drive the Americans out, and finally that the great majority, gaining confidence, united with our troops to destroy the Tagalo[g]s and the robber bands which they directed.[1]

Otis spoke for many U.S. Army officers when he insisted the Philippine War was a Tagalog rebellion in which other Filipinos had no interest. He spoke for a much smaller group when he claimed that the war was to all intents and purposes over in May 1900. As one of the first non-Tagalog areas occupied by the Army, and site of one of the earliest and most intensive Army efforts at establishing civil government, the First District of the Department of Northern Luzon was regarded as something of a showcase. But within a few months it was so badly shaken by the discovery of revolutionary control over the new governments and by a religiously inspired revolt that a year later

Otis's successor, Maj. Gen. Arthur MacArthur, reported that the district was "for many months the worst in Luzon."[2] In the interim, in the face of a determined Filipino resistance, district officers abandoned Otis's benevolent methods and replaced them with harsher ones more suited to local realities.

The First District, with a total area of some 8,000 square miles, comprised the four "Ilocano" provinces of Ilocos Norte, Ilocos Sur, La Union, and Abra, and the inland "Mountain" provinces of Benguet, Lepanto, and Bontoc. The majority of the estimated population of 531,000 was Ilocano, with some Tagalog and Chinese minorities, and was heavily concentrated on the eastern China Sea coast and the Abra River valley; in the interior were aboriginal tribesmen known collectively as Igorrotes. About 80 percent of the district was mountainous; communications were restricted to the Camino Real up the coast, some internal trails, and the Abra River. During the summer monsoon season the few roads became mud footpaths or were completely washed out. With the exception of a small garrison in Benguet, the American forces were stationed in the four Ilocano provinces and left the sparsely populated and rugged Mountain provinces alone.[3]

The Spanish considered the Ilocano provinces among the most loyal, and, with the exception of a few *ilustrados* such as Antonio Luna, there is little evidence of a strong independence movement in the north prior to 1898. During the Revolt of 1896, the Ilocanos appear to have accepted Spanish claims that this was a Tagalog insurrection, for they sent troops and supplies to aid in the fight against the Katipuneros. Despite this fidelity, Spanish officials and friars used the southern disturbances to conduct a purge of the region, arresting and torturing suspected radicals. Perhaps as a reaction to Spanish terrorism, in March 1898, Isobel Abaya, a native of Candon, Ilocos Sur, attacked the constabulary quarters and executed a Spanish priest and two friars. When this failed to generate sufficient popular support, he fled to the mountains and recruited a band of Igorrotes in Bontoc. Shortly after Abaya's abortive revolt, the destruction of the Spanish fleet and the siege of Manila rendered the Spanish position in northern Luzon untenable. In early August one of Aguinaldo's trusted subordinates, twenty-two-year-old Brig. Gen. Manuel Tinio, brought a strong force up from his native province of Nueva Ecija and captured the port city of San Fernando de La Union. Despite his youth, Tinio was a veteran revolutionary who had fought in the Revolt of 1896 and had gone into exile with Aguinaldo. Joined by much of the population, he brushed aside faltering Spanish resistance and placed the Ilocano provinces under the Philippine Republic.[4]

Tinio organized his forces to repel an expected American amphibious

First District, Department of Northern Luzon

landing on the Ilocano coast. William B. Wilcox, a U.S. Navy paymaster who visited the area shortly before the outbreak of hostilities, estimated there were 3,500 Filipino troops in the region. Perhaps more significantly, he found that not only every town but nearly every *barrio* had raised a small guard as a local defense force. While Wilcox was critical of the lack of training in the Filipino army, he was impressed with its popular support, the number of its weapons, and its large militia. Felipe Buencamino, who inspected the Ilocano province in the spring of 1899 as a special investigator for the Philippine Republic, commented that the mountainous terrain and the strong entrenchments under construction along the coast would make the area easy to defend. He also was encouraged by the military appearance of the Filipino soldiers and the popular enthusiasm for the revolutionary cause. By the fall of 1899, Tinio had raised a brigade of four battalions, each of which was furnished by one of the Ilocano provinces. At least some of these battalions were commanded by officers drawn from the provincial elite.[5]

In November 1899, Brig. Gen. Loyd Wheaton landed near San Fabian, Pangasinan, in an attempt to cut Aguinaldo's retreat and trap his remaining conventional forces. In response, the Tinio Brigade was sent south to hold open Aguinaldo's line of withdrawal. On 11 November at San Jacinto, Tinio's blocking force was attacked by Col. Luther R. Hare's Thirty-third Infantry, U.S. Volunteers (U.S.V.), one of the best units in the U.S. Army. Both sides had roughly 1,200 men, but the casualties indicate the disparity in training, equipment, and marksmanship of American and Filipino forces: the Americans lost 7 dead and 14 wounded while Tinio's men had 134 killed, over 10 percent of their total force. After the battle, Wheaton sent Maj. Peyton C. March and a battalion of the Thirty-third into the Ilocano provinces in pursuit. March's forces destroyed Aguinaldo's bodyguard at Tila Pass on 2 December and chased the Filipino president up to the Bontoc border, capturing much of his staff and family, but Aguinaldo escaped into the mountains. With his own forces badly mauled, Tinio conducted a fighting retreat north, seeking to escape over the mountains. Lt. Col. Robert L. Howze's battalion of the Thirty-fourth Infantry, U.S.V., trapped the remnants of Tinio's forces at Dingras, Ilocos Norte, on 9 December and, after a three-hour running battle, virtually destroyed the brigade.[6]

The U.S. Army thus entered northwestern Luzon less as organized occupation forces than as scattered units in confused pursuit of Aguinaldo and Tinio. While the destruction of the organized Philippine conventional forces removed visible opposition, the Americans quickly found they had new problems. The speed of their advance had made chaos of regimental and divisional organizations, and men from several commands were intermingled and under no clear authority. The troops were exhausted and many were footsore or sick; in two weeks of campaigning, one 400-man battalion was reduced to 87 men fit for duty. In La Union province the Army was plagued with what were initially perceived as Tagalogs and *ladrones*, or bandits, who cut telegraph wires, sniped, and robbed both soldiers and civilians with impunity. As Otis was quick to realize, there was an urgent need to create some form of civil-military organization to govern the newly acquired area.[7]

Because Otis believed that the Philippine War was essentially a Tagalog affair, he had great expectations for civil government in non-Tagalog areas such as northern Luzon. Otis saw pacification as entailing the restoration of order through garrisoning towns, protecting the populace, and creating a working civil government. He did not believe that Aguinaldo's partisans would continue armed resistance against these new civil governments. Assuming that the majority of the Filipino population was friendly, he believed that all that was needed was honest government and Army protection.[8]

On 20 December 1899, Otis placed Brig. Gen. Samuel B. M. Young in charge of the newly created District of North-Western Luzon and assigned him the Thirty-third U.S.V. Infantry, Third U.S. Cavalry, and a battalion each of the Thirty-fourth and Twenty-ninth U.S.V. Infantry as a constabulary force. This force was further augmented in March with the arrival of the Forty-eighth U.S.V. Infantry to replace the battalion of Twenty-ninth, giving Young about 4,000 officers and men. Young was instructed to establish civil government in his district and, specifically, to organize the towns under G.O. 43. Young, in turn, further subdivided the district into provincial commands with a military governor in command of each province and the troops in it. This basic structure was retained when the District of North-Western Luzon was renamed the First District, Department of Northern Luzon, in the reorganization of 7 April 1900.[9]

Young, who remained the district commander, was a six-foot four-inch, 250-pound, sixty-year-old veteran of the Civil War, several Indian campaigns, and the Cuban expedition. Like many senior regular Army officers, he had a meteoric career during the Civil War, rising from private to brevet brigadier general, but in the postwar Army he had stagnated as a cavalry captain for twenty years and not been promoted colonel until he was fifty-seven. In the Philippines during the northern operations of late 1899 he distinguished himself by cutting his cavalry free of its supply train and storming north to cut off Aguinaldo's retreat. Only the dilatory and hesitant conduct of Wheaton prevented Young from capturing the escaping president and bottling up the Republican Army. Despite his fine combat record, Young took command of the First District under a cloud which his own choleric temper did little to dispel. Before departing for the archipelago, he had written an ill-advised letter criticizing Otis's conduct of operations and upon his arrival he was given a severe tongue-lashing by his outraged superior. Shortly after, his transfer to brigadier general in the regulars caused him to lose his seniority in the volunteers, resulting in his being passed over for promotion to major general by his former subordinates, Wheaton and Robert Hall. Convinced that Otis and others were conspiring to destroy his career,

Young's personal bitterness, "irritable" disposition, and suspicions colored his views on everything from the manpower shortage in his district to the character of the Filipinos. He vented his frustration by advocating extreme solutions, including a controversial suggestion that the Americans adopt the methods of "European nations" such as summary executions, concentration of the civilian population, and complete military rule. Eventually, his vitriolic and often contradictory reports led his superiors to view him as an alarmist.[10]

Despite his penchant for racist remarks and repressive solutions, Young was a capable and effective district commander. He was fortunate enough to be assigned excellent subordinates, but he should be given full credit for encouraging them and weeding out incompetents. It is no accident that some of the most creative provincial counterinsurgency policies were developed under his tenure. There is no evidence that he implemented the extreme measures he advocated in his letters or that he tolerated misconduct in his theater. Although he disliked many Filipino characteristics and was critical of the Army's benevolent policies, asserting, "I do not believe that one in a hundred (surely not more) of these benighted tribes comprehend in the lowest degree the spirit or meaning of magnanimity," he enjoyed pleasant relations with individual Filipinos, especially the provincial elite and the clerics. As district commander he pioneered the introduction of new crops and diversified agriculture, demanded that loyal Filipinos be armed, and strongly advocated state-supported education. His extreme and ethnocentric statements should not obscure his humanitarian efforts or his concern for Filipinos who had endangered themselves by supporting American government.[11]

Civil administration in northwestern Luzon was coordinated at the district level by Capt. John G. Ballance. Ballance had served with Young and had impressed him as one of the finest officers in the Army. At Young's urging, Ballance was given the unwieldy title of "Chief Assistant and Advisor to the Military Governor" in February 1900. This in effect set up two channels of communication, with officers required to report on civil affairs to Ballance and on military affairs to their commanding officer. In practice, however, these lines of authority were often confused; Ballance actually functioned as Young's chief of staff, supervised district intelligence activities, and coordinated the implementation of district general orders. As confidant and occasional emissary for Young, he played a vital role in the determination and implementation of policy and perhaps moderated Young's impulsiveness.[12]

In accordance with Otis's mandate as well as Young's personal preferences, northwestern Luzon was the site of a major effort at municipal government.

On the same day the district was created, Young ordered the establishment of civil governments under G.O. 43. The practical nature of this thrust can be seen in the instructions issued to officers, who were ordered to devote at least one day to organize each municipality and to impress upon the population the necessity of forming local police to hunt down *ladrones*. They were also enjoined to remind the populace that while the U.S. Army forces were available for assistance, the main burden of self-protection lay upon the individual towns. The speed with which these civic governments were created was impressive: within three months sixty-three *pueblos* (towns) were organized, each with a *presidente*, town council, and police force.[13]

Along with an attempt to establish municipal governments went a vigorous attempt to reform district education. District headquarters ordered officers to establish schools in their towns, and monthly reports on teachers, salaries, and attendance were expected from post commanders as part of their civil report. In April, Young requested authority to hire soldiers at fifty cents a day to teach in local schools, arguing that "the benefit to the government from the knowledge of English that would be acquired would more than pay the expenses."[14] In June, he reported that there were 203 schools in his district enrolling 10,714 students out of a total school-age population of 44,716. He also outlined an ambitious program to establish two schools in each of the district's seventy-five *pueblos* and requested English teachers, building materials, and school supplies, all of which "should be maintained by the Government."[15]

Young's interest in education and civil government was shared both by his officers and Filipinos. Lt. Col. Robert L. Howze, the military governor of Ilocos Norte province, appointed a local politician, Aguedo Abayani, as civil adjutant and had the local municipal governments in the province work through him. He proudly reported that in the capital of Laoag, school attendance had climbed from 253 students in May to 625 in October, and urged building new schools and developing a Spanish-English-Ilocano primer. In many cases, officers found their enthusiasm echoed by Filipinos; one *presidente* announced he could raise 19,000 pesos for education, and in another town the commander and the local school board cooperated in building new desks, painting the school, and cleaning up the grounds. There was other evidence of Filipino satisfaction with American benevolent policies: the citizens of the *pueblo* of Santa Maria, who had earlier changed their name to Tinio, now petitioned that they be allowed to change it to Young, a request that was denied. Despite the haste with which the municipal governments and benevolent policies were established, many officers believed that they were effective: Army civil reports in early 1900 stress Ilocano satisfaction with American authority.[16]

However, the initial optimism which characterized civil government soon faded before a host of unforeseen problems. Although it set forth the basic structure for municipal government, the Army's organizational plan, G.O. 43, had serious weaknesses when put into practical application. It designated a number of industries and trades as liable for taxation, but most of these were irrelevant to the agricultural economy of the First District. At first both Ballance and Young attempted to follow the provisions of the order by insisting that municipalities provide for the salaries of their officials, teachers, and police. By June, however, Young protested that the area was "taxed to death" and stated that until finances were straightened out there was little hope of effective civil government.[17]

In addition to the inefficient tax structure established in G.O. 43, time revealed numerous other problems with military/civil government. Both Filipinos and Americans had to adjust to their new duties and responsibilities and, as one harassed officer assigned to civil duties confessed, "all matters seem unsettled and answers to questions not clear and sometimes contradictory."[18] Young commented to President McKinley that providing honest government to win over the population was difficult because the Filipinos were justifiably suspicious after decades of Spanish corruption. There were not enough officers to fill both military and civil requirements and essential services were delayed by the slowness of the Army bureaucracy in Manila to confirm local appointments or authorize essential payments. All too often, American reforms either ignored local customs or were pursued with more self-righteousness than tact. The order prohibiting cockfighting and gambling, for example, not only destroyed a major source of municipal revenue but lectured Filipinos that the "prevalence of these vices has been a serious hindrance to the mental, moral and material development of the Filipino people and their continuance will in the future prevent them from having a place among the people of modern civilization."[19] In their efforts to establish civil order and support their civic officials, some garrison officers were drawn into local rivalries or factional struggles. Often American-appointed officials proved inept or dishonest; Ballance castigated the council of Vigan for appropriating nearly all the municipal revenues for their salaries and Young cynically remarked that people voted for whoever could plunder them least. Despite his commitment to civil government, Young occasionally succumbed to fits of depression, informing McKinley that the population was "densely ignorant and utterly unfit to exercise the right of suffrage."[20] Other officers had an even more practical argument against civil government: it overlooked the still unsettled conditions in the countryside where the Army faced *ladrones*, guerrillas, and Igorrote mountaineers. Col. William P. Duvall, the commander in La Union province, bluntly stated, "The best assistance the Military authorities can now give to the schools is to guarantee to the towns a stable government and to the people personal safety."[21]

Duvall shrewdly struck at the central weakness of the early First District pacification policies based on civil government, education, and social reform: the assumption that the Ilocano provinces were peaceful and the inhabitants were eager to accept American authority. In light of the simultaneous emergence of a strong indigenous resistance in the district, it is clear that many officers overestimated the effectiveness of these benevolent measures. Garrison commanders may have been guilty of tailoring their reports to what they believed their superiors wished to hear or uncritically accepting the flattering assertions of *presidentes* and *americanistas* (pro-Americans). Other officers mistook their achievements in a particular town as indicative of the popularity of American occupation throughout the district. Unfamiliar with the language and lacking accurate sources of information, some officers accepted the visible functioning of government, schools, and sanitation projects as evidence of actual pacification. Others complacently dismissed disturbances in the countryside as the work of "small bands of thieves and robbers," and refused to acknowledge the growing signs of guerrilla resistance.[22]

Few of the American officers busily organizing the district's towns recognized that the Filipino revolutionaries were engaged in the same process. By controlling the local political structure, the guerrillas could insure that their regular troops would be fed and protected and that their agents could operate with impunity. They could build on strong foundations; the Philippine Republic had controlled the Ilocano provinces for over a year and in most places civic and revolutionary officials, who often shared a similar socioeconomic background and lived in the same towns, had reached an accommodation. Before the American invasion, municipal officials had enthusiastically supported the recruitment of soldiers, organized town guards and militia, and collected taxes. In late 1899, as Tinio's forces were driven back, they were aided by sympathetic *presidentes* and town councils, who sheltered and protected them as the American pursuit swept past. The hasty Army efforts to establish civil government in early 1900 did little to root these revolutionaries out: the Americans often confirmed the very municipal officials appointed by the Philippine Republic. When Tinio and his subordinates began reorganizing for guerrilla war, these officials were contacted, and, sometimes through exhortation or intimidation, most were won over to the revolutionary cause. In Ilocos Norte, where the Americans had few troops, the provincial commander concluded that by May "every pueblo to my certain knowledge had its insurrecto municipal government, many of their officials being the same as those put in by us."[23]

It is probable that most municipal governments initially supported the guerrillas for either patriotic or social reasons, but the element of coercion should not be underestimated. The revolutionaries recognized the threat posed by civil governments loyal to the Army and singled out for punishment those *presidentes* who collaborated with the Americans or failed to cooperate with the guerrillas. According to First District statistics, one-quarter of all the recorded assassinations of pro-American Filipinos were of civic officials. As one provincial commander pointed out, the threat of assassination was so great that "some of the presidentes prefer not to collect money for salaries, prefer not to have funds in their possession and some prefer to lie to me rather than take the chance of losing life and Municipal funds to the insurgents."[24]

Because of Aguinaldo's desire to retain northern Luzon under his own control, the revolutionary leadership remained in some flux at first. The president's precipitate retreat through the Ilocano region prevented his assuming command and left Tinio as Aguinaldo's designated subordinate. Although he was a prominant landowner, *ilustrado*, and veteran revolutionary, Tinio faced formidable obstacles in maintaining his control over the Ilocano provinces. As a Tagalog from Nueva Ecija, he was an outsider who owed his authority largely to his commission from the Philippine Republic. The destruction of his brigade in 1899 and the collapse of Aguinaldo's government left him with few personal forces and little possibility of raising new ones. Undaunted by these obstacles, Tinio began to plan for guerrilla warfare even as his regular forces were in the process of dissolution. As long as the resistance in the First District continued, Tinio issued a flood of orders coordinating the activities of provincial operations, appointing commanders, and maintaining guerrilla bands. From the beginning, he recognized the importance of controlling the *presidentes* and municipal governments and directed a great deal of attention to making certain that they cooperated with the guerrillas. He also sought to mobilize popular support through patriotic proclamations and grim warnings. American officers believed Tinio responsible for guerrilla operations throughout the district and Frederick Sexton called him "the soul of the Insurrection in the Ilocano provinces."[25]

Much of Tinio's power depended on his ability to work with such provincial commanders as Lt. Col. Juan Villamor, Col. Blas Villamor, Lt. Col. Juan Guitterez, Capt. Ignacio Peralta, Maj. Isobel Abaya, and Father Gregorio Aglipay. Most of these officers were natives of the Ilocano provinces and had close familial and social connections with the local municipal elite—in many cases they were related to the very civic officials appointed by the Americans. Juan Villamor was the most capable of these: a former officer in the Spanish Army, he had been an early proponent of guerrilla warfare, an editor for a revolutionary paper, and a delegate to the Philippine Republic's Congress. A native of Abra, he was a competent and efficient guerrilla leader, highly respected by the Army officers who faced him for his chivalry and good treatment of prisoners. His cousin Blas was also an effective guerrilla leader who operated largely on the Ilocos Sur–Abra border. The Villamors had strong local support, in part because their family was both very large and related to many of the most prominent families in the area: James LeRoy believed that their guerrillas "represented a virtual consolidation of the Ilokan [sic] principalia in a number of towns around Bigan [Vigan] and Abra."[26] In La Union province, Lt. Col. Juan Guitterez, although a Tagalog from Manila, was engaged to the daughter of the former provincial governor and with his assistance controlled many of the municipal governments. In Ilocos Sur, Capt. Ignacio Peralta was the son of a former *presidente* of Santa Cruz and Maj. Isobel Abaya was a businessman from one of the largest and most powerful families in Candon. Gregorio Aglipay, an excommunicated Ilocano priest from Ilocos Norte, was instrumental in turning the coastal towns south of Laoag into strongholds of revolutionary sentiment. Aglipay had been a key figure in Aguinaldo's government, but Tinio was "hostile to Aglipay and his pretensions" even before the American invasion. Aglipay refused to acknowledge Tinio's authority and relations between them eventually deteriorated so badly that Tinio ordered the priest's arrest.[27]

Following the pattern that occurred in most areas in Luzon, the First District guerrillas were divided into full-time partisans, or regulars, and a part-time militia, often referred to as the Sandahatan, or bolo-men. The regulars were the military elite of the revolutionary forces and were responsible for such combat operations as ambushing U.S. detachments or attacking towns. According to their instructions, they operated in small bands of 30 to 50 men, with some 200 assigned to a province and dispersed into three or four zones. Ideally, these bands belonged to much larger military organizations such as battalions or regiments and were supposed to consolidate a few times a month for a major operation. In practice, they seem to have operated in even smaller groups of 5 to 10 men whose membership and organization changed constantly. When attacked by Army patrols, guerrillas would flee for the nearest *barrio*, hide their weapons, and become "amigos."[28] The militia, or Sandahatan, acted as the intelligence and supply arm of the guerrilla organization. While the partisans were supposed to deal with the U.S. Army, the militia spied on its movements and supported the administration to insure that supplies were gathered, taxes paid, and villagers kept loyal. The militia was further divided into a small semiregular force and a number of volunteers who could be called upon for tax collecting, wire cutting, or intimidating collaborators. Living in the villages and pursuing their peacetime occupations, the militia provided both an invisible police force and a ready reserve for the guerrillas. The militia supplied the recruits to keep the regulars active, either from its own ranks or by enforcing a draft, and hid weapons and guerrillas from Army patrols. Often overlooked by Army officers concentrating on the more visible regulars, the militia was of vital importance in sustaining resistance and keeping the regulars in combat.[29]

Of equal importance with the military arm was the civil and administrative network. The regular forces were supplied and paid by contributions levied on each native and exacted by tax collectors with the help of the militia and complaisant municipal officials. In towns controlled by shadow governments, tax collectors and recruiters could operate openly, but even in garrisoned towns they were usually well known to the population. Donations and supplies were taken to storehouses and depots hidden in the hills, allowing the regulars to spend weeks in a particular area. The civil administrator, or *jefe principal*, was also responsible for enforcing proscriptions on collaboration, establishing outposts to spy on American forces, and disseminating guerrilla orders. One officer described the *jefes principales* as "the men upon whom the insurgents rely for supplies, money and men . . . they constitute their line of communications and supply."[30]

In its ideal state, regulars, militia, and *jefes* all worked together in the manner described by one officer:

> The Insurrectos have a regularly organized government throughout these districts, with a Jefe principal and assistants for each pueblo and corresponding officials for each "centro," which comprises from three to eight or ten adjoining barrios. In each "centro" is an irregular force, usually a platoon of guerrillas, who keep their arms hidden but ready to turn out at a moment's notice, either to join the regular troops of the Insurgents or to attack small bodies of Americans whenever a favorable opportunity exists. In addition there are hundreds of men—so called "hermanos" (brothers), armed with fighting (not

working) *bolos*. Besides these irregulars, who ordinarily remain at or near their homes, there were . . . not less than from four hundred to five hundred riflemen under the orders of Generals Tinio, Aglipay, Alejandrino, Natividad, Colonels Salazar, Blas Villamor, Comandante Celedeño and others.[31]

The Army attempt to pacify northwestern Luzon through civil government thus clashed with the revolutionary attempt to utilize civil government to continue resistance. In most cases, the Americans were the clear losers in the struggle for popularity and legitimacy. The speed with which the municipal governments were established, the problems inherent in their organizational structure, and the limited size of the American occupying forces created substantial problems. When these were combined with the growing Filipino resistance, the entire policy was undermined. Although some viable governments were established in areas with strong garrisons or particularly capable officers, the majority of civil administrations were not loyal to the Army but, rather, actively assisted the guerrillas.

The fragility of Army pacification was thoroughly demonstrated in La Union province in the spring of 1900. The first soldiers in the province were detachments dropped off by Young during his pursuit of Aguinaldo and Tinio. Composed often of the sick and fatigued, these small garrisons proved too weak to prevent guerrilla attacks upon the supply wagons on the coast road. They were further strained by the withdrawal of a detachment of Filipino auxiliaries for disciplinary reasons. Although Young and Otis were concerned about continuing violence in the province, its first commander, Lt. Col. Henry W. Wessells, believed that there were only "a few small bands of thieves as there are in every country."[32] Wessells complied with Young's orders to establish civil governments, but Wessells's erratic leadership left most of the responsibility in the hands of his junior officers. In the meantime, Wessells alternated between optimism and alarm: in February he complained that friendly Filipinos were being murdered, yet in March he boasted he could ride from one end of the province to the other without an escort.[33]

Neither Wessells's subordinates nor his superiors shared his confidence, and they grew increasingly skeptical as conditions in the province grew progressively worse. Although municipal governments were established and the people were outwardly friendly, Young commented that some areas of the province were "very bad" and full of guerrillas who were "amigos in the daytime." Privately, he believed that Wessells's physical infirmities, including almost total deafness, and his "incompetence" made him unfit to govern.[34] One officer in the province, Capt. Franklin O. Johnson, reported that there were at least five revolutionary organizations within ten miles of the town of Namacpacan alone. Johnson claimed that the guerrillas had a "well organized system of espionage," which reported Army movements; moreover, his own spies led him to distrust the recently elected municipal officers. He pointed out that in five weeks of activity in La Union the Army had suffered six dead, six wounded, and two missing, as well as fourteen rifles lost.[35] The province's reputation as a guerrilla stronghold was not confined to the officers who served there; shortly before he left Manila, Col. William P. Duvall was shown a map of the province by General Otis with the explanation, "This, today, is the worst part of the Philippine Islands."[36]

In early March a leader of the Guardia de Honor religious sect, Crispulo Patajo, was turned over to the American authorities by the *presidente* of Bauang as a suspected outlaw. The Guardia had been a source of trouble to the Philippine Republic in the provinces to the south because of their pro-Spanish activities, agrarian radicalism, and millennarian beliefs. Patajo, however, was apparently free of the fanaticism attributed to the sect and was considered an intelligent, pragmatic, and capable leader of La Union's Guardias. Interviewed by Lt. William T. Johnston, he denounced Bauang's *presidente* as a revolutionary agent and offered to expose the entire guerrilla military and administrative network in the area. Johnston, who was soon to demonstrate a remarkable flair for counterinsurgency intelligence, promptly released the Guardia leader and accepted his offer of help. In the next weeks, Patajo identified guerrillas living in Army-occupied towns, showed Johnston the location of supply depots, and even fought on the American side in several skirmishes. More important, he explained to Johnston the connection between the guerrilla bands and the towns that supplied and sheltered them.

In mid-March, Wessells was replaced by Duvall, who assigned Johnston the task of further investigating the connection between the Army-organized municipal governments and the guerrilla bands. Johnston and Patajo examined nine *pueblos* in La Union province, several of which were garrisoned by American forces. Johnston's findings, summarized in his 21 May report, "Investigation into the Methods Adopted by the Insurgents for Organizing and Maintaining a Guerrilla Force," was a thorough exposé of the provincial guerrilla organization. He concluded that revolutionary influence was pervasive; although the towns varied in their degree of support to the guerrillas, all of them contributed money and supplies and all did so with the connivance of their municipal governments. Within weeks of the Army's creation of municipal government, the newly appointed town officials had met with revolutionary leaders and formed guerrilla units in their towns. Over the governments organized under G.O. 43, they had superimposed their own organization of regulars, militia, and *jefes principales*. Funds were raised by taxes and by doctoring the municipal books, regular guerrilla forces were raised and quartered in the *barrios* or in camps just outside the towns, and revolutionary leaders, including Tinio, actually lived near or in La Union's villages and met frequently with the American-appointed civic officials.

The impact of Johnston's findings was considerable. The "Investigation" argued that despite the destruction of Aguinaldo's conventional forces, the Philippine War was not over and that the Army's municipal governments could not by themselves guarantee pacification. It was, in Johnston's words, "the first news that the insurrectos were actively at work organizing and the first indication that the American authorities had that the native officials of the towns and others were playing a double role."[37] MacArthur, who had recently succeeded Otis as commander in the Philippines, believed it was "altogether the best description which has reached these headquarters of the insurgent method of organizing and maintaining a guerrilla force." He incorporated many of Johnston's findings into his own annual report and later into the policies that were implemented throughout the archipelago. Indeed, MacArthur's view that the guerrillas in the field were sustained by their supporters in the towns owes most of its inspiration directly to Johnston's "Investigation."[38]

Within La Union, the investigation had an immediate effect. Duvall directed American counterinsurgency efforts at destroying not only the guerrilla bands, but their supporting infrastructure in the towns. He appointed Patajo as a chief of detectives for La Union province and authorized him to recruit his Guardia de Honor followers as a counterinsurgency vigilante force. In the next few weeks, Patajo raised between 400 and 500 volunteers who ranged throughout La Union and Benguet, often with American forces for support, and hunted down guerrilla units. These irregulars were not paid, but they were allowed to turn in any rifle they obtained for the thirty-peso reward authorized by Otis. At the same time, American soldiers with loyal native guides, usually members of the Guardia, were able to inflict substantial casualties on the regular guerrilla units.[39]

Duvall also established a provincial intelligence system that made use of Guardia de Honor, former revolutionaries, and Johnston. In early April he captured the rosters of two of the regular guerrilla companies stationed in the province, thus allowing his subordinates to "pick up insurrectos like chickens off a roost." Prisoners were given their freedom if they agreed to accompany U.S. forces and identify their former comrades. Having compromised themselves by collaboration and knowing that they risked guerrilla retaliation, they "seemed most anxious to ferret out all insurrectos in this vicinity."[40] Johnston investigated an incident in which soldiers captured more than seventy men bearing the letter C, for Katipunan, branded on their chests. For a time, the Americans feared that the guerrillas had created a terrorist secret society, but Johnston concluded that the branded men had "undoubtedly [been] made members through force or fear," and that "we are playing directly into the hands of the insurrectos if we make prisoners of this class."[41] As a result, the soldiers turned the prisoners loose and arrested the civic officials responsible for branding them.

The guerrillas' response to American counterinsurgency measures proved inadequate. As early as March, Col. Blas Villamor wrote that the Guardias were supporting the Americans more and more, and that people in the south of the province were becoming disillusioned with the revolutionary cause. The revolutionary leadership threatened to burn any towns that tolerated the presence of Guardia supporters and tried in addition to organize an anti-Guardia campaign by sending Maj. Anicela Angeles's regulars to attack the Guardia militia. When these measures failed, Tinio reversed previous policy and instructed his subordinates to conciliate the Guardias if at all possible. Patajo was not included in this amnesty; a reward of 150 pesos was offered for the head of that "traidor y terrible Americanista llamado Crispulo Patajo."[42]

The revolutionaries discovered, however, that they could not regain control of the towns, where the Guardia de Honor infrastructure had replaced their own. Ballance and Duvall had relied on Patajo for recommendations to municipal offices, and these *americanistas*—many of them Guardia partisans and some of them Patajo's relatives—permitted the Army to conduct more active operations. Leaving the towns to the protection of vigilante groups and local police forces, the Army and Guardia irregulars undertook long sweeps into the mountains. As Patajo's men moved through La Union and Benguet on patrols, they held rallies in which villagers denounced revolutionary agents, confessed previous misdeeds, embraced the American flag, bought Guardia rosaries, and joined the sect. If necessary, Patajo would establish a new government and form a Guardia militia in the town, often promoting peasants and lower-class elements and displacing the native elite. This social leveling shook the *principalía*, and, in the words of one observer, forced them to "come down from the fence" by "bringing to light all acts of disloyalty on their parts."[43]

In their support of Patajo's volunteers, officers in La Union often ignored official Army policy. Otis viewed the Guardia as "religious fanatics" and there is some evidence that he forbade Army officers to utilize their services. In addition, the officers in La Union were castigated by Brig. Gen. Jacob H. Smith, commanding in neighboring Pangasinan province, who complained about the Army–Guardia collaboration in La Union and the character of Crispulo Patajo. Smith's accusations prompted several inquiries from Manila which were evaded by Duvall and Young. With Young's complicity, officers disguised their own connection with the Guardias while pointing out the hatred that the revolutionaries bore the sectarians. To Johnston the official suspicions were irrelevant: "As to whether [Patajo] is a guardia d'honor I do not know or care."[44] Nevertheless, the alliance was further threatened in November 1900, when civil government was instituted in the province of Benguet. Phelps Whitmarsh, Benguet's new governor, complained to both MacArthur and William H. Taft about the activities of Patajo and the Guardia. Taft in turn reported to Secretary of War Elihu Root that Duvall had "produced a system of terrorism by using a secret society opposed to the insurrection and permitting its members to guide him in prosecutions that can do no good, but on the contrary, do a great deal of harm."[45] But in spite of repeated protests, the obvious success of the Guardia vigilantes precluded their dismissal. When Brig. Gen. J. Franklin Bell took command of the First District, he reversed his earlier anti-Guardia policies and continued to employ Patajo and his followers as auxiliaries; indeed, their activities were expanded outside the province.[46]

The entire controversy is instructive, for it illustrates the localization of the Army's pacification programs from province to province. Despite official policy to the contrary, officers in La Union seized the opportunity provided by an organization that was potentially hostile to the revolutionaries and therefore a potential basis for a popular militia. The provincial commander, Duvall, was astute enough to encourage Johnston's investigations of the province's civil government, an institution that had failed to produce the results expected of it. More important, he was courageous enough to act upon his subordinate's recommendations. Believing from the beginning that Filipinos were best suited to fight other Filipinos, Duvall steadily pursued his policy in the face of opposition from both the Army high command and Taft. By adapting the official policy of civil government to the realities of the situation in La Union, the Army was able to pacify the province in five months.

The war in Ilocos Norte in April 1900 demonstrates a different aspect of the guerrilla war: a popular uprising based on religious fears. The attackers were less partisans of independence than simple villagers who believed that their religion was being threatened. As in La Union province, fifty miles to the south, the war in Ilocos Norte was essentially provincial, touched off by local factors and conducted within the provincial boundaries. Similarly, the American pacification campaign was confined within the province and reflected the response of local officers to the situation in their immediate area.

The first American forces in Ilocos Norte were U.S. Marines landed at the provincial capital of Laoag to guard supplies for Young. Shortly after, Lt. Col. Robert L. Howze's battalion of the Thirty-fourth moved up the coastal road on the heels of the Tinio Brigade, defeating it on 9 December and breaking it into scattered groups. Within a few weeks, civil government was established in Banqui and Laoag, and other towns were organized in January and February. Howze, who had distinguished himself in the campaign, was appointed the military governor and speedily set to work implementing Otis's pacification policies. He appointed local officials, built schools, and sought to convince Filipinos of the benefits of American occupation. A Texan who had already won a Medal of Honor in the Indian wars and had rendered outstanding service in Cuba and the Philippines, Howze had little difficulty in making the transition from combat commander to provincial governor.

In contrast to La Union, Ilocos Norte saw little evidence of guerrilla activity for three months after its occupation. In part this was because of American weakness: a mere five companies were assigned to the province, and these were confined to five towns. Throughout January and February, much of the Army's attention was focused on civil government, not on scouting for guerrillas. As a result, much of the province lay outside the Army's patrols, and officers were dependent on information from the newly appointed *presidentes*, who claimed there were no guerrillas nearby. Nevertheless, the Americans were aware that conditions in the countryside outside the garrison towns were unsettled. Increasingly, Howze believed "there is a strong undercurrent of bad spirit and preparations for a revolt."[47]

Throughout March, garrison commanders picked up growing indications that conditions were degenerating as telegraph lines were cut, convoys attacked, and loyal Filipinos threatened. Howze found "juntas" being organized in the towns, and natives being tattooed or branded with the *C*, triangle, or circle of the Katipunan society. There was disturbing evidence that the municipal governments were disloyal or being intimidated, and a *presidente* and two suspected Army spies were murdered. The vice-*presidente* of one town was arrested for branding forty-two men in a Katipunan ceremony and another was found to be serving as a messenger for Tinio. Army intelligence picked up rumors that Father Gregorio Aglipay, a native of Ilocos Norte, was organizing the province's inhabitants through the native clergy. Aglipay was reported to have a large force in the Batac-Badoc area, and Howze reported that "everybody in that locality [were] insurrectos."[48]

The presence of Aglipay gave a religious overtone to revolutionary activities in Ilocos Norte absent in other provinces of Luzon. John Schumacher believes that, beyond Aglipay's own leadership, there is little evidence of clerical support for the revolutionaries in the Ilocano provinces. Schumacher credits this both to Aglipay's excommunication and the anticlerical policies of Aguinaldo's government, factors that alienated clerics and made them distrust Aglipay. Such views were not shared by officers serving in Ilocos Norte, who believed that Aglipay used provincial priests to disseminate propaganda, recruit men, and gather supplies. According to Howze, "the influence of Padre Aglipay continues unabated, and he has appealed to the Catholic faith of the natives, calling on them to defend Catholicism against American religion. He is branding men and forcing them to serve him. He is making a great struggle which must be met."[49] By mid-March, Howze asserted bluntly that "all padres in this province are actively supporting the Insurrection" and requested authority to "remove all padres and [have] others be sent here who do not know the people, and who are not personal friends of Aglipay."[50]

Howze's suspicions that Aglipay was planning a "great struggle" were soon borne out. On 11 April an Army patrol captured documents that outlined a provincewide revolt to take place at the end of the month. According to these plans, the citizens of Ilocos Norte, many of whom had been recently branded and enrolled as Katupunan by Aglipay's agents, would rise en masse against the occupation forces. Citizens of garrisoned towns would be joined by recruits from outlying villages and *barrios*, and together they would overwhelm the small Army forces. Although short of men, Howze sent out detachments to disrupt the guerrillas' mobilization and to prevent unified action. On 15 and 16 April, these patrols inflicted substantial losses on guerrilla concentrations in the Batac-Badoc area but, at the same time, the 30-man garrison at Batac was subjected to a night attack by an estimated 800 revolutionaries. The Filipinos set fire to the town, and charged several times, using civilians as human shields. The small Army contingent withstood these assaults from their quarters and from the church, where about 1,500 townspeople had sought refuge. According to one account, Aglipay's followers resembled "Mahdi fanatics," while another claimed that they were all drunk. Certainly their attacks against the well-armed soldiers were almost suicidal. The Americans later counted 180 dead and 135 captured. A similar attack was made on Laoag on 17 April with equal disregard for American firepower and similar casualties. Howze telegraphed his commanding officer, "Much of fighting hand to hand by fanatics worked up to pitch by Padre Aglipay and Gen. Tinio's order. They were regular dervish charges. Slaughter terrible."[51] He estimated that more than 300 Filipinos had been killed in the two days of fighting whereas the Americans had lost 3 killed and 3 wounded.

Howze responded to the Ilocos Norte revolt with a combination of magnanimity and firmness. Believing that many of the attackers were not active revolutionaries but simple villagers whipped into a religious frenzy, he tried to detach them from the guerrillas and then crush the partisans who remained. He ordered the *presidentes* of Batac and Badoc to send out word to "hombres forced to fight and who do not wish to follow the Insurrectos to come in at once and they will be pardoned."[52] After a four-day grace period in which several hundred Filipinos surrendered, Howze launched an aggressive campaign. In pursuit of guerrilla bands, U.S. patrols ravaged the district around Batac, sending women and children into the town. In one engagement on 24 April a troop of cavalry surrounded some 300 guerrillas and in a desperate battle killed 125 of them. Shortly after, the guerrillas were reported to be suffering from disease, hunger, and were so demoralized that Tinio had to come to Ilocos Norte to try to rally them.[53]

The defeat of the Ilocos Norte revolt was a great victory for the Army. The Americans counted 520 enemy dead and believed they had inflicted substantially more casualties. They had not, as in La Union, destroyed the entire infrastructure, and guerrillas continued to be a problem in the south of the province along the Ilocos Sur and Abra borders. But even if the failure of the revolt did not lead to the complete pacification of the province, it marked a turning point in the provincial war. Howze's use of patrols had preempted the revolt, preventing the revolutionaries from coordinating their assault and leading to fragmented and dispersed attacks on the U.S. garrisons. Despite the large numbers of people they had been able to recruit, the revolutionaries had not been able to destroy a single American occupation force. The fighting brought most of the guerrillas' infrastructure into the open, and the Army was able to purge revolutionary sympathizers from several municipal governments. In Laoag, captured guerrillas were whipped and mistreated by the inhabitants, "because their town, which they seem to care very much for, was attacked and threatened with destruction by the bad men of the neighboring towns."[54] Similar hostility to the guerrillas may have occurred in other towns as well and prevented them from reestablishing their clandestine organizations. In June, Howze, who had previously been pessimistic about native police, concluded that they were loyal and should be allowed to keep their weapons. Although the Batac-Badoc-Paoay area and the Dingras Valley continued to be recognized guerrilla strongholds, they were the exception to the general tranquillity of the rest of the province. The April Ilocos Norte revolt destroyed much of the guerrillas' popular support, shattered their infrastructure, and left them weakened and on the defensive.

The Ilocos Norte and La Union provincial wars made it clear that pacification measures could not stop at civil government alone. In both Ilocos Norte and La Union many municipal governments were shown to be heavily influenced, if not controlled, by the revolutionaries. In some cases the very people the Army depended on to assert American authority were clandestinely working for the enemy. Yet if civil government as the chief policy had been exposed as inadequate, officers both at headquarters and in the field were far more aware of the nature of the enemy they faced. No longer could they believe that Tagalogs and bandits were the problem; what they confronted was a localized but districtwide guerrilla resistance. In the late spring, there was increased centralization as new First District policies were sought to break up the revolutionary infrastructure and give a uniform direction to counterinsurgency within the district.

The first districtwide policies to be implemented were travel restrictions and the declaration of martial law. On 22 May 1900, First District Headquarters issued Circular Letter no. 1, requiring all males in the Ilocos and La Union to have a registration certificate. Moreover, no male inhabitant over age eighteen was allowed outside the jurisdiction of his *pueblo* without a pass from his *presidente*. People arriving or departing from a *barrio* had to report to the *barrio* head, or *cabeza*, within twenty-four hours, who in turn had to report to the *presidente*. The *presidentes* were obliged to keep a register of their *pueblos'* inhabitants and to arrest all people without passes.[55] On 15 June those sections of G.O. 100 concerning the treatment and classification of spies, war rebels, war traitors, and prisoners of war were published as a proclamation to the inhabitants. The same proclamation also contained specific prohibitions against supplying the enemy with food, shelter, and information. Ten days later, First District headquarters issued additional prohibitions on the possession or hiding of firearms.[56]

The effect of these measures was twofold. By clarifying municipal and individual responsibility, and by defining to both soldiers and inhabitants just what constituted enemy action, they allowed commanding officers to punish not just the guerrillas in the field but the *presidentes* who tolerated them and the population who supported them as well. Moreover, the publication of the laws of war outlined sanctions potentially as harsh as those imposed by the guerrillas. But in addition to this tightening of social control over the populace, the new orders forced the civil governments to become active agents of pacification, and thus placed them in direct opposition to the guerrillas. Civil government became, in effect, a means of coercion, and not merely a preparation for colonial rule. Admittedly the enforcement of these laws was sporadic, but their existence provided officers with a useful tool for selective application.[57]

Another aspect of the new centralized policies in the First District was the organization and arming of native auxiliaries. The Army had entered northwestern Luzon with Castner's Lowe Scouts, a company of American soldiers and Tagalog scouts. This unit was reformed in January 1900 with Ilocano recruits, and by August it had been built up to 250 men. These scouts established a good reputation for patrolling and intelligence work, and Young, who was dubious about arming Filipinos, asserted in December that the "scouts have served faithfully, doing splendid work."[58] Officers who worked with them were enthusiastic, and others at least conceded their necessity in the manpower-poor First District: as Col. Wirt Davis noted, "whether the native scouts can be trusted to assist the troops is problematical. This fact can be ascertained only by subjecting them to actual test. As a matter of necessity, I recommend their employment in this command."[59] In addition to the officially enlisted U.S. Army Native Scouts, other informal auxiliaries, such as Patajo's forces, served in local campaigns.

First District officers were far less enthusiastic about the establishment of a provincial police force. Under the provisions of G.O. 87, MacArthur urged commanders to make suggestions for the raising of provincial constabulary. Young, however, believed that the police were "mere creatures of the presidentes and the people in power" and proposed instead a paramilitary force modeled on Mexico's Guardia Rural, armed only with antiquated weapons, and supervised by the state.[60] In September, Divisional Headquarters, perhaps exasperated by Young's objections, declared that it "desired that this whole matter of placing arms in the hands of the natives in your district be subject entirely to your orders and control."[61] Young used this blanket authorization to table any organization of a provincial police, and as late as February 1901 district reports blamed disturbed conditions for the lack of progress in the organization or arming of the native police.[62]

In addition to Young's active obstruction, efforts to organize a district police were hindered by the lack of consensus on organization, by Army delays in supplying firearms, and by confusion over who would control the police. MacArthur's call for a provincial constabulary seemed to contradict the earlier guidelines of G.O. 43 and 40 which established municipal police. Officers shared Young's perplexity over whether native police were to be municipal guards or part of a paramilitary district constabulary, and, as a result, suggestions for their organization ranged from battalion-sized units to small squads in each town. In the absence of a coherent policy for the entire district, the police were used by individual commanders for local pacification.[63]

First District headquarters had better success in its efforts to establish a central intelligence system. Native spies had been employed from the earliest days of American occupation and Young established his own private network of paid informers, but there had been little attempt to exchange information within the district. Duvall complained that high-ranking enemy officers were allowed to escape because soldiers had no way of ascertaining their identities. Perhaps responding to the lack of centralization, in May of 1900 Ballance added the task of collecting and disseminating vital military information to his other duties. As district intelligence officer, he passed on information about suspected guerrillas, analyzed captured documents, and ordered the arrest of the agents collecting revolutionary taxes.[64]

Though no longer basing its pacification policies primarily on civil government, the Army still continued its attempts to win Filipino popular support by demonstrating the benefits of American rule. The work of organizing governments, or in the case of towns where shadow governments had been discovered, of reorganizing governments, still continued, though officers were more careful in selecting officials than before: Duvall, for example, urged the exclusion of candidates who had held office under the Philippine Republic, while Col. Marcus Cronin instructed that a new police lieutenant "be a man of property, so that we may have a hold upon him."[65] In addition, the Army undertook a districtwide program to stamp out smallpox, hiring Filipino doctors and shipping vaccine from Manila. Young and Ballance recognized that much of the unrest in the district stemmed from economic conditions, and urged their superiors to support public works programs. Referring to the troublesome area around Batac, Ilocos Norte, Ballance requested $40,000 for road repair and to provide jobs, arguing that the inhabitants were "poor and needy and having nothing, join the insurgents where by robbery and forced assessments they obtain something to eat. If work can be provided for them they will be able to provide food in a legitimate manner, and their greatest inducement to join the insurgents will be removed."[66]

The new laws and restrictions, increased emphasis on native auxiliaries, creation of a district intelligence service, and continued emphasis on civil government represented an attempt to establish more uniform pacification policies throughout the First District. Aimed at specific problems common throughout the district, the new measures demonstrated a far more sophisticated view of the situation in northwestern Luzon and indicated a great deal of innovation and adaptability at district headquarters. While the travel restrictions struck at guerrillas and their suppliers, the laws of war educated the population as to potential penalties for aiding the enemy. The early establishment of a district intelligence service recognized the vital need for reliable information, allowing district headquarters to coordinate operations against guerrilla bands while the use of the Native Scouts gave the Army auxiliaries who knew the terrain and local dialects. Finally, the continued effort at civil government offered some concessions to those Filipinos who did cooperate with the Americans.

Sophisticated as these responses might have been, they did not prevent further hostilities. At the end of the rainy season in early September the insurgents began a major offensive in the First District. Although other areas of the Philippines experienced an upsurge in combat at this time, in no other area did the revolutionary forces so openly challenge American occupation. From September to November the guerrillas inflicted almost 50 percent more casualties on the American forces than during the rest of the district's pacification.

Much of the revolutionary activity was concentrated in Abra, an isolated and mountainous province whose only access was via the Abra River. For much of the early war Abra had been one of the quietest areas, manned only by a weak and sickly battalion of the Thirty-third Infantry stationed at the capital city of Bangued.[67] The guerrilla forces were composed of two fifty-man regular companies and a local militia with perhaps 150 rifles, led by Lt. Col. Juan Villamor, the best provincial guerrilla leader in the district. Throughout 1900 Villamor had conserved these forces, concentrating primarily on controlling the towns and villages outside of Bangued, and rarely challenging the Army forces. As a member of the provincial elite, Villamor had close connections with many of the most influential people in the province. In addition, he had been quick to establish contact with municipal leaders and, with a mixture of exhortation and intimidation, to insure that they cooperated.[68]

The first indication of insurgent power in Abra came in late July when Bangued's civil government was reorganized and new elections were held.

Out of a population of some 13,000, 26 people registered and 21 voted, confirming Lt. Col. Peyton C. March, the provincial commander, in his belief that "civil government throughout this Province is more or less a farce."[69] On 28 August a company of Native Scouts was ambushed and routed near Pilar, and its American officer was killed. On 7 September Young wrote his superiors demanding more troops and claiming that "the insurrection has assumed such proportions in Abra that I do not consider it advisable to send out a detachment with less than one hundred rifles."[70] Conditions in the province grew steadily worse throughout September and October. Army patrols and guerrilla bands clashed in several sharp engagements. The crucial supply rafts operating along the Abra River, the only entrance to Bangued, were attacked, and companies attempting to clear the riverbanks ran into large enemy concentrations. The guerrillas fired into Bangued constantly from the surrounding hills. In early October, a report on the province claimed that Bangued was "at its worst": the telegraph lines had been cut, the police had fled, much of the town was destroyed, and the population was terrified. To add insult to injury, the town band deserted to the guerrillas.[71]

Although Abra was the focus of revolutionary action, the guerrillas were active elsewhere. In the Batac-Badoc area, Howze reported that "the insurgent party are kidnapping and probably killing the American party" and guerrillas virtually destroyed Army communications in September, cutting telegraph wires and poles faster than they could be replaced.[72] In the same month there were also disturbances in the Dingras Valley area and reports of partisan companies mobilizing on the border. The greatest disaster for the Americans, however, occurred in relatively peaceful Ilocos Sur on 25 October. At Cusucus, Tinio and Juan Villamor trapped an Army expedition in a narrow canyon. Lt. Charles Febiger and four other soldiers were killed, and fourteen more were wounded—the worst losses inflicted on the Army during the entire pacification of the First District.[73]

In another sense, a major casualty of the offensive was the First District commander, Brig. Gen. Samuel B. M. Young. The outbreak in August had caught him by surprise and provoked a somewhat panicky letter to his superiors, declaring that resistance had reached dangerous proportions and hinting at possible defeat. As the war showed no signs of ending, he began to advocate a harsh and repressive policy. On 11 December he openly criticized Army policy in the Philippines, claiming it was based on a false assumption of Filipino character, and urging the adoption of the "effective" methods used by the "Spanish and other European nations." Young believed it essential to "inspire rebellious Asiatics, individually and collectively, with a greater fear of the reigning government than they had of the rebels." He advocated the use of troops to fill positions in civil government, the conferring of supreme power on military commanders to make or change laws, retaliation in kind, concentration of the civilian population, devastation of guerrilla base areas, deportation, and summary execution. Young's intemperate suggestions and his reputation as an alarmist, coupled with Taft's personal dislike for Young, made the general a liability to his superiors. As a result, he was one of several senior officers either retired or promoted out of the Philippines during a command shakeup in February 1901.[74]

In response to both the guerrilla offensive and Young's requests there was a dramatic increase in American troop strength during the late fall and early winter. In August, when the guerrilla offensive started, the First District had only 3,985 officers and men, of whom 10 percent were sick. Moreover, many of the men carried as "effectives" were capable of only light duties and could not be used for patrols or expeditions. In October, troop strength had increased to 4,897 and in late November, to 5,866. With nearly a 50 percent increase in manpower in two months, the Army was able to garrison previously neglected areas and launch sustained offensive operations.[75]

Army manpower also received a boost from the increasing use of native Filipino auxiliaries. The Native Scouts grew from 4 officers and 245 men in September 1900 to 11 officers and 568 men in March 1901, largely because Divisional Headquarters in January authorized district commanders to employ as many scouts as necessary to replace the departing U.S. Volunteer regiments.[76] Besides the organized Native Scouts, First District Headquarters encouraged less formal groups of Filipino auxiliaries, whose ardor was fanned by guerrilla terrorism. Young appointed Patajo chief of detectives for the entire First District and assigned him to clear up the *barrios* near Vigan and hunt down a gang that had randomly hacked more than thirty people to death and buried them on an isolated beach. In Ilocos Sur and Abra, Patajo was utilized to recruit and lead volunteers, who were not paid wages but received thirty pesos for every rifle they turned in as well as cash bounties for capturing guerrilla officers. They had such success that the new district commander, Brig. Gen. J. Franklin Bell, was urging all provincial commanders to recruit their own native irregulars.[77]

The First District also benefited from representatives of the newly formed Federal party who arrived in the district in early 1901 and were granted permission to hold meetings in the Ilocano provinces. At public rallies, the *federalistas* urged the population to work for peace, refrain from cooperating with the guerrillas, and accept American authority. They also corresponded with revolutionary leaders and went into the mountains to induce surrenders. Bell encouraged his officers to support the Federal party because he believed this would convince intelligent Filipinos that the revolutionaries were to blame for continuing the war. In La Union, however, Duvall opposed the Federal party and his officers were "instructed to have nothing whatever to do with this organ nor any other that is merely political."[78] In contrast, Ballance believed that party representatives played an important role in negotiations with Tinio and Aglipay, and Col. William S. McCaskey, commander of Ilocos Norte, claimed that to the Federal party "more than any other influence is due the complete pacification of this province."[79] As with most pacification policies in northwestern Luzon, provincial commanders determined the actual implementation.

The Army was also able to enlist the clergy of the Ilocano provinces against the revolutionaries. Through the aid of an American chaplain, Young arranged for the Filipino clergy to take a prominent role in a series of mass meetings for civilians to take the Oath of Allegiance to the United States. In December, he presided over a ceremony involving some 2,190 former Katipunan members who took the oath and listened to "much earnest exhortation by the padres."[80] Throughout the winter, Ilocos Sur province was the site of rallies involving as few as 687 and as many as 2,200 Filipinos. Although First District directives insisted that local priests were present only to assist the military authorities, their contributions were doubtless more than mere pomp and ceremony. In one typical instance, the oath was taken on a Bible and accompanied by the kissing of a crucifix and a speech by the padre who urged his parishioners to abandon the guerrillas and turn in their weapons, and "earnestly described the advantages of peace and emphasized the solemnity and binding character of the obligation they were about to take."[81]

District Headquarters also developed a variety of methods to destroy the connections between towns and guerrillas. In some cases, the special talents of officers who had distinguished themselves in the earlier provincial wars were utilized. Johnston, who had first discovered the close ties between the towns of La Union and the revolutionaries, was given a warrant to investigate the towns in Ilocos Sur, "with a view to breaking up the secret support which had been rendered by these towns to the insurgents."[82] Special attention was paid to civic officials who failed to report guerrilla activity and post commanders were authorized to dismiss any municipal officers whom they suspected of contact with the guerrillas and, if their suspicions were strong enough, to deport them to Manila. Throughout the district, there was a new emphasis on the U.S. Army provost courts. These courts were already established in most garrison towns and had previously been used largely to deal with misdemeanors and enforce sanitary ordinances; now they were used to try suspected guerrilla supporters. Presided over by officers with slight interest in due process, they could impose strict fines or jail terms. In Candon there were as many cases tried in January and February 1901 as had been tried in all of 1900, and the penalties increased from twenty-five-peso fines to two years at hard labor. The courts were so effective that some officers, such as Col. Marcus Cronin, used them extensively: "My intention has always been to work by pressure upon officials by tracing all insurgent movements, and punishing, through military court, all aiding [the] insurgents even by not notifying us. The officials soon learn that an investigation may be postponed but never abandoned."[83]

In some areas, such as Aglipay's stronghold in the Batac-Badoc-Paoay region of Ilocos Norte, District Headquarters authorized special investigations. One such mission, led by another veteran of La Union, Capt. Daniel H. Boughton, produced a complete census and map of the district as well as enough information to implicate many of Badoc's civic officials. Armed with this, the post commander instituted a thorough purge of the area's municipal governments and by February 1901, most of the officials had been dismissed or arrested and the guerrilla infrastructure broken up. As part of the cleanup, captured guerrillas were sent into the town to identify their former comrades while Army patrols combed the area and pursued guerrilla bands. The most effective measure, however, was a decision by Badoc's commander to exploit the enmity between Tinio and Aglipay: he appointed one of Tinio's supporters, Juan Rubio, former revolutionary tax collector, as the new *presidente*. In a bitter factional battle, Rubio persecuted Aglipay's allies through a number of "highly irregular practices," including confining suspects in his own private jail, and soon had destroyed the priest's infrastructure.[84]

Another example of town pacification occurred at Bucay, Abra, a known revolutionary center, many of whose *principales* had family members serving with the guerrillas. When the town was garrisoned in November 1900, the new commander, Lt. Ezekial Williams, found it deserted and was told that the people were off cultivating their fields. The Army's campaign in Abra drove the population back into the town while forcing the guerrillas to levy more contributions to replace those destroyed. Caught between the Army and the revolutionaries, the town's officials were forced to commit themselves to one side. In December, a *principalía* delegation presented themselves to Williams and stated they wished to take the Oath of Allegiance and draw up a compact pledging support for the Army. They voluntarily placed

sentinels in the *barrios*, provided guides and spies, and urged that the population in the outlying *barrios* be quartered in the town and their crops brought
in. Over the next weeks, Bucay became involved in a virtual war with the
guerrillas. *Barrio* chiefs and inhabitants were kidnapped, a former revolutionary murdered, houses were burned, and the whole town threatened with
"sangre y muerte" [blood and death] by the local partisans under Lt. Francisco Bendito. This terrorism, however, turned the town solidly against the
guerrillas and soon armed villagers were accompanying the soldiers on expeditions. In April 1901 Bendito's hiding place was discovered by one of these
combined patrols and his band wiped out.[85]

A further, and more unpleasant, aspect of the Army's campaign to separate
civilians from guerrillas was the increasing emphasis on crop destruction. In
November, District Headquarters began confiscating and destroying rice and
foodstuffs from property owned by revolutionaries. Juan Villamor, for example, had an estimated 20,000 to 50,000 tons of rice seized. On 2 November
1900 Howze, who had been one of the most humane provincial commanders,
told his post commanders, "warn [civic officials] that the feeding, sheltering
and harboring of the Insurrecto element must at once cease, or the vicinity
will be laid to waste, even to the extent of destroying their crops. . . . The
most drastic measures will be resorted to in order to put an end to disturbances in this province."[86]

There is also evidence that some officers turned to inhumane measures.
First District Headquarters did not tolerate brutality and rigorously investigated instances where it might have occurred: when Lt. James K. Parsons
admitted that "a little persuasion was used" in one interrogation, Ballance
immediately demanded that he explain the meaning of this phrase. Parsons
replied that he had merely threatened the local officials with being deprived
of office.[87] Despite this official disapproval, from the beginning of the pacification campaign there is evidence that a few soldiers, in their desire to get
"badly needed information," were guilty of "severe treatment" of prisoners.[88]
During the pacification of La Union, Lt. Lewis M. Smith reported somewhat
admiringly that one *presidente* refused to talk "even after being strung up
three times by the neck, about six inches clear of the ground."[89] There are
also indications that guerrillas suspected of particularly heinous offenses,
such as mutilating American dead or assassinating loyal Filipinos, were shot
"attempting to escape."[90] In December, believing that his action was justified
under G.O. 100, Lt. Arthur G. Duncan executed a suspected spy without
trial at Vintar, Ilocos Norte. Duncan was brought before a board of officers
who determined that his action "was the result of not inexcusable misunder-

standing, ignorance and hasty judgment" and recommended that no further action be taken against him.[91] In the First District, such instances of torture and executing without trial, however deplorable, appear to be isolated actions by officers and men acting without the knowledge or approval of their superiors.

At the same time the Army was applying pressure to the civilian population to cut them off from the revolutionaries, it also launched a military offensive against the guerrillas. From October 1900 to May 1901, First District soldiers were kept constantly in the field in a series of large and small operations characterized by aggressive patrolling and sweeps through border areas or perceived guerrilla strongholds. Columns of about fifty men from neighboring garrisons and special mobile forces would converge on suspected strongholds, then comb the area thoroughly, establishing outposts at night. Small detachments guarded roads and trails while other groups moved into *barrios* at night and searched them, rounding up all suspects. The physical fatigue that had previously hampered such expeditions in the past was avoided by requiring the men to cover only small areas and carry only their weapons—supplies were carried by Filipinos drafted from local villages. Operations were coordinated with other provincial commands to prevent guerrillas from moving across the borders. The increase in manpower also allowed individual garrisons to provide more patrols in the immediate vicinity; their task was aided by new restrictions which forbade civilians from traveling on the roads at night. One veteran, recalling the campaign in Abra, summed it up as "on the move until they surrendered and it wasn't all fun."[92]

Very few of these operations resulted in battle, and often the soldiers had to be satisfied with destroying food and supplies, storehouses, and suspected guerrilla quarters. Initially, some officers were discouraged by the lack of combat, complaining, "it is as easy to hunt quail with an old fashioned horse pistol and without a dog, as it is to encounter the enemy under circumstances favorable to our success."[93] But as the relentless pursuit went on, they were more aware that it was taking its toll: here and there a few rifles captured or a few guerrillas killed; now and then a barracks or storehouse destroyed—this constant attrition left the guerrillas sick, hungry, and exhausted. No longer powerful forces supported by the local militia, the partisans were broken and harried and always in flight.[94] As the tempo of Army operations increased, garrison commanders received civilian delegations who disclosed the location of guerrilla hideouts or denounced members of the infrastructure. By March, one provincial commander believed that the population was thoroughly sick of the war.[95]

Much of the credit for the vigor of Army operations during the period was due to Brig. Gen. J. Franklin Bell, who was appointed to command the First District on 28 February 1901. Bell, probably the finest Army commander in the Philippine War, was a forty-five-year-old Medal of Honor winner who had already played an instrumental role in the engagements around Manila and central Luzon. A cavalryman, Bell had jumped from captain to brigadier general during his three years in the Philippines. Like Young, he was a good judge of talent, and he utilized Patajo, Johnston, and other First District veterans. At the same time, Bell's claim that the district's pacification was due to the implementation of his own methods is an exaggeration. By the time he assumed command, the guerrillas were scattered and confined to a few areas. Unlike Young, he could use small garrisons in regions cleared by local pacification campaigns while concentrating his forces on areas that were still refractory. Bell's major contribution was that he was willing and able to escalate the war to a level that the revolutionary leaders found intolerable and, once they surrendered, he was able to reconcile them to American rule. His compassion as a victor prompted one civilian to remark on "his vigorous enthusiasm for education as well as whatever might be for the general welfare of the people."[96]

Bell began operations in southern Ilocos Sur utilizing many of the personnel and policies that had worked in La Union. Duvall was placed in overall command while a new subdistrict was created under another veteran of the La Union pacification, Maj. Sedgwick Rice. In January 1901, Johnston conducted a thorough investigation and secured the names of the guerrillas' suppliers and members of the Katipunan. Patajo brought 50 of his Guardia de Honor followers in and soon recruited another 150 men. Post commanders took advantage of the historic enmity between Igorrotes and revolutionaries by providing Army garrisons to protect Igorrote villages and employing the Igorrotes to hunt down guerrillas in the mountains. On 15 April the zone guerrilla commander in Ilocos Sur, Lt. Col. Juan M. Guitterez, was captured by one of these Igorrote units. Guitterez agreed to collaborate, turning over the names of his suppliers, accompanying Johnston on his investigations, and writing to the Villamors urging their surrender. The whole operation took some five weeks and illustrates the high level of pacification expertise achieved by First District officers.[97]

The most severe operations were undertaken in Abra, which was placed under Col. Richard Comba in November 1900, with instructions from Young to prosecute the war with "the utmost rigor" and to "use the most severe measures known to the laws of war."[98] Comba quickly succeeded in scattering the Villamors' partisan units but could not capture the leaders or their guns. In mid-March 1901, he was replaced by Maj. William C. H. Bowen, who attempted to negotiate with the Villamors both through members of their family and local *presidentes*. When these overtures failed, the Army adopted both a stronger policy in Abra and a harsher view of the Villamors. Orders were given to round up all "amigos" after any engagement and question them, holding all suspects. On 9 April, Abra was placed under interdict: travel was prohibited to and from the province and all trade was cut off. Army units then began a campaign, the results of which were described by Bowen: "During the insurrection the province suffered severely; every man was either an active insurrector [*sic*] or a sympathizer, the consequence being that property had been destroyed right and left; whole villages had been burned, storehouses and crops had been destroyed, and the entire province was as devoid of food products as was the valley of the Shenandoah after Sheridan's raid during the civil war [*sic*]. The jurisdictions or comprehensions of Pilar and Villavija had been depopulated and this portion of the province had been absolutely destroyed."[99] These measures proved to be the final straw; on 21 April, Juan Villamor requested terms and was brought into Bangued the following day. On 29 April he surrendered and took the Oath of Allegiance.

Following Villamor's capitulation, there was a rush by the few remaining guerrilla leaders in the district to surrender. Tinio sent in an officer to ask for terms on 27 April and surrendered three days later. Gregorio Aglipay also surrendered on 27 April. For over a month he had negotiated with Federal party members but had steadfastly refused to commit himself. Eventually the exasperated Ilocos Norte commander sent him a note that "there would be no more talk, it was surrender or fight from then on." The former priest gave himself up two days later. A general districtwide cessation of hostilities was ordered on 1 May in order to allow guerrilla units to come in unmolested, and there was no further fighting.[100]

The suppression of revolutionary activity in the First District was one of the most complete in the Philippines: there were no reported engagements with guerrilla bands after 1 May 1901. The reports of the provincial governors stressed the peaceful conditions and the inhabitants' appreciation of Army reforms in transportation and education. Furthermore, all the major guerrilla leaders surrendered and some, such as Juan Villamor, immediately accepted positions with the U.S. government. Other former guerrillas aided the Army in hunting down *ladrones* who might have continued to disrupt the peace. The decision not to look into the wartime activities of most guerrillas also helped the American cause. Although there was some feeling among veterans that Tinio and Aglipay had been guilty of atrocities, Bell urged that they not be prosecuted.[101]

The pacification of the First District presented the U.S. Army with one of its most difficult experiences in Philippine counterinsurgency. Initially the Army believed the inhabitants favored American occupation and were hostile to the Tagalogs who composed the revolutionary leadership. As a result, the early efforts of the Army went into civil government while military needs were neglected. The outbreak of rebellion in Ilocos Norte and the discovery of the guerrilla infrastructure in La Union in the spring of 1900 changed that perception. The provincial commanders of these areas realized they faced a strong and organized resistance and undertook pacification policies designed to deal with their region's insurgency.

Pacification in the First District for most of the Philippine War was far less centralized than it was regionalized. It was, in many respects, fought province by province as each commander altered and created his own counterinsurgency methods. Much of this decentralization was due to the district's commander, Brig. Gen. Samuel B. M. Young, who left most of the actual conduct of operations to his provincial commanders. Although Manila's policies were adopted at the district level, they were often altered by provincial and post commanders. This gave First District counterinsurgency a flexibility and adaptability that was ultimately effective. The guerrilla offensive in the fall of 1900 briefly panicked the district commander but it proved only a temporary success for the guerrillas. Indeed, their very success prompted a large buildup in Army strength. Under the leadership of Young's successor, Brig. Gen. J. Franklin Bell, these essentially localized policies broke Filipino resistance and created a long and lasting peace.

3

The Nasty Little War
The Fourth District, Department of Northern Luzon

As Brig. Gen. Frederick Funston, the Fourth District's commander, noted, the war in his area was one of the most unusual regional pacification campaigns in the Philippine War:

> The condition of the country seemed perfectly normal, the towns being full of people and the usual work going on in the fields. There was not a sign of the war to be seen. . . . If anyone imagines that this was a desolated country, with the inhabitants fleeing to the woods and mountains for shelter, he is entitled to imagine again. The tendency of the people was to flock to the garrisoned towns for shelter from their own ruthless countrymen, having not the slightest fear of the troops. I have no doubt that in the year 1900 Nueva Ecija raised as much rice as it ever did; at least all suitable land was in cultivation. And yet there was a nasty little war going on all the time. It certainly was an odd state of affairs.[1]

Unlike the First District, where the Army faced a strong provincial resistance, in the Fourth District there was a weak native resistance movement which was saved only by outside intervention. In contrast to other areas in the Philippines, the revolutionaries were unable to establish shadow governments or challenge American control of the towns, and they had to rely on terrorism to intimidate the population. Under Funston, the Americans developed regional pacification policies stressing the utilization of key elements of society against the revolutionaries and rapid response to guerrilla operations.

In very brief summary, the guerrilla war in the Fourth District was a two-phase affair. In the first phase, between November 1899 and May 1900, the revolutionaries attempted to establish a politico-military organization in the towns which would supply and shelter guerrilla bands operating in the mountains. Whether through personal failings or lack of tactical skill, they were unsuccessful in this undertaking. The Americans won over much of the Ilocano population and deprived the revolutionaries of a popular base while either destroying or isolating their fragile infrastructure in the towns. Army forces also drove the guerrilla regulars from the mountains and scattered them into small and disorganized bands. In the spring of 1900, nearly the entire provincial command was captured, and the demoralized partisans hid their weapons and returned to the villages. To some Americans it appeared as if the war in the Fourth District were almost over.

The second phase of the war, from June 1900 to May 1901, witnessed the arrival of the revolutionary brigadier general Urbano Lacuna from neighboring Bulacan province. Lacuna made a belated attempt to reestablish an infrastructure of partisans, militia, tax collectors, and shadow governments. While Lacuna was surprisingly successful at this, he could neither reverse popular disenchantment nor prevent the active collaboration of key elements of society with the Americans. Morale among his fighting forces was poor, and his officers always ran the risk that when their men scattered to avoid pursuit many would remain in the towns and *barrios*. Due to the weak revolutionary organizations in the municipalities, these deserters could not be compelled to rejoin their units until the guerrillas moved back into the area. Throughout most of the second phase of the war the guerrillas were on the defensive and their military activities consisted of little more than terrorism.

The Fourth District comprised the adjacent provinces of Nueva Ecija and Principe. Nueva Ecija, by far the more important, was situated on the northeastern side of the central Luzon plain and watered by the Rio Grande de la Pampanga and its tributaries. With a population in excess of 130,000, and an area of some 2,040 square miles, it was one of the most important rice producing areas in the archipelago. Most of the land along the river had been cleared and was devoted to rice or sugar, but to the west and north and at the southeastern tip of the province, the terrain was mountainous and rough or swampy. The other province, Principe, was isolated and mountainous, with a population of only 5,200. To all intents and purposes, the war in the Fourth District was the war in Nueva Ecija.[2]

As a province with a large Tagalog population and a number of wealthy Filipinos and *ilustrados*, Nueva Ecija participated in the anti-Spanish turmoil

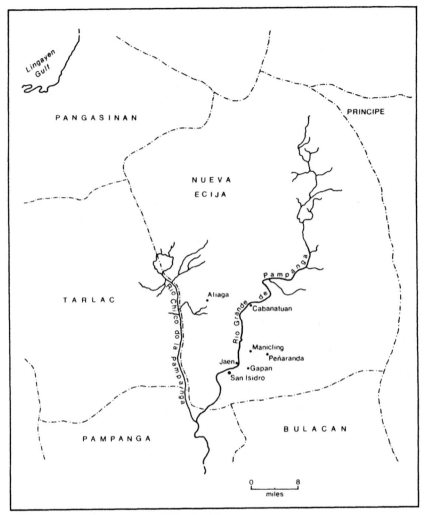

Fourth District, Department of Northern Luzon

of the late nineteenth century. Such prominent revolutionaries as Manuel Tinio and Mariano Llanera were provincial landowners. During the Revolt of 1896 the Katipuneros, under Llanera, attacked the provincial capital of San Isidro, forcing the Spanish to place the entire province under martial law. Despite a temporary lull after the truce at Biac na bato in late 1897, conditions in the region remained unsettled. Refusing to recognize the peace settlement, Brig. Gen. Ferdinand Macabulos waged a desultory war against the Spanish and claimed to control more than ninety-eight towns in central Luzon. With the arrival of the Americans and the return of Emilio Aguinaldo in May 1898, Filipino nationalists once more began concerted attacks on the Spanish. The brothers Casmirio and Manuel Tinio captured San Isidro and on 3 July 1898 proclaimed the province's independence. Nueva Ecija was part of the Philippine Republic for almost a year; indeed, San Isidro and Cabanatuan served as the temporary capitals of the government after the city of Malolos was captured by the Americans in March 1899.

Despite Nueva Ecija's active and early role, the Philippine Republic did not establish a strong administration in the province. This may be due to the fact that powerful local leaders such as Manuel Tinio sought rewards in the national government and failed to establish a strong provincial organization. Moreover, many of Nueva Ecija's soldiers were enlisted in the Republican Army and committed to the battles around Manila or to Tinio's expedition to the Ilocano provinces. Internal military preparations were minimal: a U.S. Navy observer estimated that in late 1898 there were only 300 Republican troops in the entire province. Moreover, these soldiers behaved so badly that one town rioted and took away their guns. A U.S. Army expedition in the summer of 1899 brushed them aside with disheartening ease and further diminished military support for the Republic.[3]

The Philippine cause was also weakened by internal divisions unique to Nueva Ecija. In the nineteenth century the province, which had been un-populated frontier, was settled by Tagalogs and Pampangans from the south and Ilocanos from the North, creating three mutually antagonistic groups whose ethnic tensions were ripe for exploitation by the Americans. Many of the province's Ilocanos, unlike those in the First District, were hostile to the Philippine Revolution—possibly because the Republic's leading general, the Ilocano Antonio Luna, was murdered by Aguinaldo's Tagalog bodyguard at Cabanatuan, in the very center of the province. The Pampangans, like those in their native province, remained neutral and gave mild support to the side that seemed strongest. Even the Tagalogs in the south were somewhat di-vided and some remained apathetic or hostile to the Republic.[4]

Moreover, Nueva Ecija already showed signs of the socioeconomic stress that would plague it in the twentieth century. Much of the population con-sisted of tenant farmers who were victimized by absentee landowners or who lost traditional privileges and social stability with the weakening of patron-client ties. In the 1890s there was a great deal of peasant unrest throughout central Luzon as tenants sought to achieve a more egalitarian and less exploitive society. They were alienated by the Philippine Republic's elitist economic policies and its failure to institute economic or social reforms, and many turned to such messianic and anti-Republican movements as the Guardia de Honor. Nueva Ecija's socioeconomic elite, on the other hand, may have thought the restoration of order provided by the Americans essential to maintain their political control and were willing to collaborate to secure their political and economic interests. These class divisions, when combined with the province's ethnic divisions, contributed greatly to the weakness of Filipino resistance.[5]

Under the three-zone guerrilla organization established by Emilio Aguinaldo at Bayambang on 13 November 1899, Nueva Ecija fell into the area termed "Center of Luzon" and was placed under the politico-military command of Maj. Gen. Pantaleon García. The Center of Luzon also included Bataan, Bulacan, Pampanga, Tarlac, Zambales, and Pangasinan provinces, and as a result it overlapped several U.S. Army military districts. García appointed provincial and zone commanders himself, naming Col. Pablo Padilla the politico-military chief of Nueva Ecija and Lt. Col. Casmirio Tinio a zone commander. Although García, Padilla, and Tinio were captured in the spring of 1900, Maj. Gen. Tomás Mascardo and Maj. Gen. José Alejandrino assumed control of the Center of Luzon command and Brig. Gen. Urbano Lacuna took charge of Nueva Ecija. During the war, Alejandrino's influence was largely confined to his native province of Pampanga, in part because Aguinaldo, believing Alejandrino had usurped command, ordered his arrest. As a result, other guerrilla leaders, such as Lacuna, were given a free hand to conduct their own operations. Despite their membership in the Center of Luzon command, the revolutionaries in Nueva Ecija conducted a provincial guerrilla war with little support from outside.[6]

Within the province one of the key determinants of the nature of guerrilla warfare was the poor leadership provided by the revolutionaries in the first months of the war. García, an *ilustrado* from Manila, had risen rapidly in the insurgent hierarchy during the Revolt of 1896, signing the pact of Biac na bato in 1897 and going into exile with Aguinaldo in Hong Kong. He was one of the president's most trusted subordinates, commanding an army brigade and serving as his personal chief of staff in 1899. García appears to have been a good theorist: he issued detailed instructions which urged that the Filipinos avoid conventional combat, and that they concentrate on capturing weapons and wearing down their opponents rather than seeking a quick military victory. He recognized that American civil government would be used to justify foreign occupation, and ordered all Filipinos to avoid political office or be punished as traitors. He also understood that popular support was absolutely essential, and insisted that his soldiers do nothing to lose the friendship of the populace. But despite his intellectual abilities he was a poor combat commander who, by the fall of 1899, was suffering from physical exhaustion, lingering illness, and demoralization over the complete defeat of his conventional forces. After taking over the Center of Luzon, he spent much of his time in hiding, exerting little control over his subordinates and conducting few operations. His capture on 6 May 1900, at Jaen, Nueva Ecija, was not a "deathblow to the insurgent cause" as MacArthur claimed, but instead provided an opportunity for more aggressive leadership to emerge.[7]

García's weak leadership at the top was compounded by poor guerrilla leadership within Nueva Ecija. The provincial commander, Col. Pablo Padilla, was unable or unwilling to control the misbehavior of his forces. Although a former governor of the province and a prominent figure in the war against the Spanish, he was badly beaten by the Americans during their invasion in late 1899. Moreover, he failed to take advantage of the Army's disorganization during the winter of 1899–1900 and instead suspended hostilities until February, allowing the Americans to consolidate their position. American Army officers despised him; one called him "a cruel and cowardly scoundrel" and suspected he had murdered several pro-American Filipinos. In the north of Nueva Ecija, Col. Teodoro Sandico, another *ilustrado* and veteran of the 1896 revolt, was little better. Described by Funston as a military nonentity, Sandico admitted that he was a colonel without troops. He spent much of his time in quarrels with other commanders and complained bitterly to Aguinaldo that nobody accepted his authority.[8]

From its inception, the guerrilla movement in the Fourth District was hampered by the failure of its leaders to establish a civil organization in the towns and *barrios* that could support military operations. The explanation may lie in the speed of the American advance in the fall of 1899, the lack of political and administrative skills among provincial guerrilla chiefs, or the internal divisions within Nueva Ecijan society. García and Padilla issued proclamations forbidding Filipinos to accept civil office under the Americans, but they could not enforce these decrees. Captured correspondence indicates that, unlike their counterparts elsewhere, they neglected the creation of loyal militias, shadow governments, Katipunan societies, storehouses, and village supply organizations which made up the usual Philippine guerrilla infrastructure. As a result, they had a hard time organizing such an infrastructure after the Americans had occupied the key towns. Although some guerrilla chiefs did establish ties with local *principalía* or insured collaboration through intimidation, this effort was not carried on in a systematic way throughout the province. Where an individual military leader could form such connections, he was able to secure food and shelter. Far too often, however, the revolutionaries consisted of small bands of partisans, isolated from popular support, and moving from place to place without a consistent source of supplies.[9]

The Americans invaded Nueva Ecija in May 1899 as part of their early campaigns against the main Republican army under Emilio Aguinaldo. Although Maj. Gen. Henry W. Lawton occupied the temporary capital of San Isidro on 17 May, he failed to capture the Republican government, which retreated up the river to Cabanatuan. Lawton had little trouble with the Filipino forces, whom he brushed aside with little resistance. The climate was a far more serious opponent. Undermanned and near collapse from overwork and disease, Lawton's forces withdrew and the province reverted to Republican control. The main result of this expedition was to increase the tension between Aguinaldo and his leading general, Antonio Luna, culminating in Luna's murder a month later and the equally fatal destruction of internal discipline among the Filipino troops.[10]

American forces returned to Nueva Ecija in the fall of 1899 as part of Otis's final campaign against the Republican Army in the north. Once again under Lawton, they blocked the mountain passes in the east and north of the province to prevent Aguinaldo's army from retreating into northern Luzon. Pushing aside Padilla's weak defenses, the soldiers occupied San Isidro on 19 October, but alternating low and high water, mud, and unseasonable rains stalled the advance shortly afterward. In a daring gamble, Lawton cut Brig. Gen. Samuel B. M. Young's cavalry free of the supply train and sent them north to head off the fleeing president and link up with Wheaton's forces who had landed at San Fabian. Young's horsemen swept over Nueva Ecija's demoralized Republicans and scattered them while Lawton's infantry followed behind to occupy the towns. Aguinaldo retreated to the north, barely slipping between the converging American forces, but his army collapsed and broke up, the survivors fleeing to the hills or hiding their weapons and becoming "amigos."

In their sweep through Nueva Ecija, Lawton's forces encountered little organized resistance and were somewhat surprised at the friendliness of the population. In December 1899, the new district commander rode through the province with a two-man escort and commented that the area was so peaceful that he could not tell there was a war going on. The lack of resistance allowed the Army to reorganize its chaotic administration and supply system which was now "fearfully strung out." During Young's headlong dash and Lawton's aggressive operations, Army companies and detachments had been dropped off haphazardly to guard the mountain passes, repair roads, and transport supplies for the forces operating in northern Luzon. The result was that when the Fourth District was formed in April 1900, during the Army's district organization, its 2,400-man occupation force consisted of detachments from six different U.S. Army regiments as well as the Macabebes of the Philippine Cavalry.[11]

Brig. Gen. Frederick Funston, who took command of the U.S. forces in Nueva Ecija in late December 1899, was already one of the most famous figures of the Philippine War. Although not yet thirty-five, and with no formal military training, "Fighting Fred" Funston's exploits in the Cuban insurrection and Philippine War had won him both international fame and a brigadier-generalship in the U.S. Volunteers. Unlike many regular Army generals, he had extensive experience in counterinsurgency, having fought both as a guerrilla in Cuba and against guerrillas in the Philippines. Despite his experience, or perhaps because of it, Funston was guided far more by pragmatism than any carefully developed counterinsurgency theory. He was willing to use whatever means were necessary, and if his solutions were often theatrical, they were also effective.[12]

In the first months in the province, Funston was occupied primarily with restoring order and organization to his scattered forces. He shared with all Army district commanders in the Philippines the conviction that his forces were too small and spread out, but Funston's concerns were even more valid than most of his peers. In addition to the confusion inherent in having units from six different regiments, most of whose headquarters staff were located in other provinces, Funston also had to detach a company to the isolated port of Baler in Principe. In addition, many of his men were exhausted from operations in the fall; by March 1900, the Thirty-fourth Infantry, U.S.V., his strongest force, had 12 percent of its men on the sick list. The supply system was in disarray: at one time the garrison at Cabanatuan was reduced to living off carabao (water buffalo) and rice, and other troops survived for weeks on a diet of hardtack and bacon. He was also troubled by sporadic violence from Filipino irregulars who cut the telegraph lines, sniped at soldiers, and attempted to interfere with Army control of municipal affairs "by means of interior local organizations."[13]

Funston had little time to deal with these pressing problems, for he was soon facing a strong military challenge from the revolutionaries. Perhaps encouraged by the Americans' lack of manpower and disorganization, García ignored his own instructions to avoid large battles and sanctioned an attack on Peñaranda which involved most of his regular forces. As in the Ilocos Norte revolt, the revolutionaries' security was lax and U.S. forces struck first. On 18 March 1900, an Army patrol located García and Padilla, with an estimated 400 to 700 guerrillas, at the small village of Mauiluilui. García was still in the process of mobilizing his men when an American infantry company and 50 Macabebes routed them with substantial casualties. García's forces scattered and Funston dispatched a number of expeditions into the hills, establishing a camp in a guerrilla stronghold in the northeast highlands and closing off the mountains by means of extensive patrols. Sent to pursue the fleeing Filipinos and break up a reputed enemy concentration, the soldiers found little evidence of enemy strength. Convinced that the engagement at Mauiluilui was a crushing blow, Funston optimistically predicted that he would soon drive all of the guerrillas out of the province.[14]

The American success in March demoralized the Nueva Ecija guerrillas. Some partisan bands fragmented as the men hid their guns in mountain caves and fled to the towns. Other units refused to fight and were held together only by threats of punishment: Padilla later admitted to executing several of his own men in order to enforce discipline and prevent the complete disintegration of his forces. At this point, nearly the entire revolutionary leadership was captured. Acting on a tip from Funston's excellent intelligence service, on 6 May a small patrol surrounded the town of Jaen. Among the suspects they turned up was Pantaleon García, who was so ill he was almost incapable of movement. Ten days later, the key leaders of the provincial resistance, Padilla and Casmirio Tinio, were arrested. The discouragement of the Nueva Ecija provincial leadership can be seen by the active assistance these men gave the Americans against their former comrades.[15]

Only the arrival of Brig. Gen. Urbano Lacuna in April prevented the disintegration of the insurgent cause in the Fourth District. Arriving with a force of some 200 Bulacano partisans, he quickly set to work gathering the scattered provincial forces, locating arms, and asserting his authority over the remaining guerrilla chiefs. Although born at Peñaranda in 1862, Lacuna had spent much of his adult life outside of Nueva Ecija province as an official for the Spanish colonial government. In the early months of the Philippine War he fought in the battles around Manila, serving under Maj. Gen. Pio del Pilar, a reputed outlaw, who probably gave Lacuna an excellent education in irregular warfare. Lacuna was a staunch Aguinaldo loyalist and, according to José Alejandrino, he was given the mission of killing Antonio Luna if the assassination at Cabanatuan failed. In October 1899, Lacuna was singled out by Aguinaldo for the responsibility of forming guerrilla units to block the advancing Americans in southern Nueva Ecija and northern Bulacan. For the next six months he conducted operations there before taking over the command of the revolutionary organization in Nueva Ecija. An adept guerrilla, Lacuna was a humane and chivalrous commander in his dealings with his American opponents, and he won the respect of Funston.[16]

Lacuna attempted to establish a provincial infrastructure to support his troops. He assigned Lt. Col. Isidro Carmona to collect taxes and establish contacts with influential citizens and sent messengers to key civic officials asking for contributions and support. The success of this was uneven. Lacuna did succeed in raising money and in establishing some supply networks, but he does not seem to have been able to control many of the municipal councils or to form shadow governments. In part this was because he was opposed by the early provincial revolutionary leadership which had decided to collaborate with the Americans. His failure was also due to the efforts of Funston's intelligence service and native auxiliaries, who broke up many clandestine municipal organizations. Finally, the ethnic and socioeconomic divisions within the province often meant that the population within a town was divided. In such circumstances the Americans could often secure informers who would disclose the identity of guerrilla agents. At times, Lacuna could secure the allegiance of a town council or much of the population in a locale, but his control usually depended on the immediate presence of his military forces. When the Americans moved in and the guerrillas left, the shadow governments were vulnerable. The result was that for much of the war Lacuna operated on his own—isolated and cut off from the popular support which a guerrilla needs to survive.

Lacuna realized that the attempts by García and Padilla to assault Army garrisons with massed forces had been disastrous. He substituted a strategy that would increase guerrilla morale, build up a supply system, and demonstrate to the populace that the revolutionaries still controlled the countryside. Using his Bulacano regulars as a solid core of experienced troops, he made contacts with other guerrilla leaders to conduct operations on the provincial borders. He also attempted to increase his forces by informing guerrillas in Tayabas province that they were now under his authority and they should immediately come north to aid him. Lacuna also developed a variety of harassing tactics which made life miserable for the Americans. In May 1900, his men began to fire into garrison towns at night, thus making maximum use of their poor marksmanship and faulty ammunition. In a slightly more spectacular attempt to impress the population, Maj. Tomás Tagunton attacked San Isidro, killing several civilians in the fighting. Unlike García, Lacuna kept his forces dispersed and the Americans were unable to locate the perpetrators of "this deviltry."[17]

Lacuna was greatly aided during this reorganization by events in the neighboring Fifth District. Two weeks after Tagunton's raid on San Isidro, Capt. Charles D. Roberts was captured at Santa Lucia, Bulacan, by guerrillas and shortly afterward, an Army patrol was badly punished by the brothers Simon, Alipio, and Pablo Tecson. Army headquarters in Manila ordered Funston to strip his garrisons, form a mobile column, and cooperate with Brig. Gen. Frederick D. Grant, commander of the Fifth District, to hunt down the guerrillas responsible and rescue Roberts. Although Funston believed the operations had little chance of success, he dispatched nearly a quarter of his available manpower for operations in the Fifth District. Throughout June, Army units pursued the guerrillas, encountering stiff resistance and recapturing only a few Americans. During the same month Funston sent most of his remaining soldiers into the mountains to destroy an important supply center. The result was that there were very few Army forces in Nueva Ecija available to conduct operations against the provincial guerrillas.[18]

Lacuna attempted to take advantage of the lack of Army manpower and the summer rainy season by concentrating his forces and attacking isolated Army garrisons. Although the strategy may have been sound, the execution was badly flawed. As in the Mauiluilui engagement, the Americans struck first: on 14 June, a patrol located Lacuna's forces as they were assembling near Peñaranda and administered a severe defeat, killing twenty-two men and capturing sixteen rifles. On 4 July, Col. Pablo Tecson and Lacuna joined forces and attacked Manicling, a town recently garrisoned by a small detachment and lacking any defenses. To prevent U.S. reinforcements, the guerrillas also attacked Gapan and Peñaranda. There was some hard fighting at Manicling, but in all three towns the attacks were beaten off with large guerrilla losses. These engagements cost the guerrillas heavily in men and ammunition and eroded much of the morale that Lacuna had built up.[19]

This activity prompted a quick American counteroffensive aimed at driving the guerrillas into the mountains, forcing them either to disperse or give battle far from the towns. On 21 July, a provisional force of Macabebes and infantry destroyed Lacuna's largest permanent camp after a stiff fight that left thirty-six guerrillas dead and seven Americans wounded. A day later, another patrol located an arsenal and captured 24 rifles, 300 pounds of gunpowder, and vital reloading machinery. In late August, Army forces cooperated in a giant sweep of the Pampanga-Bulacan-Nueva Ecija border area, destroying storehouses and scattering guerrilla bands. In the north, the surrender of Lt. Col. Roberto Grassa removed virtually all revolutionary forces on the Nueva Ecija-Pangasinan border. The guerrillas also suffered a major loss when Lt. Col. Isidro Carmona, Lacuna's chief tax collector, was captured at Gapan with much of Lacuna's administrative correspondence. This in turn led to the discovery of much of the fragile guerrilla supply organization and to the arrest of the entire Gapan infrastructure. By August, Lacuna's attempt to build up a provincial organization was in shambles. Army intelligence reported increased guerrilla desertions, with more than 100 rifles captured or surrendered. Forced to the border regions, Lacuna was soon asking Lt. Col. Alipio Tecson for more rifles and Col. Pablo Tecson complained that American operations had left his partisans without ammunition and food.[20]

The failure of his summer attacks and the success of the American counteroffensive forced Lacuna to fall back on the tactics he had developed in May. Revolutionary agents visited prominent *principales* and urged them to support the guerrillas, threatening retaliation if they failed to do so. The guerrillas resumed their nocturnal sniping into U.S.-occupied towns and their harassing of Army patrols and supply trains. Most towns suffered from guerrilla attempts to set fire to houses and *americanistas* were singled out as the targets for assassination and property destruction. This incendiarism proved ineffective in preventing collaboration, but in November, Lacuna extended it to the property of people who withheld active support or shirked paying the guerrilla tax collectors. He also attempted the destruction of entire towns, ordering Jaen burnt to ashes on the allegation that its inhabitants were spies for the Americans. On 2 January 1901, Tagunton's guerrillas burnt 200 houses in San Isidro because the population refused to contribute food or money. The American casualties were negligible during these attacks but "the situation of the people who had taken refuge in the garrisoned towns was in many ways pitiable."[21]

The evidence suggests that most guerrilla terrorism in the Fourth District was counterproductive. The Americans did not halt their military operations in order to protect the towns, rather they increased them. Throughout the winter and early spring they inflicted significant casualties on the revolutionaries while, with the exception of one stiff skirmish in May involving the Macabebes of the Philippine Cavalry, suffering negligible losses themselves. More important, Nueva Ecija's *principales* decided that the guerrillas posed a major threat to their safety: by January, Funston reported that the "better class" of Filipinos were in favor of the Americans and hostile to the guerrillas and that "there is a very decided tendency to actively aid us."[22] In February, the "principal men" of ten *pueblos* wrote to Lacuna stating that the population was sick of war; they threatened to form vigilante groups against him if he did not surrender. In one town, guerrillas who attempted to get food were killed and their rifles turned over to the Americans.[23]

During the winter of 1900–1901, the revolutionary cause in the Fourth District was clearly lost. Most of its prominent leaders, such as Lt. Col. Joaquin Natividad and Maj. Antonio Mendoza, surrendered, and others, such as the officer responsible for most of the incendiary attacks, Maj. Tomás Tagunton, were killed. Army patrols captured many demoralized partisans and entire companies of guerrillas laid down their weapons. In January alone, the Americans counted 135 rifles captured and 24 surrendered, more than the total obtained in the four previous months. Partisan bands were forced to the border areas in the southeast where they were harried by Army expeditions from several districts. Those guerrillas that remained "devoted all their energies to keeping away from the troops" and virtually no engagements occurred between 28 January and 19 May 1901. Indeed, Lacuna found it necessary to threaten his officers with punishment for allowing Army forces to travel through their areas unmolested. But by April his own officers were deserting him, and in the neighboring provinces leaders such as José Alejandrino, the Tecson brothers, and Isidro Torres surrendered. Despite the hopelessness of his cause, Lacuna held out until 19 May, when, after prolonged negotiations, he finally capitulated.[24]

While his men were mopping up resistance in Nueva Ecija, Funston led the most famous military operation of the Philippine War. Acting upon captured correspondence received from the isolated command at Principe, Funston with a small group of U.S. Army officers and a Macabebe company set out to capture Emilio Aguinaldo. Having captured much of Lacuna's correspondence, Funston forged papers that identified the officers as prisoners and the Macabebes as their guards. The expedition landed on the coast of Isabella province and worked their way into Aguinaldo's headquarters. The Filipino leader was captured without serious resistance and taken off to Manila, where he soon issued a proclamation accepting American authority and calling for an end to the fighting. The immediate significance of this capture is unclear. Funston believed that Lacuna began surrender negotiations only after he received a personal letter from Funston in mid-April with Aguinaldo's peace proclamation attached. However, the destruction of Lacuna's headquarters on 18 March, the surrenders of Alejandrino, Torres, and Sandico in April, and pressure from the Nueva Ecija Federal party may have been of far more importance to Lacuna than Aguinaldo's proclamation.[25]

The successful pacification campaign waged by Funston and his fellow officers was the result of counterinsurgency methods and policies that exploited provincial conditions and enemy weaknesses. Because the guerrillas never established a strong infrastructure throughout the district, the Army was not forced to spend much of its time rooting out *jefes principales* and shadow governments in the occupied towns. Moreover, unlike officers in other areas, Funston did not attempt to use civil government as a pacification measure until the military situation had been resolved. Instead, he relied on a well-organized intelligence service, rapid response to guerrilla actions, and the inclusion of key elements of the population in their own defense. Funston himself never articulated these policies and it is quite possible that he never consciously developed them into a coherent pacification strategy. He was primarily a charismatic commander who personally conducted military operations in the field while relying on informal contacts with the local elite, former guerrillas, and the Ilocanos for civil pacification. Although a vocal advocate of repression, his actual conduct was characterized by lenient surrender terms, rewards for collaboration, and personal friendship. Against a deeply rooted popular guerrilla movement he may well have proved an abysmal failure, but in the pursuit of Lacuna's regulars, Funston was a resounding success. Pragmatic and flexible, he could quickly exploit the opportunities the guerrillas gave him to launch operations for "exterminating the Goo Goos."[26]

Funston's intelligence system was, in his own words, "hard to beat," and it gave him valuable information on enemy plans and concentrations. He established social contacts with former or captured leaders in order to gain information on guerrilla organization. Quite early in his tenure he created a native secret service whose efficiency he promoted by making large payments for vital information: the Filipinos who located Pantaleon García, for example, were paid 200 pesos for their help, and the guide who led him to the hidden papers of the Philippine Republic received 150 pesos. Funston also bribed revolutionary agents; on one occasion he bought off one of Lacuna's couriers who turned over correspondence implicating several prominent Filipinos in San Isidro. Aware that his agents were vulnerable, he did his best to protect them from guerrilla retaliation. When four of his spies were kidnapped, he retaliated by seizing four male members from the family of a prominent guerrilla and put them on bread and water. His district intelligence service was bolstered by fine field intelligence from garrison commanders. Capt. Frank A. Sullivan, the commander at Aliaga, was one of the most enterprising: he kept a list of suspects on file, enabling his patrols to identify guerrillas who were posing as civilians. The effectiveness of Fourth District intelligence is best illustrated in the capture of Emilio Aguinaldo. The location of Aguinaldo's headquarters was first discovered by a garrison commander in Principe who captured key documents. From then on, from the forging of letters from Lacuna, to the development of the deception plan, to the actual expedition itself, the entire operation shows a smoothly functioning and capable intelligence service at work.[27]

The success of U.S. Army intelligence in the Fourth District owed a great deal to the revolutionaries' own carelessness. The consistent failure of the guerrillas to protect the identities of their supporters contributed greatly to their inability to form an effective infrastructure. In several instances a budding guerrilla organization was compromised by the capture of key documents. As mentioned earlier, Funston disrupted Lacuna's attempt to establish a support network in San Isidro by bribing one of Lacuna's messengers. In June 1900, Lt. Frank A. Jernigan's Ilocano Scouts located Casmirio Tinio's correspondence for the two years in which he headed the clandestine organization in Nueva Ecija. According to Col. Lyman W. V. Kennon, this gave the names and organizations of the entire civil-military organization as well as "a very complete idea of the existing military conditions in this province."[28] The capture of Lt. Col. Carmona, delegated by Lacuna to establish a supply system, compromised much of the guerrilla civil organization. In October, the Americans captured much of Lacuna's administrative papers, "implicating natives in San Isidro and [Jaen] as well as revealing a well organized spy system."[29]

Funston also used his intelligence network to plan and conduct fast, hard-hitting military operations against the guerrillas. Early in 1900, he organized a twenty-five man unit called the "Headquarters Scouts" which, in addition to scouting, served as a personal escort and as a quick strike force. Funston was very fond of this unit and used it on a number of operations against guerrilla bands: on several occasions, he happily led it into battle. He also made good use of the Philippine Cavalry (Macabebes) and Ilocano Scouts assigned to the district. The Ilocanos were familiar with the countryside and could often obtain information from townspeople or relatives. Both units were especially valuable during the rainy season and in mountainous and swampy terrain where the American heavy infantry was often slowed down. In addition, the Filipino troops performed a variety of special operations: on one occasion, a small group of Macabebes disguised themselves as bull-cart drivers and ambushed a guerrilla band levying tolls on provincial roads.[30]

In rather startling contrast to the revolutionaries' growing terrorism, Funston evolved from an advocate of harsh and rather indiscriminate repression into a humane and sympathetic commander who made increasing efforts to insure that military consequences fell only upon the guerrillas and their active supporters. The change in his treatment of wire cutting offers a good example. In January 1900, his policy was to arrest the village headmen and burn down the houses immediately around the cut, with the provision that if the problem continued, the entire village would be burned. There are hints that even more drastic measures were occasionally "discreetly administered."[31] By January of 1901, however, Funston wrote, "The wire is not often cut in this District, probably three times a month which certainly is not often considering a state of war. It is always done by a small band and usually in an uninhabited locality. It is improbable that they remain anywhere in the vicinity and hunting down the three or four men who have probably done it is a very futile performance. I cannot see the expediency of burning the barrios in the vicinity of where a wire has been cut as the damage is almost invariably done by people from elsewhere. I think the unarmed and defenseless people in the barrios could not prevent wire cutting if they were so disposed."[32] His tolerance paid off in public support: in San Antonio a guerrilla who demanded that the people tear up wire was seized by the townspeople and taken to the Americans. Funston also protested the mistreatment of Filipino civilians by U.S. soldiers from other districts; but in this he was hampered by the belief of his immediate superior, Maj. Gen. Loyd Wheaton, that officers who reported American misconduct were somehow soft on the guerrillas. Funston, however, had come to believe that effective military operations could go hand in hand with conciliating the population and he attempted to insure this.[33]

Funston was less tolerant of the guerrillas themselves or of people he suspected of aiding them. He shared with Brig. Gen. Samuel B. M. Young a penchant for advocating rigorous measures. Funston gave strict orders that his troops follow the laws of war and that "care be taken that in all efforts to obtain information from natives that no action be taken not in accordance with [General Orders 100]."[34] Nevertheless, Funston and the troops under him were guilty of some very harsh policies, especially early in his tenure. In early March 1900, a soldier was killed by bolo-men in front of several witnesses who refused to point out the culprits. In retaliation, the Americans rounded up all the natives within a 200-yard radius including a woman who was 20 feet from the site but claimed to have heard nothing. Lt. Henry A. Ripley, who led the investigation, suggested that "extreme measures may jog her memory" and requested authority to burn her house. Probably as a result of such methods, Ripley succeeded in obtaining a confession from one of the assailants.[35] Burning civilian houses never became the common, even accepted, policy that it did in southwestern Luzon, but it was still practiced by American soldiers, especially in the early months of 1900. On one occasion the town of Candaba was set afire and there was some doubt whether guerrillas or drunken U.S. soldiers were to blame. In another instance, Capt. George C. Gibson burned several houses after discovering guerrilla weapons because "the inhabitants in their usual lying manner told us that they were there to work in the palay fields, none of which were near the houses."[36] Even Kennon, an advocate of conciliating the population, excused the burning of houses as "inevitable" as long as the country was infested by "robbers."[37] When a Filipino commander executed five American prisoners of war, Funston directed that no quarter be given to his troops, and, somewhat contradictorily, that all prisoners from this unit were to be held for trial. When he surprised two guerrillas in the act of killing captured Macabebe scouts, he publicly hung them without trial. He informed one Filipino that if he broke his Oath of Allegiance to the United States he would be shot and later, when Teodoro Sandico was negotiating his surrender, Funston's aide suggested: "better take him prisoner or better still kill him."[38] These harsh measures, however deplorable, were apparently accepted by Funston as necessary to demonstrate to both the guerrillas and the population that the Americans could and would retaliate.

Funston also tried to integrate important segments of Nueva Ecija society into counterinsurgency activities. Despite his lack of interest in the more benevolent aspects of American occupation, Funston was able to draw on considerable Filipino support throughout his tenure. He later commented that one of the "unique features" of the war was the "pleasant social relations between the officers of the American garrisons and the better class of people in the towns."[39] One factor contributing to these congenial relations was Funston's overlooking the *principales'* secret contributions to the guerrillas which they made either from patriotism or to protect their property and lives. He occasionally summoned a prominent resident and told him the exact amount he had contributed to the guerrillas, sending him back to his home presumably impressed by both Funston's knowledge and generosity. His preferential treatment of the native elite was indicated by his willingness to overlook even obvious violations: he requested clemency for the *presidente* of one town who had been sentenced to five years in prison for aiding the guerrillas on the grounds that he was "under duress of the strongest kind." His close relations with the elite increased through the war, in part due to guerrilla terrorism, and prompted one revolutionary chief to comment that since both Ilocanos and Tagalogs "of importance" were so hostile to the guerrillas "it will be necessary that four or five lives be taken in each town."[40]

Perhaps because of his ties with the local landowners and town elders, Funston was able to utilize the services of former revolutionaries who wished to resume their place among the provincial elite. The original Nueva Ecija guerrilla command had not been distinguished by a strong commitment to Filipino independence and after their capture many collaborated against Lacuna. After their surrender Padilla and Lt. Col. Joaquin Natividad helped organize the Federal party in the province and warned Lacuna that they would aid the Americans against him. Lacuna's terrorism strengthened this tie between former revolutionaries and the Americans. Casmirio Tinio, who after his capture had been restored to a civil office in his native town of Licab, wavered between aiding his former comrades and collaboration with the Army to such an extent that in October the Americans considered arresting him. Tinio, however, was under even more pressure from the revolutionaries: Sandico demanded support and made a personal visit, threatening to kill him and destroy Licab. Tinio, probably against his own instincts, became an informer and gave Funston information on the strength and composition of the guerrilla forces in his area. Within a few months, Tinio had become so tied to the Americans that when three of Sandico's partisans attempted to find refuge in Licab they were killed by Tinio and their weapons turned over to the Americans.[41]

Funston encouraged the support of former guerrillas by giving lenient surrender terms. Initially he opposed any negotiations with the enemy, but with his customary adaptability he learned to use his former adversaries to speed district pacification. He insisted that the surrender be complete and officers who surrendered were expected to bring in their men and arms with them or risk being sent back to round them up. Natividad and Mendoza, for example, spent several days persuading their fellow guerrillas to come in with their rifles. But having surrendered, a guerrilla leader could find he had given up very little. Casmirio Tinio was maintained as a *principale* despite U.S. suspicions that he was still collaborating with the guerrillas. Although he was suspected of murdering several Filipinos, Pablo Padilla was allowed to go free. Lt. Col. Roberto Grassa, also suspected of several assassinations, was given a virtual amnesty in the hope that it would encourage others to surrender. Teodoro Sandico, only allowed to surrender after he produced a considerable number of rifles, was released immediately and allowed to go to Manila. Such generosity was in sharp contrast with guerrilla intimidation and doubtless explains why many Filipinos collaborated with Funston. Lacuna's surrender was perhaps the most important result of Funston's lenient policy. The revolutionary and his officers were promised complete amnesty, allowed to keep their side arms, and given immediate liberty and freedom to travel. Afterward, Funston "spent many hours in pleasant reminiscence" with his former adversaries.[42]

In addition to the collaboration of the provincial elite and policies designed to win over former guerrillas, Funston also made excellent use of the locally raised Ilocano Scouts. The original impetus for these units came from Col. Lyman W. V. Kennon, commander of the Thirty-fourth Infantry and a man who took great pride in his title of "Father of the Ilocanos." Recruited primarily in the northern part of Nueva Ecija, these units performed exceptionally well. They took part in many of the Army's expeditions and operations, and served as translators, escorts, and outposts as well as protecting the Ilocano community from retaliation. They also tied much of the Ilocano community to the American cause, hampering guerrilla efforts to organize the population in the north. Kennon described them as "entirely trustworthy, orderly, enthusiastic to learn, brave in action and loyal to the United States."[43]

The American–Ilocano alliance began in late 1899 during the U.S. offensive when Kennon was forced to use Ilocano prisoners of war to transport supplies and build roads. This brought him into a close working relationship with the influential Ilocano leader, Francisco Madrid, who was soon recruiting more Ilocano construction workers from Nueva Viscaya province, an activity that led to his assassination early in 1900. Kennon realized that Madrid's killing had alienated much of the Ilocano community. He arranged for Francisco's son Bruno to return home with an American pass to bury his father, believing that "with proper management and through him or his companions the Ilocanos may be made assured friends of the United States."[44]

Both Kennon and Funston soon became convinced that the Ilocanos could be trusted as armed auxiliaries, and on 15 January 1900, Funston proposed that 100 Ilocanos be raised as native scouts. Kennon, however, quickly moved beyond this modest proposal and began to press actively for the immediate enlistment of much larger Ilocano forces. In March he claimed that the district's American soldiers were insufficient for a protracted guerrilla war and that native forces were necessary to support them. To demonstrate the Ilocano's loyalty, Kennon pointed to the recent murder of Madrid as well as the alleged historic hatred between Tagalogs and Ilocanos. Otis dismissed his suggestions, stating flatly that native troops were not expedient at the time and authorizing only a few guides. Undaunted, Kennon set to work, and by June had recruited a company of 50 Ilocanos armed with Springfield rifles under Lt. Frank Jernigan.[45]

In addition to the Ilocano Scouts, the Americans relied on the Ilocano populace as guides, construction workers, and bearers. On 1 September 1900, a group of Ilocano boatmen and 4 Ilocano Scouts successfully held off nearly 100 guerrillas at Villacorta after their U.S. Army escort had fled. Kennon in particular favored Ilocanos in appointments to municipal offices and ordered his officers to do the same. When Americans operated near Ilocano towns they were instructed not to molest "peaceful citizens" because "it is desired to win and retain the friendship of every Ilocano."[46] He also formed Ilocano volunteers into a paramilitary force to serve with the American garrisons, acting as both a town militia and auxiliaries. The revolutionaries reacted by murdering key leaders and Ilocanos suspected of collaboration, in one instance decapitating an old woman and burying two men alive. This terrorism seems only to have tied the Ilocanos closer to the Americans.[47]

Kennon's enthusiasm for Ilocano auxiliaries led him into several conflicts with superiors over pacification policies. He remained a persistent advocate of the use of native forces and constantly urged the recruitment of more Ilocano Scouts, whom he saw as vital paramilitary auxiliaries to the undermanned Army units. He became involved in a dispute with MacArthur over the latter's inexplicable refusal to pay the authorized thirty-peso rewards to some Ilocanos who had led U.S. forces to more than 100 rifles. After almost six months of wrangling, Kennon finally secured payment. He even tried to bypass Funston and enlist the aid of Taft and Wheaton when he felt Funston was blocking the recruitment of more Ilocanos. Funston, aware that there were not enough American officers to command even the existing Army companies, eventually had to call attention to Kennon's breaches in military protocol. Nevertheless, Kennon's lobbying did secure an authorization for more troops. Wheaton, who was hostile to the use of native soldiers, conceded in September 1900 that the Ilocanos in Nueva Ecija "have so far committed themselves to the American cause that some confidence may be placed in the *probability* that they will remain loyal" (emphasis in original) and urged that they be increased to 240 men.[48] Three months later, Funston requested that this number be doubled and claimed that the Ilocanos had never lost a man or gun in over a year and had captured more weapons than any other unit in the district.

A final and less commendable aspect of the use of Ilocano Scouts was the relatively free hand that both they and the Philippine Cavalry were given against suspected guerrillas. Funston made it clear that he would tolerate no revolutionary misconduct against his native auxiliaries and, as mentioned, he summarily executed two Filipino officers who were caught murdering Native Scouts. He was less prompt in punishing the misbehavior of his own forces. Ilocano volunteers were accused of being secret members of the Guardia de Honor and of shooting and torturing suspects.[49] The Macabebes in the Philippine Cavalry also had a vicious reputation. On one occasion, while their American officer was sick, they subjected the townspeople of San Francisco to "numerous and atrocious outrages during the 24 hours they were garrisoned there."[50] Wheaton was furious at this misconduct and ordered Funston to "enforce discipline on these savages at all hasards [sic]." Funston did little beyond reprimanding the officer responsible, pointing out that such conduct negated the otherwise good record of his men. Although he did not encourage his auxiliaries to mistreat guerrillas, he probably felt that the threat of Macabebe and Ilocano retaliation was an important factor in persuading other Filipinos to collaborate with the Americans.[51]

Unlike General Young's First District, Funston's Fourth District was not viewed as a showcase and he was not subjected to the same pressures to establish municipal government. Funston did not create an office to handle civic affairs as Young did and there was no officer in the district with powers comparable to Ballance's. He delegated most district administration to his aide, Capt. Erneste V. Smith, while he took to the field at the head of expeditions or with his beloved Headquarters Scouts. Smith, who was expected to serve as a chief of staff, adjutant, intelligence officer, line commander (he was responsible for the capture of Pantaleon García), and a number of other duties, was unable to devote much attention to civil affairs. Either through Funston's own preferences or through the disorganization that he initially faced, he delayed the implementation of civil government under either G.O. 40 or G.O. 43 for most of 1900. As a result, in some instances civil government was established by officers working through an informal system of town councils. Maj. William C. Brown, for example, held a meeting on 25 June with the council of Malabar to discuss such issues as the tax on the local railroad, whether to teach English in schools, and how best to complete the local roads. In July 1900, Funston announced that sixteen towns were ready for organization under G.O. 40, but by October only ten of these had held elections; moreover, these elections were so poorly attended that in one town only fourteen people cast votes. In other towns, the elections were postponed due to bad weather or invalidated by the election of unqualified officials. Nevertheless, by December Funston reported every town government operational and "as far as reported the system appears to be working fairly well."[52]

The Fourth District's commander was also indifferent to the possible uses of Filipino native police as an aid to American pacification. Despite orders from Manila to form municipal police forces, in July 1900, Smith reported that nothing had been done to organize or arm them. Under some pressure from his superiors, Funston armed the police force of Peñaranda in October as a test case but disarmed it in December after two pistols were lost, and he argued that the unsettled state of affairs militated against arming any more native police.[53] The success of Army military operations and the recovery of the two pistols caused him to reverse himself in January. Thereafter he became an enthusiastic convert, and in March he claimed that the police had materially aided the Army forces. Other officers noted that *presidentes* used the police as servants and that their low wages and bad armament led to very inefficient law enforcement. The civil governor who replaced Funston reported that in January 1902 only ten of the province's twenty-three towns had an armed police force and that the situation needed urgent remedy.[54]

Funston also neglected using his military forces as agents of social reform. Fourth District Headquarters made great efforts to insure that roads were built, but ignored such other aspects of civic action as schools, sanitation projects, and medical care. As a result, the initiative was left to individual officers who often displayed an ethnocentric desire to improve the lot of their charges. Maj. John A. Baldwin spoke for some officers when he sarcastically requested that "in our noble efforts at teaching these barefoot children of a primitive civilization the rudiments of sanitation, I have the honor to request that the Subsistence Department be [ordered] to clear up around its warehouse."[55] Yet Baldwin subjected the town of San Isidro to a complete reform campaign which featured extensive street cleaning, the prohibition of hard liquor, and the requirement that people washing in rivers and streams wear bathing trunks. Like many officers, Baldwin's interest in social reform had both an idealistic and a pragmatic rationale: "Self-interest is the foundation on which a people must be expected to accept a foreign government. The schoolhouse, together with just and enlightened treatment must be relied on to regenerate these people and lead them in true paths of civilization."[56]

Funston's lack of attention to civil government, native police, and schools indicates that he felt these measures were irrelevant to the pacification of the district. In most districts, these nonmilitary measures were undertaken primarily as practical methods to obtain popular support or compliance. For a variety of other reasons, however, Funston could boast by January 1901 that "there is now here a good public sentiment in favor of the American authorities, a fact which has been manifested in numerous ways. The people are tired of disturbances and want the country pacified. The rebels in arms no longer have the support of the general public."[57] Unlike officers in other districts, Funston did not face a strong guerrilla movement that was sustained by support from the towns. Whereas many towns in the Philippines were ruled by a shadow government which controlled the population through a mixture of patriotism and intimidation, in the Fourth District the tendency of the people was to flock to the Army-garrisoned towns for shelter. Guerrilla tactics, which took the form of incendiary attacks on towns and property destruction, appear to have backfired and only increased support for the Americans. In addition, the American–Ilocano alliance not only won over much of the north, it also insured that in any provincial town where Ilocanos lived the Americans could often find information and support. Thus, the main incentive which might have pushed Funston toward civic action and social reform, that of the necessity of destroying the guerrillas' hold on the loyalty of the population, was lacking. Believing there was little need for such methods, Funston either ignored them or assigned them very low priority.

Despite his disinterest in nonmilitary pacification, Funston's counterinsurgency methods were well suited to the regional guerrilla war he encountered in the Fourth District. In this he was fortunate that the resistance he faced was weak, internally divided, and often poorly led. Unlike officers in the First District, he confronted neither a strongly developed guerrilla military organization, an entrenched infrastructure, nor, with the exception of Lacuna, skilled opponents. In contrast to most district commanders, Funston had a very easy task. Yet he should be credited with the intelligence and drive to make the most of his situation. From the very first, he established an effective intelligence network and created elite units capable of reacting to sudden opportunities; in two crucial instances he was able to break up guerrilla offensives by attacking first. Moreover, he embraced a wide variety of pacification methods, many of which focused on mobilizing the district's population behind the Americans. By conciliating powerful ethnic and social groups, using native auxiliaries, and conducting military operations which struck at the guerrillas but left the populace relatively untouched, he was able to virtually destroy opposition in slightly more than a year.

The Army's pacification campaign in the Fourth District was among its least difficult. Many of the accepted methods of guerrilla resistance—the shadow governments, Katipunans, assassination, and so on were never able to seriously challenge the American control. Faced with a divided populace and a dispirited resistance and given pragmatic and competent leadership, the Americans in the Fourth District structured a campaign that exploited Filipino weaknesses. With his opposition so weak, Funston had a far easier task than Young did. Indeed, had he been given a few more troops he might easily have ended the war in mid-1900 shortly after the capture of García. It is difficult not to conclude that, regardless of Funston's colorful personality, the Fourth District was a backwater. This is not to deny that for the people concerned the war was, in Funston's words, a "nasty little war," in which guerrilla terrorism, the Army's burning of houses, and Macabebe outrages contributed greatly to the suffering of the inhabitants. Yet on both sides, Americans and Filipinos contributed to make it a much less nasty war than it could have been.

A rare photograph of combat in the Philippine War. Most fighting consisted of such skirmishes between U.S. patrols and small bands of guerrillas. (National Archives 111-RB-1246)

Maj. Gen. Arthur MacArthur, commander of the U.S. Army forces in the Philippines during the height of the guerrilla war. (Courtesy of U.S. Army Military History Institute)

Brig. Gen. Samuel B. M. Young, commander of the First District, Department of Northern Luzon. (Courtesy of MacArthur Memorial)

Brig. Gen. Frederick Funston (fourth from left), commander of the Fourth District, Department of Northern Luzon, in the field. (Courtesy of U.S. Army Military History Institute)

William T. Johnston, one of the U.S. Army's counterinsurgency experts, as a U.S. Military Academy cadet in 1891. Johnston played a key role in the pacification of two districts. (Courtesy of U.S. Army Military History Institute)

Brig. Gen. Manuel Tinio's forces which operated in the First District, Department of Northern Luzon. (Courtesy of MacArthur Memorial)

U.S. soldiers with a captured guerrilla officer. The guerrillas seldom wore uniforms and could easily pass as "amigos." (Courtesy of U.S. Army Military History Institute)

Bicol auxiliaries and a U.S. Army sergeant bring in a suspected guerrilla in the Third District, Department of Southern Luzon. (Courtesy of U.S. Army Military History Institute)

Brig. Gen. Juan Cailles and his guerrillas surrender to the Americans in June 1901. Cailles led the guerrilla resistance in Laguna province. (National Archives 111-SC-98028)

Maj. Gen. Miguel Malvar, the most effective guerrilla commander in Luzon.
(National Archives 111-SC-98029)

4

Stalemate in Bicolandia
The Third District, Department of Southern Luzon

Col. Walter Howe's summation of counterinsurgency in the Third District, Department of Southern Luzon, illustrates the frustration felt by officers serving in southeastern Luzon:

> The garrisons were in all cases so small that no man could be spared to hold the interior towns as they were captured, and the inevitable result followed. Towns captured on one day were of necessity evacuated on the next; and any native who gave information or in any way showed friendship for the Americans was killed by the revolutionaries, who immediately returned and reoccupied the towns, and a district which could have been kept in comparative peace if more troops had been furnished, was repeatedly fought over, repeatedly captured, and as often given up for want of sufficient force to hold it. As a matter of fact the regiment held the ground upon which any part of it happened to stand, but no more.[1]

The war in the Bicol (Bicolandia) region was a unique regional war with few similarities to other areas. Unlike their compatriots elsewhere, the district's revolutionary leadership did not challenge the Army's occupation of the towns but instead withdrew with the civilian population into the hills. Aided by formidable terrain and the inadequate strength of the Army, they pursued a defensive strategy which precluded a quick military solution and caused the pacification campaign to become a virtual stalemate.

The Third District encompassed the three provinces of Ambos Camarines (consisting of the recently joined Camarines Norte and Camarines Sur), Albay, and Sorsogon, a total area of some 5,400 square miles. Situated on a narrow peninsula and barely joined to the rest of Luzon, southeastern Luzon is a distinct cultural region known as "Bicolandia," geographically divided by volcanic mountains and large embayments into several semiautonomous sub-regions. The area's isolation is further compounded by dense vegetation, poor roads, and rugged hills presenting an almost impenetrable barrier to overland travel. Although roads link such important cities as Legaspi and Nueva Caceres, many areas of Bicolandia are joined to the rest of Luzon only through waterborne communications. Despite these geographic barriers, the area is united by a common language and traditions which create a distinct Bicol culture.[2]

Southeastern Luzon assumed world importance in the mid-nineteenth century with the commercial cultivation of abaca (Manila hemp) for an international market in cordage. The harbors of Legaspi, Sorsogon, Bulan, and Tabaco became key ports for the hemp trade; interior towns such as Iriga, Ligao, and Oas developed into prosperous trading centers and Albay, Sorsogon, and the Lagonoy district of the Camarines became the centers of abaca production. The commercial cultivation of abaca also increased the prosperity of the lowland rice-growing areas of Ambos Camarines which became responsible for feeding the population working in the abaca fields and ports. By 1900, southeastern Luzon's economy was tied both to interna-tional markets and to the smooth functioning of internal trade—a sharp disruption in either could lead not only to economic hardship but to severe food shortages.[3]

The Philippine Revolution in Bicolandia, with the exception of the Cama-rines, was noteworthy chiefly for its lack of bloodshed and bitterness. The economic benefits of the abaca and food trade provided comparative pros-perity, and many of the religious grievances that prompted rebellion in other areas of the Philippines were absent. The Franciscan order did not possess large estates and the diocese of Nueva Caceres was unique in having native Filipino priests occupying half the parishes. In 1896, Albay sent volunteers, money, and supplies to fight against Aguinaldo's Katipuneros in the belief that they represented an effort by the Tagalogs to dominate Luzon. Spanish volunteers managed to dispel much Bicol good feeling by brutally suppress-ing a small outbreak near Daet, Ambos Camarines, in November 1897. When Spanish authority throughout the archipelago collapsed in the summer of 1898, the provincial elite in Albay assumed control in September, allowing the Spanish governor to depart freely. In Sorsogon there was a similarly peaceful political transfer as the Spanish governor handed over his authority to Father Jorge Barlin. In Ambos Camarines, perhaps as a result of the atrocities the year before, political change was more violent and stained by the murder of more than 100 Spanish prisoners of war. Having freed them-

Third District, Department of Southern Luzon

selves from foreign control, the local *principalía* established provincial governments and regional militia and pledged their loyalty to the new Philippine Republic.[4]

As in the Fourth District, Department of Northern Luzon, the Republican leaders in Bicolandia were unable to translate their political control of the area into an effective military posture. In September 1898, Aguinaldo appointed his fellow Caviteano and loyal supporter, Maj. Gen. Vito Belarmino, to military and political command of the region. An early member of Aguinaldo's Katipunan faction, Belarmino was a brigadier general during the Revolt of 1896 and served as a combat commander and as an administrator in the short-lived first Republican government. After going into exile with Aguinaldo in Hong Kong, he returned in 1898 to command a division against the Spanish at Manila. In addition to Belarmino, other military commanders also arrived to put the area firmly in the hands of the Philippine Republic. In the Camarines provinces, the capable Brig. Gen. Vicente Lukban established a local defense force before being sent to the Visayan Islands. He was replaced by the less-efficient Brig. Gen. Wenceslao Viniegra. Brig. Gen. José Ignacio Paua, a native Chinese who had distinguished himself as an ordnance officer and fighter, arrived to insure that the profits from the hemp trade flowed to the new government. Through the continued export of abaca and the efforts of Paua, southeastern Luzon was able to send considerable sums of money to the new government.[5]

Beyond dispatching these officers, the Republic did little to put the area on a military footing. Aguinaldo's government contributed only 180 rifles, barely enough to arm two companies, leaving the area with such a shortage of arms that in all of Albay province it was estimated there were no more than 250 rifles. With such inadequate armament, Belarmino's efforts were limited to fortifying the major ports and attempting to form an army equipped with machetes, bows and arrows, and spears. In the fall of 1899, his defensive plans received a further setback when the Americans blockaded Philippine hemp ports, severely inhibiting the region's prosperity and creating economic distress among the inhabitants. Moreover, the revolutionaries suffered from internal divisions: Paua complained to Aguinaldo that the revolutionaries were abusing the Chinese by robberies and forced contributions. Thus, for a variety of reasons, despite more than a year of independence, the Philippine forces were militarily ill-prepared for the American expedition that arrived in January 1900.[6]

The objective of the American invasion of the Bicol region was, in the words of its commander, "to render a sufficient quantity of hemp available for the American market as soon as possible."[7] The blockade may have hurt Bicol prosperity, but it also created severe repercussions within the U.S. cordage industry and caused the War Department to cable its "urgent inquiries and anxiety here about hemp."[8] Accordingly, on 15 January 1900, Otis assigned Brig. Gen. William A. Kobbé to occupy the hemp ports of Tabaco, Legaspi, Donsol, and Bulan in Albay and Sorsogon and establish civil government and customs services. The choice of Kobbé, one of the chief advocates of benevolent pacification, indicates both the importance with which Otis viewed the reestablishment of the hemp trade and his belief that pacification in southeastern Luzon would consist primarily of establishing effective civil government.[9]

On 20 January Kobbé's expeditionary force, comprising the Forty-third and Forty-seventh U.S.V. Infantry, and Battery G, Third Artillery, occupied the port of Sorsogon without resistance. According to later reports, the revolutionary high command ordered the town burned, but the local commander disobeyed and withdrew to the interior with most of the townspeople. The following day Bulan and Donsol were occupied by Maj. Hugh D. Wise's battalion of the Forty-seventh, giving the Army effective control of Sorsogon province's key hemp ports. While most of the Filipino forces retreated into Albay province, irregulars continued to stay near the towns and harass American patrols. Foreshadowing the pattern throughout the district, the Americans stationed at Donsol found it impossible to persuade the inhabitants to return, in part because the soldiers themselves were under attack by snipers and arsonists. Despite the easy landings at Sorsogon, the desertion of the towns and the immediate beginning of guerrilla warfare hinted that pacification in southeastern Luzon would be a difficult and lengthy undertaking.[10]

The 23 January amphibious assault on the port of Legaspi, Albay, gave further indications of the firmness of the local resistance. Under Belarmino and Paua, the Albayanos had constructed an elaborate system of trenches reinforced with captured Spanish cannon. Fortunately for the U.S. soldiers, Paua devoted insufficient attention to his flank defenses, and a small American force landing to the north was able to turn his left wing. The Bicols fought with reckless disregard for casualties, and it was only after vicious hand-to-hand fighting that they were driven out of Legaspi and the neighboring towns of Albay and Daraga. The battle was costly in both lives and property: the Americans counted fifty-three Filipino dead and a number of buildings destroyed, largely by naval gunfire. In the following days Kobbé's forces garrisoned other strategic lowlands towns, encountering sniping and ambushes as they patrolled the countryside.[11]

Having seized the major hemp ports in Albay and Sorsogon provinces, Kobbé quickly set to work reestablishing the hemp trade. On 27 January he declared the ports of Sorsogon and Donsol open and, three days later, Bulan, Albay, and Legaspi. To encourage business he established liberal laws on the transportation of hemp and agricultural products. Kobbé also made sincere attempts to win over the population. He forbade American troops to enter native houses, ordered captured Filipinos turned loose, and stressed "the importance of conciliating the inhabitants of your neighborhood in encouraging them to pursue their usual avocations."[12] His subordinates complied with this, and late in January Wise assured Kobbé that at Donsol "there has been no looting, no destruction nor no molestation of the property of absent natives."[13]

Admirable though the emphasis on normality, trade, and rapport may have been, it hardly reflected Kobbé's precarious position. His expeditionary force consisted of only two regiments, and he took the Forty-third with him when he left the Bicol region to occupy the Visayan islands of Leyte and Samar on 25 January. The Forty-seventh was broken up and assigned to garrison seven large towns in Albay and Sorsogon with slightly more than 1,000 soldiers. Belarmino's forces soon moved back into the neighboring *barrios*, harassing the isolated Americans with snipers and incendiaries and threatening to attack. The Forty-seventh's garrisons lacked sufficient forces to create an effective buffer zone; one officer noted, "I can chase the Insurrectos for miles in any direction, but must afterwards come back and they follow."[14] In early February, the garrisons at Legaspi, Donsol, Albay, and Daraga were attacked; Donsol and Albay were burned, and at Daraga the small Army force came close to being overwhelmed by the Filipinos. On hearing these reports, Kobbé remarked that native resistance had "exceeded in stubbornness and aggressiveness any fighting since the outbreak in February 1899. They are skillfully led, have had no experience in fighting Americans, and have been idle a year under frequent reports of revolutionary victories in the north."[15]

The first two weeks of Army occupation in Albay and Sorsogon established a pattern that was to continue for much of the district's pacification. Belarmino's forces could not drive or burn the Americans out of the towns, nor could they face the better-armed soldiers in combat without prohibitive casualties; but they could keep the population in the hills and prevent the Americans from reestablishing the hemp trade. The Army, for its part, could not achieve a decisive military victory. Although U.S. soldiers claimed to have killed more than 200 guerrillas in the ten days of fighting after the landings, they could not disperse the enemy forces who perched just outside their lines and continued to plague them. Kobbé had taken the Forty-seventh's transport with him, forcing the troops to carry all their own supplies and effectively precluding sustained operations. Lacking forces to garrison the inland towns, patrols could only conduct brief forays into the countryside, but at night they would have to return to their isolated towns. In the meantime, soldiers soon learned that the hemp fields and hills were not only almost impassable, but they provided excellent cover for snipers. Since neither side could defeat the other, a stalemate soon developed.[16]

As the occupation of Albay and Sorsogon provinces came to a standstill, a new Army expeditionary force under Brig. Gen. James M. Bell (no relation to J. Franklin Bell) was dispatched to Ambos Camarines to complete the occupation of the hemp ports. On 20 February 1900, the Fortieth and Forty-fifth U.S.V. Infantry landed in San Miguel Bay, occupying the provincial capital of Nueva Caceres two days later. Suspecting that Belarmino's forces were dependent on food stored at Nueva Caceres, the Americans quickly cut his supply lines into Albay province. With the exception of a small engagement at Libmanan, there was little military resistance; but as the expeditionary forces moved into the populous valleys, the inhabitants fled to the mountains. Almost immediately the stalemate that had emerged in Albay was repeated. With few exceptions the Filipino forces avoided battle and contented themselves with sniping from the hills or attempting to burn occupied towns. The withdrawal of the Fortieth Infantry in mid-March for service in Mindanao left the Forty-fifth as undermanned as the Forty-seventh and unable to do more than hold on to the towns it had captured.[17]

To a large extent, the emergence of a military stalemate was the result of a conscious decision by the Filipino revolutionary leadership. Having failed to prevent the Army landings at the beachheads or the occupation of many of the towns, they now planned to frustrate American control by deserting the towns and having civilians move to inland villages or the mountains. One captured proclamation urged Filipinos in Sorsogon to withdraw to the mountains where "the Americans cannot reach us and we can have our own government." The revolutionaries attempted to keep the populace away from the Army with a mixture of patriotism, propaganda, and intimidation. Citizens were urged to avoid all contact with the invaders and only go into occupied towns to purchase essential supplies. They were told that the soldiers would subvert the Catholic religion and murder and plunder indiscriminately. Those Filipinos who returned had their property destroyed or were threatened with horrible reprisals.[18]

At the same time the civilian population were leaving the towns, Belarmino decided that the revolutionary military forces should withdraw to the mountains and avoid all combat except in the most favorable circumstances. In part this strategy reflected his belief that the war would be won either in central Luzon or in the United States with the election in 1900 of Democrat William Jennings Bryan. Moreover, in the early months of the war Belarmino was considering the possibility of surrender. In his mid-fifties and suffering from a disease that would leave him almost blind, he was physically incapable of an active military role, and he delegated many decisions to subordinates, especially his aide, Col. Ramon Santos. In spite of his long military experience, and in contrast to Manuel Tinio or Miguel Malvar, Belarmino was not interested in coordinating guerrilla forces or developing uniform policies throughout the region. His captured correspondence gives little indication that he exercised much control over his subordinates and, except for a warning against serving on American civil governments, he appears to have been more worried about the moral danger of gambling than the physical danger of enemy troops. In common with Tinio, he was hampered by the fact that he was an outsider without strong social connections and as a result, he depended a great deal upon the cooperation of his subordinates. Neverthe-less, a 1902 Army intelligence report credited him with having great influ-ence among the Bicol population, especially among the *principales*. Certainly his adoption of a defensive strategy was an excellent decision and contributed greatly to the sustained resistance in the Third District. Moreover, after his early wavering he steadfastly held to the cause of independence and contin-ued fighting long after other revolutionary leaders had surrendered.[19]

Belarmino's guerrilla forces consisted of a combination of regulars and militia, or Sandahatan, commanded by an officer corps that was dispropor-tionately Tagalog *principalía*. A study of 31 leaders in the Camarines revealed that 22 were Tagalog or came from Tagalog regions, and only 5 were Bicols—the only non-Tagalog to achieve high rank was Lt. Col. Ludovicio Aréjola.[20] Under these officers were a few partisan units which lived in the mountains in bands of between 10 and 100 men, about one-third of them supplied with rifles. During active U.S. operations, these regulars would disperse and become civilians or break up into small groups which moved constantly. The Sandahatan lived in *barrios* and villages outside the American zone and "were engaged in cultivating the soil for the subsistence of the riflemen and them-selves, posing as our friends, but acting as spies, and only assembling at stated times, or when specifically called upon for a kidnapping or marauding expedition."[21] They also dug mantraps and trenches, served in their villages as the revolutionaries' enforcement arm, and supplied outposts for the guer-rilla camps, using carabao horns and "bamboo tomtoms" to warn the guerril-las of the soldiers' approach. They made the Army officers feel that they were living in a fishbowl; as Col. Walter Howe commented in April: "I cannot send out 10 men in the middle of the night without it being known before they have gone a mile."[22]

The guerrillas used a variety of methods to inflict casualties on the Army while avoiding losses of their own and to confine the Americans to the deserted towns. The region's dense vegetation, low hills, and few roads allowed them to set ambushes and snipe at Army patrols almost routinely: one Army escort on the Legaspi-Ligao road reported that they were fired on from all the "usual places on the road and in fact we had to fight our way through . . . every column that goes through the hills loses men."[23] Despite the limited number of rifles, poor marksmanship, and the "tin-can ammuni-tion" used by the guerrillas, they not only inflicted casualties but forced Army patrols to constantly deploy and engage in the exhausting and time-consum-ing work of sweeping the hills and hemp groves. The troops also discovered many trails that hid artfully designed mantraps: on a single patrol, soldiers found forty spring-traps designed to drive a hidden spear through the unwary victim's chest.[24] Belarmino further hampered Army expeditions by ordering his partisans to assault American-occupied towns when the garrisons went on patrol or to launch incendiary attacks to burn the soldiers out. Within the towns soldiers were threatened by individual assailants. One sentry was decapitated by an apparently harmless "hombre" who had concealed a long knife in a basket. Belarmino's chief of staff, Col. Ramon Santos, even proposed poisoning U.S. garrisons with a solution made from a native fruit, but this his fellow commanders refused to sanction. All in all, American troops could agree with one district commander that "this is indeed a strange sort of warfare."[25]

Resistance was maintained by a system of taxes and voluntary or enforced contributions, chiefly on hemp and agricultural products, which funded the purchase of rice and supplies. Recognizing the importance of the abaca trade, Belarmino's headquarters declared on 19 April that all merchants trading it must purchase a license from the revolutionaries. Howe estimated that the guerrillas collected one peso per bale on each of the 500 bales that came into Legaspi daily, though he took some comfort from the fact that most of this was lost through corruption. They also harvested hemp from the fields of suspected *americanistas* and sold it to middlemen, with the result that a steady stream of contraband hemp flowed out, either from small ports that lacked U.S. garrisons or under the ineffective supervision of U.S. Army customs officers.[26]

Americans serving in southeastern Luzon were infuriated by the illicit hemp trade and fumed at their superiors' failure to support vigorous measures. The most obvious solution to cutting this source of money and supplies, the closing of all hemp ports and a blockade on trade, was repeatedly refused by Manila and Washington. The Third District's commander, Brig. Gen. James M. Bell, urged the closing of the hemp ports because "the greater portion of the hemp shipped from these ports is actually owned by the insurgents or their sympathizers and . . . is sold in Manila for the benefit of the insurgents."[27] After his own investigation in the fall of 1900, MacArthur also urged closing the ports on the grounds that "if hemp could not get out or rice in, two powerful interests would operate for tranquilization."[28] But Secretary of War Elihu Root, believing that the hemp trade was necessary to protect American cordage needs, resolutely prohibited any interference in the hemp trade. As a result, the guerrillas continued to benefit from the contraband trade until the end of the war.

Despite their early success in isolating the Army and establishing a thriving trade in contraband hemp, the revolutionary strategy had serious long-term weaknesses. In separating the populace from the Army, the guerrillas forfeited all chance of establishing an underground resistance in the garrison towns. The *presidentes*, priests, or other local authorities who supported the guerrillas remained with the guerrilla forces, leaving few of the *principales* to establish and lead the shadow governments, clandestine Katipunans, and *barrio* militias that enforced authority in most American-occupied towns in the Philippines. While initially successful, in time the depopulation campaign, the withdrawal of their military forces to the mountains, and the failure to establish support systems in the towns all contributed to weaken the guerrillas. Although they might occupy the highlands with relative impunity, nearly all the food-producing areas were in the lowlands under Army occupation, and by conceding the hemp ports, they effectively cut off much of the population from its source of income. As a result, the guerrillas and the civilians who stayed with them spent an inordinate amount of time simply avoiding starvation. Those Filipinos who refused to flee or returned to their towns in the face of guerrilla threats had clearly decided that accommodation with American authority was possible and that Army garrisons could protect them. In consequence, although an individual town might retain but a fraction of its original inhabitants, those who chose to live there were confirmed *americanistas*.[29]

These weaknesses would appear only with time, for in the early months of 1900 the American position looked much worse than that of the guerrillas. Their mission was one of the clearest of any regional pacification force in the Philippines: to open the hemp ports, insure that an adequate supply of hemp reached the U.S. market, and establish civil government. However, the forces in the district were initially far too weak and poorly supplied even to meet these limited objectives. Although they had accomplished the first step, "it became evident that possession of the ports was not possession of the interior, nor did it insure peace in the garrisoned places themselves."[30] Indeed, there was reason to believe that in the beginning the chief beneficiaries of the restoration of the hemp trade were the revolutionaries. The American soldiers' final task, the establishment of civil government, was irrelevant as long as the population remained in the mountains.

To compound the Army's difficulties, the commander in southeastern Luzon, Brig. Gen. James M. Bell, was beset by personal problems. After his successful invasion of the Camarines, he was appointed to the command District of South-Eastern Luzon in late March which was renamed the Third District on 1 May 1900. Born in 1837, and commissioned during the

Civil War, Bell had served on the western plains against the Sioux, Cheyenne, Kiowas, and other Indian tribes. The rigors of campaigning in the tropical Philippines proved too much for the old veteran, and by early summer his aide confided that Bell was physically "breaking up." He was forced to take a leave of absence from June to September and was replaced on 28 February 1901, retiring from the Army almost immediately afterward. Furthermore, he was handicapped by a lack of support in Manila and from his immediate superior, Maj. Gen. John Bates, commander of the Department of Southern Luzon. Both MacArthur and Bates failed to provide Bell with essential supplies and men and disregarded many of his suggestions. Moreover, communications within the Third District were so primitive that many towns within the same province were linked only via Manila. As a result, Bell was forced to act more as director of operations than as battlefield leader. He decided upon many of the key pacification policies but left their implementation to officers serving in the field. Fortunately for Bell, he shared with Young in the First District the blessing of capable subordinates who were able to construct effective regional pacification methods and develop their own policies.[31]

The initial operations following the occupation of the ports soon established American-held enclaves around the towns and left the countryside under the control of the guerrillas. The early months were devoted to consolidating the American position and enticing the population back, and to a few expeditions against known guerrilla strongholds. In March an Army expedition destroyed Belarmino's fortified camp at Malabog, Albay. That same month, Paua, whose relations with Belarmino had deteriorated since the U.S. invasion, surrendered with several members of an influential Albayano family, the Imperials, who had been prominent guerrilla officers.[32] These successes were small compensation for the continuing inability of the Americans to defeat the guerrillas decisively. In April, Bell toured the Third District and concluded that the guerrillas "infest the whole country, terrorizing the people and driving them from their homes. Many cases are reported of the murders of natives and Chinamen who have shown friendship for the Americans."[33] Most officers in the area shared their commander's pessimism and believed that "we are governing just the spots we sit upon."[34]

A chief cause of this military stalemate was the critical manpower shortage in the Third District. This itself was the outgrowth of Otis's decision to occupy the entire archipelago immediately after Aguinaldo's defeat. Perhaps convinced that the Bicols would welcome the Americans, Army headquarters starved Bell for troops despite his frequent calls for reinforcements. By mid-May, the American forces consisted of the Forty-seventh Infantry and the Forty-fifth Infantry, a company of the Thirty-seventh U.S.V. Infantry, a squadron of the Eleventh U.S.V. Cavalry, and a detachment of artillery: a total of 2,600 troops to pacify a native population of 600,000. Otis argued that both Kobbé and Bates felt this was enough and that Bell was pessimistic, but soldiers in the district insisted they needed more men and believed it impossible to pacify the area with such limited troop strength.[35]

The terrain and climate of the Bicol region proved to be almost as much of an adversary as the insurgents and greatly encouraged the early stalemate. Although there were a few overland routes between the provinces, they were often blocked or in need of major repairs and internal communications were so poor that Col. Howe complained he was out of touch with much of his Forty-seventh Infantry for most of his tour of duty. Dense tropical vegetation, abaca groves, hills, bays, and rivers created a terrain so rough that a sniper could be ten feet away and virtually invisible from the soldiers that pursued him. Cavalry was useless, and on infantry patrols the flanking parties could not move through the brush and hills quickly enough to keep up with the main force marching on the roads. The result was that Filipino snipers could creep up to within a few yards of the patrol and fire with relative impunity. In the inland valleys, men collapsed from the summer heat and entire garrisons were reported to be too exhausted for operations. To further complicate matters, the fall monsoon season was accompanied by typhoons which restricted seaborne operations and washed out most of the roads. Conditions during this season were so bad that divisional headquarters advised a suspension of operations.[36]

Yet a third factor was the inadequacy of Army logistical support. The Army's commissary department never overcame the difficulties of sending supplies by water from Manila to southeastern Luzon. As a result, critical shortages left troops in some areas without adequate food for months. Rations arrived so rotten they were immediately condemned; in one memorable (but not atypical) incident, soldiers at Nueva Caceres were able to salvage only 10 out of the 195 crates of potatoes that had been shipped. Equally bad was the supply system within the district, and much of the food that did arrive often could not be easily distributed. The regionwide rinderpest epidemic, which broke out in mid-1900, was a double curse: it killed off domestic draft animals and also denied the troops fresh meat. The expeditionary forces were not provided with large wagons and thus were forced to use numerous small supply trains, tying up troops in escort duty and providing the guerrillas ample opportunity for ambushes and sniping. In some areas, such as the Iriga district, the garrisons were dependent upon native boatmen who were often robbed by the insurgents. The Army's failure to pay most garrisons meant that for over six months the men could not buy food themselves. Medical supply services during the first half-year of occupation were even worse. Kobbé appropriated most of the Forty-seventh Infantry's medical supplies for his expeditionary force and replacements did not arrive till fall. Officers who sought to buy essential medicine for their men out of their own funds found that there was none to be had for any price.[37]

These problems, each one serious enough by itself, compounded and recompounded to cripple the Army and encourage the guerrillas. Moreover, they precluded any buildup for the sustained operations which alone could break the stalemate. On those rare occasions when contact with the enemy had been maintained, the troops ran out of supplies in a few days and had to break off with "slight tangible result."[38] Lack of supplies and rough conditions took a considerable toll on the men: in Donsol, for example, six months of service rendered half the garrison unfit for active duty. Bad food, inadequate rest, nonexistent medical supplies, and the strain of guerrilla warfare produced a general breakdown in the Forty-seventh: "This condition is not altogether due to the climate, but is largely due to the intense strain they have been under, which has acted in two ways: some have been rendered nervous and unfitted by it, others seem to have grown callous and indifferent, willing at any time to take undue risks, but it has, generally speaking, affected the health of the regiment as a whole."[39] Until these inadequacies of manpower, supply, and communications could be redressed, the Army could not launch a sustained effort to challenge guerrilla control of the hills. With their military options circumscribed, officers turned to pacification policies that needed no large expenditures of men and supplies.

As we have noted, a fundamental assumption that underlay district policy was that the Bicol population did not support the predominantly Tagalog guerrilla leadership and could be won over to American rule with humane treatment. Although there is a certain truth to Norman Owen's observation that "at times American officers were convinced that 'the entire native element' was against them," it is probable that Lt. Col. James Parker spoke for most of his fellow officers when he declared, "It is my earnest belief that once convinced of the beneficent motives of the United States all resistance by the mass of the people will cease."[40] Most Army officers in the Bicol region attributed the resistance to the Tagalogs and believed the Bicol population was either pro-American or terrorized by the guerrillas/Tagalogs. Col. Joseph H. Dorst, commander of the Forty-fifth Infantry, went so far as to urge "the deportation of every Tagal[og] who has been brought into the province by the rebel government."[41] Lt. Col. Charles C. Starr believed that Belarmino and other Tagalogs were only continuing the war for their personal enrichment and argued that "the confiscation of the property of these Tagalo[g] leaders which lies in their home provinces would do more to bring many of them to their senses than anything else."[42] The most extreme proponent of this view was Parker, who argued, quite mistakenly, that "the insurrection [in the Lagonoy district] is kept alive by about 200 Tagal[og]s, whom the mass of the inhabitants fear and hate."[43]

This view of the populace as divided into malevolent or misguided *insurrectos* on the one hand and potentially friendly natives on the other helped channel much of the Army's pacification policies into gaining the support of the population. Kobbé's initial orders had stressed the importance of establishing civil government and attempts were made in Albay and Sorsogon immediately. But the mass evacuation of the towns had rendered futile the standard model of government under G.O. 43. Kobbé's successor, Bell, wisely decided that "unsettled conditions" precluded organization under either G.O. 43 or 40 and on 27 April he substituted his own variant, G.O. 7. This required the post commander to do no more than appoint a *presidente* and organize a municipal police force; other municipal offices, though not required, could be added as the situation warranted. In its simplicity and flexibility, G.O. 7 could be quickly implemented even in towns with only a fraction of their inhabitants. It did not require post commanders to deal with taxation, municipal ordinances, or town boundaries, but only with maintaining order. Most important, it centered all authority in the post commander and the *presidente*, and required them to work together.[44]

As a result of G.O. 7, *presidentes* became the middlemen between the Army and the populace. They quickly learned that cooperation could yield substantial personal benefits: increased prestige, a visit from Bell, or a public ceremony to award them a baton of office. There were also far more lasting rewards: in Iriga the *presidente* was authorized to select not only all the municipal officers, but also to promote gambling at the town fiesta; further, he was resolutely backed in a conflict with the local padre. Commanders lent troops to deal with town troublemakers and insured that the *presidentes'* property outside the town was respected. When the Army adopted strict controls over rice and hemp, the local *presidentes* were in an ideal position to make huge profits through licenses and fines.[45]

In return, the *presidentes'* greatest contribution was their ability to convince much of the population to move back into towns. This frustrated the guerrilla strategy and made those who stayed in the hills increasingly discontented. In addition, from quite early in the American occupation, individual *presidentes* cooperated more fully than was usual elsewhere on Luzon. They supplied spies and guides and prevented their own townsmen from smuggling food or information to the revolutionaries. Some formed vigilante units and sent them into the hills, forcing the people still hiding to come in, and burning guerrilla food caches. Others provided vital information and advice or wrote to the guerrillas in the hills to offer to negotiate their surrenders or threaten them with destruction. In numerous other ways, individual *presidentes* contributed to Army pacification of southeastern Luzon. It was fitting that when Bell stepped down as commander his final address praised the *presidentes* for their great support.[46]

The second great target of concentration was the native clergy. Although Bell's official policy was to avoid all influence in religious matters, his subordinates found that "if the Priest can be made to come back to his house and live the natives will follow and remain quiet."[47] Local U.S. commanders made great efforts to secure priests for their local churches, realizing that "a thoroughly good man would be of very material assistance to us in the pacification of the district."[48] Capt. Arlington U. Betts even considered kidnapping a priest for his town, but after some negotiations he was able to settle on a less dramatic solution. Once they were established, the priests proved very effective in calming the populace, urging support for American policies, recommending reliable people, and establishing good relations between soldiers and civilians. For their part, officers supported the clergy with medicine, passes, and concessions to their parishioners. John Schumacher, in his impressive study of the Filipino clergy during this period, has argued that "nowhere else was there such widespread and effective support of the Filipino clergy for the Revolution." However, the bulk of Army source material indicates that as the U.S. occupation became more entrenched the clergy increasingly came to an accommodation with the Americans.[49] By late 1900, cooperation between officers and priests was the rule, not the exception, and at least one revolutionary fumed at the support given the Americans by the "Machiavellian" priests.[50]

Less successful were the Army's attempts to organize and arm the local police forces as provided for in G.O. 7. Shortly after he took command, Bell armed the police of four towns in Ambos Camarines and required them to cooperate with U.S. patrols on operations outside their towns. As a result of this experiment, the police from one town found several caches of supplies, and those from another fought off a guerrilla attempt to disrupt the Fourth of

July fiesta. Encouraged by this, in May 1900, Bell requested 200 rifles for a district constabulary; but despite MacArthur's announced intention to support armed native police, he rejected Bell's appeal and it was not until November that an inadequate supply of 200 shotguns arrived. Without the support of his superiors, Bell found it impossible to establish a districtwide native police organization; and throughout 1900, it was left up to individual officers to organize and arm municipal police and employ them as local conditions warranted.[51]

To compensate for the lack of native police, officers turned to recruiting auxiliaries from the population of the garrison towns. Proposals to develop a more formal native military organization of Bicol Scouts were ignored by MacArthur, and it was not until March 1901 that Native Scout units were established. Col. Dorst summed up some of the frustration at these delays when he argued that "an organization of armed natives is essential to help us." He urged that it be organized at once: "There are plenty of men who have compromised themselves for us repeatedly and of whose loyalty there can be no reasonable doubt, and at the same time they have shown they are brave. They are acquainted with the people of the community and know amigos from rebels, and also know a stranger when they see him. They cannot be induced, however, to get far away from the immediate presence of troops because they have no guns. . . . They may not do much fighting but as spies and guides they would be most valuable in getting reliable information for troops and make the country insecure for rebels."[52] In the absence of official support, local commanders gave weapons to *presidentes* or armed their guides while they were on patrols. They also developed their own intelligence networks from former guerrillas and spies and formed volunteer units in their garrison towns. Although offically recognized Native Scout units were not recruited until 1901, there were many Filipinos who served with the U.S. forces as irregulars in 1900.

Much of the cooperation between *presidentes*, priests, and Army officers in the Third District was due to the relatively good conduct of American soldiers. Both Kobbé and Bell were convinced of the importance of conciliating the inhabitants and underscored that the troops behave themselves. Bell issued strict orders against entering houses, violating the rights of peaceable citizens, or appropriating property, and he insisted that all supplies be paid for. During the fighting that accompanied the occupation, many officers tried to avoid inflicting unnecessary casualties, sending interpreters or prisoners to the guerrillas to persuade them to depart. When Maj. Hugh Wise encountered a guerrilla band near Donsol on 14 February, he did not fire and notified his superiors: "You will see from this report and from former reports that I have adhered to the General's policy of trying to conciliate these people, and have refrained from firing upon such organized forces ... in hopes that they were ignorant misguided men who would return to their peaceful occupations when they found us forbearing and found that we would not shoot them on sight."[53]

With the advent of civil government this emphasis on benevolence became even greater. Army officers placed in command of provinces or towns took their responsibilities seriously and tried their best to look after their people. Dorst put this into its strongest form when he declared, "Everything that concerns the welfare of the people is [of] as much interest to me as matters affecting the welfare of a company are to its captain."[54] This is not to assert that the conduct of Americans was perfect: on occasion they looted and made indecent proposals to women, and evidence shows that on one occasion they hung prisoners by their thumbs to make them talk. Such incidents of bad conduct, however, were relatively minor and uncommon. To a degree unusual in a guerrilla war, the U.S. Volunteers in southeastern Luzon remembered that "the enemy was the insurrecto with gun or bolo—not the simple people caught between the lines."[55]

Faced with the problem of convincing the population to return from the mountains, officers sought to show the benefits of American rule through the establishment of schools, markets, and civic projects. Some officers believed that "the school proved the key" and educational reform became a major element of district pacification.[56] Under Bell, the schools "received early and constant attention" and the general personally directed the publication of a Bicol-English grammar book. Due to the district's poor supply system, officers were often short of the books and monies available to other areas, but they showed commendable ingenuity in resolving these problems. Lt. Col. Starr used captured guerrilla taxes to pay for a new schoolhouse, and Maj. William C. Forbush confiscated a revolutionary's vacated house for a schoolroom.[57] Other officers built roads and bridges, established newspapers, and supervised the distribution of food when starvation threatened some districts. Army doctors who treated Filipinos and dispensed scarce medicines helped win over the population; according to Capt. Augustus C. Hart, "our attempts to give them medical assistance have been most gratefully accepted and have created good feelings among them."[58]

The emphasis on civic government and social reform, a policy that in part reflected American weakness, gradually won much of the population back to the town. In some areas, such as the Lagonoy district, the Bicols returned almost immediately, and within a month of the Army occupation civic officials were elected, police forces and schools were established, and the priest was conducting religious services. But the population of Nabua, Camarines, returned only after an Army campaign had destroyed most of the food in the countryside and the *presidente* had threatened to go after them with his own forces.[59] At Donsol the process was much slower and required much more patience. The population fled with the arrival of the Army in February and the 100 families who returned to the town were supported largely through the efforts of Maj. Hugh D. Wise. Lacking any funds of his own, and with his men unpaid since their arrival, Wise put the inhabitants to work rebuilding burned-out houses and paid them in captured rice. It was not until 21 August 1900 that a few native hemp boats arrived and were allowed to sell their goods, and were given rice to take back to the interior. News of this good treatment spread and within a few days the town was once again filled and a heavy trade in hemp resumed. Donsol's officers skillfully exploited the situation by treating the hemp sellers well and sending medicine to those in the mountains, for they realized such benevolence would "shake the confidence of the masses in the men who are the cause of the present suffering."[60]

Members of the Federal party cited the American good behavior when they negotiated surrenders. The *principales*, who provided much of the support for the revolution, realized their social and economic interests could be served under U.S. rule and "played an important role in the acquiescence of Albay to American colonialism."[61] The soldiers' behavior refuted guerrilla claims of American atrocities, and, when this conduct was coupled with the rapid implementation of civil government, the result was undoubtedly to convince many Bicols to return to the towns. The Army was soon in a position to use their good reputation to achieve military ends. As Col. James Lockett smugly observed: "The pompous bearing and vain boasting of the *insurrecto*, when feeling secure, and his aptitude for strategic moves to sylvan retreats on the approach of danger, has not been entirely lost on the observant but dazzled native, who has also had many opportunities for contrasting the humane treatment extended by the Americans with what he receives from his patriotic fellow countrymen."[62]

At the same time they were emphasizing civil government and the conciliation of the native populace, soldiers were also developing military procedures that would break the stalemate in southeastern Luzon. The shortage of available troops, the guerrillas' extensive use of outposts, and Belarmino's defensive strategy militated against large operations. Instead, the Army increasingly relied on small patrols that could move at night or travel off the main trails to surprise outposts and search the isolated *barrios* where the guerrillas lived. A growing fleet of naval gunboats and steam launches allowed the Americans to conduct operations on the extensive waterways and coasts of the Bicol region: soldiers would land near a hostile village and surround it, taking prisoners and destroying guerrilla supplies. Many of these patrols used native guides, often the clients or servants of *presidentes* or *principales* who had accepted American sovereignty. In Albay, "Wray's Scouts," a composite force of twenty men under the leadership of Lt. George M. Wray, "struck fast, hard, often, near and far, and were a menace to every guerrilla band within marching distance."[63] As Americans were rotated out, Wray replaced them with Filipino guides or former guerrillas until the unit was fully integrated.

These new tactics were complemented by an intensification of the campaign that sought to cut the revolutionaries off from the food-producing areas controlled by the Army. Officers were quick to realize that "the food problem troubles the insurrectos more than any other," but Bell's enforced absence from June to October 1900 left a vacuum of leadership at the very time when many regional officers were developing their own policies to curb the hemp and rice trade.[64] The result was that although Third District Headquarters did little beyond passing a decree allowing the destruction or confiscation of all guerrilla storehouses, garrison commanders were adopting far harsher policies. In many towns, food traders were required to be people of known loyalty, to obtain passes, and to have their products weighed both on arrival and departure. In April 1900, Wise, on his own initiative, prohibited a steamer with a cargo of rice from landing at the unoccupied town of Pilar. In the same month, a company of the Forty-fifth raided a clandestine market established on Lake Bato and drove the guerrillas back across the lake. In April the commanders at Legaspi and Tabaco forbade oil, cigarettes, and rice from leaving the towns, forcing the guerrillas to withdraw into the interior for lack of food a month later.[65] In the Iriga valley of the Camarines, a major rice-producing area, Army officers and *presidentes* collaborated on developing the food-restriction policies. *Presidentes* issued orders fixing food prices, prohibiting the sale of rice and salt to anyone outside the town, and closing down all the stores outside the town limits. Although the garrison provided support, most of the restrictions were enforced by the *presidentes* and native police. In Guinobatan and other towns in Albay, post commanders established convoys to escort people to market and prevent the revolutionaries from levying taxes. These successes encouraged other officers to develop regional policies and to expand them in collaborative efforts with officers in different areas.[66]

American officers balanced this new effort to stop the flow of food from their towns with an equal emphasis on destroying guerrilla supplies in the countryside. Although harassed by snipers and ambushes, U.S. patrols, often with native help, continued to seek out hidden fields and storehouses. When it could concentrate enough manpower, the Army sent large crop-destruction expeditions into known enemy areas. Although some commanders tried to bring confiscated rice back for the civilian population, most food could not be transported and was destroyed where it was found. At least one veteran, who believed that the Bicol population and the soldiers had previously enjoyed friendly relations, felt that the Army's increasing burning of fields and farms led many Filipinos to dislike the Americans.[67] Occasionally the soldiers found entire valleys devoted to cultivation, but even if they discovered little, these crop-destruction raids inflicted a steady drain on the guerrillas' supplies and forced them to devote much of their energy to searching for food. Sandahatan units, for example, had to be disbanded and ordered to plant crops, doing no military service beyond weekly guard duty. The new pressure on their already scanty food supply circumscribed the breadth and duration of their movements and forced them to leave *americanista* towns alone and move constantly to new areas.[68] The increasing guerrilla demands on the populace for food alienated popular support and provoked many people to return to the garrisoned towns. One high-ranking guerrilla officer captured in December testified that his rations had consisted of two pints of rice a day, and he commented that the Americans fed their prisoners better than the guerrillas fed their troops.[69]

The regional food-restriction campaigns were aided, ironically, by the rinderpest epidemic which struck the local livestock in mid-1900. The disease not only killed off the scanty fresh meat supply for soldiers and Filipinos, it prevented plowing during the summer planting season because of the deaths of draft animals. Moreover, the stricken animals tended to die in rivers and streams, polluting the water supply. In the Camarines, upon which much of the Bicol region depended for grain, Bell estimated that only 10 percent of the normal rice crop was planted in 1900. At Iriga, it was believed that 90 percent of the cattle died during the summer, and at San José de Lagonoy, an officer noted in July, "cattle are dying all over the country and it looks as if we will have not only insurgents to contend with but famine and pestilence in addition."[70] In an effort to preserve livestock, Belarmino issued a proclamation forbidding the killing of animals except to feed his troops. Army garrison officers made arrangements for importing rice from merchant companies and the Americans eventually sent a total of 10,000 *piculs* of rice, or some 1,300,000 pounds, to the Lagonoy district alone.[71]

In the winter of 1900–1901, reinforcements allowed the Army to undertake larger operations and for the first time seriously challenge the guerrillas deep in the mountains. In November an expedition attacked Belarmino's headquarters near Jovellar, Albay. Although the expedition encountered few guerrillas, it destroyed food supplies and scattered the guerrillas so badly that Lt. Col. Starr boasted, "There are not more than 100 insurrectos left in this Province and the fight has been whipped out of them."[72] The Americans also launched a major effort in Sorsogon province, where small patrols were landed by steam launches at towns on the water while other troops swept the mountains.

For the most part, these patrols inflicted few casualties and received none themselves, but they destroyed food caches and crops and penetrated previously unpatrolled areas. In one of the major successes, a small force virtually cleared the adjacent island of Catanduanes when it surrounded the town of Baras and captured eleven rifles and twenty-seven prisoners, including "Rogue" Bustos, the revolutionary governor. In February, detachments from Sorsogon were transported on the U.S.S. *Don Juan de Austria* in an amphibious raid on the island of Burias, where they arrested the entire guerrilla supply organization.[73] Similar operations in the Camarines destroyed Aréjola's headquarters and most of his food supplies. The guerrillas were "constantly chased and harassed" and complained that they could sleep no more than one night in any place because of the pressure from Army patrols.[74]

The Americans were aided in these operations by the allies they had gained during the period of military stalemate. Priests played an important role in quelling resistance. In Bulan, for example, Father Casiano Vera delivered a speech urging his parishioners to assist the Americans. The next day, a Federal party chapter was formed and many people signed the Oath of Allegiance.[75] In Oas, the town priest held a mass attended by both the *presidente* and U.S. officers, urging the populace to assist the Army. The parish priest of Minalabac played a key role in the negotiations between American officers and Lt. Col. Aréjola.[76] The Americans were also aided by *presidentes* such as Esteban Delgado of Ligao, who issued a proclamation warning those people still in the hills that if they did not return to the towns within eight days, the U.S. soldiers would burn their houses in the countryside and shoot them like animals; the result, according to a guerrilla leader, was that many people fled to the towns.[77] Bartolomé Roa, *presidente* of Oas, issued a similar proclamation and, with a troop of sixty armed volunteers, burned guerrilla crops.[78] *Presidentes* also recruited townsmen as auxiliaries for the Army: in some towns, post commanders armed policemen and used them to defend the *barrios*; other Filipino auxiliaries accompanied Army forces on expeditions into the hills.[79]

The campaign in Sorsogon province is a good example of the Army's ability to combine military operations, benevolence, and cooperation from influential Filipinos to achieve a successful regional pacification. In the winter of 1900–1901, the Americans launched extensive military operations against the small ports that furnished the guerrillas with food and the guerrillas' sanctuaries in the hills. As a result, by late January 1901 Lt. Col. Emetirio Funes, the revolutionary commander in the province, found his forces reduced to slightly over 100 men, 23 rifles, and 673 cartridges. That month, on the prompting of the priest of Bulan, a delegation of the Federal party began to deliver speeches urging a stop to the fighting. These speeches were well received in Irocin, a town near Funes's hideout, and the *federalistas* soon established direct contact with Funes's partisans. Promised a complete pardon and given full military honors by the Army commander, Funes marched his troops in on 21 February, and within a few days was out in the field "actively engaged in the work of pacification."[80] Officers in Sorsogon then turned their attention to Maj. Esteban Fulay, Funes's chief subordinate, who was given a one-week armistice and the incentive of the release of 55 prisoners upon completion of surrender terms. Fulay surrendered at Gubat on 2 March with 49 officers and 240 men, but only 2 rifles, and was given a huge fiesta. Through a clever application of military force, face-saving ceremonies, and Filipino support, the Army had virtually ended provincial resistance in Sorsogon by mid-March. According to Howe, the "most cordial relations" existed between Army officers and former revolutionaries who declared they were tired of fighting and determined not to have any more trouble.[81]

Other Army campaigns pursuing similar policies yielded similar successful results. In the Camarines, Aréjola was pressured by expeditions that penetrated areas where he had previously been secure and destroyed his food supply. Although his forces numbered some 800 men, they had only 43 rifles and had little recourse but to flee. After establishing contact through the aid of a parish priest, Lt. George Curry and Lt. George Van Horn Mosely had a personal meeting with Aréjola and persuaded him to surrender on 23 March 1901. He then cooperated in securing the surrender of most of the other guerrilla units in the Camarines.[82]

In view of the success of a pacification policy combining active military operations with leniency and negotiations, it is painful to describe the Army's final campaign against Belarmino. Constantly harassed by the Americans in Albay, Belarmino's forces crossed into Sorsogon and launched an abortive attack on the small garrison of Donsol on 25 May, which was beaten off with no American casualties. The American response was characterized by unusual harshness—perhaps out of a general exasperation with Belarmino's refusal to surrender and perhaps because U.S. Army regulars had replaced the volunteers of the Forty-fifth and Forty-seventh Infantries. In any case, the ensuing operations not only demonstrated the Army's ability to retaliate but exposed the guerrillas' inability to protect their civilian followers. Sending columns out to scour the countryside and destroy all supplies, the soldiers struck at both Belarmino's forces and Filipino civilians. Within three weeks, they had destroyed 19 towns, 800 outposts and storehouses, and large quantities of rice and hemp; they killed 150 guerrillas, captured 100, and forced 900 more to surrender.[83] Meanwhile, other units moved on Belarmino's last refuges in the Jovellar area of Albay. Isolated and steadily pursued by Americans and Native Scouts, Belarmino's partisans, some 300 riflemen with almost no ammunition, began to collapse and many surrendered to the Americans. Belarmino finally called a halt to the fighting and capitulated on 4 July.[84]

Belarmino's surrender did not end all guerrilla resistance in southeastern Luzon, and for the rest of 1901, the Army was engaged in mopping-up operations. In northern Camarines, Maj. Lorenzo W. Cooke and a battalion of the Twenty-sixth U.S. Infantry fought three recalcitrant guerrilla bands until the fall of that year. In the southern part of the province, the Army had to conduct a campaign against Maj. Elias Angeles, who had disregarded Aréjola's instructions to surrender, which lasted until September. In this expedition the Army was assisted by the *presidente* of Magarao, who volunteered fifty municipal police to hunt down the guerrillas. No sooner were these last campaigns over than Army units were sent into Sorsogon to deal with another outbreak of violence. A former revolutionary known only as Caloche had broken his parole and convinced his followers that through magical talismans, or *anting-anting*, they would be invulnerable to American bullets. For the next two years, self-proclaimed revolutionary and religious leaders maintained a sputtering guerrilla warfare which was not suppressed by the Philippine Constabulary until 1903. These movements, lacking a strong tie with either the Philippine Republic or the resistance under Malvar, may be better categorized as agrarian unrest than part of the Philippine War. They were reflections of the turmoil and displacement within Philippine rural society after three years of constant warfare.[85]

The pacification campaign waged by the U.S. Army in the Third District was an impressive combination of flexibility, benevolence, and pragmatic counterinsurgency methods. Denied adequate manpower or resources and dealing with an opponent who avoided a military decision, district officers were faced with a stalemate throughout the first half of 1900. Turning to nonmilitary pacification methods and implementing flexible but effective civil governments, cultivating *presidentes* and priests, establishing social reforms, and emphasizing good conduct, the Army was able to demonstrate to the Bicols that American rule "was tolerable and even potentially beneficient."[86] As a result, many influential Filipinos abandoned the revolutionaries and cooperated with the Americans. Coupled with these humanitarian pacification policies were new tactics and counterinsurgency policies designed to deprive the guerrillas of food and supplies. The tactics developed in southeastern Luzon stressed the use of small patrols which moved through the *barrios* and kept the guerrillas constantly on the move. Local commanders also established food restrictions and turned to crop destruction to starve the guerrillas out of the mountains. They were thus able to demonstrate the dire consequences for people who did not accept colonial authority while holding out the benefits of American rule.

The pacification of southeastern Luzon is an excellent instance of Army regional counterinsurgency in the Philippine War. The Army officers and troops who served there had to overcome formidable obstacles. They had to deal with the frustration of facing an enemy who refused to stand and fight and with superiors who sent them inadequate manpower and supplies. The climate, terrain, and diseases all contributed to sap the effectiveness of the soldiers and to diminish the already small forces. Despite this, officers in the Third District were able to establish pacified enclaves, win over much of the populace, and weaken the resistance substantially. With few exceptions, relations between soldiers and Filipinos were characterized by friendliness and humanitarianism. The pacification of the Bicol region offers an exemplary chapter in the annals of counterinsurgency in the Philippine War.

5

War in the Tagalog Heartland
The Second District, Department of Southern Luzon

On 26 August 1901, Brig. Gen. James F. Wade outlined in considerable detail the reasons behind the protracted guerrilla warfare in his department:

> The forces of the insurrection are not kept in the field, except a few men who accompany the higher officers. The majority of them live at home, even in and about the towns we occupy. When wanted, they are warned through their system of signals and runners and gather at night at some designated place. The number is limited only by the number required or by the number of rifles within reach. The common soldier wears the dress of the country; with his gun he is a soldier; by hiding it and walking quietly along the road, sitting down by the nearest house, or going to work in the nearest field, he becomes an "amigo," full of good will and false information for any of our men who may meet him.[1]

Wade's explanation for the continued turmoil in the Second District, Department of Southern Luzon, was written months after the effective end of the war in the rest of Luzon. From the mountains of Ilocos Norte to the abaca groves of Albay, the main guerrilla forces had surrendered. Throughout the archipelago, new civil governments were assuming control and police were replacing the Army as the bulwarks of American colonial authority; but in this region, only a few hours' travel from Army headquarters in Manila, resistance continued unabated. Well led, popularly supported, and sustained by a highly developed infrastructure, the guerrillas in the Second District appeared able to make good their promise to fight on for another ten years. The war in southwestern Luzon was to be the greatest challenge to Army regional pacification on the entire island. In the end it would be defeated only by one of the most thorough and controversial pacification campaigns of the Philippine War.

The Second District comprised the three provinces of Batangas, Laguna, and Tayabas, an area of some 4,200 square miles with a 1903 census population of almost 560,000 people. Batangas and Laguna, with their sister province of Cavite, were in Wade's words, "the most thickly settled and the richest in southern Luzon, the home of the Tagalo[g]s and the birthplace of the insurrection.[2] The southern province, Batangas, with an area of 1,108 square miles, was the most populous, with roughly 311,000 inhabitants. The northern province of Laguna, with an area of 750 square miles, had a population of about 170,000. Tayabas, stretching east along a narrow peninsula to Ambos Camarines, had a total area of 2,334 square miles but a population of only 109,780. Cottage industries flourished and the region produced an abundance of rice, sugar, coconuts, and fish. But as the Americans were to learn to their cost, the terrain was ill-suited for military operations, ranging from wet rice paddies, foothills, lakes, seacoast, and jungle, to volcanic mountains. Moreover, the area was extremely unhealthful; the summer monsoons made malaria and dysentery so prevalent that some American garrisons would be reduced to less than half their strength. The combination of high population density, difficult terrain, and disease resulted in some of the most difficult campaigning in the Philippines.[3]

During the late nineteenth century, southwestern Luzon was swept by nationalist and anti-Spanish activity. The region's landholding elite sought political reforms that would protect their local economic and social status from encroachment by the Spanish and the religious orders. The educated elite dominating local politics was influenced by European nationalism and Philippine reformist thought and began demanding a more active role in colonial government. The peasants also were disenchanted with Spanish rule, and sought solace in millenarian movements which mingled radical social reform with dreams of a Christian utopia. With this heritage of discontent and reformist thought, it is not surprising that many of the region's inhabitants were receptive to the message of Andres Bonifacio and Emilio Aguinaldo. When the Katipuneros revolted in 1896, many of the area's inhabitants joined in, plaguing the Spanish with virulent guerrilla war in Batangas and Laguna. The peace settlement at Biac na bato provided only a

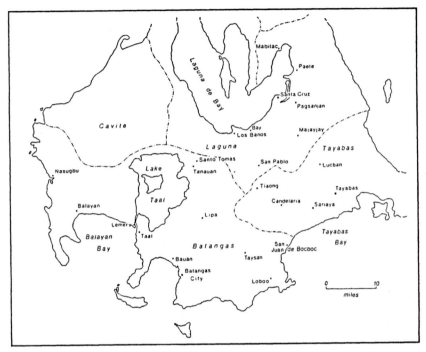

Second District, Department of Southern Luzon

temporary lull, and when Aguinaldo returned the local forces quickly routed
the Spanish and established Filipino governments pledged to support the
new Philippine Republic. Thereafter, the region provided recruits and leaders for the Republican armies which surrounded first the Spanish and then
the Americans in Manila.[4]

Despite the region's proximity to the capital city, it was relatively untouched by the outbreak of hostilities between Filipinos and Americans in
February 1899. The Americans concentrated their efforts north of Manila,
neglecting incipient Philippine revolutionary forces and governments to the
south. Such Army operations as were conducted were designed chiefly to
drive the revolutionaries back and prevent any threat to Manila from the
south. These sporadic sweeps quickly bogged down, perhaps leading both
revolutionaries and the general population to doubt the American ability to
sustain prolonged operations.[5] Thus for almost a year the provincial revolutionary leaders were able to centralize their authority, to discipline the military forces, and to insure the compliance of the population. They established
military forces in each town, collected arms, and settled relations between

local civil and military leaders. The result was that Batangas and Laguna, and to a lesser extent Tayabas, were far better organized and prepared for a sustained guerrilla war than were the other areas of Luzon.

Not until January 1900 did an Army division, under the command of Maj. Gen. John C. Bates, invade southwestern Luzon. Bates followed an ambitious plan, dividing his forces into two brigades, one of which, under Brig. Gen. Loyd Wheaton, was to hold the Republican forces in Cavite, while the second, under Brig. Gen. Theodore Schwan, would swing along the west coast of Laguna de Bay and establish a defensive line. With the trap set, Wheaton's forces would move forward, driving the revolutionaries into Schwan's waiting outposts. The troops carried through their assigned maneuvers, but the Filipinos contented themselves with a few abortive battles and then melted away. Bates's soldiers captured few prisoners and, somewhat to the surprise of the Americans, the march quickly became "for the most part, a vigorously conducted triumphal procession for the posting of garrisons."[6] Cavite, Batangas, Laguna, and most of western Tayabas were occupied by early February, but it soon became apparent that occupation and pacification were very different problems.

For the first months of occupation in 1900 the Army maintained the organization used in the January invasion; officers reported to a confusing variety of expeditionary brigades. On 10 April, Divisional Headquarters in Manila made the provinces of Batangas, Laguna, and Tayabas part of the Department of Southern Luzon and designated them as the Second District. For a few weeks the district was under Wheaton, but he soon left to take command of the Department of Northern Luzon, and Col. William E. Birkhimer temporarily succeeded him. Brig. Gen. Robert H. Hall replaced Birkhimer on 28 June 1900, and headed the district until 10 April 1901, when the three provinces were combined with Cavite province and renamed the First District.

The departmental commander, Maj. Gen. John C. Bates, was almost sixty and had served in the Civil War, several Indian campaigns, and the Cuban occupation. An able diplomat, he had negotiated a treaty with Moro leaders which kept them quiet for much of the Philippine War. Despite this varied civil and military experience, Bates proved a mediocre commander who was criticized by Taft for his excessive pessimism, his suspicion of Filipino civilians, and his failure to appreciate the effect of revolutionary terrorism. Bates developed neither a strategy nor counterinsurgency policies and failed to encourage his subordinates who did. He opposed such innovative measures as arming local police forces, raising Native Scouts, or giving cash bounties to loyal Filipinos.[7]

Bates's lack of direction was not initially apparent because from May until June the Second District was in the capable, if authoritarian, hands of Birkhimer. An expert at military government who had already received a Medal of Honor for his exploits in the Philippines, he was disliked by his fellow officers as "cold blooded and selfish" and "a damned old nasal-toned fool."[8] He realized that pacification would be a long and complex process in which the Army had to pursue political as well as military goals. In March he had argued: "We must take care of the good and law abiding people who are now coming back and quieting down on their little farms all about, else we will lose that confidence in us that sound policy requires we should inspire and pursue."[9] The Americans should pursue the practical policy of "killing armed insurrectos and ladrones and showing all people by our armed presence everywhere, that we are masters of the country and intend to remain so."[10] Nevertheless, abuses of civilians would not be countenanced because they were "inimical to the good interests of the United States in its efforts to establish friendly relations."[11]

Hall, who replaced Birkhimer in June, lacked his predecessor's intelligence and drive, and offered no compensating virtues. Although he graduated from the U.S. Military Academy before the Civil War, by the Spanish-American War Hall had risen no further than colonel of an infantry regiment. His existing correspondence gives no indication of any strategic plans and his annual report is a simple chronology with appended reports. He failed to support his subordinates' policies and to investigate their claims, leaving Col. Cornelius Gardener to carve out a virtually independent subdistrict in Tayabas. Hall may have been physically incapable of active command: in 1901 he was replaced for medical reasons and retired shortly afterward. There can be little question that Hall's apathetic leadership of the district, when coupled with Bates's conservatism at the departmental level, greatly magnified the already large obstacles to Army pacification.[12]

Under Bates and Hall were some 5,000 troops, making the Second District, although still undermanned, among the strongest in Luzon. Five U.S. Volunteer regiments were stationed there: the Twenty-eighth commanded by Birkhimer in southeast Batangas; the Thirtieth under Gardener in Tayabas; the Thirty-seventh under Col. Benjamin F. Cheatham in northwest Laguna and Tayabas; the Thirty-eighth under Col. George S. Anderson in southwest Batangas; and the Thirty-ninth under Col. Robert L. Bullard in north-central Batangas and eastern Laguna. With the exception of Cheatham, all the regimental commanders were professional officers, U.S. Military Academy graduates, and all had extensive service in the prewar Army, Cuba, or the Philippines. The company officers and soldiers contained many veterans of the National Guard and Spanish-American War, rigorously selected to insure they were physically and mentally prepared for the tropics.[13]

Initially, they faced little resistance; there was some desultory skirmishing, caused primarily by patrols clashing with partisan bands or intruding into revolutionary strongholds. In February, after returning from a ten-day hike in which the only enemies he encountered threw down their guns and surrendered, Capt. John L. Jordan wrote that the war was virtually over except for some mopping up. While soldiers searched the mountains and paddies, the revolutionaries had apparently yielded: although there were eleven engagements in February 1900, there were only five in March and one in April. The inhabitants of the towns, who had fled at the approach of the Americans, returned to their homes, and the Army, lulled by this inactivity, turned its attention to establishing the municipal governments, sanitation projects, schools, police forces, and other civil government services.[14]

The brief attempt to implement municipal governments in the spring of 1900 revealed a number of problems. Officers found that towns were destitute and unable to pay civic salaries or impose taxes. Birkhimer believed that the civic organization outlined in G.O. 40 and G.O. 43 was unnecessarily complicated and its conditions impossible to fulfill: under a strict interpretation of the orders there were very few Filipinos whose property holdings qualified them as electors. One Laguna town had 23 men qualified to vote out of nearly 5,000 inhabitants; another had only 3. A further problem was the refusal of the *principales* to participate. As Gardener pointed out, "whenever we rebuild civil government in towns and cities we must necessarily use the very element we have kicked out, that is, prominent Filipinos to fill local offices."[15] However, officers soon found that the "leading people . . . declined to take any part in [the] organization of a civil government."[16] Without the support of the elite, the Americans could seldom find qualified people to govern the towns. Frustrated and impatient, and increasingly aware of the revival of armed resistance, garrison officers procrastinated, circumvented their instructions, or appointed town officials without elections. Lt. Arthur W. Orton recalled organizing one municipality in which he simply "rounded up all the natives and required that they elect a Mayor and Vice-Presidente and City Council. Then [he] went back to Los Baños and let them run their own town."[17]

The strongest advocate of civil government was Gardener, commander of the Thirtieth U.S.V. Infantry and de facto governor in Tayabas province. Gardener was sympathetic to the Filipinos, and in a private letter to the antiimperialist Hazen S. Pingree, he criticized the American soldiers for their racism and recommended that the Philippines be given independence. His empathy for the Filipinos may have contributed to his alienation from his fellow officers, but a more probable cause was that during the invasion he had accused soldiers in other units of looting while turning a blind eye on the transgressions of his own men. When he entered Tayabas, Gardener pledged to establish civil government, and he made great efforts to fulfill his promise; early in his tenure he began meeting after church with leading citizens and town officials to discuss civic matters. In order to cultivate the *principales*, he directed that "considerable latitude be exercised and men of family, influence and education be enrolled even if they do not pay quite the amount in taxes."[18] Thereafter, he filed glowing reports about the development of government in Tayabas which culminated in his 8 February 1901 declaration that "the Province is ripe for, and should have, civil government . . . as soon as practicable."[19] He received his wish; Tayabas was placed under civil government a month later and Gardener made its first governor.

Despite Gardener's enthusiasm, the experiences of his officers indicate that even when both provincial commander and post commander were committed to civil government they faced almost insurmountable difficulties. The case of the town of Lucban, Tayabas, commanded by Maj. Matthew F. Steele, is illustrative. Steele was initially quite optimistic about the possibility of civil government, but his ability to converse with the *principalía* in Spanish soon made him aware of their fears. In April, when Gardener ordered his officers to conduct elections in their towns, Steele wrote to his wife that he did "not expect a single person to vote" because "the edge of a bolo and the hand of an assassin are the price they would pay for taking that oath and holding office under American rule."[20] When successive attempts at forming a government failed, an exasperated Gardener suggested that Steele follow his example and lock all the local *principalía* in a room, refusing to let them out until they had formed a government. Steele attempted this, but the *principales*, perhaps forewarned, first elected the leading revolutionary in the local jail and then their three greatest enemies. After this fiasco, Steele's further efforts were largely invalidated in late August when one of the leading *principalía* was kidnapped, an event which Steele admitted had the "desired effect" of making everyone in the town afraid to come near the Americans.[21] Despite Steele's problems, in September Gardener reported that most of Tayabas's towns, including Lucban, were ready for civil government and that Lucban was ready for reorganization under G.O. 40. Yet when Steele attempted to organize the town under this plan and appointed electors, they responded by fleeing to another town. Shortly afterward, Steele compelled one person to become the *presidente*, but the man went to Manila and appealed to Bates, who informed Steele: "It is not the desire of the Department Commander that friendly natives should be placed in jeopardy by assuming office when we cannot assure their immunity from those who are still antagonistic; such offices should be assumed voluntarily."[22] On 20 December, Steele responded to Gardener's prodding with a blunt explanation of the key problem in forming civil government: "I have tried every argument to persuade various citizens to accept the office of *Alcalde* [mayor] but without success. They are all afraid of the ducut [assassination]. Every principal man in Lucban has some property in the sementera [area outside of town] and they all claim they would not be able to visit these sementeras if they accepted the office. And they claim also that the insurgents would take away and destroy all their rice and other things in the sementera. They all say but for this they would gladly accept the office and they hope the conditions will soon be such that they can accept this office without risk of their lives and property. I believe thay are honest in their protestations and that they are well disposed toward us."[23]

Contributing to the problems of civil government was the Army's failure to develop an organized armed native policy which might have protected the towns. Much of this failure was self-inflicted: throughout 1900, Bates was hostile to any plan to distribute firearms to the police and obstructed the formation of municipal police forces throughout the Department of Southern Luzon. Hall also opposed any such force, believing that the Tagalogs would be disloyal. Soldiers serving in the district echoed these misgivings; throughout the war there were several who opposed any arming of native police in southwestern Luzon.[24] Moreover, among those officers who supported police there was no consensus about organization: within the Thirty-ninth Infantry, for example, the colonel wanted municipal police forces, one of his battalion commanders opposed any police, and another favored a large provincial constabulary. Birkhimer supported a paramilitary Guardia Civil and urged officers to begin training small groups in preparation for the withdrawal of the U.S. Volunteer units. There was also a great deal of debate over police armament and many officers echoed the sentiments of the departmental commander that "they should not be armed with weapons which could be used against us in case they prove treacherous."[25]

In Tayabas, Gardener pushed through the organization of police with the same fervor he had shown for civil government. Much of his enthusiasm was due to his belief that disturbances in Tayabas were caused by *ladrones* and that there were no guerrillas in the province. He argued that the towns were pro-American but needed protection which the American soldiers, due to their many other duties, were incapable of giving. In June 1900, he ordered police forces formed in the town of Tayabas and armed them with rifles issued by the Thirtieth Infantry. He also urged his superiors to authorize a special police force that would be paid by the U.S. Army and would operate throughout the province. In addition, he pressured his subordinates, including the harried Steele, to form volunteer police forces to patrol against incendiaries and bandits. Although Gardener did not succeed in winning approval for a provincial constabulary or even making all his subordinates create municipal police, his efforts were impressive and gave Tayabas a far better police force than elsewhere.[26]

With the exception of Tayabas, few towns gained native police forces in the Second District in 1900. A districtwide report in December revealed that most had very small, underpaid police forces armed only with bolos and clubs; another report on Laguna province indicated that many had no police force at all.[27] In response to the departure of the volunteer regiments and MacArthur's orders of 29 December 1900, to the effect that the formation of an armed police be regarded as "emergency work," there was some renewal of effort. But this was hindered by the discovery that the Ordnance Department had no pistols or shotguns for distribution.[28] Hall's investigations revealed that in February 1901, despite MacArthur's orders, there was "a lack of uniformity of organization and pay in the existing force, as well as opinions of the commanders in the matter of the pay and armament of the proposed organizations."[29] Opposed by the district's high command and lacking any unity, the creation of native police fell on the shoulders of dedicated garrison commanders. Until the wholesale reorganization of the provinces themselves in mid-1901 in preparation for civil government, the police remained a negligible factor in Army pacification.

Second District officers had better luck in their efforts to implement social reforms. A departmental circular requesting opinions on education elicited agreement on the necessity of education but little consensus on the type of schools to organize, the curriculum, or the role of the American government. Most officers supported Lt. Col. Charles J. Crane's view that "the natives are very desirous to have good schools and . . . [our] assistance in that particular will aid very materially to lessen opposition to our authority."[30] Gardener held that "it is education which lifts up a people," and urged the residents of Tayabas to send their children to the United States for schooling.[31] Owing to the efforts of committed Army officers, schools were established in many towns, and children of all social classes were taught by native teachers or soldiers. The lack of class distinction, coupled with a refusal to tolerate religious instruction, provoked some opposition from the *principales* and clergy, but officers still believed that the schools were much appreciated.[32]

Although they were carried out with commendable enthusiasm and occasional local success throughout 1900, Army experiments in the Second District with such nonmilitary pacification policies as civil government, police, and social reform were generally unsuccessful. In some respects this was because many of what the Americans considered reforms were either done for the Army's benefit or were carried out with scant regard for local sensibilities. Many Filipinos found the new municipal governments and police forces a poor substitute for the more autonomous ones they had enjoyed under the Philippine Republic. Some reforms, such as restricting cockfighting, gambling, and prostitution were imposed as much to preserve the morale of the soldiers as the morals of the Filipinos.[33] Commanding officers who reestablished the Spanish corvée and drafted civilian labor to build and maintain roads or clean up towns were justly resented by the people who were conscripted.[34] This is not to say that all reformers had selfish motives: Army doctors treated sick Filipinos and established clinics and Gardener sent his regimental doctor to all the *barrios* in his area without charge, claiming, "I am convinced that just mere pills will be more effective than bullets in undermining the insurgent leaders' authority."[35] Yet although he remained convinced as late as December 1901 that "true loyalty and contentment could only come under a benign civil government," his optimism was ill-founded. Medicines, roads, and education may have been popular with the Filipinos, but they were insufficient to draw popular support away from the revolutionaries. Increasingly, the majority of soldiers in the district grew disenchanted with policies based only on benevolence and agreed with Capt. Jordan: "This business of fighting and civilizing and educating at the same time doesn't mix very well. Peace is needed first."[36]

Army efforts at civil government were further hampered by soaring sick lists. As the summer rainy season began in late May, Bullard's belief that southwestern Luzon was "an awful region of known contagious and tropical diseases" was borne out.[37] The hardest hit units were the Thirty-seventh, which had a sick report of 25 percent, and the Thirtieth and Thirty-ninth, with about 30 percent reported sick for much of the summer. Despite Gardener's efforts to retain them, by fall over 200 soldiers of the Thirtieth had been evacuated to Manila and either placed in hospitals or sent back to the United States for early discharge.[38] Worse, some garrisons suffered disproportionately. The company stationed at Paete, Laguna, had only 30 men fit for duty out of a strength of 101 and the company at Tiaong, Tayabas, had less than 10 men capable of active duty, and many of the sick were pressed into service.[39] Malaria, dhobie itch, tropical ulcers, dysentery, and other diseases sapped the vitality of the soldiers and soon reduced entire garrisons to emaciated, feverish invalids. Medical care was often inadequate, and in more isolated areas consisted of little more than erratic doses of quinine. Because of the poor supply system, many of the sick failed to receive the special diets and supplies that were necessary for recovery; they stayed sick, and healthy men then broke down because of increased duty and lack of rest.[40]

The fragility of the Army's accomplishments in social reform and civil government was demonstrated in the summer of 1900, when the desultory attacks of the previous few months accelerated sharply. Instead of occasional sniping, guerrillas began to fire into towns, ambush supply wagons, and openly assassinate collaborators in an effort to destroy Army civil government as well as influence the presidential elections in the United States. Second District forces had fifty-four engagements between June and August with twelve soldiers killed and twenty-eight wounded, in sharp contrast to only eleven engagements between March and May with one soldier killed and two wounded.[41] In early June, Cheatham commented that there was "undoubtedly renewed activity among the insurgents, taxes are being collected and soldiers impressed, the towns that are not occupied by the Americans and were full of men a month ago are now practically deserted except for the women and children."[42] Crane noted this new guerrilla activity and its advantages for the Army when he commented that in Batangas, "the impression of Filipinos here is that the order is now to fight and that we may look for more activity from the insurgents. This will be [best] for us: the situation during the past two months was not natural."[43] Others were worried about the guerrilla activity; Bullard wrote in his diary: "Hostilities almost resumed, so active have insurgents become," and Birkhimer summed up the situation: "we control within the line of our bayonets, but no further."[44]

The revolutionary resurgence in the Second District owed its strength to a well-balanced and flexible system sustained by the superiority of the revolutionary leadership, a capable military force, good tactics, the support of the native elite, and the suppression of local collaboration with the Americans. Maj. Gen. Miguel Malvar and Brig. Gen. Juan Cailles, *Jefes Superiores Politico-Militares* of Batangas and Laguna provinces, respectively, were capable, intelligent, and ruthless commanders. Malvar, a native Batangueño, was a prosperous landowner and member of the *principalía*. Charismatic, a dedicated patriot, and an able organizer, he was probably the most capable adversary the Americans faced in the Philippine War. Born in 1865, a brigadier general at thirty, in 1896 he raised a guerrilla band for Aguinaldo from his native town of Santo Tomas. He soon made a reputation not only as a military leader but as an intransigent hard-liner who opposed anything short of complete independence.[45] Cailles, the son of an Anglo-Indian mother and a French father, was a former Cavite schoolteacher. Fiery and impetuous, he shocked U.S. Army officers at Manila by denouncing American ambitions and declaring, "War, war, is what we want." Promoted to brigadier general in 1899, at the age of thirty-three, he served as governor of Laguna where, like Malvar, he exercised his duties as provincial chief with an iron hand, controlling his civil and military officials with exhortation and force.[46]

Both Malvar and Cailles understood the principles of guerrilla warfare and developed similar strategies in their respective provinces. Neither sought a battlefield decision against the invaders; from the beginning, their policy was to deny the Americans control of both the populace and the countryside. They concentrated upon establishing and maintaining a clandestine support system in the occupied towns and the *barrios*, and upon rigorously enforcing orders against participation in American civil government through appeals to patriotism or, when necessary, kidnapping, property destruction, and assassination. Both men avoided combat unless clearly advantageous militarily or politically, such as the attacks they staged to influence the U.S. elections, and to demonstrate "that in the Philippines they were protesting with rifles."[47]

Under Malvar and Cailles was an officer corps also distinguished by its long service and military ability. Nearly all were natives of Batangas, Laguna, or Tayabas, and they were often connected to the revolutionary leadership by strong familial, business, or personal ties. In Batangas, for example, the officer corps was "in a real sense Malvar's corps, since many of its members were his relatives or intimate friends."[48] Despite Malvar's insistence that the guerrilla leaders were "modest landholders," the bulk of evidence suggests that they came from the more substantial propertied interests in their provinces.[49] Many field officers, including Malvar, had been town or provincial officials under the Spanish or Republican regimes. Their prewar political and economic status allowed them to recruit soldiers from among their fellow townsmen or the tenants of their estates. In some cases political and military authority were so indivisible that the civic officials also led the resistance. In Batangas, the *presidente* of one town took to the hills with his troops, and another town had a guerrilla band whose "government and administration [were] under the control of the local presidente who organized it."[50] Resistance in the Second District thus was led by the most powerful segments of the community.

These officers drawn from the *principalía* commanded partisans and militia recruited, supported, and quartered in their native towns and *barrios*. Some of the partisan units retained their connections to the preinvasion Philippine Republic conventional forces: according to a commander in Tayabas, in early 1900 they were broken up and stationed in towns "with express orders to go out and fight throughout their jurisdiction."[51] After the invasion the revolutionary leadership ordered villages to form new guerrilla units. Malvar's 27 October 1900 proclamation, entitled "Guerrilla Warfare. Instructions," gave detailed directions for the creation and maintenance of these forces. He directed each town to raise a column from the local population and turn over all firearms for its use. These forces would be proportionately stationed in company strength in the main town and surrounding *barrios* so they could obtain recruits, supplies or rice, and money and yet "not be burdensome, and the campaign [can] continue as long as the ambitious Americans wish." Malvar insisted that civil officials exercise a great deal of control over the operations of their town's column; not only was civil government to be established "to its normal condition" but officers were instructed to "have the chiefs of columns always act in concert with the civil authorities of the towns." He also ordered officers to prevent pursuit by constructing secret crossings and movable bridges over rivers, ravines, and mountains and to fight from ambush, taking advantage of difficult terrain.[52]

The *principales* who dominated the officer corps commanded companies whose ranks were filled with laborers and townspeople of little wealth or education. Although some units were organized with ambitious tables of organization featuring battalion and regimental designations, the typical partisan unit seldom had more than fifty or sixty permanent guerrillas with perhaps twenty rifles. These forces lived in camps or outlying *barrios* and were supplied by taxes and contributions levied on the town. They were composed of young bachelors and held together by a few veterans tied to their officers by long service, deference, and patron-client bonds. When more manpower was needed, recruits were called together from other companies, drafted from nearby villages, or collected by press gangs among those individuals too poor or powerless to avoid conscription. The case of Gregorio Tixon, described by his *barrio* chief as "unmarried . . . a servant . . . [and an] orphan . . . willing to en-list [*sic*] since he has no money to pay for a substitute" is probably typical.[53] One veteran who served for almost five years explained: "We were fighting because our officers told us to fight. We obeyed our leaders. There was no alternative. If we did not obey, we would be punished."[54]

Although better equipped than most in Luzon, the revolutionary command was hampered by an inadequate supply of arms and ammunition. Both Cailles and Malvar were advocates of firepower over numbers; Malvar restricted the number of bolo-men to 30 percent of company strength, and claimed in 1901 that he had 7,000 firearms. Certainly they enjoined their men to protect their firearms and enforced stiff penalties on anyone who surrendered them. Most guerrillas only used their weapons when on operations; otherwise the rifles were ingeniously hidden in hollowed out bamboo, fields, trees, streams, caves, and even graveyards. Not surprisingly, such exposure to the elements transformed many of the weapons into "an interesting lot of junk" and made them useless.[55] Ammunition was in critical demand; Cailles reported he had many rifles but only twenty rounds per man. Cartridges were manufactured from tin strips and filled with crude gunpowder mixed from matchheads and local sulphur. In the words of one cavalryman, guerrilla firearms and ammunition were "crude affairs but could be very dangerous at close quarters."[56] However few their numbers, these weapons were more than sufficient to enforce guerrilla authority in the towns and *barrios* and to maintain resistance indefinitely. As one officer noted, "as long as we are unable to capture their rifles we cannot consider them pacified."[57]

Recognizing that they were overmatched, the revolutionaries sought to prolong the war rather than defeat the Army in the field. On 14 January 1900, Lt. Col. Mariano Cabrera criticized "formal" warfare and urged a "guerra de emboscadas" (war of ambushes) to exhaust the enemy.[58] Later, when his military position worsened, Malvar moved even further toward a strategy of prolonged and desultory guerrilla war. He realized that the psychological and political presence of armed revolutionary forces was more important than their military actions; as long as guerrilla bands existed, the Americans could not count on the loyalty of the populace or establish a secure colonial government. He urged his forces to fight only from ambush and to avoid combat whenever the outcome could be unfavorable. In 1902, he urged that if the guerrillas had 100 cartridges they should use no more than ten a year and thus prolong the war for ten years.[59]

Although outnumbered and outgunned, the guerrillas skillfully exploited one of their major tactical advantages: their ability to fight a prolonged war. Their forces were virtually independent of each other; Army operations against one column would have little effect on another raised by neighboring villages. Officered by the local elite and recruited from a small area, the guerrilla bands had strong unit cohesion and made maximum use of the limited number of rifles. Moreover, the close ties between officers and civil officials meant that a guerrilla unit could be expanded as long as the town officials remained loyal. The dispersion of a town's company into smaller squads stationed in surrounding *barrios* insured both an adequate source of supplies and an effective means of intimidating potential *americanistas*. Moreover, the scattered forces could quickly assemble, strike, and disperse, secure in the knowledge that local inhabitants, many of whom were relatives or friends, would deny all information to the American pursuers. As Lt. Col. Charles J. Crane concluded: "this country offers so many hiding places that the insurgents do not have to go far to obtain perfect concealment. And as a rule, after leaving the scene of combat they conceal their weapons and appear as innocent amigos. Most of them live at home and work at their ordinary vocation, those who are not at home live in houses already occupied by their friends and all appears to be one family in each house. All this makes it almost impossible to find any particular band that has committed a certain depredation."[60]

The revolutionaries also made effective use of terrorism. In contrast to Funston's Fourth District, terrorism in southwestern Luzon was directed against individuals as well as property. Some attempts were made to demoralize the Americans through atrocities upon Army prisoners, but most terrorism was intended to punish Filipinos who worked for the Americans, to serve as a warning for potential collaborators, and to demonstrate the Army's inability to protect civilians.[61] Many terrorist actions, especially the killing of collaborators, were not indiscriminate but rather directed against specific targets, carried out in front of numerous witnesses, and publicized heavily. By publicly assassinating an Army guide or a collaborating *presidente*, they not only removed a dangerous threat but deterred potential *americanistas*.[62]

Publication of this policy was frequent and systematic from the beginning of the American occupation. Numerous proclamations asserted that traitors, people who surrendered weapons, *ladrones*, and other malefactors would be punished with death. Bulletins cited the killing of *americanistas* or criminals as evidence of the guerrillas' power to enforce their threats.[63] In addition to proclamations, the revolutionaries relied heavily on terrorist action itself as a form of propaganda. *Americanistas* who lived in U.S. Army-held towns could be executed in full view of their neighbors. One guide was boloed while walking in a large crowd, another was cut down in the market, and a third was stabbed at the cockpit.[64] However, if the U.S. garrison or the public attitude made a public execution too risky, the revolutionaries were content to kidnap the victim, and either hold him hostage or kill him in the hills.[65]

Perhaps the sole opponent of terrorism as a policy was Col. Buenaventura Dimaguila, a commander in Tayabas. Appealing over the heads of Cailles and Malvar to Lt. Gen. Mariano Trías, Dimaguila charged that assassinations were alienating the people, that guerrillas were committing numerous abuses, and that wealthy contributors had all fled. He argued that the assassination of officials left only the worst elements willing to serve in government. Dimaguila's protest may reflect a feud with Cailles as much as humanitarian sentiment. Its apparent uniqueness suggests unanimity within the guerrilla leadership on the utility of terrorism, as well as the Army's inability to mount an effective deterrent.[66]

Many American officers were convinced that the revolutionary leadership not only advocated assassination as a policy, it supervised the killings. Certainly some Filipinos were killed on their direct orders: Cailles's letter book indicates that he personally ordered or approved the execution of twenty-nine Filipinos between August 1900 and April 1901. If or how he enforced these death sentences is more difficult to determine. Some Americans, in southwestern Luzon and elsewhere, believed that a secret Mandodukut society was masterminding assassinations throughout the Philippines. However, beyond instructing followers to learn the verb *dukut* [kill or destroy], the correspondence of regional guerrilla leaders is devoid of references to the Mandodukuts and the Army was never able to prove the existence of such a group. It appears that although assassinations may have been ordered by Cailles or Malvar, they were performed as individual actions against local enemies and not by agents of a secret society.[67]

The actual number of civilians killed by the guerrillas in Batangas, Laguna, and Tayabas is impossible to determine. Many may have been killed by *ladrones* with only the slightest connection to the independence movement.[68] Others' deaths or kidnappings went unreported; their fate was discovered only later through captured papers. In the fall of 1900, American commanders were asked to forward estimates of local assassinations and assaults to Taft's Philippine Commission. From a partial collection of these reports, Brig. Gen. Hall estimated that in 1900, only 17 civilians were assassinated and 106 assaulted for sympathizing with the Americans. There is no comparable statistical data for 1901 or 1902, but U.S. Army investigations of a few selected towns late in the war show that there had been several killings that previous commanders had not reported. As indicated, Cailles authorized 29 killings in a period of nine months and the commanding officer at Calamba,

Laguna, estimated that 51 Filipinos had been killed in his town alone. The records are contradictory and incomplete and the total number of assassinations and assaults in the Second District will probably never be known.[69]

Whatever the actual number, the mere threat of such retaliation seems to have vitiated American attempts to establish civil government or secure popular support. Steele's problems at Lucban have already been detailed and may serve as an example of what went on throughout southwestern Luzon. The elections at the town of Batangas, for example, were effectively blocked when two guerrillas set fire to several buildings. The commanding officer noted bitterly, "It is not likely now that anyone will accept the office of local Presidente at elections set for Sunday night."[70] At Pila, Laguna, the garrison commander found all the potential officeholders terrified of being killed and steadfast in their refusal to have anything to do with American civil government. As Maj. Frederick K. Ward pointed out, the guerrillas "have [the] aid of every inhabitant of the country for information, etc. They continue to dominate the inhabitants and compel their aid, active or passive, for the simple reason that their punishments for failure to comply are much more than any practiced by us, or permitted to us under the laws of civilized warfare."[71]

Complementing the revolutionary military forces was the most developed support system in all Luzon. Like the military system, it drew its strength from the municipalities. Initially all cooperation with the Americans was forbidden and any native official who served the Americans was subject to death. Army counterpressure, occasionally exerted through threats to destroy towns that failed to form governments, led to a more moderate policy. From mid-1900 on, the guerrillas usually allowed town councils to form municipal governments under U.S. authority, provided that these continued to give clandestine support. Thereafter, town officials consulted or notified their local revolutionary leaders about their appointment to office and either secured approval or replacement. In some cases this was carried to an extreme: the guerrilla commander met with the *principales* to draw up a list of candidates who were then "elected" under the auspices of American civil government.[72] Since guerrilla bands were raised and officered by the municipal elite, their leaders were well acquainted with local politics and could appoint sympathetic officials. In some cases they might select their relatives or business partners. If the area's forces were commanded by an outsider, he could usually summon a *junta* of prominent men and solicit their recommendations for tax collectors and recruiters. Once the local civilian organization was established, it was allowed to function relatively independently as long as it produced supplies, information, and shelter.[73] In many towns the guerrilla infrastructure paralleled the American civil government; the local *presidentes* and town officials, outwardly friendly, held commissions in the revolutionary forces, and *barrio* chiefs collected taxes for both revolutionary and American governments. In one case the post interpreter informed the guerrillas of the identity of collaborators, and in another, the municipal police served as couriers for the guerrillas and reported to them all Army movements. Indeed, the revolutionaries made an effort to integrate civil and military duties throughout southwestern Luzon so that officials and officers could switch readily from one side to the other.[74]

The revolutionary municipal governments supported the guerrillas with food, money, and supplies, which were paid for through a number of taxes. In 1901, Malvar ordered the establishment of a uniform taxation system based on a head tax, a 10 percent tithe on the rice crop, and a tax on the churches. He also urged special "taxes," such as the requirement that couples who wished to get married must donate a rifle. Local commanders instituted taxes in their areas or demanded additional supplies and services; some collectors stated that they had been instructed to collect as much as 30 percent of the rice harvest. In addition, they relied greatly on donations and voluntary contributions from the *principalía*, who could arrange emergency loans and supplies.[75] They also collected money by fining collaborators, kidnapping people for ransom, issuing licenses to gambling establishments, and collecting road tolls. These extra levies were necessary because clearly many of the official taxes were not collected regularly, largely due to the poverty of the population. Nevertheless, on the whole the insurgent tax-collection system worked well; and it was not until the U.S. Army began its population concentration campaign in 1902 that the guerrilla forces went short of food or supplies.[76]

The strength of this infrastructure lay in the support of the educated, landholding provincial elite. In contrast to other areas of Luzon, where at least a segment of the upper class felt that its interests were best served by the Americans, those in southwestern Luzon were strong backers of the guerrillas. As we have noted, most of the officer corps—and the civil officials who subverted American political control—belonged to this group. We have also indicated how important contributions from the *principales* were to the revolutionaries' taxation system. Glenn A. May argues that the provincial elite's strong commitment was due to a variety of factors: patriotism, self-interest, and what he has termed the "nephew/neighbor factor," the personal and familial connections that tied the *principales* in the field to those who remained in the American-occupied towns. Indeed, so great was the role of the *principalía* that he has concluded that in Batangas "the primary impetus for the resistance came from the elite and that without their active participation, there would have been relatively little opposition to the American occupation."[77]

The role of the clergy, the other influential class in southwestern Luzon, is much less clear. John Schumacher has suggested that it was "precisely the organized cooperation of the clergy that had much to do with the fact that the guerrillas were able to hold out so long in the southern Tagalog provinces."[78] Much of the clerical resistance to the Americans may reflect the clergy's own social position as members of the elite, or "class [of] . . . monied mainstays of the insurgents." Lt. Col. Charles J. Crane summed up a number of Army prejudices when he stated, "It is to the interest of the Priest and the rich to keep the black Tagal[og]s in utter ignorance, and thus prolong the war. With peace they must take lower seats."[79] As Schumacher has demonstrated, some clergymen actively gave the guerrillas physical, financial, and moral support, even abandoning their parishes to serve in the field. Most conspicuous were the parish priests of Taal and Lemery, who defied the orders of their superiors and fled with the statue of the Virgin of Casaysay, an object of considerable veneration to many Batangueños. Others contributed money to the revolutionary forces or hid guerrilla weapons and supplies.[80]

There is equal evidence that clergymen and Army officers often aided each other. The padre at Sariaya acted as a spy for the Americans "on the quiet," and was so successful in his deception that Malvar sought him out to request additional funds.[81] One guerrilla officer complained that the priest of Pila had "seduced" the population into supporting the Americans. Other priests acted as intermediaries in the surrender negotiations for partisan officers or convinced their townspeople to return to American-held villages. When a U.S. battalion left San Pablo, Laguna, the padre presented it with a beautiful flag and made a speech of thanks. In turn, American officers secured the release of parishioners or relatives who had run afoul of the Army authorities. The role of the Tagalog clergy was ambiguous, and both resistance and collaboration were common.[82]

The revolutionary organization in southwestern Luzon was the best organized and best led, and had the most popular support of any in the island. Some officers might contemptuously refer to "bare-foot, shirt-tail, half-armed Filipinos," but the more intelligent shared with Birkhimer a grudging respect for their foes: "I owe it to our rebel enemy to say that, from their standpoint, I regard their scheme of warfare as nearly perfect. In the facility with which they can play the insurrecto-amigo act they have an immense advantage. Their facilities for recruitment and their plans for receiving money and supplies are not to be despised."[83]

Having spent the early months of 1900 organizing their military forces and support structure, the revolutionaries increased the level of violence against American garrisons in the summer. Generally they limited their operations to ambushes, wire cutting, and sniping, but occasionally they concentrated their forces and launched a major attack on a supply train or Army post. The small garrison at Taal, Batangas, was attacked on 6 July by an estimated 400 guerrillas under Malvar. Although the U.S. commander had been warned by both the *presidente* and neighboring officers, he apparently took no precautions and 6 soldiers were wounded. The garrison took revenge a few days later, when it located the guerrillas and attacked them with the aid of a gunboat, killing 38. Birkhimer noted, however, that the victory netted few lasting results, and concluded bitterly: "We cannot destroy the rebels because they have concealed their arms and are the most obsequious of amigos."[84]

To prevent the guerrillas from concentrating large forces and overrunning isolated posts, the Army launched several attacks on suspected strongholds. One of the most sought-after targets was the headquarters of Cailles. In late May and early June, expeditions moved into northeastern Laguna near the Morong and Infanta provincial borders; the Thirty-seventh Infantry under Cheatham surrounded and searched four towns and swept the country thoroughly, but found neither Cailles nor his base camps. In August, however, a native guide showed the Americans the guerrilla's headquarters. The soldiers of the Thirty-seventh Infantry and Eleventh Cavalry had a sharp fight before the revolutionaries fled, leaving 5 dead and 8 rifles, as well as valuable papers.[85] The Americans clashed with Cailles again at Mabitac, Laguna, on 17 September, when 40 soldiers from the Thirty-seventh and 90 from the Fifteenth Infantry made made a frontal attack on an estimated 800 guerrillas. Cheatham had proposed a flanking attack, with the inexperienced Fifteenth, under Capt. David D. Mitchell, acting as a diversionary force. Mitchell, who had spent less than two days in the Philippines, abruptly changed this plan and sent his men across an exposed causeway flanked on either side by flooded rice paddies. The soldiers were cut to pieces; the Americans suffered 21 killed and 23 wounded. MacArthur privately told Taft that had Mitchell not been killed he would have been court-martialed.[86]

To counter the revolutionary resurgence, the Army relied on a combination of large expeditions and sweeps and small-unit actions and tactics. Birkhimer voiced the common belief that they had to take the offensive, stating that when soldiers were in the field the populace was inclined to peace, when they were inactive the Filipinos became "insolent" and guerrilla activity flourished.[87] With the exception of the instances mentioned, the guerrillas' refusal to stand and fight limited most American offensive operations to constant patrols and "roundups." Operating at night, a patrol would make a quick march, surround a *barrio*, and then conduct an intensive house-to-house search for weapons, supplies, suspects, and correspondence. Church records were used to verify the people found in each house. The inhabitants were interrogated, often by a paid interpreter or former guerrilla, and suspects were marched away to jail. On occasion, the population of an entire city was rounded up and hundreds of people interrogated or detained. Although the majority of searches yielded no rifles or guerrillas, they kept the revolutionaries on the move, disrupted their infrastructure, and demonstrated the Army's considerable powers of harassment. As Birkhimer explained, "we do not know insurrectos and bad men from good ones, so we are often compelled to arrest all alike and bring them in here to be sorted out; in this way the good are temporarily inconvenienced, but only temporarily. But even this evil has its good side: the people find that the United States authorities are liable to overhaul them at any moment and it has a salutary, lasting effect."[88]

From the harassment of the roundup, Army counterinsurgency tactics escalated to the destruction of houses and property. The burning of buildings was practiced by both sides; moreover, many U.S. soldiers were inclined to believe that destroying the Filipino's nipa-and-wood houses did not constitute serious property damage. Officially, only buildings used exclusively as rebel barracks were to be burned on operations, but these orders were often disregarded or given considerable leeway in their interpretation. By June 1900, it was common for soldiers to burn surrounding houses if they discovered cut telegraph wires or supply depots or if the houses served as cover for snipers. Many officers accepted the practice as a legitimate form of retaliation. Birkhimer, who had vigorously protested the burning of a village in March, justified the policy in June when Gardener made a similar protest. Although he claimed during one operation that "destruction of property was . . . effected in such manner as to impress these people with the absolute knowledge that we wage war only on the rebels and their military supplies," it is doubtful that the Filipinos who had their property destroyed appreciated his distinctions.[89] Other officers were even less restrained; on one expedition against Cailles's headquarters, Cheatham urged that his troops be allowed "to burn freely and kill every man who runs."[90] Although his suggestion was rejected, there are disturbing implications in the fact that as early as May, well before the peak of guerrilla activities, such a proposal could be made with impunity—and to District Headquarters.

Other pacification methods or policies were developed by individual commanders. Maj. George T. Langhorne offered to free prisoners if their families would turn in their rifles. Company commanders mounted their troops for sudden raids or used gunboats to track down guerrilla hideouts located along the lakes and seacoast. In Tayabas, a picked force under Capt. Charles P. Newberry served as a mobile column that went wherever guerrillas or *ladrones* were reported. Operating in the hills and jungles for weeks at a time, they drew supplies and replacements from the other garrison towns.[91] Surprisingly, only a few officers at that time advocated any restrictions on food and supplies. Col. George S. Anderson proposed the "thorough destruction of all stores that may serve as subsistence to the Insurgent Army" but his suggestion was not adopted.[92] In May 1900, Gardener ordered all food in the *barrios* and small farms brought into the municipalities and stored, restricting families to a small portion for personal use. His efforts were not duplicated in other areas, and there was no concentrated effort to cut the guerrillas' food supply until Bell's controversial campaign more than a year later.[93]

The Army's intelligence system reflected the lack of central direction that characterized pacification in the Second District during 1900. Its impact upon Army operations is unclear, largely because officers were ordered to avoid written references that might implicate their sources. In April, shortly before Hall replaced him, Birkhimer recommended the establishment of a district intelligence service, but the duties of this office were never clarified and there is little evidence in post records that it distributed information. Bates and Hall made little effort to structure an effective intelligence service even to the extent of a centralized record of possible revolutionaries.[94]

Most intelligence activities were handled at the company or regimental level, where, despite the lack of official support, garrison officers developed intelligence services in their towns and provinces which were often quite effective. Civic officials were expected to contribute information on guerrilla activities and were held responsible if storehouses or barracks were discovered in their area. Several *presidentes* placed the safety of their towns above other loyalties and gave the Americans warning of guerrilla attacks. Besides this, officers established their own informant networks, relying on captives, guides, and spies, as well as interrogations. Moreover, rewards were offered for the capture of prominent guerrillas, though Bates turned down Hall's suggestion for a 1,000-peso prize to any Filipino who could capture Cailles.[95]

The Army encountered substantial difficulties in obtaining accurate information in southwestern Luzon. The Americans' ignorance of the Tagalog language and the threat of retaliation prevented Filipinos from giving information to Army patrols. One officer gave some indication of this problem, as well as a description of accepted Army methods of obtaining information: "We cannot use spies here as Americans are about twice as large as Filipinos, [of a] different color and will never be able to learn their dialects. Not a native will under any circumstances give us any information about the insurgents not even if they are threatened with death or having their houses burned and they will always give notice of our approach."[96] Officers found that some informants had little concept of numerical strength or were prone to exaggerate, perhaps in order to increase the value of their information. As a result, garrison commanders received panicky messages reporting huge concentrations of *insurrectos* about to sweep down on their towns. Bullard forwarded one such message with the caution that it should be read "for what it is worth, which I believe is nothing."[97] Nevertheless, the revolutionaries worried about the growing effectiveness of Army intelligence and devoted much of their own effort to identifying and removing informers.[98]

The formation of Native Scouts proved to be just as difficult as the creation of intelligence services. In other regions of Luzon, the Army was able to exploit ethnic, religious, or class divisions to recruit effective Filipino auxiliaries. In the Second District, however, the elite's support for the revolutionary cause and fear of guerrilla retaliation, often public and atrocious, discouraged enlistment. The departmental commander, Bates, as we have seen in the neighboring Third District, was skeptical about the use of any Filipino scouts, and Hall did little to encourage their enlistment. In addition, many officers were uncertain about the wisdom of entrusting Tagalogs with weapons that might be used against the Americans. One officer suggested the Army use only a few Tagalog guides and recruit scouts among the Macabebes and other more loyal groups. So great was this suspicion that supporters of Native Scouts would qualify their recommendations: "I have not full faith in the honesty or truth of any Tagalo[g] even after enlistment in our service but the act of enlistment separates him from his people, and makes him a marked man, and apostates have always proven very zealous. And if not fighting for us these same people are naturally assisting our enemy. . . . Finally it is the old plan so often used to advantage of dividing the strength of the enemy and having them fight each other."[99] Given these doubts and the scarcity of recruits, it is not surprising that neither Native Scout units nor irregular forces were raised in the Second District. The Tagalog units that did appear in June 1901 were recruited in other provinces.

The guerrilla resurgence did produce one important development in Army counterinsurgency theory. With the growing recognition that the enemy was not "the ignorant Tagalo who handled the knife," but rather the "persons of influence" who controlled his actions, individual officers began urging the implementation of measures against the upper classes.[100] Col. Cheatham advocated that palm trees in the Majayjay area should be cut down in retaliation for the destruction of telegraph wires: "I believe this plan will be effective for the cocoanut groves are owned by the wealthy and influential class who can control the actions of the rabble if they desire to do so, the trees are a source of great revenue to them and they value them accordingly, whereas burning the houses does not reach the guilty parties."[101] The belief that the *principales* were responsible for continued resistance would have an important impact on Army pacification policies in southwestern Luzon in 1901.

By the fall of 1900, Army pacification efforts throughout the Second District had failed in most of their goals. Lulled by their easy conquest and weak resistance, Second District Headquarters had concentrated on civil government and social reform at the expense of counterinsurgency. With some exceptions, civil government, native police, and social reforms had proven insufficient to win popular support. Because of a mixture of fear and loyalty, the bulk of the population gave more heed to revolutionary directives than to the Army's. Nonmilitary pacification failed so miserably that almost no Filipinos in the district took advantage of MacArthur's amnesty.[102] In the absence of strong leadership from Bates and Hall, responsibility for the conduct of the war and the development of policies devolved upon regimental and company commanders with the result that pacification was fragmented and uncoordinated. Nevertheless, there was some room for cautious optimism. The Army had weathered the guerrilla resurgence and occasionally inflicted severe tactical defeats on the revolutionaries. Officers developed and improved small-unit tactics and established networks of spies, informers, and guides. As the monsoon season ended and the sick lists declined, the now-veteran troops in the Second District began to mount a counteroffensive of their own.

The extensive changes throughout the Philippines in the last few months of 1900 and early months of 1901 brought substantial changes to the Second District. McKinley's reelection and the subsequent issuing of G.O. 100 signaled a more severe policy throughout the archipelago. Resistance in other areas of Luzon was virtually eliminated by July 1901, allowing the Army to turn its full attention to the southwestern region. Within the Second District, efforts to establish municipal governments and police forces were increased, and the Federal party began winning over converts to the American cause. In addition, the Americans were able to keep consistent military pressure on the revolutionaries. Although the U.S. Volunteer regiments were withdrawn at the beginning of 1901, they were replaced by regular Army forces with little diminution of actual strength. By mid-1901, most of the First and Sixth U.S. Cavalry, the Fourth, Eighth, Twenty-first, and Thirtieth U.S. Infantry, and several coast artillery units were stationed in southwestern Luzon.[103]

The old Second District disappeared in April 1901, when the Army decided to consolidate the four provinces of Tayabas, Batangas, Laguna, and Cavite into the newly designated First District, Department of Southern Luzon. This reorganization also saw Brig. Gen. James F. Wade replace Bates as departmental commander. Wade, a cavalryman with extensive service in the frontier Army during the Indian campaigns, possessed a much better understanding of the nature of Philippine guerrilla war than Bates. The newly organized district also benefited when Brig. Gen. Samuel S. Sumner replaced Hall. Although he would later be criticized for a lack of vigor, Sumner was more decisive and innovative than his predecessor. Sumner and Wade's task was ostensibly eased when civil government was granted to Tayabas and Cavite, a decision that left the Army free to concentrate on Laguna and Batangas. In Cavite, the surrender of Trías and his forces in March 1901 ended most resistance in the province, and in Tayabas the situation was deceptive: the few engagements (only nineteen from February 1900 to January 1901), the apparent success of civil government, and the fact that much of the western province was in the Bicol region led to the assumption that its population was less recalcitrant than that of Batangas and Laguna.[104]

The new year also saw a shift in the momentum of the guerrilla war at the operational level. Before the presidential election in the United States, the level of guerrilla and Army activity stayed quite high: there were ten engagements in September and eleven in October 1900; some towns were subject to repeated sniping and attacks. However, by October, in some areas, American units had seized the initiative and the engagements were increasingly the result of Army patrols' discovery of guerrilla bands. With the end of the monsoon season, the Army sick lists decreased and the better weather made expeditions easier. No longer confined to the immediate vicinity of their garrisons, the Americans moved into the countryside, often sending expeditions into areas they had previously left alone.[105]

Army tactics in 1901 retained the developments of 1900, but were implemented with more expertise and experience. Roundups were both more thorough and more effective; and small patrols and large expeditions attempted to keep the enemy forces dispersed and far from the support of the townspeople. Although the Army scored some conspicuous successes, such as the capture of Cailles's papers, for the most part engagements were confined to long-range skirmishing in which the Army suffered few casualties but inflicted little physical damage. But these operations, although not spectacular, inexorably forced Malvar's forces back into southeastern Batangas and the border area where Batangas, Laguna, and Tayabas join.[106]

In all of this, the forces in southwestern Luzon benefited greatly from MacArthur's emphasis upon breaking up the guerrillas' supply system and nullifying the role of the "prominent families." Conditions in the district closely paralleled those described by MacArthur, with the revolutionaries sustained largely through the aid of the civilian population. General Order 100 outlined the duties and responsibilities of noncombatants and called for strict penalties against both guerrillas and their supporters. Moreover, MacArthur directed the Army to concentrate its operations less on the elusive partisans and more toward seeking out and destroying the infrastructure. With an "approved manner of conducting war" thus clarified, officers believed their superiors would support a harsher and more ruthless policy in the district.[107]

An unfortunate result of this was an increasing blurring of the lines between civilian and military targets. As we have seen, property destruction had already become a quasi-acceptable form of retaliation among soldiers in the field; now its use was apparently accepted at higher levels. Sumner listed guerrilla storehouses as legitimate targets for destruction and ordered: "In case troops are fired on from any barrio, it will be burned unless advisable to preserve it for our future use."[108] He did attempt to stop the burning of crops and houses by soldiers, believing that such action "entails hardship and starvation on the peaceful inhabitants," but was willing to sanction retaliatory burnings against specific targets.[109] When an American guide was murdered in the marketplace at Bauan and witnesses refused to give information, Sumner authorized the burning of the marketplace. The soldiers, furious at the death of their "mascot," also burned fourteen houses and only stopped the fire when it threatened their own quarters.[110]

Another grievous consequence of this blurring of military and civilian targets was the resort to excessive force, and occasionally to torture, as a way to secure information. As the guerrilla war dragged on, Bullard's fear that "ultimately we will be driven to the Spanish method of dreadful punishment on a whole community for the acts of its outlaws which the community systematically shields and hides, *always*" appeared to be increasingly justified.[111] Hitherto—according to both revolutionary documents and their own personal reminiscences—the soldiers in the U.S. Volunteer regiments had been well behaved and enjoyed good relations with the few Filipinos they were able to befriend. One of these volunteer officers, Maj. Matthew F. Steele, stated: "I have never burnt a house yet or cut a tree, or whipped a native or hung one, and I don't intend to. If we can't conquer these savages without resorting to Spanish methods, my notion is we had better quit these islands, and let them have them."[112] But the regulars who replaced the volunteers in 1901 had fewer scruples and the use of torture increased in 1901 and 1902.

Physical mistreatment and torture were never sanctioned by either Divisional Headquarters in Manila or district headquarters, and there were constant warnings against it; but it clearly occurred. The most infamous torture was the "water cure," which consisted of forcing water down the victim's throat until he agreed to divulge the required information. An Army investigation in 1902 concluded that some soldiers had given Filipinos the water cure, but smugly concluded that in "comparatively few instances is there evidence that a commissioned officer was present."[113] Given the prevalence of testimony in private papers, courts-martial, and other Army investigations, it is impossible to concur with this judgment. An Army board called to investigate Gardener's allegations that torture was widespread heard testimony from both Americans and Filipinos which suggested that in Tayabas alone, between October and December 1901, there were seventeen cases of physical abuse involving eight U.S. officers.[114]

Richard J. Welch has argued that in the Philippine War most such atrocities were "inspired by anger, boredom, and racial animosity."[115] However, in southwestern Luzon the use of the "water cure" was not the result of random individual sadism. Rather it appears to have been both a means of retaliation and a distressingly common manner of interrogation among officers assigned to intelligence work.[116] Unlike most other districts, the Army did not have access to a group or class of Filipinos disenchanted with the revolutionaries and willing to cooperate. As Sumner complained, "the inhabitants of Laguna are as a class very loyal to General Cailles and it is impossible to obtain any information that might lead to his capture, to an almost equal extent the people of Batangas guard the safety of General Malvar."[117] Moreover, the ability of the revolutionaries to assassinate collaborators infuriated the Americans and discouraged other collaborators. Veterans of the Second

District knew that the guerrillas could impose much stricter, and bloodier, sanctions than were permitted the U.S. Army under the laws of war. In this situation, they viewed the "water cure" as a means of compulsion that could, at least temporarily, overcome either patriotism or fear.[118]

Other, less drastic, measures to improve the gathering of information were also taken at this time. Departmental Headquarters sent the district sixteen photographs of Cailles with instructions to see that they received wide distribution. Photographs of other revolutionary leaders were thereafter sent to post commanders along with physical descriptions, habits, and known locations.[119] On 22 December 1900, American forces captured Trías's papers and obtained the names of all the commissioned officers in southern Luzon. Army headquarters sent a list of 560 guerrilla officers to post commanders in February 1901, with orders to report on their whereabouts. The discovery of Cailles's papers on 26 April 1901, provided vital information about his hideouts and supply service, and the information was put to immediate use. Sumner informed his garrison commanders of the exact number of rifles in their areas and directed them to "arrest principal men of town and endeavor to make them produce them."[120] The increasing and effective use of spies and former revolutionaries caused the guerrillas to spend more of their time attempting to uncover potential informers. These actions, while still not as complete as many officers wished, gave military intelligence in the southwestern Luzon far better organization and direction.

In addition to these military measures, the Army continued to work on civil government as a means of cutting off the guerrillas from the population and establishing pro-American government at the local level. As it had in 1900, the Army approached this mission with mixed emotions. Sumner and Wade largely continued the policies of their predecessors and avoided giving active encouragement to the establishment of civil government. Officers who organized towns often found that some *presidentes* dragged them into local feuds. In other towns the guerrillas attempted, and often succeeded, in subverting civil organization by having their own nominees appointed or by executing unsympathetic *presidentes*. Yet on the whole, there were grounds for some optimism. In one town, the *presidente* captured five rifles and in another several inhabitants assisted the Army to bring about the surrender of local guerrilla bands. In contrast to 1900, when the district had been almost impossible to organize, by 1901 there were towns that were recognizably loyal to the Americans. The Army would soon be able to turn its full attention to those recalcitrant towns controlled by the guerrilla infrastructure.[121]

The Army made steady improvements in the organization of Filipino police, partly in response to pressure from headquarters in Manila, which declared in December 1900 that the establishment of a native police force was an "emergency measure" and that its members would be compensated from insular funds. The Army exerted further pressure on post commanders in May by a divisional directive that ordered them to report on the weapons, pay, uniforms, and status of their police forces.[122] As a result, serious, if somewhat unwilling, attention was devoted to the project. Although MacArthur's replacement, Maj. Gen. Adna R. Chaffee, wanted the Ordnance Department to control the distribution of pistols and shotguns to the police, shortages in this department threw this burden on individual garrison officers.[123]

On the whole, Wade's comment that "our experience in the use of natives for police work has not been entirely satisfactory" was an apt description of the American effort to create loyal police.[124] There were some conspicuous successes, however. In one town, the *presidente* purchased five revolvers to distribute to the new police force, and in another the police, armed with weapons borrowed from the infantry garrison, were responsible for more arrests than the soldiers were. Lt. Traber Norman, despite his misgivings about arming the Tagalogs, organized a 22-man municipal police force and gave pistols to its officers and noncommissioned officers. In general, in 1901 officers approached the formation of local police units with far more enthusiasm and patience than they had in 1900. As a result, although they experienced temporary frustration they were willing to continue supporting the policy. Norman, for example, learned that his chief of police had collaborated with a revolutionary officer to arrange the kidnapping of two policemen. His solution was to dismiss the offenders but to retain the rest of the policemen. Lt. Patrick A. Connolly, who had to disarm the police in his town when they failed to arrest *ladrones*, immediately began restructuring and arming a new town police force. If the district police forces were not entirely satisfactory, they were far more so than they had been in 1900.[125]

Another source of assistance was the Federal party, whose representatives appeared in the district in February and March. Several of these had been revolutionaries who had close personal relations with both the local elite and the guerrillas. They were authorized by the Army to organize chapters of the Federal party and to open negotiations with the guerrillas. Although they failed to secure the surrender of Cailles and Malvar, they were more successful with several subordinate officers and their troops. They also impressed Army officers with the capable manner in which they won over the populace in previously hostile towns.[126] The guerrillas viewed the party as a serious threat and tried to kill its leaders and prevent its spreading. A *federalista* was among the five "traitors" executed at Sampaloc by Cailles in April 1901. In Laguna, one of Cailles's chief subordinates, Lt. Col. Pedro Caballes, authorized the arrest and execution of all party members, and shortly afterward he requested permission to burn towns where a chapter had been organized. Another commander authorized the immediate elimination of all *federalistas* and the destruction of any town which supported them. Not surprisingly, one party organizer felt "that his personal safety [would] only be assured by the immediate presence of American troops wherever he [went]."[127]

The effects of the municipal governments, local police, and *federalistas* were cumulative and increasingly the populace was split off from the revolutionaries. Mariano Lopez, a prominent Batangueño, worked to convince guerrillas to surrender even though his brother served as an partisan officer. The guerrillas' shadow *presidente* of Pagsanjan, together with his followers, took their rifles under pretext of going to cut telegraph wires and deserted to the Americans. Caballes complained that all the influential people in that town had gone over to the Americans, and urged that the town be burned. The loss of Pagsanjan was an especially bitter pill for Cailles, as he had previously praised the *presidente* and town for their revolutionary sentiments. Perhaps as a result of incidents like this, Cailles retracted his December proclamation, which required that any Filipino who worked for the Americans report within thirty days or face execution; now he assured *presidentes* they would be pardoned after Philippine independence.[128]

For the guerrillas, the new American activity and the increasing restlessness of the civilian population coincided with two other setbacks. In neighboring Cavite province, extensive negotiations between officers and Lt. Gen. Mariano Trías, the commander of southern Luzon, culminated on 15 March 1901. Trías surrendered not only himself but most of his men and arms, and Cavite was soon declared pacified. A few days later, Funston and a band of Macabebe Scouts captured Emilio Aguinaldo. Both nationalist leaders believed that continued resistance was futile; Trías wrote to Malvar urging his capitulation, and on 19 April Aguinaldo issued a proclamation, "To the Filipino People," declaring his acceptance of U.S. sovereignty.[129]

In consequence, the revolutionaries in southwestern Luzon were forced to develop a new rationale to justify their continued resistance. According to Lt. Col. Noberto Mayo, they were ready to follow Trías and surrender, and awaited only a decision from Malvar. However, Cailles and Malvar had been acting as virtually independent provincial warlords since the American invasion, and were not constrained by the actions of Trías or Aguinaldo. On 4

April Malvar asked Cailles to convene a meeting of all the leaders who remained and vowed to continue the fight until the Americans were worn down by "esta guerra interminable."[130] On 12 April he issued his proclamation, "Brothers and Companions in the Strife," in which he announced he had succeeded Trías as commander in southern Luzon. Although modestly denying his own talents, he stated that unless he assumed this authority the independence movement would collapse. He also made a direct popular appeal for mass support, claiming that neither education nor social status were necessary to patriots. On 13 July he declared himself commander in chief of all forces in the Philippines and urged all Filipinos to take up arms against the Americans.[131]

Malvar moved quickly to consolidate his position and to organize resistance in southwestern Luzon along more efficient lines. In open letters to Trías and Aguinaldo, he publicized his assumption of command, justifying it as the alternative to demoralization. Although he notified guerrilla leaders in other provinces of his new authority, he made no effort to direct operations outside of Batangas.[132] On 28 April he announced a thorough reorganization of the military forces in southern Luzon, establishing a draft of 1 man for each 100 inhabitants, levying taxes on every citizen, creating a reserve, and offering to commission private citizens who recruited and armed their own forces. In addition, he published new regulations for the guerrillas, altering their composition and prescribing tactics that emphasized ambush and protracted warfare.[133]

Malvar's decision confirmed the regional nature of the war. From his headquarters in Tayabas, near the Batangas and Laguna borders, he provided organizational leadership in a steady stream of orders and resumés governing the resistance in southwestern Luzon. However, much of this was inspirational; and his provincial and zone commanders appear to have operated relatively independently. Indeed, despite his later claims, some of Malvar's orders either appear to have been written for propaganda purposes or reflect a considerable ignorance about actual conditions in the field. It is doubtful, for example, whether any guerrilla chief in late 1901 had time to follow his instructions to oversee the vaccination of all the children in his area or hire a doctor to inspect all his troops.[134]

Malvar and Cailles made a major effort to reorganize the guerrilla military forces and infrastructure in Tayabas province. Lacking a strong provincial leader, Tayabas had been commanded by a Batangueño, Col. Eustacio Maloles, who was Malvar's brother-in-law. Throughout 1900, Maloles had exercised little control over his subordinates and conducted few operations.

In August 1900, Lt. Col. Emilio Zurbano challenged Maloles and asserted that he was now the political-military chief of the province, a claim disputed by Col. Buenaventura Dimaguila, who considered himself under the authority of Trías, and by Col. Marcelo Rada, who operated independently. This squabbling dissipated the military effort, leading Gardener, the American provincial commander, to believe that Tayabas was clear of revolutionaries.

In January 1901, Malvar divided the province into three zones under Col. Mariano Castillo in the west, Col. Dimaguila in the northeast, and Lt. Col. Zurbano in the southeast. In April Cailles moved his forces into northern Tayabas where they were joined by those of Zurbano at Sampaloc. The guerrillas occupied the town for three days, holding a dance and executing five Filipinos for various offenses. Cailles declared Zurbano the new commander of eastern Tayabas and promised that from then on the Laguna forces would aid the inhabitants of Tayabas against the Americans. This reorganization only appears to have increased the factionalism; Rada apparently retired, Maloles and Dimaguila surrendered shortly afterward, and Zurbano surrendered in July. The guerrillas in Tayabas remained disorganized and fragmented, and the revolutionary strength in the province continued to be its civil infrastructure, not its military forces.[135]

The capitulation of Maloles, Dimaguila, and Zurbano indicates that among a growing number of revolutionaries there was an increasing exhaustion and willingness to abandon the struggle. There had been virtually no surrenders among the top guerrilla leadership in 1900, but already there were several within the first months of 1901. According to Lt. Col. Bernardo Marques, "they surrendered for various things; some because they tired of staying in the field; some through fear and because they lost hope; because some of them had been injured or lost their health through life in the field and some because their families obliged them to surrender."[136] Dimaguila surrendered because of a feud with Cailles, because of a U.S. promise to release his uncle from a jail, and because newspapers had reported he was negotiating, thus putting him in jeopardy with other guerrillas. Zurbano surrendered "because he saw the scantiness of [their] resources and believed further resistance would be useless."[137]

The most important surrender was that of Cailles on 24 June 1901. It was probably as much a surprise to the Army as it was to the revolutionaries. As late as 15 April he had proclaimed that he would never surrender. Eleven days later, however, an Army expedition had captured most of his papers, compromising the entire guerrilla infrastructure in Laguna. He may also have been affected by the capture of his personal secretary, who wrote him a letter requesting his surrender and enclosing a copy of Aguinaldo's proclamation. Erroneous newspaper reports that he was negotiating may have influenced his decision as well. In early June, Cailles sent a trusted subordinate to arrange the terms and probably secured a blanket pardon. Shortly after, he surrendered at Santa Cruz with some 100 officers, 500 men, 140 civilian officials, and 400 rifles. Cailles had been viewed as the most dangerous of the revolutionaries, and MacArthur believed his capitulation was "very important, as it is most probable [that the] pacification [of] all southern Luzon [would] follow quickly."[138]

Although the surrender was indeed "very important," pacification did not follow as quickly as hoped. The guerrilla organization, as Trías's departure had shown, was too informal, personalized, and localized for one commander to control. Some of Cailles's subordinates, particularly Lt. Col. Martin Cabrera, refused to accept the surrender terms and remained in the field with Malvar. In Tayabas, owing to Malvar's efforts at another reorganization in the summer of 1901, the surrender of Maloles and Zurbano seems simply to have moved subordinate commanders up a notch. By 1901, warfare in southwestern Luzon had become so localized that many guerrillas had little contact with anyone outside of their immediate area.[139]

In the face of the increasing strength of the Americans and their own growing weakness, the surviving revolutionaries determined to maintain a very low level of insurgency, returning to their villages, hiding their weapons, and becoming civilians again. Although not actively challenging the Americans, they continued to maintain their hold on the population's loyalty. Taxes were still collected, shadow governments maintained, and assassinations still arranged in occupied towns. Malvar's small partisan bands, some 500 or 600 regulars, moved constantly, seldom concentrating, but obtaining food quite easily from secret storehouses in the mountains and from sympathetic villages. With some 3,500 rifles hidden, and with strict injunctions against wasting ammunition, Malvar was convinced he could hold out for another ten years. Sumner believed that Malvar could not "concentrate a force of any magnitude or hold the men together for any time, nor is he likely to risk any general engagement with our troops, his policy is one of negative opposition as far as our Government is concerned, and a reign of terror as far as the natives."[140]

Malvar's decision to drag out the war contributed to growing feeling of frustration within the Army. The rest of the archipelago, except for Samar, was quiet; Aguinaldo had been captured; and the only remaining obstacle was Malvar's stubborn resistance. Although officers serving in southwestern Luzon could see that great strides had been made, they were irritated by the continued presence of guerrilla bands, the presence of hostile civilians in the garrison towns, and the ability of guerrillas to strike at *americanistas*. Sumner appeared to have no solutions: "There are few means at hand to impress these people with the disadvantage of warfare unless we burn the barrios, destroy the food, and subject them to personal torture which is inhuman and unwise, they are purely an agricultural people, and have no general commercial or public system that can be interrupted to their detriment."[141] The headquarters in Manila had lost confidence in both him and Wade. Taft reported: "General Wade is incompetent and General Sumner under him is not very much better," and Chaffee, who succeeded MacArthur in June, complained that Sumner lacked vigor and had "accomplished nothing with Malvar of consequence." For Chaffee, already under pressure because of the attack on American troops at Balangiga in Samar and reports of renewed trouble in the north, the "standstill" in Batangas was intolerable and demanded a quick resolution.[142]

The November 1901 reorganization of Army forces into Separate Brigades gave Chaffee the chance to abolish Wade's position and place Brig. Gen. J. Franklin Bell in command of the newly created Third Separate Brigade. Bell, as we have seen, had already proven himself as both a fighter and a district commander in the First District and was acceptable to both civil and military authorities. The newly formed brigade's area of operations comprised most of the provinces around Laguna de Bay: Morong, Cavite, Batangas, Laguna, and Tayabas, as well as the large islands of Mindoro and Marinduque and some smaller island groups. Bell was assigned 7,622 soldiers from the First and Sixth U.S. Cavalry and Second, Eighth, Twentieth, Twenty-first, Twenty-eighth, and Thirtieth U.S. Infantry, and 680 troops from the Macabebe, Ilocano, and Tagalog Native Scouts. In addition, he was allowed to bring with him a staff of junior officers familiar with his methods.[143]

Bell's policies were well designed to contain the insurrection waged by Malvar in southwestern Luzon; from the beginning, the objective was established, the enemy clearly identified, and the measures to be used outlined. Moreover, through his 1 December 1901 speech to the brigade's officers, telegraphed circulars, and personal communications, Bell succeeded in exercising a personal supervision over the campaign that no other district commander duplicated. He believed that "the insurrection in this brigade continues because the greater part of the people, especially the wealthy ones, pretend to desire but in reality do not want peace."[144] He therefore structured a pacification campaign designed to "make the existing state of war and martial law so inconvenient and unprofitable to the people that they will earnestly desire and work for the reestablishment of peace and civil government, and for the purpose of throwing the burden of the war upon the disloyal element."[145] In his military policies, Bell stressed that while surrenders were important, the "primary and most important object of all our operations in this brigade is to obtain possession of the arms now in the hands of the insurgents."[146] The capture of arms would not only cripple the active revolutionaries, but also prevent the hundreds of "amigos" now posing as civilians from resuming guerrilla warfare.

Bell also sought to break up the insurgent civil organization by compelling municipal officials and other members of the traditional elite into supporting the Army. He claimed that "the common people amount to nothing. They are merely densely ignorant tools, who blindly follow the lead of the principales."[147] Accordingly, he struck at figures of influence and authority in the community, the priests, *principales*, and civil officials. Just as the guerrillas had practiced selective terrorism to insure compliance, Bell used selective retaliation for the same ends. The provincial elite were presumed guilty; they were held responsible for the behavior of their townspeople and subject to punishment for any infractions. They could be arrested and held for trial not only for their own actions, but for the actions of guerrillas in their area. If an *americanista* was assassinated and they failed to identify the killers, they could even be executed, although in fact none were. If a telegraph wire was cut, their houses were to be singled out for burning. The only "acceptable and convincing evidence of the real sentiments of either individuals or town councils should be such acts publicly performed as must inevitably commit them irrevocably to the side of the Americans by arousing the animosity and opposition of the insurgent element."[148]

In order to "make the people want peace, and want it badly," Bell instituted measures that ranged from mild to severe harassment. The ports of Batangas, Laguna, and Tayabas were closed, trade or travel on the public roads prohibited, and the payment of rents for Army-occupied buildings suspended. Troops in the field could commandeer transportation and bearers without payment. The Spanish corvée for public works was reinstituted and the rich were required to pay a fine to avoid working. Bell disarmed the police and cut off the extra pay they received from insular funds, often the majority of their salaries, unless they actively assisted the Army. Henceforth, revolutionary officers were permitted no terms but unconditional surrender, and even then only if they brought their men and weapons, and agreed to collaborate. Captured guerrillas were to be tried before the provost marshals and could lighten their sentences only by offering valuable information, serving as guides, or securing the surrender of other guerrillas or weapons.[149]

Bell's most controversial policy was to herd the populace into "protected zones." This concentration was a radical step, but it had been attempted previously on a limited scale in some areas of Luzon. Bell had isolated a few villages during the Abra campaign of 1901, the population of Marinduque Island had been briefly concentrated, and the town of Bauan, Batangas, had voluntarily relocated its outlying *barrios* in November. Although he had considered the idea, Sumner believed that terrain and the number of inhabitants precluded "the possibility of inaugurating any system of concentration or any thorough control of the food supply."[150] Bell thought otherwise. He announced the implementation of concentration in Telegraphic Circular no. 2 on 8 December 1901, authorizing post commanders to establish a zone in each town where inhabitants from "sparsely settled and outlying barrios" could be quartered. He allowed them until Christmas Day to bring in all their animals, rice, and possessions, and urged commanders to help them as much as possible. After that period, all property, livestock, and food found outside the zones were subject to confiscation.[151]

In practice, concentration was accomplished relatively easily, largely because commanding officers were given considerable flexibility in implementing it and because of Bell's own efforts to prevent suffering. Towns of recognized loyalty were given special privileges and were exempt from many of the regulations. In Paete, for example, the commander reported that there had been no guerrilla activity for ten months and that with only 100 men he could not possibly enforce the concentration orders. He allowed the inhabitants to work in the hemp fields and only required them to come into the village at night. In other cases, officers implemented a few measures and then used the threat of further concentration to force *presidentes* to turn over hidden rifles.[152] To discourage epidemic diseases, Bell instituted a vaccination program for an estimated 300,000 Filipinos. He also directed that the utmost care be taken to secure a plentiful supply of food and instructed his commanders to build storehouses, establish fair food prices, and prevent hoarding and speculation. He encouraged public works projects in which men in the camps could labor on public projects and be paid in rice. The Army shipped a large quantity of rice to southwestern Luzon, and this was either sold at cheap prices or given to the destitute in the zones.

Although concentration proved effective as a counterinsurgency technique, its cost in human suffering was unquestionably high. While Army officers, such as Col. Arthur L. Wagner, claimed that the camps were healthy and not overcrowded, the news that the Army had implemented "reconcentration" shocked many Americans. Antiimperialist newspapers made unfavorable comparisons between Bell and the Spanish general Valeriano "Butcher" Weyler in Cuba in the 1890s, and Senator A. O. Bacon read an anonymous letter referring to clouds of vampire bats swirling over the dead in the concentration camps in the Philippines. Despite the efforts of Bell and his fellow officers to ameliorate conditions, people forced into the camps were overcrowded and suffered from food shortages and sanitation that ranged from poor to appalling. Glenn A. May, who has made the most thorough study of mortality during this time, estimates that malnutrition, poor sanitary conditions, disease, and demoralization may have cost as many as 11,000 Filipino lives and made the population susceptible to the cholera epidemic of 1902.[53]

Although concentration remains Bell's own grim contribution to the war, many of his other policies were chiefly improvements of earlier methods. For example, he strengthened and centralized the intelligence services and at the same time took advantage of improvements in the Army's Philippine-wide intelligence services. Manila's Division of Military Information under Capt. Ralph Van Deman synthesized reports, analyzed captured documents, and provided pictures and descriptions of known revolutionaries. Intelligence at the district and brigade level benefited from the work of Sumner, whose projected Bureau of Information was established on 23 September 1901 in Batangas and Laguna to coordinate and disseminate information to post commanders. Bell's policies forced many former guerrillas to supply information and serve as guides. Captured officers, perhaps threatened with provost court prosecution, were required to make up lists of all their rifles and account for every officer in their command. This information was often invaluable; in one instance a prisoner revealed maps of guerrilla storehouses and hiding places. The Third Brigade also benefited from G.O. 294 of 28 September 1901, a long overdue order which designated a post intelligence officer charged with collecting information on the surrounding terrain, the sentiments of the inhabitants, and the dispositions of guerrilla bands. These officers were soon providing the Manila headquarters with information on the situation in each town and province as well as much needed local tactical intelligence for quick raids and roundups.[54]

Bell utilized some of his most effective intelligence officers in the brigade and post provost courts. Provost marshals operated in Batangas and Laguna and raided Tayabas and Cavite to arrest suspects. Allowed considerable leeway in their procedures, granted the power to try civilians and assess maximum penalties of two years in prison or 1,000 pesos in fines, the provost courts could readily punish any Filipino suspected of supporting the guerrillas. Bell appointed six brigade provost officers who had served with him in northwestern Luzon, including Capt. Daniel H. Boughton, who had broken up Aglipay's guerrillas, and Capt. William T. Johnston, who had been a key figure in the La Union counterinsurgency campaign.[155]

Johnston's experiences give an indication of how the Third Separate Brigade's provost marshals operated. After reporting to Bell in January, he was sent to Lipa, Batangas, which Bell called "the worst town in the brigade," and where his investigations soon proved "that all of the influential people in that town had been all the time actively engaged in assisting and prolonging the insurrection." Johnston arrested 172 inhabitants implicated as revolutionary tax collectors, releasing 1 man for every two rifles surrendered, and holding others hostage until the surrender of the local guerrilla forces. He also required the *principalía* to write a letter repudiating the revolutionaries and promising to remain loyal, a document that was then sent to Manila and given considerable publicity as a "spontaneous action." Not satisfied with written promises, Johnston formed a 60-man unit of Filipino "volunteers" he armed with captured guns and used as guides; after purging Lipa in two weeks, he moved on to Tiaong where he performed another and even more publicized cleanup.[156]

In those areas outside the provost marshals' purview, local post commanders instituted similar measures. Bell's policies were designed to punish the influential Filipinos—a task for which some Army officers had difficulty in restraining their enthusiasm. The commanding officer in Pagsanjan "arrested all rich people believing that they supported the insurgents on the outside," and there is ample testimony that his example was followed by others.[157] Col. Arthur Wagner noted that the rich had "lost heavily" during the campaign: "They undoubtedly yearn earnestly for peace and for the first time they are trying to bring it about. They deserve but little sympathy in their unhappiness, for it is they that have sustained the war, and it is but just that the pinch of concentration should be felt by them."[158] Although manifestly unjust, Bell's measures did accomplish their central purpose: to put intolerable pressure upon the native elite who supported the guerrillas. Faced with the loss of their wealth and social prestige, most civil officials and *principales* came to a rapid accommodation with American authority.

Bell's authorization to deport undesirable individuals from their villages was highly convenient to both provost marshals and post commanders. Convicted or suspected civil officials and *principales* were placed in local jails or sent to Malagi Prison, located on a rocky and desolate island, where they were subject to stringent physical and disciplinary conditions. Funds above fifty pesos were confiscated, and they were forced to wear a brass identification number and work in a rock quarry which soon reduced their clothes to rags. In addition to these humiliating measures, they were made responsible for the behavior of the other prisoners.[159]

As Army provost marshals and garrison commanders purged the towns of civilian sympathizers, Army forces in the fields harried the guerrilla forces with extensive military operations. The primary target for Bell's soldiers were the Loboo Mountains, which run roughly south of a line from the town of Batangas to San Juan de Bocboc and which served as a secure sanctuary for Malvar's partisans. When Army expeditions penetrated the area, they found it teeming with storehouses; one expedition in November 1901 destroyed over 50,000 pounds of unhulled rice in two days. However, the rugged terrain, the poor trails, and problems of supply effectively prevented sustained operations; fewer than half of the soldiers on a June 1901 expedition completed the march—the rest dropped out from sore feet, exhaustion, and disease. Sumner, whose operations forced Malvar back into this area, bitterly noted: "Malvar can live indefinitely in this stronghold surrounded by enough followers to make a show of government. And unless his supplies are interrupted and the people made to feel the danger and hardships of his presence, they will probably acquiesce in the control assumed by him."[160]

Despite its importance, when the Third Separate Brigade moved into the Loboo area the guerrillas made little attempt to defend their sanctuary. In December 1901, an Army scout detachment made a thorough reconnaissance of the area, marching at night, keeping their movements secret, and locating and occasionally destroying supplies. Armed with their information, an expedition under Col. Almond B. Wells formed a cordon from Batangas to Taysan and then swept into the mountains. The soldiers traveled light, their food and supplies carried by conscripted Filipinos. In one week's operations they killed only nine revolutionaries but confiscated or destroyed an estimated 1 million tons of rice and palay, 6,000 houses, 200 carabao, 680 horses, and 800 cattle. They went back again with orders from Bell to conduct operations "having for a common object the complete clearing out of every vestige of animal life and every particle of food supply found within the region embraced by lines connecting San Juan, Taisan [sic], Loboo, and the sea."[161] American expeditions and patrols continued to operate in the mountains until mid-January, and thereafter constantly kept patrols in the area. By March the Americans were receiving aid from many of the former Loboo guerrillas and patrols were finding only a few discouraged civilians.[162]

The Loboo Mountains operations, as well as other Army operations aimed at the destruction or confiscation of food supplies, were intended not only to destroy guerrilla stores but also to provide food to the reconcentrated towns. Some officers in the field tried to send the food back into the towns, but the storehouses were often located on mountains or in jungles far from any town. Wells made great efforts to get as much rice as possible into the towns, but in his operations between 23 March and 1 April he still destroyed 180,000 pounds of palay and 60,000 pounds of corn. Other commanders seem to have been less concerned with providing food for the "reconcentrados." Pvt. Frederick Presher described one such raid on one village in reprisal for guerrilla disturbances: "All small barrios and isolated shacks were burned, all live stock rounded up or destroyed, bannana [sic] and orange groves and growing crops destroyed. Several square miles of territory were laid to waste."[163] Similarly, Lt. Samuel W. Widdifield conducted patrols, "burning everything capable of housing an hombre in sight."[164]

These operations were assisted by increasing numbers of Filipinos, who were now willing to aid the Americans openly. Some of these new allies were poor men attracted by the rewards: thirty pesos for each rifle and five or ten pesos for revolutionary officers. Bell's decision to cut the extra pay of policemen who did not actively aid the Army resulted in several municipal police forces' taking an active role in counterinsurgency operations. In some villages the inhabitants, tired of the endless cycle of guerrilla exactions and Army retaliation, formed vigilante committees and drove the guerrillas from their towns.[165] Significantly, however, much of the American support came from the native elite, who abandoned the revolutionaries in the face of Bell's pressure. For example, it was the "prominent hombres" and "leading citizens" of Bauan who sacked neighboring towns, not the Army troops who accompanied them.[166] Cailles, who after his surrender helped organize a unit of several hundred volunteers to accompany Army forces on expeditions in Laguna, was one of the most active of these new supporters. Although the general population may have remained sympathetic to Malvar and the idea of Philippine independence, Bell's measures had made a significant number defect to the Americans. Indeed, when Malvar surrendered, he claimed that the major factor in his decision was the realization that he was now being pursued by the "people."[167]

The cumulative effect of Bell's campaign was devastating. An Army communiqué in March described Malvar as out of contact with most of his partisans and spending most of his time in hiding.[168] His forces were no better off: dispersed, hungry, and harried by both the Army and the formerly loyal populace. After a month of the brigade's operations, surrenders became common; in January most of the insurgents in western Batangas capitulated, many testifying about the effectiveness of Bell's measures and their own demoralization. One major surrendered sixty-six rifles and his men confessed to "being entirely out of their chief article of food, rice."[169] In some units there was open mutiny: one officer was killed by his second in command when he attempted to prevent his troops' surrender.[170]

Malvar finally submitted on 16 April 1902, an action that Reynaldo Ileto argues was due to Malvar's belief that he and the population were "faced with the prospect of genocide."[171] Glenn A. May believes that Malvar arranged with Bell to turn himself in for 1,800 pesos.[172] The effective cause of Malvar's surrender was clearly the Army's relentless pursuit. The guerrilla general himself conceded that the chief causes of his capitulation were "the measures of General Bell . . . reconcentration, the complete cleaning up of food supplies outside the towns, persecution of the insurgent soldiers by the people, the search for myself by the people, and the demoralization of my troops."[173]

Testimony to the thoroughness of Bell's campaign can be found in the statistics of the Third Separate Brigade's activities. Between 1 December 1901 and 30 April 1902, the dates of the campaign, 210 guerrillas were killed and 139 wounded, 64 officers and 835 men were captured, and 413 officers and 2,560 men surrendered. The Army captured 629 rifles and received 2,264 through surrenders. This last figure is the most significant, for the loss of firearms effectively deprived the few remaining revolutionaries of the means to sustain resistance to American rule.[174]

The pacification campaign in Batangas, Tayabas, and Laguna remains one of the most controversial episodes in a controversial war. Only days after their announcement, Gardener charged that Bell's policies and the Army's pacification measures were "sowing the seeds for perpetual revolution."[175] John Schumacher has called it an "infamous" campaign, and Leon Wolff, Russell Roth, and Stuart C. Miller have detailed its cruelty and brutality.[176] But it has had its defenders as well: John Gates has praised Bell's campaign as "a credit to the American army in the Philippines and a masterpiece of counter-guerrilla warfare."[177] May, one of the few scholars to work with primary source material, offers this judgment: "It was, on both sides, an ugly guerrilla war."[178] Curiously enough, with the exception of Gardener, very few contemporaries who served there—revolutionaries as well as Americans—challenged the necessity of Bell's campaign. By their own admission, the guerrillas were prepared to fight on for years, with potentially even more catastrophic results for the population. Moreover, given the strength of Malvar's support, the adroitness of his strategy, and the difficulties of campaigning in southwestern Luzon, there appeared little hope for the Army to pacify the area through a policy of attraction. Bell's policies seem, in the balance, to have been economical and moderate, in the sense that they avoided the extremes that might have occurred—extremes both of racist brutality and squeamish hesitation. As a result, the war was not prolonged unnecessarily through an overabundance of caution or delicacy, and doubtless many lives were spared in consequence; nor was it conducted generally with the viciousness that appeared sporadically on either side. It may have been "an ugly guerrilla war," but it was not conspicuously so; and for this, some credit must be given Bell and his troops.[179]

The Army's pacification campaign in southwestern Luzon was by far the longest, most costly, and most difficult pacification campaign in Luzon. The resistance was well organized and well led, and possessed invaluable support from the native elite. Influential Filipinos in the Tagalog provinces, to a degree unmatched in the rest of the island, equated patriotism with support for the guerrillas. Hiding behind the population, living for the most part as "amigos" and only occasionally engaging in active operations, and using terrorism, particularly the public killing of collaborators, the guerrillas effectively inhibited any Filipino cooperation with the Army. Not until the Army created equal pressure and fear of punishment did the revolutionaries lose control. Many of the key elements that characterized Army pacification in other areas of Luzon were either unsuccessful or impossible in southwestern Luzon. The Americans could recruit no ethnic or religious minorities to fight the revolutionaries; nor would any group of loyal and influential Filipinos serve as a civil government and deny the guerrillas the use of their villages. Information, one of the most valuable commodities in a guerrilla war, was especially hard to obtain. As Col. Wagner stated, the Army was a "blind giant," powerful enough to destroy the enemy, but unable to find him.[180] In many respects Batangas and Laguna in the fall of 1901 were at the same stage of pacification as other districts had been a year earlier. The key difference was that by late 1901 the Army was under great pressure to end the Philippine War immediately, and the high command was willing to sanction measures that would have been rejected in 1900.

John Gates's statement that Bell's campaign represented "pacification in its most perfected form" implies that it was the culmination of a gradual evolution in Army pacification during the Philippine War.[181] However, it would be more fitting to state that the campaign in southwestern Luzon demonstrates both the regional nature of Filipino resistance and the regional counterinsurgency policies developed by the Army to combat it. The circumstances that impelled Bell's policies—the guerrillas' support among the native elite, their effective use of terrorism, their willingness to continue a desultory war for years, their capable leadership—were all unique to the southern Tagalog provinces. Bell's pacification methods were a direct response to the specific circumstances that characterized this regional war. They represented not a master plan for counterinsurgency but Bell's recognition of the uniqueness of the guerrilla war in southwestern Luzon. The true culmination of Army pacification policy in the Philippine was in this realization that counterinsurgency methods needed to be adapted to the regional guerrilla warfare in Luzon.

6

Provincial Guerrilla Resistance and American Pacification

With the collapse of Aguinaldo's regular forces in late 1899, the U.S. Army in the Philippines was broken up into small garrisons, freeing officers in the provinces from direct control. This decentralization was not intentional, but was almost inevitable given the small U.S. forces, ambivalent policies, rugged terrain, and poor communications. These officers soon found that official policies of benevolence or nonmilitary pacification had to be either altered or abandoned altogether. In place of these officially sanctioned policies, they began to develop and implement their own counterinsurgency methods which reflected their understanding of the realities of the guerrilla war in their immediate locales. The success of these local policies and methods expanded Army control throughout the region, until by 1901 clearly regional counterinsurgency campaigns emerged. These district campaigns effectively crushed the Filipino resistance in most of Luzon and prepared the ground-work for the end of the war in 1902.

Army headquarters in Manila initially perceived the First District, Department of Northern Luzon, as a friendly region whose Ilocano populace was hostile to the Tagalog-dominated Philippine Republic. A special Army administrator, Capt. John G. Ballance, was appointed to control civil affairs and the Army attempted to win over the population through civil government, schools, roads, and social reform projects. Within a few months, however, the discovery that many of the civil governments were actually controlled by the guerrillas and the outbreak of a religiously inspired revolt led to a reappraisal of district pacification. In two provinces, La Union and Ilocos Norte, the Americans fought short but very intensive campaigns which effectively cleared much of these provinces from guerrilla influence. These campaigns were managed by local officers with little direction from outside. However, District Headquarters, responding to this evidence of guerrilla strength, instituted a series of comprehensive policies: declaring martial law, holding civic officials accountable for the actions of their townspeople, and restricting travel. In the fall of 1900, the revolutionaries launched a brief offensive, concentrated primarily in the previously quiet province of Abra and led by the provincial commander, Lt. Col. Juan Villamor. Army response was immediate and drastic, entailing the destruction of crops and the concentration of the populations of some villages. This pacification campaign proved successful, and the First District was completely pacified by the late spring of 1901.

In the Fourth District, Department of Northern Luzon, the provincial guerrilla resistance was both weak and poorly led. Early guerrilla resistance collapsed in the spring of 1900, and many of the former insurgents came to terms with the Americans. Thereafter, resistance came from an outside force of guerrillas under the command of Brig. Gen. Urbano Lacuna. Lacuna never established an infrastructure in the towns, and for much of the war he was confined to the hills. His attempt to insure popular compliance by terrorism ultimately backfired, and the Americans, well led by Brig. Gen. Frederick Funston, were able to capitalize on both anti-Tagalog and anti-terrorist feeling. Utilizing active military operations, local support, and a fine intelligence network, Funston reduced the guerrillas to a negligible threat by 1901. The guerrilla resistance in the Fourth District was always fragile, and Funston's intelligent leadership insured that it remained so.

In the Third District, Department of Southern Luzon, the Army faced a very different form of revolutionary strategy. After their unsuccessful attempt to prevent the American landing, the guerrillas withdrew to the hills with much of the population. Thereafter, they refused to be drawn into military engagements with the Army and devoted most of their efforts to controlling the countryside. American pacification evolved into a two-pronged strategy designed to entice the civilian population back into the towns while making the hills untenable for the guerrillas. The soldiers relied on benevolent policies such as civil government and schools and at the same time enlisted local support through the *presidentes* and native police. They also sought to cut the guerrillas' food supply and harry them with small patrols. By 1901 this had succeeded to such an extent that the revolutionaries were forced to launch attacks on towns occupied by U.S. troops. The American counteroffensive broke up the guerrilla bands and caused most of them to surrender by mid-1901.

In the Second District, Department of Southern Luzon, the Americans confronted a far more powerful and united resistance led by the provincial elite. In contrast to other areas, the guerrillas were well led and able to establish a strong infrastructure in the Army-occupied towns. The Tagalog composition of the population and the support of the native elite gave the guerrillas much more popular support than elsewhere in Luzon. Early attempts at civil government, native police, or social reforms were countered by guerrilla infrastructures and terrorism. Indifferent Army leadership at the highest levels prevented a unified strategy and led to fragmented operations throughout 1900. The Americans had more success in 1901, forcing the surrender of key guerrilla officers and driving the guerrilla forces back into a few isolated areas. A large number of revolutionaries, however, refused to surrender and tried to prolong the war indefinitely with desultory operations under Maj. Gen. Miguel Malvar. In late 1901, the Americans, under Brig. Gen. J. Franklin Bell, responded with the most thorough and complete district pacification of the Philippine War. Using telegraphic circulars to enunciate his policies, Bell implemented a complete counterinsurgency campaign designed to separate the guerrillas from the population. He established population reconcentration zones, sent large expeditions into guerrilla strongholds, used provost marshals to break up town infrastructures, destroyed food supplies, and forced the native elite to commit themselves to the Army. These counterinsurgency policies had their desired effect, and guerrilla resistance collapsed within a few months.

All four of these campaigns were fought virtually independently. In the final campaigns in southeastern Luzon, Bell used several officers who had had wide experience in counterinsurgency warfare in the First District. He also utilized methods, such as concentration camps, food and travel restrictions, and Filipino auxiliaries, which had been implemented elsewhere. His campaign, however, was one of the most clearly regional campaigns fought. It was designed specifically for the situation in Batangas, Laguna, and Tayabas in late 1901. Faced with a protracted war, Bell instituted measures designed to smash enemy resistance as quickly as possible. Unfortunately, in the process a great deal of hardship was inflicted on the civilian population. Bell's policies did not represent a perfection of Army pacification methods, but rather a clear recognition that the war in each of these three provinces was unique and required the creation of unique and distinct regional pacification policies.

Filipino nationalist scholars claim that the Philippine War represents the Filipino people in arms, but, as we have seen, the Filipino guerrilla resistance was essentially regional and decentralized. Guerrilla district commanders tended to develop a base in one province and delgate guerrilla activities in other areas to subordinates. Thus, although Mariano Trías was in charge of all of Southern Luzon, he restricted his activities to Cavite province. Somewhat similarly, Vito Belarmino, who was in charge of the entire Bicol region, confined himself to Albay. Realizing the limitations of their authority, these commanders gave their provincial chiefs a virtual free hand. The strongest guerrilla commanders were provincial leaders such as Juan Villamor, Miguel Malvar, and Juan Cailles, who were natives of the provinces in which they fought and had strong personal connections to important segments of the population. They were virtually independent, obeying superior authority only if it suited the realities of their region. Provincial commanders, in turn, often delegated authority to zone commanders, as Lacuna did with Tómas Tagunton in the Fourth District. Where no strong provincial authority existed, guerrilla authority fragmented or devolved upon the strongest local chief, and guerrilla resistance in the province would center in one or two towns or a specific region such as the Batac-Paoay area of Ilocos Norte. The evidence does not support the conclusion that Aguinaldo controlled the guerrilla resistance. Rather, it indicates that neither Aguinaldo nor anyone else controlled the conduct of the war beyond the boundaries of their respective provinces.

There was a great deal of variation in both the strategy and methods used by the guerrillas. While the basic objectives of the Filipino nationalists were clear and included prolonging the war, avoiding large battles, harassing small patrols and garrisons, and preventing the Americans from exercising civil authority, there was no archipelago-wide strategy for achieving these objectives. Belarmino's decision to contest the American landings on the beaches and his decision to abandon the towns were at variance with Malvar's decision to disperse his forces and develop a supporting infrastructure in the towns. Although all guerrillas tried to control the population, the methods they used to insure compliance varied greatly. The guerrillas in La Union attempted to construct a carefully organized infrastructure that would function as a shadow government, ostensibly cooperating with the Army while actually aiding the guerrillas. In Ilocos Norte, Aglipay sought to organize Katipunan societies and challenge the Americans through direct military attack. In central Luzon, Lacuna used terrorism directed primarily at property in an effort to swing the population back to the guerrillas. In southwestern Luzon, the guerrillas withdrew the population from the Army-occupied towns. In southeastern Luzon, Malvar and Cailles relied on support from the elites and the intimidation of collaborators.

This disunity in the conduct of the guerrilla war is even more apparent if we look at the guerrillas' civil organization or infrastructure. There were certainly revolutionary supporters in most towns in Luzon throughout the Philippine War. It is also probable that if there were no American garrisons, or if the post commanders were lax, a guerrilla band could have probably collected taxes, secured supplies, and even sought shelter in most outlying *barrios* on the island throughout 1900 and 1901. But it could not have done this for long without fear of being denounced unless there was a well-developed system of compliant civic officials, tax collectors, and militiamen. Such a system existed only in the First District, Department of Northern Luzon, and the Second District, Department of Southern Luzon. In the Third District, Department of Southern Luzon, and the Fourth District, Department of Northern Luzon, no such system was developed and the occupied towns became centers of pro-American sentiment. Thus in both a military and an organizational sense, one of the characteristics of Filipino guerrilla resistance was its lack of uniformity.

It also appears that, from the Filipino side, the Philippine War was not a "people's war" either in the Maoist sense or the sense that it had the support of the vast majority of the Filipino people. This is not to say that the majority of the Filipino population did not want independence, but rather that the existing revolutionary leadership was unable to maintain a hold on Filipino loyalty. The U.S. Army's constant presence among the population, its efforts to implement civil government and social reforms, and its ability to coerce Filipinos through property destruction, imprisonment, and, in several instances, physical abuse proved stronger than revolutionary ideology or intimidation. In every district studied here, with the exception of the Tagalog region, the Army was able to enlist and utilize a substantial number of Filipino supporters. Some of these were ethnic or religious groups disenchanted with the abuses or policies of Aguinaldo's government. They joined the Americans for reasons that they viewed as more important than the cause of independence. In the First District, the Guardia de Honor allied with the Army to protect itself from revolutionary persecution. In the Fourth District, a number of Ilocanos joined the Americans both from fear of Tagalog domination and because the guerrillas had murdered their leader. In the Bicol region, many *presidentes* and townspeople, including a substantial number of policemen and volunteers, joined the Americans to protect their towns. Only in the Second District, thanks to the strong support of the *principales* for the revolutionary leaders, did the Army face a united population.

The Army was often able to enlist the aid of provincial elites against the guerrillas. These were not the "plutocrats" or *ilustrados* who have been criticized by Filipino nationalist scholars, but rather *presidentes*, civic officials, merchants, and landowners. These people viewed the war as disruptive, and revolutionary control as either undesirable or not worth the necessary sacrifices. The U.S. Army's growing willingness and ability to inflict social, economic, and physical pressure forced these Filipinos to accommodate themselves to American rule or risk destruction. In many cases, Army civil governments and reforms demonstrated the benevolent aspects of American rule or allowed these people to retain most of their privileged status. Guerrilla terrorism alienated them, and in some towns, such as Bucay, Abra, these *principales* were drawn into a virtual civil war against the guerrillas. The support of these provincial leaders, who also provided the bulk of support for the revolutionaries, was a vital factor in the Army victory and indicates both the divisions within Philippine society and the lack of unanimous popular support for the revolutionaries throughout Luzon.

The Army also received either active help or passive cooperation from many Filipino clergymen. Only in the First District, and then only in Ilocos Norte where Aglipay was in the field, did religious issues play a leading role in the resistance. Even in this district, the Americans, and especially Young, were able to enlist the clergy's aid in the pacification campaign. In the Fourth District there are no references to clerical hostility to the Americans. In the Third District, the clergy, with the exception of four guerrilla-priests, often aided American pacification. In the Second District, some of the clergy, perhaps reflecting either their own political views or their position as part of the provincial elite, opposed the Americans. Others, however, collaborated with the Army and helped win over their parishioners to American rule. Thus, although it is clear that some clergymen were active guerrillas, there is insufficient evidence to support the conclusion that the clergy as a corporate body supported the guerrillas. Most of the evidence in Army operational records seems to indicate an opposite conclusion: as a corporate body the clergy was more likely to cooperate with the Americans than with the revolutionaries. John Schumacher has argued convincingly that the Filipino clergy was initially one of the most revolutionary groups in the islands. However, as the Army demonstrated its ability to hold territory, the clergy, in common with their parishioners, gradually abandoned their revolutionary sentiments and came to an accommodation with American rule.

The U.S. Army showed itself a competent counterinsurgency force able to adjust and adapt to the challenges it faced in the Philippines. A key to this success was the ability of officers to construct pragmatic pacification policies designed to meet the realities of the guerrilla war in their towns, provinces, and districts. Although they received some guidance from Manila, they were given both the freedom and the opportunity to adopt centralized policies to their needs in their regions. In many cases they did not hesitate to reject policies that they knew would be impractical. Army civil government is one example of this regional adaptation of central policies. In the First District, the one district where the headquarters in Manila's insistence on civil government as the primary means of pacification was rigidly followed, it was quickly abandoned in the face of guerrilla resistance. Funston refused even to begin organizing civil government until the Fourth District was virtually pacified. In the Bicol region, Brig. Gen. James M. Bell developed his own form of civil organization which was both practical and simple.

Another aspect of Army flexibility was the willingness of regional officers to use Filipino auxiliaries. These officers were quick to form alliances with groups and individuals in order to secure the tranquillity of their areas. The clearest example of this was in La Union province, where the Army allied with the Guardia de Honor against the guerrillas. Funston's use of the Ilocano Scouts and the use of Bicol volunteers in the Third District are further illustrations. Individual officers often carried out these actions in the face of obstruction from Manila or Departmental Headquarters. Army officers in the provinces ignored their lack of official support, however, and developed informal units of auxiliaries and volunteers.

The study of the Army's pacification of the Philippines offers many lessons for military theorists in the field of guerrilla warfare. A pre-Maoist rural insurgency was defeated by an Army lacking a strong centralized counterinsurgency strategy. Indeed, the key to the Army's success was its lack of adherence to rigid doctrines or theories and the willingness of its officers to experiment with novel pacification schemes. By relying, albeit unintentionally, on the intelligence and ability of its garrison and provincial commanders, the U.S. Army threw the burden of pacification on the very people who had to deal with it. In the Philippines there were no helicopters or radio communications to insure that each subordinate followed his instructions to the letter. Most officers were isolated, and in some areas it took almost six months for an officer's superiors to read his situation reports and comment on them. This lack of official control aided pacification. It not only forced individual officers to be responsible for the pacification of their areas, but also prevented interference from their superiors, particularly in Manila.

Another aspect of Army pacification important to current guerrilla studies is the value of experience. Throughout the Philippine War, Army officers and their troops were kept in one district, often in the same town, for much of their term of service. They learned to deal not only with the problems of terrain and climate but with the local guerrilla resistance and the local population. While they complained bitterly of their isolation and lack of support, this isolation and the smallness of the garrisons they commanded forced them to establish contacts among the population. After serving in one area for a few months, they soon developed a practical understanding of the key obstacles to pacification and the best methods to overcome them. Their extended service allowed them the opportunity to experiment with innovative and individualized counterinsurgency methods. The rapid end of the guerrilla war in Luzon attests to their success.

A final lesson for students of guerrilla warfare is the necessity of achieving a decisive military victory over guerrilla forces. Although benevolent policies such as education, self-government, and social reforms may win over the populace and demonstrate an alternative to the revolutionaries, they cannot succeed until military superiority is achieved. In all four of the districts studied in this book, the Army attempted to implement nonmilitary pacification policies. These were crucial in obtaining support from the Filipino populace, especially key minorities and social classes. At the same time, the Army could not fully develop these policies until the guerrillas had been defeated or neutralized. As long as the guerrillas could rely on civilian support, whether inspired by patriotic motives or fear, pacification was impossible. It was only when the Army could separate the guerrillas from the civilians and prevent the guerrillas from disrupting civil organization that social reform was possible. Officers in the Philippines, no matter how benevolent their intentions, realized that the military objective, the defeat of the guerrillas, was the most essential of their tasks.

Notes

Forms and Abbreviations Used in Citations

The majority of the material for this book can be found in the following record groups at the National Archives: in Washington, D.C., Records of the Adjutant General's Office (Record Group 94); Records of the Office of the Inspector General (Record Group 159); Records of the Bureau of Insular Affairs (Record Group 350); Records of U.S. Army Mobile Units, 1821–1942 (Record Group 391); Records of U.S. Army Overseas Operations and Commands, 1898–1942 (Record Group 395); in Suitland, Maryland, Records of the Judge Advocate General's Office (Record Group 153). To provide ease of reference, citations from these sources will give the number of the record group and, where applicable, the series number. For example, the citation 395/5583 refers to Record Group 395, series 5583, and the citation 94/117 refers to Record Group 94, series 117. Citations for each Record Group 395 series will be identified the first time they appear by the title given to the series which appears in the National Archives, "Preliminary Inventory of the Records of U.S. Army Overseas Operations and Commands, 1898–1942 (Record Group 395)," and thereafter as 395/series number.

Abbreviations

1D	First District
2D	Second District
3D	Third District
3SB	Third Separate Brigade
4D	Fourth District
8th A.C.	Eighth Army Corps
Adj.	Adjutant
AG	Adjutant General
AAG	Assistant Adjutant General
AAAG	Acting Assistant Adjutant General
ANJ	Army and Navy Journal
Bk	Book

Brig.   Brigade
Btln.   Battalion
C.G.   Commanding General
ChAst   Chief Assistant
C.O.   Commanding Officer
C.S.   Chief of Staff
Div.   Division
DivPhil   Division of the Philippines
DMI   Division of Military Information
DNL   Department of Northern Luzon
D.P.   Department of the Pacific
DSL   Department of Southern Luzon
G.C.M.   General Court-martial
G.O.   General Order
Hq   Headquarters
IB   Independent Brigade
Inf.   Infantry
I.O.   Intelligence Officer
LR   Letters Received
LS   Letters Sent
MilSec   Military Secretary
n.d.   No Date
OCA   Office of Chief Assistant
OMG   Office of the Military Governor
OMI   Office of Military Intelligence
P.B.   Provisional Brigade
P.L.   Presidente Local
PIR   Philippine Insurgent Records
PIR SD   Philippine Insurgent Records, Selected Documents
S-D   Subdistrict
SMG   Secretary to the Military Governor
TS   Telegrams Sent
U.S.V.   U.S. Volunteers
WD   War Department Reports

Chapter One

1. Cosmas, *An Army for Empire*, p. 117.

2. Maj. Gen. Wesley Merritt to William McKinley, 15 May 1898, U.S. Army, *Correspondence Relating to the War with Spain*, 2:646 (hereafter cited as *CWS*).

3. All quotations from William McKinley to Secretary of War, 19 May 1898, *CWS*, 2:676–78. Gates, *Schoolbooks and Krags*, pp. 6–7.

4. Trask, *War with Spain*, pp. 369–90, 404, 439–41, 470; Cosmas, *An Army for Empire*, pp. 117–21; Gates, *Schoolbooks and Krags*, pp. 3–7; Welch, *Response to Imperialism*, pp. 3–10.

5. Phelan, *Hispanization of the Philippines*; LeRoy, *Americans in the Philippines*, 1:6–82; Oades, "Social and Economic Background of Philippine Nationalism"; Larkin, "Philippine History Reconsidered," pp. 613–24; Wickberg, *Chinese in Philippine Life*; Zaide, *Philippine Revolution*; Figuracion, "Background and Development of Philippine Nationalism"; Kalaw, *Philippine Politics*, pp. 1–68; Schumacher, *Revolutionary Clergy*, pp. 1–47. The U.S. War Department, *Pronouncing Gazetteer*, contains a wealth of information about the Philippines in 1903.

6. Agoncillo, *Revolt of the Masses*; Ileto, *Payson and Revolution*, pp. 93–139; Kalaw, *Philippine Politics*, pp. 68–93; Kennon, "Katipunan of the Philippines," pp. 208–20; Guerrero, "Understanding Philippine Revolutionary Mentality," pp. 240–56; Schumacher, "Recent Perspectives," pp. 447–54; Fernandez, *Philippine Republic*, pp. 13–23; LeRoy, *Americans in the Philippines*, 1:82–90, 100–101; 119–20; James A. LeRoy to Capt. John R. M. Taylor, 16 May 1904, PIR SD 1306.1. John R. M. Taylor provides an interesting perspective in Taylor, *Philippine Insurrection*, pp. 27–34 FZ, 80–100 FZ, 1–8 LY. Taylor's work, which consists of a two-volume history and three volumes of documents or exhibits, was never published, hence the unique pagination system. It exists on microfilm at the National Archives, Microcopy 254, PIR, reel 9.

7. Achútegui and Bernad, *Aguinaldo*, p. 48.

8. Zaide, *Philippine Revolution*, pp. 141–52; Fernandez, *Philippine Republic*, pp. 27–31; Agoncillo, *Revolt of the Masses*; Aguinaldo and Pacis, *A Second Look at America*, pp. 18–28; Bain, *Sitting in Darkness*, pp. 154–73; Ragsdale, "Coping with the Yankees," pp. 127–31; Welch, *Response to Imperialism*, pp. 11–12; Taylor, *Philippine Insurrection*, pp. 27–33 FZ.

9. "Decree—Regulations for the Organization of the Sandahatan Forces," 11 November 1897, Taylor, *Philippine Insurrection*, Exhibit 50, pp. 52–55 LY.

10. Zaide, *Philippine Revolution*, pp. 153–66; Fernandez, *Philippine Republic*, pp. 32–47; Aguinaldo and Pacis, *A Second Look at America*, pp. 27–28; Schumacher, *Revolutionary Clergy*, pp. 48–64; Ileto, *Payson and Revolution*, pp. 130–39, 155–95; LeRoy, *Americans in the Philippines*, 1:79–138; Taylor, *Philippine Insurrection*, pp. 27–40 FZ, 11–79 LY, "Constitution of Biac-na-bató," 5 November 1897, ibid., Exhibit 47, pp. 49–51 LY; Achútegui and Bernad, *Aguinaldo*, pp. 422–553.

11. "Untitled," Exhibit 66, p. 68 LY, and Ferdinand Macabulos, "Statement," 10 July 1898, Exhibit 130, pp. 50–1 MG, both in Taylor, *Philippine Insurrection*; Trask, *War with Spain*, pp. 398–410; Fernandez, *Philippine Republic*, pp. 47–51, 129–42; Ragsdale, "Coping with the Yankees," pp. 28–54; Ataviado, *Philippine Revolution in the Bicol Region*; Owen, "Winding Down the War in Albay," pp. 557–61; May, "Filipino Resistance," pp. 533–36; Larkin, *Pampangans*, pp. 119–28; Chaput, "Leyte Leadership in the Revolution," pp. 3–5; Schreurs, "Surigao, from General Aguinaldo to General Bates," pp. 57–68; Guerrero, "Luzon at War."

12. Fernandez, *Philippine Republic*, pp. 59–71; Trask, *War with Spain*, p. 404; Braisted, *United States Navy*, pp. 42–47; Spector, *Admiral of the New Empire*, pp. 88–90; Gould, *Spanish-American War and President McKinley*, p. 61; Cosmas, *An Army for Empire*, p. 192; Welch, *Response to Imperialism*, pp. 12–14; "Statement of Admiral George S. Dewey, U.S.N.," U.S. Congress, Senate, *Affairs in the Philippines*, pp. 2926–84 (hereafter cited as Senate, *Affair*); Aguinaldo and Pacis, *A Second Look at America*, pp. 29–66; Emilio Aguinaldo, "Untitled," Taylor, *Philippine Insurrection*,

Exhibit 2, pp. 2–8 MG; Emilio Aguinaldo, "To all Civilized Nations and Especially to the Great North American Republic," ibid., Exhibit 71, pp. 71–73 LY; Zaide, *Philippine Revolution*, pp. 173–74, 215–18. The correspondence between Dewey and his superiors can be found in U.S. Congress, House, *Annual Reports of the Navy Department . . . 1898*, pp. 102–13.

13. Brig. Gen. Thomas Anderson to AG, U.S. Army, 18 and 21 July 1898, *CWS*, 2:809. For Anderson's relations with Aguinaldo, see Gates, *Schoolbooks and Krags*, pp. 18–20; "Report of General Anderson," 29 August 1898, U.S. Congress, House, *Annual Reports of the War Department . . . 1898*, pp. 54–56.

14. "Report of Gen. Wesley Merritt," 31 August 1898, U.S. Congress, House, *Annual Reports of the War Department . . . 1989*, p. 40.

15. Brig. Gen. Thomas A. Anderson to AG, U.S. Army, 14 July 1898, *CWS*, 2:779–80.

16. Trask, *War with Spain*, pp. 411–22; Gates, *Schoolbooks and Krags*, pp. 17–22, 32–34; Taylor, *Philippine Insurrection*, pp. 34–40 AJ; Cosmas, *An Army for Empire*, pp. 236–42; Sexton, *Soldiers in the Sun*, pp. 36–46; Emilio Aguinaldo to Brig. Gen. Thomas V. Anderson, 13 and 14 August 1898, *CWS*, 2:813–14; Emilio Aguinaldo to Maj. Gen. Wesley Merritt, 21 August 1898, ibid., 2:817.

17. Maj. Gen. Wesley Merritt, "Memorandum for Major Bell," n.d., *CWS*, 2:818. Merritt's proclamation can be found in House, *Annual Reports of the War Department . . . 1898*, pp. 49–50.

18. Morgan, *William McKinley*, p. 368; Leech, *In the Days of McKinley*, pp. 209–12, 323–28, 345–47, 361–63; May, *Imperial Democracy*, pp. 243–62; LaFeber, *New Empire*, pp. 361–62, 408–17; Gould, *Spanish-American War and President McKinley*, pp. 63, 85, 99–100; Welch, *Response to Imperialism*, pp. 6–10; Trask, *War with Spain*, pp. 452–54.

19. William McKinley to Secretary of War, 21 December 1898, *CWS*, 2:858–59.

20. G.O. 3, Hq, D.P., 8th A.C., 9 August 1898, House, *Annual Reports of the War Department . . . 1898*, p. 50.

21. Col. Irving Hall to AAG, 2d Btln. 2d Brig., 18 August 1898, ibid., p. 78; Gates, *Schoolbooks and Krags*, p. 32; Miller, *"Benevolent Assimilation,"* pp. 58–59; Sexton, *Soldiers in the Sun*, pp. 64–78.

22. Report of Major General E. S. Otis, U.S. Army, Commanding the Division of the Philippines, and Military Governor of the Philippine Islands, September 1, 1899, to May 5, 1900, in U.S. Congress, House, *Annual Reports of the War Department . . . 1900*, p. 203. For an overview of Otis's tenure in Manila, see Bolton, "Military Diplomacy and National Liberation," pp. 99–104; Gates, *Schoolbooks and Krags*, p. 32.

23. Maj. Gen. Elwell S. Otis to AG, Washington, 1, 2, and 4 January 1898, *CWS*, 2:866–68.

24. William McKinley to Maj. Gen. Elwell S. Otis and Admiral George Dewey, 8 January 1899, ibid., 2:873.

25. May, "Why the United States Won the Philippine-American War," p. 365; Agoncillo, *Malolos*.

26. Emilio Aguinaldo, "Proclamation," Taylor, *Philippine Insurrection*, Exhibit 399, pp. 14–15 KU; Fernandez, *Philippine Republic*, pp. 66–70, 104–14; Zaide, *Philippine Revolution*, pp. 199–201; Maj. Gen. Elwell S. Otis to AG, U.S. Army, 12 January

1899, *CWS*, 2:908–9; May, "Why the United States Won the Philippine-American War," pp. 368–69.

27. Sexton, *Soldiers in the Sun*, pp. 79–90; Gates, *Schoolbooks and Krags*, pp. 76–77.

28. Sand-30, "Trench, Parapet, or the 'Open,' " p. 480.

29. Sexton, *Soldiers in the Sun*, pp. 103–61; *ANJ* 37 (7 April and 2 June 1900); Gates, *Schoolbooks and Krags*, pp. 79–114; Ragsdale, "Coping with the Yankees," pp. 212–18.

30. Taylor, *Philippine Insurrection*, p. 78 AJ; Emilio Aguinaldo, "Proclamation," 20 June 1898, Exhibit 37, ibid., pp. 29–30 MG; Emilio Aguinaldo, "Proclamation," 30 July 1898, Exhibit 133, ibid., pp. 52–53 MG.

31. Foronda, intro. to Kalaw, *An Acceptable Holocaust*, p. vi.

32. Taylor, *Philippine Insurrection*, pp. 32 AJ, 76–91 AJ; Alejandrino, *Price of Freedom*; Wilcox, *Through Luzon on Highways and Byways*, p. 194; Zaide, *Philippine Revolution*, pp. 277–81.

33. Alejandrino, *Price of Freedom*, pp. 120–24, 131–33, 141–59; Lt. C. N. Murphy, "Death of Antonio Luna," PIR SD 861.3; Antonio Mabini to Ambrosio Moxica, 26 April 1899, PIR SD 1021.2.

34. *WD* 1900 1:2:63, 169; *ANJ* 36 (4 March 1899); "Autobiography," Corbin Papers.

35. "Report of Major-General E. S. Otis, U.S. Army, Commanding the Division of the Philippines and Military Governor of the Philippine Islands," *WD* 1900 1:4:199–347; "Report of an Expedition to the Provinces North of Manila, P.I., during the Months of September, October, November, and December, 1899, Maj. Gen. Henry T. Lawton, Commanding," ibid., 1:6:6–417, includes "Report of an Expedition into the Northern Provinces of Luzon, October 11, 1899, to January 5, 1900, by Brig. Gen. S. B. M. Young, U.S.V., Commanding," pp. 262–94; "Report of Operations of Second Division, Eighth Army Corps, From May 31, 1899, to April 6, 1900, by Maj. Gen. Arthur MacArthur, U.S.V., Commanding," ibid., 1:8:14–526.

36. *WD* 1900 1:4:366–67, 369–95; "Report of an Expedition into the Province of Cavite, January 4 to 31, 1900, by Brig. Gen. Loyd Wheaton, U.S.V., Commanding," ibid., 1:6:625–39; "Report of Operations in the Provinces of Cavite, Morong, Batangas, Laguna, and Tayabas, January 4 to February 8, 1900, by Maj. Gen. J. C. Bates, U.S.V., Commanding First Division, Eighth Army Corps," ibid., 1:6:640–59; "Report of Operations of Schwan's Expeditionary Brigade in the Provinces of Cavite, Batangas, Laguna, and Tayabas, January 4 to February 8, 1900, by Brig. Gen. Theodore Schwan, U.S.V., Commanding," ibid., 1:5:387–564.

37. *WD* 1900 1:4:395–96; "Report of an Expedition to Occupy and Open Hemp Ports in the Philippine Islands, January 18 to April 8, 1900, by Brig. Gen. W. A. Kobbé, U.S.V.," ibid., 1:7:7–41.

38. "Report of an Expedition to the Provinces of North and South Camarines, February 12 to March 1, 1900, by Maj. Gen. J. C. Bates, U.S.V.," ibid., 1:6:660–65.

39. Taylor, *Philippine Insurrection*, pp. 29–32 HS, 47–51 HS; Gates, *Schoolbooks and Krags*, p. 128; *WD* 1900 1:5:59–60.

40. "Annual Report of Maj. Gen. Arthur MacArthur, U.S.V., Commanding Division of the Philippines, Military Governor in the Philippine Islands," *WD* 1900 1:5:59–76; "Orders for a Guerrilla Column commanded by Major Villamor," 1900,

PIR SD 51.7; Taylor, *Philippine Insurrection*, p. 46 HS; "Plan of Combat," January 1900, Exhibit 1030, ibid., p. 41 GV; Maj. Gen. Pantaleon García, "Instructions for Guerrillas and Flying Columns," 25 November 1899, Exhibit 1020, ibid., p. 37 GV; Ambrosio Flores, "Instructions for the Organization of a Corps of Guerrilla Militia," 5 January 1900, PIR SD 1198.10; Brig. Gen. Urbano Lacuna to Majors and Captains Commanding Companies of 1st and 2d Btlns., 7 December 1900, PIR SD 658.4; Maj. Tomas Tagunton to Captains Commanding Guerrilla Btlns., 29 November 1900, PIR SD 658.3 For the importance attached to the U.S. presidential elections and the adoption of operations designed to influence them, see Taylor, *Philippine Insurrection*, p. 31 HS; Brig. Gen. Juan Cailles to Col. Pablo Astilla, 6 August 1900, Exhibit 1084, ibid., p. 57 GV; Emilio Aguinaldo to Calixto Villacorta, 27 June 1900, Exhibit 997, ibid., p. 27 GV; Col. Teodoro Sandico to Lt. Col. Casimiro Tinio, 20 July 1900, Exhibit 1080, ibid., p. 56 GV; Emilio Aguinaldo to Brig. Gen. Isidro Torres, 8 July 1900, PIR SD 527.8; Emilio Aguinaldo to Brig. Gen. Francisco Macubulos, 27 June 1900, PIR SD 527.2; Emilio Aguinaldo, "To the Filipino Generals, Field and Line Officers, and Soldiers," 29 October 1900, PIR SD 1037.2; Ragsdale, "Coping with the Yankees," pp. 304–9.

41. Gates, *Schoolbooks and Krags*, pp. 97–98, 156–57. For the organization of the "new" Katipunan, see Taylor, *Philippine Insurrection*, p. 33 HS; Emilio Aguinaldo, "To the Katipunan," 15 July 1898, Exhibit 60, ibid., pp. 37–38 MG; San Miguel to Acting Military Chief, 6 December 1899, Exhibit 1022, ibid., p. 37 GV; Ambrosio Flores, "Instructions," 5 January 1900, PIR SD 1198.10; "Reglamento del Katipunan de los Hijos del Pueblo," 28 September 1900, PIR SD 673.1; Villamor, *Inedita Cronica*, pp. 69–72; Perfecto Clemente to Monico Andres, 28 September 1900, PIR SD 673.1.

42. Capt. Delphey T. E. Casteel to Wife, 14–20 October 1900, Casteel Papers.

43. Major Edgar Z. Steever to C.O., Vigan, 20 July 1900, 395/5583, Vigan, Ilocos Norte, LR, Feb. 1900 to Dec. 1902, LR 1286. Gates, *Schoolbooks and Krags*, pp. 156–66; May, "Why the United States Won the Philippine-American War," pp. 361, 365–71; May, "Filipino Resistance," pp. 536–48; *ANJ* 38 (20 October 1900).

44. *WD* 1900 1:5:61–62; Ileto, *Payson and Revolution*, pp. 197–209; Isobel Abaya, "Ilocanos Proclamation," 1900, PIR SD 521.1; "Proclamation of Lt. Col. Emilio Zurbano, Military Governor of Tayabas, to his Fellow Citizens," 23 April 1901, Taylor, *Philippine Insurrection*, Exhibit 1154, p. 81 GV; Gates, *Schoolbooks and Krags*, pp. 161–62; Gatewood, *Black Americans*, p. 287; Lt. Col. Emilio Zurbano, "To the Worthy North American Citizens in these Islands," 25 September 1900, Taylor, *Philippine Insurrection*, Exhibit 1097, pp. 61–62 GV.

45. Felipe Calderon to the U.S. Philippine Commission, 25 November 1900, Root Papers, Special Correspondence. For Filipino terrorism and U.S. reaction, see Gates, *Schoolbooks and Krags*, pp. 164–69; Senate, *Affairs*, pp. 69–70; Simeon Villa to Chiefs of the Philippine Guerrillas, 15 November 1900, Taylor, *Philippine Insurrection*, Exhibit 1115, p. 68 GV; Worcester, *Philippines Past and Present*, pp. 226–47; *ANJ* 38 (8 September 1900); LeRoy, *Americans in the Philippines*, 2:228–46. For a discussion on "agitational terrorism," see Thomas P. Thornton, "Terror as a Weapon of Political Agitation," in Eckstein, ed., *Internal War: Problems and Approaches*, pp. 71–99.

46. Sturtevant, *Popular Uprisings*, pp. 115–29; Brig. Gen. Manuel Noriel, "Proclamation," 1 October 1900, Taylor, *Philippine Insurrection*, Exhibit 1100, pp. 62–63 GV; *ANJ* 37 (14 and 26 May 1900); Col. Luther Hare to Anon., 28 January 1900,

endorsement on report by Maj. Thomas Ashburne, 94/117, 33d Inf. LS Bk 1, LS 24; "Report of Operations on San Luis Road Against Ladrones," Maj. James H. Parker to AG, 2D, DSL, 26 April 1900, 395/2408, 2D, DSL, LR, Nov. 1899 to Apr. 1901, Box 1; Col. William Howe to AG, IB, 1st Div., 8th A.C., 6 April 1900, 395/2420, 3D, DSL, LR, Jan. 1900 to Nov. 1901, LR 6. General Pio del Pilar was perceived as a bandit by many American officers, see Sexton, *Soldiers in the Sun*, pp. 149–50.

47. Funston, *Memories of Two Wars*, p. 386. May, "Filipino Resistance," pp. 548–51; Schreurs, "Surigao, from General Aguinaldo to General Bates," pp. 67–68; Chaput, "Leyte Leadership in the Revolution," pp. 6–9; Brig. Gen. Manuel Tinio to Lt. Col. Vicente Salazar, 22 April 1901, PIR SD 909.8; Brig. Gen. Urbano Lacuna to Adj., Btln. Lorenzo Tomayo, 19 May 1900, PIR SD 345.3.

48. William McKinley to Secretary of War, 21 December 1898, *CWS*, 2:859.

49. *WD* 1900 1:4:448. For similar sentiments, see *ANJ* 37 (9 June 1900); Maj. Gen. Elwell S. Otis to AG, Washington, D.C., 15 February 1900, *CWS*, 2:1144; Maj. Gen. Elwell S. Otis to Secretary of War, 10 April 1900, ibid., 2:1159; "Statement of General Elwell S. Otis," Senate, *Affairs*, pp. 732–73. Otis's optimism was shared by others, see *ANJ* 37 (28 April, 26 May, 9 June 1900). For the division of Luzon into departments and districts, see Hq, DivPhil, G.O. 1, 7 May 1900, in *WD* 1900 1:4:442–44; *ANJ* 37 (7 May and 9 June 1900).

50. Maj. George T. Langhorne to Col. Robert L. Bullard, 28 July 1900, 395/2408, Box 1, LS 381. For text of G.O. 40 and G.O. 43, see Senate, *Affairs*, pp. 111–28; Lt. William R. Smedberg to Capt. William A. Burnside, 7 January 1900, 395/2148, 1D, DNL, Letters and Telegrams Sent, Dec. 1899 to Apr. 1900, LS 27.

51. Brig. Gen. Samuel B. M. Young to MilSec, 28 June 1900, 395/2167, 1D, DNL, LS Relating to Civil Affairs, Jan. 1900 to Sept. 1901, LS Bk 1, LS 259.

52. *ANJ* 37 (9 June 1900); *WD* 1900 1:4:448–561; Gates, *Schoolbooks and Krags*, pp. 128–49; Owen, "Winding Down the War in Albay," pp. 579–85.

53. *WD* 1900 1:4:61; quote "useful agencies" from Lt. Col. Enoch Crowder to C.G., DSL, 5 February 1901, 395/2330, DSL, General Correspondence, Apr. 1900 to Nov. 1901, LR CA225; Gates, *Schoolbooks and Krags*, pp. 194–95. For MacArthur's criticism of Otis's strategy, see William H. Taft to Elihu Root, 14 July 1900 and 18 August 1900, Taft Papers, series 21.

54. Maj. Gen. Arthur MacArthur to AG, Washington, D.C., 31 August 1900, *CWS*, 2:1203–4; *WD* 1900 1:5:65–66; *ANJ* 38 (29 December 1900); Ragsdale, "Coping with the Yankees," pp. 298–304. In the Department of Northern Luzon, for example, of the 1,241 surrenders over half came from the pacified Second District while the troublesome First District had only 78, see Hq, DNL to SMG, 17 September 1900, 395/2130, Hq, DNL, LS, Apr. to Dec. 1900, LS 674.

55. Brig. Gen. Frederick Funston to AG, DNL, 8 October 1900, 395/2261, 4D, DNL, Letters and Endorsements Sent, Jan. 1900 to Oct. 1901; Lt. Col. James M. Parker to Col. Arthur Wagner, 4 October 1900, 395/2330, LR A1926.

56. Lt. Samuel P. Lyon to Mary P. Lyon, 13 January 1901, Lyon Papers.

57. William H. Taft to Elihu Root, 14 July 1900, Taft Papers, series 21.

58. Maj. Gen. Arthur MacArthur to AG, 19 September 1900, *CWS*, 2:1211.

59. Capt. John L. Jordan to Mother, 30 September 1900, Jordan Papers; Maj. Gen. Arthur MacArthur to AG, 28 September 1900, *CWS*, 2:1214.

60. *ANJ* 38 (10 November 1900).

61. Elihu Root to Secretary of State, 2 November 1900, 94/349329.

62. *WD* 1901 1:4:91–92. For a copy of G.O. 100, see Senate, *Affairs*, pp. 971–82. For MacArthur's intention to issue it, see Maj. Gen. Arthur MacArthur to AG, Washington, D.C., 25 December 1900, *CWS*, 2:1137–38. For an analysis of G.O. 100, see Hartigan, *Lieber's Code and the Law of War.*

63. *WD* 1901 1:4:90. Brig. Gen. Thomas H. Barry to C.G., DNL, 395/2133, DNL, General Correspondence, 'A' Series, Apr. 1900 to Nov. 1901, Box 18, LR 20693.

64. Gates, *Schoolbooks and Krags*, p. 206. Sexton, *Soldiers in the Sun*, p. 251; Taylor, *Philippine Insurrection*, pp. 19–20 HS.

65. Lt. Col. James H. Parker to Theodore Roosevelt, 18 November 1900, series 1, reel 7, Roosevelt Papers; Brig. Gen. Samuel B. M. Young to AG, DNL. 17 January 1901, 395/2150, 1D, DNL, Letters and Telegrams Sent, Apr. 1900 to Nov. 1901, vol. 4, LS 83; Sherwood Coleman to Theodore Roosevelt, 10 January 1901, Roosevelt Papers, series 1, reel 8; Brig. Gen. Merritt Barber to C.G., DNL, 22 September 1900, 395/2130, LS 702; Col. Edward B. Williston, Provost Marshal to C.G., DNL, 20 June 1900, 395/2269, 4D, DNL, LR, Apr. 1900 to Oct. 1901. For the lack of a previous American policy on prisoners, see LeRoy, *Americans in the Philippines*, 2:256. For the issuance of G.O. 100 in other areas before MacArthur's proclamation, see G.O. 24, Hq, DSL, 5 June 1900, in Senate, *Affairs*, p. 40; Funston, *Memories of Two Wars*, pp. 331–35; *ANJ* 37 (14 April 1900); "Proceedings of a Board of Officers Convened Pursuant to a Telegram from Hdqrs. 1st Dist., Dept. Northern Luzon, dated Vigan, P.I., Nov. 24, 1900," 21 December 1900, 395/4047, Laoag, Ilocos Norte, Letters and Telegrams Received, 1900–2, LR 4496.

66. *WD* 1901 1:4:94–96, 114–25; Hq, DivPhil to C.G., DNL, 11 March 1901, 395/2269, Box 2. For deportation policy, see William H. Taft to Elihu Root, 18 September 1900, Taft Papers, series 21; Maj. Gen. Henry Corbin to Maj. Gen. Arthur MacArthur, 26 December 1900, Roosevelt Papers, series 1, reel 8. For new surrender policy, see Provost Marshal General to C.O., 2 January 1901, 395/2408, Box 3, LR 8. For the Federal party, see "Platform of the Federal Party December 21 1900," Senate, *Affairs*, pp. 310–19; Taylor, *Philippine Insurrection*, p. 46 HS; Steinberg, *Philippines*, pp. 45–48; Ragsdale, "Coping with the Yankees," pp. 316–19; PIR SD 899.

67. Maj. Gen. Arthur MacArthur to AG, Washington, D.C., 4 January 1901, *CWS*, 2:1241–42. Troop strength figures from 153/12184.

68. *WD* 1901 1:4:92–106; "Annual Report of Maj. Gen. Adna R. Chaffee, U.S. Army, Commanding Division of the Philippines, and Military Governor of the Philippine Islands," *WD* 1901 1:7:8–11. For a summation of the 1901 campaign, see Gates, *Schoolbooks and Krags*, pp. 225–43.

69. Gates, *Schoolbooks and Krags*, pp. 238–39; Maj. Gen. Henry C. Corbin to Maj. Gen. Arthur MacArthur, 16 March 1901, *CWS*, 2:1259; Maj. Thomas Ward to Maj. Gen. Adna R. Chaffee, 21 June 1901, ibid., 2:1286. For Chaffee's plans and the organization of Separate Brigades, see *WD* 1902 1:9:187–88.

70. G.O. 66, 4 July 1902, *CWS*, 2: 1352–53. For the campaign in Samar see Gates, *Schoolbooks and Krags*, pp. 249–56; Schott, *Ordeal of Samar*; Fritz, "Before the 'Howling Wilderness,'" pp. 186–90; Welch, *Response to Imperialism*, pp. 138–41. Many

officers believed that the "Balangiga massacre" proved that the Philippines were not yet ready for civil government. The massacre was also cited as evidence that the Americans could not trust the Filipinos and as a justification for the implementation of more rigorous policies throughout the archipelago. The Samar campaign of 1901–2, which was conducted with great severity, furnished the antiimperialist press with a great deal of material for their charges that the Army was pursuing atrocious and brutal policies throughout the Philippines.

71. Welch, *Response to Imperialism*, pp. 133–47.

Chapter Two

1. *WD* 1900 1:4:334–35. James R. M. Taylor quoted this passage and asserted that "this is what took place everywhere else in the archipelago except in the extreme south," Taylor, *Philippine Insurrection*, p. 11 HS; Anon., "District of North Western Luzon, P.I.," *ANJ* 37 (14 April 1900); LeRoy, *Americans in the Philippines*, 2:204–5. A much condensed version of this chapter appeared in Linn, "Provincial Pacification in the Philippines, 1900–1901," *Military Affairs* 51 (April 1987):62–66.

2. Maj. Gen. Arthur MacArthur to AG, 30 April 1901, *CWS*, 2:1274. For Otis's view of northwestern Luzon and Philippine resistance after 1900 see Senate, *Affairs*, pp. 733–34; Maj. Gen. Elwell S. Otis to Secretary of War, 10 April 1900, *CWS*, 2:1159; *WD* 1900 1:4:448–49, 560–61.

3. Figures on population are taken from Brig. Gen. Samuel B. M. Young to AG, DNL, 7 September 1900, Young Papers, Box 6. Maj. John G. Ballance estimated the populations by province as Abra—36,523; Illocos Norte—140,443; Ilocos Sur—151,400; La Union—103,297. This gives a total of 431,663 inhabitants of whom 113,700 were males eighteen and over; see Maj. John G. Ballance to AG, DNL, 28 February 1901, 395/2167, vol. 3, LS 326; "Report of the Provincial Governor of Abra," 16 December 1901, 350/3599, "Abra" File; "Report of Aguedo Agbayani, Governor of the Province of Ilocos Norte, Luzon," 1 November 1902, 350/3601, "Ilocos Norte" File; "Report of Julio Agcaoli, April 2, 1903, giving for the year 1903 the General Conditions, etc., in the Province of Ilocos Norte," 2 April 1903, ibid. For the geography of the Ilocos regions see Wernstedt and Spencer, *Philippine Island World*, pp. 328–61. For a good account of climatic and geographic obstacles, see Lt. Col. Robert L. Howze to Chief Engineer of the Division, 9 July 1900, 395/4043, Laoag, Ilocos Norte, Letters and Telegrams Sent, Jan. 1900 to Dec. 1902, LS Bk 1.

4. "Memorial on Behalf of Isabel Abaya," 23 January 1899, PIR SD 682.2; Mariano Llanera to Emilio Aguinaldo, 7 August 1898, Taylor, *Philippine Insurrection*, Exhibit 88, p. 43 MG; "Events in December 1877," ibid., Exhibit 65, p. 65 LY; "S. S. Saturnus" File, PIR SD 1148.4; PIR SD 1024; Zaide, *Philippine Revolution*, p. 222.

5. Felipe Buencamino, "Notes of a trip of inspection," 3 April 1899, PIR SD 742.2; "Memoria de las defensas de Ambos Ilocos," 17 March 1899, PIR SD 687.1; "Memoria de las defensas Ilocanos-Union," PIR SD 687.3; Felipe Buencamino to Emilio Aguinaldo, 17 April 1899, PIR SD 679.12; Villamor, *Inedita Cronica*, pp. 9–11; Col. William S. McCaskey to Brig. Gen. J. Franklin Bell, 1901, 395/4043, LS Bk 5, LS 1792; Wilcox, *Through Luzon on Highways and Byways*, pp. 193–99. James LeRoy's

criticism of Wilcox as an observer should be noted, see LeRoy, *Americans in the Philippines*, 1:334–35.

6. *WD* 1900 1:6:277–88, 528–60; Maj. Peyton C. March to AG, Cavalry Brig., 1st Div., 8th A.C., 8 December 1899, *WD* 1900 1:6:330–34; Lt. Col. Robert L. Howze to AG, Cavalry Brig., 1st Div. and 8th A.C., 5 January 1900, 395/4043, LS Bk 1; "Report on the Defense of Vigan, Luzon, P.I., December 4, 1899, by Lieut. Col. James Parker, Forty-Fifth U.S. Volunteer Infantry," *WD* 1900 1:7:138–51; Tafton MS; Letter of 27 December 1899, Nixon Letters; McCutcheon, *Drawn from Memory*, pp. 161–65; Kalaw, *An Acceptable Holocaust*, pp. 49–55. According to Felipe Buencamino, Tinio had only 350 men at San Jacinto and lost 47, see Maj. James Parker to Maj. Gen. Samuel B. M. Young, 11 July 1902, Young Papers, Box 3, "Official Correspondence" File.

7. *WD* 1900 1:4:321–29, 449, 1:6:285. For indications of the exhaustion and scattering of American forces, see ibid., 1:6:330–33; *Jawbone* (February 1938).

8. For Otis's views of the importance of civil government and garrisoning as a means of pacification, see *WD* 1900 1:4:448–49, 560–61; *ANJ* 37 (16 June 1900).

9. Hq, DivPhil, G.O. 1, cited in *WD* 1900 1:4:442–44; *ANJ* 37 (2 February 1900). For the organization of the District of North-Western Luzon see G.O. 3, OMG of North-Western Luzon, 9 January 1900, 395/2172, 1D, DNL, General and Special Orders, Jan. to Apr. 1900.

10. For the quarrel between Otis and Young, see Sexton, *Soldiers in the Sun*, pp. 176–77; Brig. Gen. Samuel B. M. Young to Theodore Roosevelt, 1 April 1900; Brig. Gen. Samuel B. M. Young to Senator T. R. Carter, 1 May 1900; Capt. John G. Ballance to Brig. Gen. Samuel B. M. Young, 17 April 1900, all in Young Papers, Box 6, "Private File." For Young's comments on his "irritable" disposition, see Brig. Gen. Samuel B. M. Young to Marjorie and Elizabeth [daughters], 18 December 1899, Young Papers, "Uncatalogued Material." Quote "European nations" from Brig. Gen. Samuel B. M. Young to AG, DNL, 28 December 1900, 395/2150, LS Bk 3, LS 3421. Carefully selected portions of Young's suggestions can be found in "Report of Brig. Gen. J. Franklin Bell, Commanding First District, Department of Northern Luzon," *WD* 1901 1:5:30–36. John Gates believes that Young's proposals were the "most radical suggestions made by any officer," Gates, *Schoolbooks and Krags*, p. 189. For Otis's comments on Young's alarmism see Maj. Gen. Elwell S. Otis to Secretary of War, 10 April 1900, *CWS*, 2:1159.

11. Quote "I do not believe" from Brig. Gen. Samuel B. M. Young to Gen. George M. Sternberg, 7 April 1900, Young Papers, Box 6, "Private File." See also Brig. Gen. Samuel B. M. Young to MilSec, 28 June 1900, ibid., Box 6, "Private File," LS 143; Brig. Gen. Samuel B. M. Young to AG, DNL, 24 November 1900, 395/2133, LR 19208; Brig. Gen. Samuel B. M. Young to Secretary of Agriculture, 10 October 1900, ibid., LR 16268; Brig. Gen. Samuel B. M. Young to AG, DNL, 4 February 1901, 395/2167, vol. 3, LS 223.

12. Capt. John G. Ballance to C.O., Laoag, 7 February 1900, 395/2167, vol. 1, LS 16; Capt. John G. Ballance to AG, 28 February 1900, 395/2157, 1D, DNL, Letters and Telegrams Received, Dec. 1899 to Apr. 1900, LS 48; Brig. Gen. Samuel B. M. Young to C.S., 21 December 1899, *WD* 1900 1:4:323. Ballance was appointed chief of staff in December 1900 and in May 1901 was placed in command of the First

District, see Hq, 1D, DNL, G.O. 21, 17 December 1900 and G.O. 11, 25 May 1901, 395/2173, General Orders, Special Orders, and Circulars, Apr. 1900 to Nov. 1901.

13. Capt. John G. Ballance to AG, DNL, 13 September 1900, 395/2167, vol. 2, LS 570; *ANJ* 37 (2 February 1900); Lt. William Smedberg to Maj. Samuel M. Swigert, 20 December 1899, 395/2148; Lt. William Smedberg to Capt. George F. Hunter, 30 December 1899, ibid.; Brown, *Diary of a Soldier in the Philippines*, pp. 147–48; Brig. Gen. Samuel B. M. Young to William McKinley, 4 July 1900, Young Papers, "Private File," LS 152. For Young's reports on civil government see Brig. Gen. Samuel B. M. Young to Maj. Cunliffe H. Murray, 11 January 1900, 395/2167, vol. 1, LS 3; Brig. Gen. Samuel B. M. Young to AG, DNL, 6 May 1900, 395/2150, vol. 1, LS 166; Brig. Gen. Samuel B. M. Young to MilSec, 28 June 1900, and Brig. Gen. Samuel B. M. Young to William McKinley, 4 July 1900, Young Papers.

14. Capt. John G. Ballance to SMG, 16 April 1900, 395/2167, vol. 1, LS 120.

15. Brig. Gen. Samuel B. M. Young to MilSec, 28 June 1900, Young Papers; Capt. John G. Ballance to C.O., Laoag, 7 February 1900, 395/2167, vol. 1, LS 16. For samples of officers' reports on education see 395/2184, Descriptive Book of Towns in the Provinces of Ilocos Sur (north), Ilocos Sur (south), and Union, May to Nov. 1900. For other examples of Young's interest in education, see Brig. Gen. Samuel B. M. Young to William McKinley, 4 July 1900, Young Papers; Brig. Gen. Samuel B. M. Young to AG, DNL, 24 November 1900, 395/2133, LR 19208; Brig. Gen. Samuel B. M. Young to AG, DNL, 4 February 1901, 395/2167, vol. 3, LS 223.

16. Capt. John G. Ballance to C.O., Candon, 1 March 1900, 395/2157, LS 25; Lt. Col. Robert L. Howze to Capt. John G. Ballance, 20 May 1900, 395/4043, LS Bk 1; Brig. Gen. Samuel B. M. Young to MilSec, 11 January 1900, 395/2167, vol. 1, LS 3; Capt. Frank L. French to Post Adj., Laoag, 30 November 1900, 395/4047, Box 1, LR 447; "Province of Ilocos Norte-Laoag," 395/2180, Extracts of Monthly Reports Received from Inspecting Officers; Col. Lyman W. V. Kennon to ChAst, 1D, DNL, 10 February 1901, 395/2158, 1D, DNL, LR, Apr. 1900 to Oct. 1901, Box 24, LR 2763; *ANJ* 38 (25 May 1901); Maj. Thomas Q. Ashburn to AG, Vigan, 9 January 1900, 395/3061, Bangued, Abra, LS Relating to Civil Affairs, Jan. 1900 to Aug. 1901; Lt. William Coffey to Adj., 1st Btln., 33d Inf., 7 April 1900, 395/2157, LR 1269.

17. Brig. Gen. Samuel B. M. Young to MilSec, 28 June 1900, Young Papers. Lt. Col. Robert L. Howze to ChAst, 1D, DNL, 1 June 1900, 395/4043, LS Bk 1. For correspondence on the district's financial problems see 395/2167.

18. Capt. John Howard to Col. Robert L. Howze, 8 February 1900, 395/2167, vol. 1, LS 10.

19. Circular Letter no. 14, 14 August 1900, 395/2174, 1D, DNL, General Orders, Special orders, and Circulars, 1900–1901, Box 1. Brig. Gen. Samuel B. M. Young to William McKinley, 3 March 1900, Young Papers.

20. Brig. Gen. Samuel B. M. Young to William McKinley, 4 July 1900, Young Papers. See also Brig. Gen. Samuel B. M. Young to Lt. Col. Robert L. Howze, 13 March 1900, 395/2173; Lt. Col. Robert L. Howze to AG, D.P., 13 May 1900, 395/4043, LS Bk 1; Capt. George E. Dodd to Adj., Vigan, 27 June 1900, 395/5582, Vigan, Ilocos Sur, Registers of Letters and Telegrams Received, Feb. 1900 to Jan. 1903, LR 234; Capt. John G. Ballance to José Rivero, 25 July 1900, 395/2167, vol. 2,

LS 361; "Report of Lt. John W. Ward," encl. in Maj. John G. Ballance to C.O., Civil S-D, Vigan, 14 December 1900, 395/5589, Vigan, Ilocos Sur, LR Relating to the Civil Government, Mar. 1900 to Oct. 1901, Box 1, LR 994; Lt. Francisco Bendito to Jefe Americano del Destacamento de Bucay, 15 February 1901, 395/3064, Bangued, Abra, LR, 1900-1901; *ANJ* 37 (10 March 1900). For U.S. expeditions against the Igorrotes, see *WD* 1900 1:6:730–73; Tafton MS.

21. Col. William P. Duvall to ChAst, 28 May 1900, 395/5617, San Fernando, La Union, Letters, Telegrams, and Endorsements Sent, Jan. 1900 to Sept. 1906, LS Bk 1, LS 669. Col. William P. Duvall to Capt. John G. Ballance, 4 June 1900, ibid., LS 719; Maj. John G. Ballance to AG, DNL, 28 February 1901, 395/2167, vol. 3, LS 326.

22. Col. Luther R. Hare to AG, District of North-Western Luzon, 15 February 1900, 395/5578, Vigan, Ilocos Sur, Letters and Endorsements Sent, Feb. 1900 to Dec. 1902, vol. 1. Hare, in fact, continued to perceive the guerrillas as the "ladrone contingent" until he left the First District, see Col. Luther R. Hare to AG, 1D, DNL, 3 June 1900, ibid. For reports on early guerrilla activities, see Maj. Thomas Ashburn to Adj., 33d Inf., 22 February 1900, 395/2157, LS 629; Capt. Julio Tinio to P.L.'s of Taguidin, Sevilla, Santa Cruz, etc., 21 March 1900, PIR SD 598.1.

23. Brig. Gen. Manuel Tinio, "Proclamation," 20 March 1900, PIR SD 353.6, and Tinio's correspondence with Pantaleon Gonzales, 15 June 1900, PIR SD 353.4; Saturnio Singson, 15 June 1900, PIR SD 353.5; Pedro Legaspi, P.L., 3 October 1900, PIR SD 353.7; P.L., Santa Cruz, September 1900, PIR SD 576.9; P.L., Candon, September 1900, PIR SD 576.9. Quote "every pueblo" from Lt. Col. Robert L. Howze to Capt. John G. Ballance, 20 May 1900, 395/4043, LS Bk 1.

24. Lt. Col. Robert L. Howze to ChAst, 1 June 1900, 395/4043, LS Bk 1. For statistics on assassinations see Senate, *Affairs*, p. 1001.

25. Sexton, *Soldiers in the Sun*, p. 265. For information on Manuel Tinio, see Wilcox, *Through Luzon on Highways and Byways*, p. 168; PIR SD 353, "Manuel Tinio, Brigadier General" File, PIR SD 576, "Manuel Tinio" File, and PIR SD 1024, "Tinio, M." File; "Proclamation Published in San Fernando de Union of Aug. 2, 1898," PIR SD 1024; "Events in December 1897," Taylor, *Philippine Insurrection*, Exhibit 65, p. 65 LY; "Notes for the History of the Glorious Epopée of the Independence of the Philippines," ibid., Exhibit 70, pp. 70–71 LY; Capt. George A. Dodd to [AG, 1D, DNL], Young Papers, Box 5, LR Bk 1, LR 574; Brig. Gen. J. Franklin Bell to AG, DNL, 28 March 1901, 395/2150, LS Bk 4, LS 540.

26. LeRoy, *Americans in the Philippines*, 2:206. Booth, *My Observations and Experiences*, pp. 58–59

27. Quote "hostile to Aglipay" from Schumacher, *Revolutionary Clergy*, p. 108. For information on Juan Villamor, see Villamor, *Inedita Cronica*; PIR SD 522, "Juan Villamor" File, and PIR SD 628, "Abra" File. For information on Aglipay, see PIR SD 909, esp. Brig. Gen. Manuel Tinio to Lt. Col. Vicente Salazar, 22 April 1901, PIR SD 909.8; Capt. George A. Dodd to [AG, 1D, DNL], 14 May 1900, Young Papers. For other officers, see Col. Marcus Cronin to Adj., Vigan, 4 December 1900, 395/3402, Candon, Ilocos Sur, LS, Feb. 1900 to Jan. 1902, LS 554; Col. William P. Duvall to AG, 1D, DNL, 28 December 1900, 395/5617, LS Bk 3, LS 2037. For the

native elite's connections with the guerrillas, 395/5594, Vigan, Ilocos Sur, List of Natives Connected with the Insurgent Government, 1900.

28. Lt. Col. Robert L. Howze to AG, Vigan, 31 July 1900, 395/4043, LS Bk 1; Villamor, *Inedita Cronica*; Brig. Gen. Manuel Tinio to Lt. Col. Joaquin Alejandrino, 8 September 1900, PIR SD 576.1; "Diary supposed to be written by Lt. Col. Vicente Salazar," PIR SD 367.9; Maj. Peyton C. March to Col. Luther R. Hare, 6 May 1900, 395/2158, LR 394; Francisco Caledonia to Commanders of Flying Columns, 12 March 1900, PIR SD 353.11; "Orders for a Guerrilla Column Commanded by Major Villamor," 1900, PIR SD 51.7; "Report of Asst. Surgeon Theodore Bath," 24 October 1900, 395/2133, LR 20047; "Official Memorandum: Antonio Singson," Lt. William R. Smedburg to C.O., Vigan, 12 January 1901, 395/2150, vol. 4, LS 49; "Declaración del Capitan de Sandahatan, Victoriano Avila," "Declaración del soldado Pablo Arce," "Declaración del soldado Batolomé Aspa," taken by Crispulo Patajo, encl. in Maj. John G. Ballance to C.O., Vigan, 16 February 1901, 395/5583, Box 3, LR 1125.

29. "Revolutionary Military Code," captured by Maj. Edgar Z. Steever, 6 July 1900, 395/2133, LS 14873; Capt. William Graves to Adj., Vigan, 27 March 1901, ibid., LR 8814; Col. William P. Duvall to AG, Vigan, 1 May 1900, 395/2158, LR 236.

30. Capt. Earl C. Carnahan to Adj., Bangued, 13 April 1901, 395/3059, Bangued, Abra, LS, July 1900 to Jan. 1902, Box 1, LR 244. Brig. Gen. Manuel Tinio to P. L. Piddig, 17 May 1900, PIR SD 353.10; Brig. Gen. Manuel Tinio to Lt. Bonifacio Fernandez, 2 March 1901, Exhibit "E" in Maj. John G. Ballance to C.O., Vigan, 13 April 1900, 395/5583, Box 3, LR 2075; "Receipts for rice, supplies," PIR SD 745.2; "Papers Captured at Collago, Abra," 8 December 1900, 395/2133, LR 1097; Col. Wirt Davis to Maj. John G. Ballance, 27 December 1900, 395/5578, vol. 5.

31. Maj. Edgar Z. Steever to C.O., Vigan, 20 July 1900, 395/5583, Box 1, LR 1286.

32. Lt. Col. Henry W. Wessells to AG, 31 January 1900, 395/2157, LR 257. *WD* 1900 1:4:324–25; Woolard, "Philippine Scouts," pp. 39–42.

33. Lt. Col. Henry W. Wessells to AG, 10 February 1900, 395/5617, vol. 1, LS 27; Lt. William T. Johnston, "To Whom It May Concern," 13 June 1901, 94/ACP 417696, Crispulo Patajo File; Capt. William T. Johnston, "A Brief Record of Services Since 1898," 94/ACP 4625, William T. Johnston File (hereafter "Brief Record").

34. Brig. Gen. Samuel B. M. Young to AG, 8th A.C., 25 January 1900, 395/2148, LS 119; Brig. Gen. Samuel B. M. Young to AG, Washington, D.C., 3 July 1900, Young Papers, Box 6, "Private File," LS 150; Lt. Milton H. Hollingsworth to Adj., 1 February 1900, 395/2157, LR 348.

35. Capt. Franklin O. Johnson to AG, Vigan, 6 March 1900, 395/2157, LR 684.

36. "History of the 48th Infantry, U.S. Volunteers," Col. William P. Duvall to AG, U.S. Army, 24 June 1901, 94/187.

37. Johnston, "To Whom It May Concern," 94/ACP 417696. Lt. William T. Johnston, "Investigation into the Methods Adopted by the Insurgents for Organizing and Maintaining a Guerrilla Force by First Lt. W. T. Johnston, Third U.S. Cavalry" (hereafter "Investigation"), *WD* 1900 1:7:257–64; Capt. Philip H. Stern to Adj., San Fernando, 16 March 1900, 395/2157, LR 19; Capt. Philip H. Stern to AG, 18 March

1900, ibid., LR 996. For background on the Guardia de Honor, see Guerrero, "Luzon at War," pp. 185–212; Sturtevant, *Popular Uprisings*, pp. 96–114; LeRoy, *Americans in the Philippines*, 1:346–47, 2:208–9. For sources on the relations between the Guardia de Honor and the Republican government see PIR SD 94.1; PIR SD 168; PIR SD 1006; PIR SD 2015.

38. Maj. Gen. Arthur MacArthur, comment on Johnston, "Investigation," *WD* 1900 1:7:264–65. For indications of Johnston's influence on MacArthur's views and policies, see ibid., pp. 61–62; Brig. Gen. Thomas H. Barry to C.G., DSL, 19 December 1900, *WD* 1901 1:4:93; Maj. Gen. Arthur MacArthur to AG, Washington, D.C., 25 December 1900, Roosevelt Papers, series 1, reel 8. John Gates argues that Johnston's report only confirmed MacArthur's own conclusions on the nature of the guerrilla war, see Gates, *Schoolbooks and Krags*, pp. 194–95.

39. Col. William P. Duvall to AG, 16 April 1900, 395/2157, LS 1423; Brig. Gen. Samuel B. M. Young to AG, Bautista, 2 May 1900, 395/2150, vol. 1, LS 133; Capt. William A. Hankins to Adj., 2d Btln., 48 Inf., 2 May 1900, 395/2158, LR 682; Capt. Alexander V. Richardson to Adj., 48th Inf., 8 May 1900, 395/2158, LR 678; Lt. Lewis Smith to C.O., Co. "I," 48th Inf., 9 May 1900, 395/2133, LR 6413; "Report of Engagement near Vagalin, Province of Union, Luzon, P.I., May 27, 1900, by Lieut. W. T. Johnston, Third U.S. Cavalry, Commanding Troop M," *WD* 1900 1:7:270; "Diary of Events, May 6, 1900 to June 14, 1900," 94/228225; 94/187, "History of the 48th Inf.," p. 11.

40. Lt. Edwin M. Suplee to Adj., San Fernando, 21 April 1900, 395/2158, LR 86; quote "chickens" from Col. William P. Duvall to AG, 4 April 1900, 395/2157, LR 1113. Lt. William T. Johnston to Adj., 5 April 1900, ibid., LR 1232; Juan Baltazar to Col. William P. Duvall, 5 April 1900, ibid., LR 1338; Leon Jacunda to "The General," 2 May 1900, 395/2158, LR 457.

41. Lt. William T. Johnston to Post Adj., 22 May 1900, 395/2158, LR 829. Maj. A. L. Dade to AG, DNL, 7 May 1900, Young Papers, Box 6, "Private File," LR 274.

42. Lt. Col. Juan Guitterez to Capt. Ignacio Peralta, 4 November 1900, Taylor, *Philippine Insurrection*, Exhibit 1109, p. 66 GV; Natalio Valencia, "Proclamation," 13 November 1900, PIR SD 564.4; Col. William P. Duvall to AG, 1D, DNL, 28 December 1900, 395/5617, vol. 3, LS 2037; Brig. Gen. Samuel B. M. Young to AG, DNL, 25 December 1900, 395/2150, vol. 3, LS 3303; Brig. Gen. Manuel Tinio to Lt. Col. Joaquin Alejandrino, 8 September 1900, PIR SD 576.9; Col. Blas Villamor to Capt. Anacleto Mendoza, encl. in Col. William P. Duvall to AG, 1D, DNL, 6 June 1900, 395/2133, LR 6014; Col. Blas Villamor to Maj. Pablo Bustamente, 30 March 1900, encl. in Capt. William Hankins to Adj., 2d Btln., 48th Inf., 2 May 1900, 395/2158, LR 682; "Coboar," PIR SD 1006.6; Anon., "Proclamation," 18 April 1900, PIR SD 168.9; Col. William P. Duvall to Hq, 1D, DNL, 15 May 1900, 395/2158, LR 679; Brig. Gen. Samuel B. M. Young to AG, D.P., 29 March 1900, in *WD* 1900 1:4:332; Col. William P. Duvall to AG, Vigan, 11 July 1900, 395/2158; Lt. Hugh Thomason to Adj., 15 May 1900, 395/2158, LR 550; Lt. William T. Johnston to Adj., 5 April 1900, LR 1231; Col. William P. Duvall to AAG, 20 March 1900, LS 996; Col. William P. Duvall to Adj., Vigan, 3 April 1900, LR 1103, all in 395/2157; Capt. A. D. Beight to Sr. Bartolome Vaguer, 3 April 1900, 395/5617, vol. 1, LS 185.

43. Phelps Whitmarsh to Maj. Gen. Arthur MacArthur, 9 September 1900, in

"Correspondence on Civil-Military Relations in Benguet," 350/2368.5; Mulrooney, "No Victor, No Vanquished," pp. 213–22. For Guardia operations, see Maj. John G. Ballance to C.O., San Fernando, 6 December 1900, 395/2167, vol. 2, LS 895; Francisco Veracruz to Civil Governor, 10 December 1900, 395/5589, Box 1, LR 410; Maj. John G. Ballance to C.O., Civil S-D, Vigan, 11 December 1900, 395/5589, LR 400; Brig. Gen. Benjamin A. Alvord to Hq, 1D, DNL, 6 November 1900, 395/2158, LS 819; Brig. Gen. Samuel B. M. Young to AG, U.S. Army, 23 January 1902, 94/ACP 417696. For prosecutions of civic officials who aided the revolutionaries, see 395/5644, San Fernando, La Union, Register of Charges and Specifications for Cases Tried in the Provost Court, Mar. 1900 to Apr. 1901.

44. Johnston, "Investigation," *WD* 1900 1:7:263. *WD* 1900 1:4:338–39; Brig. Gen. Jacob H. Smith to AG, DNL, 3 November 1900, 350/2368.5; Col. William P. Duvall to Maj. John G. Ballance, 24 January 1901, 395/2133, LR 675. See also Duvall's comment that both he and officers in La Union have not recruited Guardia de Honor though some men belong to it. His policy has been to ignore "secret societies" in "our native helpers," Col. William P. Duvall to AG, 12 April 1900, 395/2157, LR 1321.

45. William H. Taft to Elihu Root, 10 October 1900, Taft Papers, series 21. Phelps Whitmarsh to Maj. Gen. Arthur MacArthur, 9 September 1900, 350/2368.5; Brig. Gen. J. Franklin Bell to AG, DNL, 25 April 1901, 395/2133, LR 9233; 94/187, "History of the 48th Inf."; Johnston, "Brief Record," 94/ACP 4625.

46. For the often bitter correspondence over the retention of Patajo's men, see 350/2638.5; Brig. Gen. J. Franklin Bell to C.O., San Fernando, 5 April 1901, 395/2488, LR 38; Brig. Gen. J. Franklin Bell to AG, DNL, 25 April 1901, 395/2133, LR 9233.

47. Lt. Col. Robert L. Howze to AG, Vigan, 7 March 1900, 395/4043, LS Bk 1. Lt. Col. Robert L. Howze to Civil Governor, Vigan, 19 February 1900, ibid. For early civil government, see Lt. William Smedberg to Capt. George K. Hunter, 30 December 1899, 395/2148, LS 2; Col. William S. McCaskey to Brig. Gen. J. Franklin Bell, 395/4043, LS Bk 4, LR 1762.

48. Lt. Col. Robert L. Howze to Lt. Grayson Heidt, 16 March 1900, 395/4043, LS Bk 1. Quote "juntas" from Lt. Col. Robert L. Howze to AG, Vigan, 20 March 1900, ibid. For further correspondence see Lt. Col. Robert L. Howze to Lt. Cleveland C. Lansing, 16 March 1900; Lt. Col. Robert L. Howze to AG, Vigan, 26 February, 30 March, and 13 April 1900; Lt. Col. Robert L. Howze to Maj. Edgar Z. Steever, 26 February 1900, all in ibid.; *WD* 1900 1:7:237–39.

49. Schumacher, *Revolutionary Clergy*, pp. 114–15; quote "the influence of Padre Aglipay" from Lt. Col. Robert L. Howze to AG, Vigan, 22 March 1900, 395/4043, LS Bk 1.

50. Lt. Col. Robert L. Howze to AG, Vigan, 15 March 1900, 395/4043, LS Bk 1. *WD* 1900 1:4:313–16; Brig. Gen. Samuel B. M. Young to Maj. Gen. Arthur MacArthur, 19 April 1900, 395/2150, vol. 1, LS 12. James LeRoy suggested that the revolt in April was the responsibility of Aglipay and that the regular guerrillas did not take part, see LeRoy, *Americans in the Philippines*, 2:205. For the confused relations over Aglipay's authority see Col. William S. McCaskey to Brig. Gen. J. Franklin Bell, 3 May 1901, 395/4043, LS Bk 4, LS 1456; Lt. Col. Robert L. Howze to Brig. Gen. Samuel B. M. Young, 12 October 1900, ibid., LS Bk 2, TS 321; Brig. Gen. Manuel

Tinio to Lt. Col. Vicente Salazar, 2 April 1901, PIR SD 909.8; Santiago Espiritu to Lt. Rosendo Valido, 24 April 1901, PIR SD 909.8.

51. Lt. Col. Robert L. Howze to Col. Lyman W. V. Kennon, 18 April 1900, 395/4043, LS Bk 1. Quote "Mahdi fanatics" from *ANJ* 37 (21 July 1900). For other accounts, see "Report of an Engagement at Batac, Province of Ilocos Norte, P.I., April 16, 1900, by Capt. C. J. Rollis. Thirty-Fourth U.S.V. Infantry," *WD* 1900 1:7:225–28; "Report of Engagement at Batac, Province of Ilocos Norte, Luzon, P.I., April 16 and 17, 1900, by Lieut. Grayson Heidt, Third U.S. Cavalry," ibid., pp. 229–30; *ANJ* 37 (23 June 1900); Lt. Col. Robert L. Howze to AG, Vigan, 18 April 1900, 395/2157, LR 1469; Unsigned [Lt. Col. Robert L. Howze] to AAG, 1D, DNL, 3 May 1900, 395/4043, LS Bk 1. Howze believed that "many of them were drunk and all were fanatically crazy," *WD* 1900 1:7:238.

52. Lt. Col. Robert L. Howze to Maj. Julius A. Penn, 20 April 1900, 395/4043, LS Bk 1.

53. Capt. George A. Dodd to Brig. Gen. Samuel B. M. Young, 25 April 1900, 395/2158, Box 1, LR 5; Brig. Gen. Samuel B. M. Young to AG, 26 April 1900, 395/2150, vol. 4, LS 64. For Tinio's arrival in Ilocos Norte, see Lt. Col. Robert L. Howze to AG, Vigan, 26 May 1900, 395/4043, LS Bk 1; *WD* 1900 1:7:239; Brig. Gen. Samuel B. M. Young to AG, 26 April 1900, 395/2150, vol. 4, LS 64.

54. Lt. Col. Robert L. Howze to AAG, 1D, DNL, 21 May 1900, 395/4043, LS Bk 1. For the aftermath of the revolt, see Lt. Col. Robert L. Howze to AAG, 1D, DNL, 3 May 1900; Lt. Col. Robert L. Howze to AG, Vigan, 26 May 1900; Lt. Col. Robert L. Howze to ChAst, 1 June 1900; Lt. Col. Robert L. Howze to AG, Vigan, 11 June 1900; Lt. Col. Robert L. Howze to AG, 28 June 1900; Lt. Col. Robert L. Howze to AAG, 1D, DNL, 30 June 1900, all in 395/4043, LS Bk 1. See also the civil reports on police improvement in 395/2180, 1D, Extracts of Monthly Reports Received from Inspecting Officers.

55. Hq, 1D, DNL, Circular Letter no. 1, 22 May 1900, 395/2174. This was modified on June 7 to restrict travel of males age eighteen to sixty, Circular Letter no. 3, 7 June 1900, 395/2173. Circular 1 was not issued in Abra until November, see Post Hq, Bangued to ChAst, 8 November 1900, 395/3059, LS 411; Circular Letter no. 11, Office of ChAst, 11 July 1900, 395/2174.

56. Office of ChAst, "Proclamation," 15 June 1900, 395/5583, Box 1; Office of ChAst, Circular Letter no. 7, 25 June 1900, 395/2174.

57. For examples and criticism of the lax enforcement of these orders see Lt. Frederick E. Coe, Provost Marshall to Adj., Vigan, 31 August 1900, 395/5583, Box 1; Maj. John Howard to Adj., San Fernando, 5 November 1900, 395/2884, Aringay, La Union, LR, June 1900 to Apr. 1901, LR 455; Maj. John G. Ballance to C.O., Civil S-D, Vigan, 15 February 1901, 395/5589, LR 221; Maj. John G. Ballance to C.O., Vigan, 16 February 1901, 395/2150, vol. 4, LS 277. In Cabuagao, Ilocos Sur, there was a total of two cases in 1900 to 1901, and these were suspects found on a sweep of a guerrilla stronghold, 395/3268, Cabuagao, Illocos Sur, Charges and Specifications for Cases Tried by the Provost Court, 1900–1901. For provost court reports on enforcement, see 395/5644; 395/2986, Badoc, Ilocos Norte, Record of Charges and Specifications for Cases Tried in the Provost Court, Nov. 1900 to June 1901.

58. Brig. Gen. Samuel B. M. Young to AG, DNL, 10 December 1900, 395/2150,

vol. 3, LS 3042. Woolard, "Philippine Scouts," pp. 17–18, 42–43. For recruitment of Native Scouts, see Brig. Gen. Thomas Barry to C.G., DNL, 19 January 1901, 395/2133, LR 1091; "Correspondence Relating to the Organization of Native Scouts and Police," 94/369141; OMG, G.O. 17, 14 April 1900, 395/2172; Capt. John F. Green to Anon. [AG, 1D, DNL], 20 April 1900, Young Papers, Box 5, Bk 1, LR 35; Capt. John F. Green to AG, 30 April 1900, 395/2158, LR 229; Lt. Col. Robert L. Howze to AG, Vigan, 395/2157, LR 1201; Col. William Duvall to AG, 5 April 1900, ibid., LR 1150. For Castner's Scouts, see Lt. Joseph Castner to Brig. Gen. Samuel B. M. Young, 2 April 1900, Young Papers, Box 6, "Private File," LR 249; *WD* 1900 1:4:327, 332; Lt. Joseph C. Castner to Adj., Vigan, 15 March 1900, 395/5582, LR 257.

59. Col. Wirt Davis to Maj. John G. Ballance, 27 December 1900, Young Papers, Box 4, LR 6882. Capt. John F. Green to AG, Vigan, 5 October 1900, 395/2158, LR 4006; Ward, "Use of Native Troops," pp. 793–805; Capt. John F. Green to AG, Vigan, 25 October 1900, 395/2158, LR 4806; Brig. Gen. Samuel B. M. Young to AG, DNL, 3 December 1900, 395/2150, vol. 3, LS 2921; Col. Wirt Davis to C.S., Hq, 1D, DNL, 3 April 1901, 395/5578, vol. 7, LS 1120; Lt. John A. Ward to Adj., Santa Maria, 19 April 1901, 395/2133, LR 9645. For volunteer units, see Hq, DNL, G.O. 22, 29 December 1900, 395/2173.

60. Brig. Gen. Samuel B. M. Young to AG, DNL, 31 January 1901, 395/2167, vol. 3, LS 202; Brig. Gen. Samuel B. M. Young to AG, DNL, 30 July 1900, 395/2133, LR 10899. For Young's comments on the dangers of arming Filipinos, see Brig. Gen. Samuel B. M. Young to AG, DNL, 7 February 1901, 395/2150, vol. 4, LS 210.

61. Brig. Gen. Benjamin A. Alvord to C.G., 1D, DNL, 23 September 1900, 395/2130, LS 703.

62. Brig. Gen. Samuel B. M. Young to AG, DNL, 30 July 1900, 395/2133, LR 10899; Hq, DNL to C.G., 1D, DNL, 15 August 1900, 395/2130, LS 603; Brig. Gen. Samuel B. M. Young to AG, DNL, 13 September 1900, 395/2167, vol. 2, LS 576; Maj. Gen. Loyd Wheaton to AG, DivPhil, 30 September 1900, 395/2130, LS 724; Brig. Gen. Samuel B. M. Young to AG, DNL, 13 October 1900, 395/2167, vol. 2, LS 680; Maj. Gen. Loyd Wheaton to SMG, 30 November 1900, 395/2130, LS 884; Brig. Gen. Samuel B. M. Young to SMG, 10 January 1901, 395/2133, LR 361; Maj. Gen. Loyd Wheaton to AG, DivPhil, 27 January 1901, 395/2130, LS 941; Brig. Gen. Samuel B. M. Young to AG, DNL, 31 January 1901, 395/2167, vol. 3, LS 203; Brig. Gen. Samuel B. M. Young to AG, DNL, 7 February 1901, 395/2133, LR 3837; Maj. John G. Ballance to AG, DNL, 28 February 1901, 395/2167, vol. 3, LS 326.

63. Lt. Col. Enoch H. Crowder to C.G., 1D, DNL, 20 June 1900, 395/2130, LS 437; Maj. Edgar Z. Steever to CO, Vigan, 20 July 1900, 395/5583, Box 1, LR 1286; Lt. Col. Robert L. Howze to AG, Vigan, 15 September 1900, 395/4043, LS Bk 2, TS 135; Col. William P. Duvall to AG, 1D, DNL, 9 July 1900, LR 2125; Lt. Col. Robert L. Howze to AG, Vigan, 19 July 1900, LR 2102; Col. Wirt Davis to AG, 1D, DNL, 22 July 1900, LR 2143, all in 395/2158; Maj. Gen. Arthur MacArthur to AG, 28 May 1900; *CWS*, 2:1172–73.

64. Maj. John G. Ballance to C.O., San Fernando, 15 May 1900, 395/2157, LS 137; Maj. John G. Ballance to C.O., Bangued, 11 December 1900, 395/2150, vol. 3, LS 2562; Maj. John G. Ballance to C.O., Vigan, 14 September 1900, 395/2150, vol.

4, LS 71; Maj. John G. Ballance to C.O., Ilocos Sur, 29 February 1901, ibid., LS 321; Maj. John G. Ballance to Brig. Gen. J. Franklin Bell, 4 April 1901, ibid., vol. 5, LS 582; Col. William P. Duvall to AG, 16 April 1900, 395/2157, LR 1922. For Young's private sources, see Brig. Gen. Samuel B. M. Young to Marjorie [Mrs. John H. Gibbons], 21 March 1900, Young Papers, "Uncatalogued Material."

65. Col. William P. Duvall to AG, Vigan, 6 July 1900, 395/2158, LR 1819; quote "be a man of property" from Col. Marcus Cronin to Capt. Edmund Davis, 12 June 1900, 94/117, 33d Inf., LS Bk 2, LS 730.

66. Capt. J. G. Ballance to AG, DNL, 20 August 1900, 395/2167, vol. 1, LS 446. For U.S. Army efforts against smallpox, see Capt. J.G. Ballance to C.O., Namacpacan, 23 July 1900, ibid., LS 246; Capt. J. G. Ballance to C. O., Candon, 23 July 1900, ibid., LS 349. For continuing civil government, see Capt. J. G. Ballance to MilSec, 15 September 1900, ibid., vol. 2, LS 570.

67. Capt. Frederick Hadra to Post Adj., Bangued, in Lt. Col. Peyton C. March to Post Adj., Vigan, 17 August 1900, 395/2158, LR 3188; Col. Marcus Cronin to AG, 1D, DNL, 10 November 1900, ibid., LR 5280; Musgrove, "Brief History of the 33rd USVI"; *Jawbone* (February 1936).

68. "Orders for a Guerrilla Column Commanded by Major Villamor," 1900, PIR SD 51.7; Juan Villamor to Brig. Gen. Manuel Tinio, 25 May 1900, PIR SD 522.2; "Projecto de un Codigo deseñales de dia y noche para las guerrillas de Abra," n.d., PIR SD 628.1; Unsigned [Maj. William C. H. Bowen] to AG, 1D, DNL, 2 May 1901, 395/3059, LS Bk 1, LS 92; Lt. Col. Juan Villamor, "Proclamation," 14 February 1900, encl. in Maj. Thomas Ashburn to Adj., 33d Inf., 22 February 1900, 395/2157; Lt. Col. Juan Villamor, "To the Suffering Inhabitants of Abra," and Julio Borbon, "To the Public of Bangued," captured 10 October 1900, 395/2133, LR 17497; Col. Blas Villamor, "Inhabitants of Abra," 10 January 1901, 395/3064, Box 1.

69. Lt. Col. Peyton C. March to Maj. John G. Ballance, 2 and 31 August 1900, 395/2161, 1D, DNL, Copies of Telegrams (Ciphers) Sent, Dec. 1900 to Mar. 1901, LS 18 and 21; Lt. Col. Peyton C. March to Maj. John G. Ballance, 31 August 1900, ibid., LS 21; Lt. Col. Peyton C. March to ChAst, 6 September 1900, 395/3061, LS 23.

70. Brig. Gen. Samuel B. M. Young to AG, DNL, 7 September 1900, Young Papers, Box 6, "Personal" File, LS 167; Brig. Gen. Samuel B. M. Young to Mr. V. G. Way, 2 November 1900, ibid.; Lt. Col. Peyton C. March to Post Adj., Vigan, 5 September 1900, 395/3059, LS 171; Brig. Gen. Samuel B. M. Young, endorsement on LR 4107, 5 November 1900, vol. 3, LS 2424. Juan Villamor behaved very chivalrously in this fight, burying the American commander, Lt. Henry N. Way, and sending his class ring to the Americans. He also released the eight Native Scouts he captured, see Lt. Col. Peyton C. March to Post Adj., 5 September 1900, 395/3059, vol. 1, LS 71; J. V. [Lt. Col. Juan Villamor] to Lt. Col. Peyton C. March, n.d., Young Papers, Box 6, "Private" File.

71. "Province of Abra," 10 October 1900, 395/2180. According to captured documents, Juan Villamor ordered the *presidente* of Bangued to evacuate all noncombatants from the town, see Julio Borbon, "To the Public of Bangued," 1900, 395/2133, LR 17497. For reports on engagements and conditions in Abra, see Lt. Col. Peyton C. March to Capt. William R. Smedberg, 5 September 1900, 395/2158, LR 3151; Capt.

Charles W. Van Way to Post Adj., Bangued, 6 September 1900, *WD* 1901 1:5:46–47;
Capt. William R. Smedberg to Lt. John W. Ward, 19 September 1900, 395/2150, vol.
3, LS 1605; Brig. Gen. Samuel B. M. Young to AG, DNL, 24 September 1900, ibid.,
LS 1650; "Report of Capt. Frederick Hadra, Ast. Surgeon, 33d U.S.V.I.," 26 October
1900, 395/2133, LR 20045; C.O., Vigan to [AG, 1D, DNL], 8 October 1900, Young
Papers, Box 5, LR Bk 4, LR 4108; Capt. William R. Smedberg to Lt. Howard, 3
December 1900, 395/2150, vol. 3, LS 2923; Lt. Col. William L. Luhn to Adj.,
Province of Abra, 6 December 1900, 395/3064; 94/187, "33rd Inf. History." In
November attacks on the Abra River were so serious that U.S. forces were stationed
along it every time rafts were sent, see Lt. William Lowe to Capt. William F. Martin,
10 November 1900, LS 412; Lt. Col. Peyton C. March to Lt. Howard C. Price, 13
November 1900, LS 417; Lt. Stephen M. Hackney to Capt. William F. Martin, 16
November 1900, LS 424, all in 395/3059.

72. Lt. Col. Robert L. Howze to AG, Vigan, 2 and 8 September and 10 October
1900, 395/4043, LS Bk 2, TS 154, 197, and 313; Lt. Col. Robert L. Howze to C.O.,
Batac, 27 September 1900, TS 207, ibid.; Lt. Col. Robert L. Howze to Lt. Harold B.
Howard, 23 and 25 September 1900, 395/2150, vol. 3, TS 1639 and 1661; "Province
of Ilocos Norte—Dingras," September 1900, 395/2180; "Report of Captain R. K.
Evans," 23 August 1900, 94/338335.

73. Brig. Gen. Samuel B. M. Young to AG, DNL, 25 October 1900, 395/2150,
vol. 3, LS 2206. Lt. Grayson V. Heidt to AG, DNL, 26 October 1900, ibid., LS 2220;
"Report of Ast. Surgeon Thomas Bath," 7 November 1900, 395/2133, LR 20047;
ANJ 38 (30 March 1901).

74. All quotations from Brig. Gen. Samuel B. M. Young to AG, DNL, 17 January
1901, 395/2150, vol. 4, LS 83. Brig. Gen. Samuel B. M. Young to Theodore
Roosevelt, 28 November 1900, Young Papers, Box 6, LS "Personal" File, LS 190;
Brig. Gen. Samuel B. M. Young to AG, DNL, 11 December 1900, 395/2150, vol. 3,
LS 3066; Brig. Gen. Samuel B. M. Young to Henry C. Corbin, 28 November 1900,
Young Papers, Box 6, LS 189. For Young's initial letter, see Brig. Gen. Samuel B. M.
Young to AG, DNL, 7 September 1900, ibid., Box 6, LS "Personal" File, LS 167;
Jessup, *Elihu Root*, pp. 340–41.

75. Troop strength figures in the First District are incomplete. These figures are
taken from 395/2181.

76. Col. Wirt Davis to C.S., 7 March 1901, 395/5578, vol. 6, LR 804; Col. Lyman
W. V. Kennon to C.S., 9 February 1901, 395/4043, LS Bk 3, LS 405. For authorization of Native Scouts, see Brig. Gen. Thomas Barry to C.G., DNL, 19 January 1901,
395/2133.

77. Brig. Gen. J. Franklin Bell to C.O., Aringay, 5 April 1901, 395/2488, LR 38;
Brig. Gen. J. Franklin Bell to Col. Wirt Davis, 24 April 1901, 395/2150, vol. 5, LS
704; 94/187, "History of the 48th Inf."; Maj. John G. Ballance to C.O., Vigan, 16
February 1901, 395/2150, vol. 4, LS 277; *WD* 1901 1:5:35; *ANJ* 38 (6 April 1901);
Hq, DivPhil, G.O. 83, 27 April 1901, in Senate, *Affairs*, pp. 1155–60.

78. Capt. A. D. Beight to C.O., Aringay, 3 February 1901, 395/2884, LR 49. Brig.
Gen. J. Franklin Bell to AG, DNL, 28 March 1901, 395/2150, vol. 4, LS 540; Maj.
John G. Ballance to C.O., Vigan, 15 March 1901, 395/5589, Box 2, LR 388–97.

79. Brig. Gen. John G. Ballance to AG, DNL, 8 June 1901, 395/2150, vol. 5, LS

903; quote "more than any other influence" from Col. William S. McCaskey to AG, 1D, DNL, 29 May 1901, 395/4043, LS Bk 4, LS 1766.

80. Brig. Gen. Samuel B. M. Young to Maj. Gen. Loyd Wheaton, 2 December 1900, 395/2180, vol. 3, LS 2894; Brig. Gen. Samuel B. M. Young to Maj. Gen. Loyd Wheaton, 17 January 1901, Young Papers, Box 6, "Private" File, LS 201.

81. Col. Wirt Davis to C.S., 1D, DNL, 11 March 1901, LS 830; Col. Wirt Davis to AG, 1D, DNL, 28 January 1901, LS 276; Col. Wirt Davis to Maj. John G. Ballance, 22 February 1901, LS 654; Capt. Henry L. Ripley to C.O., Candon, 25 February 1901, LS 693; Capt. Henry L. Ripley to C.O., Cabuagao, 11 March 1900, LS 845, all in 395/5578, vol. 6; *ANJ* 38 (2 March 1901); Maj. John G. Ballance to C.O., Ilocos Sur, 25 February 1901, 395/3150, vol. 4, LS 333. The guerrillas may have been reacting to these ceremonies when they kidnapped Padre Ambrocio Miria in Candon, see Capt. James S. Butler to Lt. Frank D. Tompkins, 24 January 1901, 395/3402, vol. 2, LS 155.

82. Capt. Henry L. Ripley, Adj. to C.O., Santa Maria, 17 April 1901, 395/5578, vol. 7, LS 1259; Capt. Dennis E. Nolan to C.O., Ilocos Sur, 17 April 1901, 395/2150, vol. 5, LS 668; 94/187, "History of the 48th Inf.," p. 2; Capt. Daniel H. Boughton to Adj., 1 December 1900, 395/4047, Box 1, LR 5390.

83. Col. Marcus Cronin to Adj., Vigan, 11 December 1900, 395/3402, LS 576. For the work of courts, see 395/3410, Candon, Ilocos Sur, Record of Charges and Specifications for Cases Tried by the Provost Court, Feb. 1900 to July 1901. Maj. John G. Ballance to C.O., Vigan, 19 January 1901, 395/2150, vol. 4, LS 92; Capt. Henry L. Ripley to Mrs. Elenteria Florentina, 18 February 1901, 395/5578, vol. 6, LS 622; 395/5594; Maj. John G. Ballance to C.O., Civil S-D, Bangued, 13 January 1901, 395/3064, Box 1; Maj. John G. Ballance to C.O., Civil S-D, Vigan, 15 February 1901, 395/5589, LR 221; Col. Wirt Davis to Maj. John G. Ballance, 9 January 1901, 395/5578, vol. 5, LS 92; Brig. Gen. Samuel B. M. Young to AG, DNL, 15 January 1901, 395/2150, vol. 4, LS 77.

84. Brig. Gen. J. Franklin Bell to C.O., Badoc, 1 June 1901, 395/2150, vol. 5, LS 877; Hq, Civil S-D, Ilocos Norte, to ChAst, 1D, DNL, 10 February 1901, Kennon Papers; Col. Lyman W. V. Kennon to C.O. Batac, 13 February 1901, LS 495; Col. William S. McCaskey to C.S., 1D, DNL, 21 February 1901, ibid., LS 583; Lt. Col. Robert L. Howze to C.S., 10 January 1901, TS 116, all in 395/4043, LS Bk 3; Capt. Daniel H. Boughton to Adj., 1 December 1900, 395/4047, Box 1, LR 539.

85. *WD* 1901 1:5:39; Lt. Ezekial J. Williams to Adj., Bangued, 20 April 1901, 395/3064, Box 1; Maj. John G. Ballance to C.O., Bangued, 12 November 1900, ibid. For Bendito's proclamations, see Lt. Francisco Bendito to Habitants of Bucay, n.d., 1901, ibid.; Lt. Francisco Bendito to Jefe Americano del Destacamento de Bucay, 15 February 1901, ibid. Bendito also told the Americans he would boil them in oil or tie them to anthills, see Peter Konrad Questionnaire.

86. Lt. Col. Robert L. Howze to C.O.'s, 2 November 1900, 395/4043, LS Bk 2, LS 52. Maj. John G. Ballance to C.O., Bangued, 2 November 1900, 395/2150, vol. 3, LS 2562; Maj. John G. Ballance to C.O., Bangued, 12 November 1900, 395/5583, Box 2, LR 3640; Maj. John G. Ballance to C.O., Vigan, 17 November 1900, 395/2150, vol. 3, LS 26365; Capt. Henry L. Ripley to C.O., Santa Maria, 1 April 1901, 395/5578, vol. 7, LS 1236; Capt. Henry L. Ripley to C.O.'s, 21 April 1901, ibid., LS

1379. For restrictions see Col. Wirt Davis to AG, 1D, DNL, 1 October 1900, ibid., vol. 3, LS 1942.

87. Lt. James K. Parsons to Post Adj., Vigan, 20 June 1900, 395/5582, vol. 2, LR 744; Lt. James K. Parsons to AG, 28 June 1900, ibid.

88. Lawrence Benton Questionnaire.

89. Lt. Lewis M. Smith to C.O., Company I, 48th Inf., 9 May 1900, 395/2158, LR 793. For evidence of the use of torture, see Peter Konrad Questionnaire; Tafton MS.

90. Col. William P. Duvall to AG, Vigan, 3 and 4 April 1900, 395/2157, LR 1103 and 1120; "Diary supposed to be written by Lt. Col. Vincent Salazar," PIR SD 367.9.

91. Col. Lyman W. V. Kennon to AG, 1D, DNL, 3 December 1900, 395/4043, LS Bk 2, LS 609. "Proceedings of a Board of Officers Convened Pursuant to Telegram from Hdqrs. 1st Dist., Dept. Northern Luzon, dated Vigan, P.I., Nov. 24, 1900," 395/2047, Box 1, LS 4496; Lt. Col. Robert L. Howze to AG, Vigan, 21 November 1900, 395/4043, LS Bk 2, TS 541.

92. George O. Burwell Questionnaire.

93. "Report of Major Edgar Z. Steever," 30 December 1900, 395/2133, LR 3837; *WD* 1901 1:5:75; Col. Wirt Davis to Maj. John G. Ballance, 31 January 1901, 395/5578, vol. 6, LS 369.

94. This overview of Army operations is taken from *WD* 1901 1:5:30–100; Brig. Gen. Samuel B. M. Young to AG, DNL, 11 December 1900, 395/2150, vol. 3, LS 3216; Capt. Henry L. Ripley to Maj. Edgar Z. Steever, 1 October 1900, 395/5578, vol. 3, LS 1932; "Report of Capt. E. Carnahan," 10 December 1900, 395/2133, LR 3837; Col. Richard Comba to Maj. John G. Ballance, 21 December 1900, Young Papers, Box 5, LR Bk 4, LR 6719; Lt. Col. Robert L. Howze to C.O., "K" Co., 34th Inf., 4 October 1900, 395/2158, LR 4719; Lt. Harold P. Howard to Maj. Edgar Z. Steever, 1 October 1900, 395/2150, LS 1771; Col. Lyman W. V. Kennon to AG, Vigan, 29 November and 5 December 1900, LS Bk 3, TS 591 and 650; Lt. Col. Robert L. Howze to Brig. Gen. Samuel B. M. Young, 1 October 1900, TS 249; Lt. Col. Robert L. Howze to AG, Vigan, 15 October 1900, TS 329; Capt. Harry W. Newton to C.O., Badoc, 30 November 1900, TS 593, all in 395/4043, LS Bk 3; Capt. R. T. Ellis to C.O., Vigan, 7 December 1900, 395/2158, LR 6263; Capt. Henry L. Ripley to C.O.'s, Cabuagao, etc., 11 November and 24 December 1900, 395/5578, vol. 5, LS 2605 and 2851–58; Col. Richard Comba to C.S., 1D, DNL, 5 January 1901, 395/3059, LS 4; Col. Wirt Davis to Maj. John G. Ballance, 26 February 1901, 395/5578, vol. 6, LR 900.

95. Col. Richard Comba to C.S., 1D, DNL, 1 March 1901, 395/3059, Box 1, LS 26; Capt. Earl C. Carnahan to Adj., Bangued, 13 April 1901, 395/3064.

96. W.E. Chapman, "Report of the Schools in the Province of Abra, 16 December 1901, 350/3599, "Abra" File. For Bell's later life, see Raines, "Major General J. Franklin Bell and Military Reform." For Bell's comments, see *WD* 1901 1:5:37. Bell quoted Young's correspondence to indicate the seriousness of the situation but left out the sections in which Young explained that the situation was much better. Compare Bell's citations of Brig. Gen. Samuel B. M. Young's 28 December 1900 letter in *WD* 1901 1:5:33–34 with the actual letter, Brig. Gen. Samuel B. M. Young to AG, DNL, 28 December 1900, 395/2150, vol. 3, I ; 2421. Young, for example, states the situation is "much improved" and that the guerrillas have broken into small bands and

their leaders are hiding. See also Young's more optimistic appraisal of the district in Brig. Gen. Samuel B. M. Young to AG, DNL, 7 February 1901, ibid., vol. 4, LS 210.

97. *WD* 1901 1:5:37–41, 95–100; Col. William P. Duvall to Capt. Richardson, 7 January 1901, 395/2884, LR 13; Lt. Dennis E. Nolan, Adj. to C.O., Ilocos Sur, 17 April 1901, 395/2150, LS 668; Maj. John G. Ballance to C.O., Vigan, 395/5583, Box 3, LR 2124; Johnston, "Brief Record," 94/ACP 4625; 94/ACP 417696; 94/187, "History of the 48th Inf.," pp. 1–2.

98. Col. Richard Comba to Maj. John G. Ballance, 24 December 1900, Young Papers, Box 3, vol. 4, LR 6808. Brig. Gen. Samuel B. M. Young to Maj. Gen. Loyd Wheaton, 17 January 1901, ibid., Box 6, "Private" File, LS 201; "Report of Col. Richard Comba," encl. in Brig. Gen. Samuel B. M. Young to AG, DNL, 7 February 1901, 395/2133, LR 3837; Col. Richard Comba to C.S., 1D, DNL, 1 March 1901, 395/3059, vol. 1, LS 26.

99. "Report of the Provincial Governor of Abra," 16 December 1901, 350/3599, "Abra File." For final operations in Abra, see Maj. William C. H. Bowen to C.S., 1D, DNL, 1 April 1901, 395/3059, vol. 1, LS 45; Capt. Stephen M. Hackney to C.O.'s, Abra, 31 March 1901, 395/3059, vol. 1, LS 41; Hq, 1D, DNL, G.O. 6, 9 April 1901, 395/2173; Capt. Earl C. Carnahan to Adj., Bangued, 13 and 21 April 1901, 395/3064; Maj. William C. H. Bowen to Officer in Charge of Civil Affairs, 22 May 1901, 395/2133, LS 11549; *ANJ* 39 (7 September 1901); Peter Konrad Questionnaire; Maj. John G. Ballance to C.O., Province of Abra, 8 March 1900, 395/2150, vol. 4, LS 414; Col. Blas Villamor to Col. Richard Comba, 17 March 1900, 395/3064; Brig. Gen. J. Franklin Bell to AG, DNL, 28 March 1901, 395/2150, vol. 4, LS 540; *WD* 1901 1:5:37–38; Maj. William C. H. Bowen to C.S., 1D, DNL, 1 April 1901, 395/3059, vol. 1, LS 45; Villamor, *Inedita Cronica*, pp. 30–133. The surrender ceremonies are described in "Major" [Maj. William C. H. Bowen] to AG, 1D, DNL, 9 May 1901, 395/3059, vol. 1, LS 80.

100. Quote "there would be no more talk" from Col. William S. McCaskey to Brig. Gen. J. Franklin Bell, 25 April 1901, 395/4043, LS Bk 4, LS 1315. Brig. Gen. Manuel Tinio to Lt. Col. Vicente Salazar, 2 April 1901, PIR SD 909.8; Brig. Gen. Manuel Tinio to Lt. Dionisio Reyes, 25 February 1901, encl. in Maj. John G. Ballance to C.O., Vigan, 3 April 1901, 395/5583, Box 3, LR 2105; Col. William S. McCaskey to C.S., 27 April 1901, ibid., LS 1335; Capt. Lewis M. Lewis, Adj., 20th Inf. to C.O.'s, Dingras, Banna, and Salsona, 24 April 1901, ibid., LS 1292; Col. Wirt Davis to Maj. John G. Ballance, 23 March 1901, 395/5578, vol. 7, LS 996; Brig. Gen. John G. Ballance to AG, DNL, 8 June 1901, 395/2150, vol. 5, LS 903; Brig. Gen. William S. McCaskey to Capt. John R. M. Taylor, 14 August 1904, PIR SD 1306.10. For the amnesty, see Brig. Gen. John G. Ballance to AG, DNL, 8 June 1901, 395/2150, vol. 5, LS 903; Lt. Frank A. Wilcox to C.O.'s, La Union, Abra, Ilocos Norte, Ilocos Sur, 1 May 1901, 395/5583, Box 4, LR 2529.

101. Brig. Gen. J. Franklin Bell to C.O., 3d Cav., 13 May 1901, 395/2150, vol. 5, LS 778; Brig. Gen. J. Franklin Bell to C.O., Ilocos Sur, 26 May 1901, 395/2150, vol. 5, LS 853; Capt. Henry L. Ripley, Adj. to C.O., Cabuagao, 27 May 1901, 395/5578, vol. 7, LS 1597. For former guerrillas helping the Army see Col. William S. Mc-Caskey to Brig. Gen. J. Franklin Bell, 1 May 1901, 395/4043, LS Bk 4, LS 1400. For

provincial reports, see Senate, *Affairs*, pp. 192–94, 212, 350–51; 429–33, 461–70, 498–500.

Chapter Three

1. Funston, *Memories of Two Wars*, pp. 314–15. A shortened version of this chapter appeared in Linn, "Guerrilla Fighter: Frederick Funston in the Philippines, 1900–1901," *Kansas History* 10 (Spring 1987): 2–16.

2. Capt. Augustus C. Macomb to AG, DNP, 16 March 1902, 395/2635, Hq, DNP, General Correspondence, Nov. 1901 to Oct. 1902, Box 6, LR 7454; Wernstedt and Spencer, *Philippine Island World*, pp. 371–73, 631; Kerkvliet, *Huk Rebellion*, pp. 1–25; Larkin, "Philippine History Reconsidered," p. 614. Principe province has since been incorporated into Quezon (Tayabas) province.

3. Ferdinand Macabulos, "Statement," 10 July 1898, Exhibit 130, Taylor, *Philippine Insurrection*, pp. 50–51 MG, 22 AJ; "Acta de la proclamación de la independencia de la provincia Nueva Ecija," 3 July 1898, PIR SD 345.1; Zaide, *Philippine Revolution*, pp. 116–17, 126; Guerrero, "Luzon at War," p. 203; L. M. Lacundola to Emilio Aguinaldo, 18 April 1899, PIR SD 192.3; Wilcox, *Through Luzon on Highways and Byways*, p. 197.

4. Funston, *Memories of Two Wars*, p. 319; Larkin, *Pampangans*, p. 126; William H. Taft to Elihu Root, 13 September 1900, Taft Papers, series 21; Gleeck, *Nueva Ecija*, pp. 6–7. In 1960 out of Nueva Ecija's total population of 608,300 some 386,700 were Tagalog speaking, 205,000 Ilocano speaking, 10,400 Pangasinan or Pampango speaking, and 6,200 spoke another language. It is quite possible that the proportion of the Tagalog-speaking people has increased substantially from the 1900 level, see Wernstedt and Spencer, *Philippine Island World*, pp. 622–23.

5. May, "Why the United States Won the Philippine-American War," pp. 365–67. For the antipathy of peasants toward the Republican regime in central Luzon, see Guerrero, "Luzon at War," pp. 144–49, 164–204. For the conditions of the peasantry in Nueva Ecija and later revolts see Ileto, *Payson and Revolution*, pp. 259–313; Sturtevant, *Popular Uprisings*, pp. 70–72, 131–38, 175–92; Kerkvliet, *Huk Rebellion*, esp. pp. 1–25. John A. Larkin argues that the Pampangans, when faced with a similar situation, opted for the security of American rule, see Larkin, *Pampangans*, pp. 119–26. For the collaboration of the elite with the Americans, see Funston, *Memories of Two Wars*, pp. 355–56; Brig. Gen. Frederick Funston to AG, DNL, 2 January 1901, 395/2263, 4D, DNL, TS, Jan. 1900 to Aug. 1901, Box 4.

6. "Decree Appointing Pantaleon García to the Supreme Command in Central Luzon," 2 November 1899, PIR SD 243.2; Taylor, *Philippine Insurrection*, p. 49 HS; Maj. Gen. Pantaleon García, "Appointments," 9 January 1900, ibid., Exhibit 1037, p. 44 GV; Maj. Gen. Pantaleon García to Lt. Col. Casmirio Tinio, 3 January 1900, PIR SD 243.3. García's appointment from Emilio Aguinaldo is in PIR SD 243.2. For José Alejandrino's assumption of authority, see Brig. Gen. José Alejandrino to Isidro Torres, 1 July 1900, PIR SD 323.11; Brig. Gen. Tomás Mascardo to Brig. Gen. José Alejandrino, 1 November 1900, PIR SD 625.1.

7. Quote "death blow to the insurgent cause" from *ANJ* 37 (25 June 1900). Hq, 34th Inf. to C.O., "K" Co., 34th Inf., 13 April 1900, 395/2790, Aliaga, Nueva Ecija, LR, Apr. to Aug. 1900, LR 35; Maj. Gen. Pantaleon García to Brig. Gen. Isidro Torres, 2 February 1900, PIR SD 243.11; Maj. Gen. Pantaleon García to Brig. Gen. Isidro Torres, 10 February 1900, Taylor, *Philippine Insurrection*, Exhibit 1044, pp. 45–46 GV; Maj. Gen. Pantaleon García, "Decree," 15 April 1900, ibid., Exhibit 1054, p. 48 GV; *WD* 1900 1:4:59–60, 62; Maj. Gen. Pantaleon García, "Instructions for Guerrillas and Flying Columns," 25 November 1899, PIR SD 243.6; Capt. Erneste V. Smith to AG, 4D, 7 May 1900, 395/2133, LR 5166; *ANJ* 37 (12 May and 25 June 1900). For background of García, see Zaide, *Philippine Revolution*, pp. 294–95; Gleeck, *Nueva Ecija*, p. 6; Funston, *Memories of Two Wars*, p. 318.

8. Quote "cruel and cowardly scoundrel" from Brig. Gen. Frederick Funston to AG, DNL, 17 May 1900, 395/2263, Box 1. Funston, *Memories of Two Wars*, pp. 319, 357; "Diary of Events, May 6 to June 14, 1900," 94/228335; Col. Pablo Padilla to Lt. Col. Casmirio Tinio, 21 January 1900, PIR SD 51.8; Col. Teodoro Sandico to Lt. Col. Casmirio Tinio, 20 July 1900, Taylor, *Philippine Insurrection*, Exhibit 1079, p. 56 GV; Brig. Gen. Frederick Funston to AG, DNL, 25 May 1901, 395/2262, 4D, DNL, Copies of LS, Apr. 1900 to Oct. 1901, LS 2759; *WD* 1900 1:4:360–61. Padilla admitted to executing several of his own men, see Brig. Gen. Frederick Funston to AG, DNL, 20 May 1900, 395/2263, Box 1. For Padilla's interference in local affairs, see Lt. Col. Pablo Padilla to Marcelino García, 13 January 1900, PIR SD 498.1. For complaints on the behavior of Padilla's men, see Ferdinand Madrid to Col. Pablo Padilla, 17 February 1900, PIR SD 345.4.

9. For examples of guerrilla proclamations, see Maj. Gen. Pantaleon García to Brig. Gen. Isidro Torres, 2 February 1900, PIR SD 243.11; Maj. Gen. Pantaleon García to Brig. Gen. Isidro Torres, 10 February 1900, Taylor, *Philippine Insurrection*, Exhibit 1044, pp. 45–46 GV; Maj. Gen. Pantaleon García, "Decree," 15 April 1900, ibid., Exhibit 1054, p. 48 GV; Lt. Col. Casmirio Tinio to Captain of Detachment at Margan, 26 March 1900, PIR SD 480.12; *WD* 1900 1:5:62; Capt. Willard D. Newbill to AG, San Isidro, 7 February 1900, 94/117, 34th Inf., LS Bk 1, LS 214; Lt. Col. Casmirio Tinio to Jefe Local of Toro and Santa Rita, 17 March 1900, PIR SD 51.9. The revolutionary central leadership did authorize the formation of Katipunan societies and militia, but there is little indication these orders were ever implemented, see Ambrosio Flores to Marcelo García, 5 January 1900, Taylor, *Philippine Insurrection*, Exhibit 1035, p. 43 GV.

10. *WD* 1899 1:4:119–21. For Luna's killing, see May, "Why the United States Won the Philippine American War," pp. 362–63; Lt. C. N. Murphy, "Death of Antonio Luna," PIR SD 861.3; "El Commercio," 23 July 1903, PIR SD 1021.6; Kalaw, *Development of Philippine Politics*, pp. 205–16; Sexton, *Soldiers in the Sun*, p. 166; Zaide, *Philippine Revolution*, pp. 315–17; Taylor, *Philippine Insurrection*, p. 43 AJ; Alejandrino, *Price of Freedom*, pp. 149–59; Bain, *Sitting in Darkness*, pp. 189–90.

11. Quote "fearfully strung out," from Maj. Gen. Henry W. Lawton to CS, 17 November 1899, *WD* 1900 1:4:263. For U.S. operations in Nueva Ecija see, ibid., pp. 217–38, 262–88; ibid., 1:6:6–404; Col. Lyman W. V. Kennon to Lt. Col. Clarence R. Edwards, 8 December 1899, 94/117, 34th Inf., LS Bk 1, LS 164; Emilio Aguinaldo to Lt. Col. Casmirio Tinio, 18 October 1899, PIR SD 1198.1; Woolard, "Philippine

Scouts," pp. 24–41. For evidence of Republican demoralization see the captured correspondence in PIR SD 299.1; Alejandrino, *Price of Freedom*, p. 191; Funston, *Memories of Two Wars*, p. 313; *WD* 1900 1:5:46. For Army confusion, see Col. Lyman W. V. Kennon to Maj. Gen. Loyd Wheaton, 8, 9, and 10 December 1899, 94/117, 34th Inf., LS Bk 1, LS 172, 174, 182, 183; Funston, *Memories of Two Wars*, p. 313. For the organization of the Philippine Cavalry, see Woolard, "Philippine Scouts," pp. 56, 77–88. The Macabebes, natives of the town of Macabebe, Pampanga, had served as elite troops for the Spanish, see Coffman, "Batson of the Scouts," p. 70.

12. For biographical material on Funston see Funston, *Memories of Two Wars*; Crouch, "The Making of a Soldier"; Crouch, *A Yankee Guerrillero*; Bain, *Sitting in Darkness*. For Funston's popularity with his soldiers, see Ganzhorn, *I've Killed Men*, pp. 147–208; Elston Mitchell Questionnaire; William H. Taft to Elihu Root, 14 July 1900, Taft Papers, series 21.

13. Capt. Erneste V. Smith to C.O.'s, San Fernando, etc., 20 January 1900, 395/2263. Col. Lyman W. V. Kennon to Maj. Gen. Arthur MacArthur, 27 December 1899, LS Bk 1, LS 217; Col. Lyman W. V. Kennon to AAAG, 3d Brig., 2d Div., 8 A.C., 13 March 1900, LS 363; Col. Lyman W. V. Kennon to Col. Charles Keller, 4 February 1900, LS Bk 1, LS 199; Col. Lyman W. V. Kennon to AG, San Isidro, 21 March 1900, LS Bk 2, LS 398, all in 94/117, 34th Inf., LS Bks; Brig. Gen. Frederick Funston to Col. Lyman W. V. Kennon, 29 March 1900, 395/2262; Capt. Erneste V. Smith to AG, 2d Div., 31 January 1900, 395/2263, Box 1; Maj. John Baldwin to AG, 3d Brig., 2d Div., 1 March 1900, 395/4965, San Isidro, Nueva Ecija, LS, Feb. 1900 to July 1906.

14. Brig. Gen. Frederick Funston to AG, 2d Div., 21 March and 28 March 1900, 395/2262; "Reports of Operations of the Thirty-fourth Infantry, U.S.V. in the Provinces of Nueva Ecija and Bulacan, Luzon, P.I., March 16 to August 30, 1900, by Maj. Joseph Wheeler, Jr., Thirty-fourth Infantry, U.S.V.," *WD* 1900 1:7:365–67; Maj. Joseph E. Wheeler, "Report of Expedition and Engagement, March 18 1900," 7 April 1900, 395/2133, LR 4516; Capt. Erneste V. Smith to AG, DNL, 21 March 1900 395/2263, Box 1; Brig. Gen. Frederick Funston to AG, DNL, 25 May 1901, 395/2262, LS 2759.

15. Brig. Gen. Frederick Funston to AG, 2d. Div., 6 April 1900, 395/2263, Box 1; Maj. John A. Baldwin to AG, 3d Brig., 2d Div., 27 February 1900, 391/1728, 22d U.S. Inf. LS Bk; Capt. Erneste V. Smith to AG, 4D, DNL, 7 May 1900, 395/2133, LR 5166; Brig. Gen. Frederick Funston to AG, DNL, 20 May 1900, 395/2263, Box 1; Brig. Gen. Frederick Funston to AG, DNL, 25 May 1901, 295/2262, LS 2759; Funston, *Memories of Two Wars*, pp. 347–48; Hq, 34th Inf. to C.O., Co. "K," 34th Inf., Aliaga, 13 April 1900, 395/2790; Capt. Erneste V. Smith to Brig. Gen. Frederick Funston, 6 May 1900, 395/2262; *ANJ* 37 (12 May and 25 June 1900); "Diary of Events 5/6/00 to 6/14/00," 94/338335; Capt. Erneste V. Smith to Capt. Robert W. Dowdey, 10 March 1901, 395/2263, Box 4; Lt. Col. Casmirio Tinio to Brig. Gen. Frederick Funston, 26 September 1900, PIR SD 480.9.

16. "Settlement of a Check for 200,000 pesos," Taylor, *Philippine Insurrection*, Exhibit 78, p. 77 LY; Emilio Aguinaldo to Col. Urbano Lacuna, 29 October 1899, ibid., Exhibit 706, p. 46 GR; Brig. Gen. Frederick Funston to AG, DNL, 28 May 1900, 395/2263, Box 2; Brig. Gen. Frederick Funston to AG, DNL, 28 June 1900,

395/2263; Brig. Gen. Frederick Funston to AG, DNL, 25 May 1901 395/2262, LS 2759; Manuel, *Dictionary of Philippine Biography*, pp. 239–41; LeRoy, *Americans in the Philippines*, 2:213: "Brig. Gen. Urbano Lacuna" File, PIR SD 658; Alejandrino, *Price of Freedom*, pp. 158–59.

17. Brig. Gen. Frederick Funston to AG, DNL, 14 June 1900, 395/2263, Box 2; Capt. Erneste V. Smith to Brig. Gen. Frederick Funston, 12 May 1900, 395/2263, Box 1; Brig. Gen. Urbano Lacuna to Adj., Btln. Lorenzo Tugcay Tamayo, 19 May 1900, *WD* 1900 1:7:120.

18. Funston, *Memories of Two Wars*, pp. 348–54, 357–59; "Report of Engagement on Mount Balubad, Province of Bulacan, P.I., June 11, 1900, by Brig. Gen. F. D. Grant, U.S.V.," *WD* 1900 1:7:115–20; Ganzhorn, *I've Killed Men*, pp. 176–82; Col. Lyman W. V. Kennon to AG, 4D, DNL, 14 June 1900, 395/3248, Cabanatuan, Nueva Ecija, LS, Mar. 1900 to Dec. 1901, LS 117.

19. *WD* 1900 1:7:370–71; Hq, 4D, DNL to AG, DNL, 14 June 1900, Folder P-3, Funston Papers; Lt. Harry W. Newton to Capt. William D. Newbill, 19 June 1900, 395/2269, LR 873; Funston, *Memories of Two Wars*, pp. 359–65; Ganzhorn, *I've Killed Men*, pp. 182–84; *ANJ* 37 (25 June 1900).

20. Col. Pablo Tecson to Brig. Gen. Isidro Torres, 23 and 28 August 1900, PIR SD 545.1 and 545.3; Brig. Gen. Urbano Lacuna to Lt. Col. Alipio Tecson, 1 August 1900, PIR SD 591.2; Maj. Joseph E. Wheeler to AG, 4D, DNL, 26 August 1900, 395/2269; Brig. Gen. Frederick Funston to AG, DNL, 24 June 1900, 395/2633, Box 2; Capt. Erneste V. Smith to AG, DNL, 27 July 1900, ibid.; Brig. Gen. Frederick Funston to AG, DNL, 25 May 1901, 395/2262, LS 2759; *WD* 1900 1:7:372–76.

21. Funston, *Memories of Two Wars*, p. 373. Maj. William C. Brown to Helen Brown, 26 January 1901, Brown Papers, Box 2; Brig. Gen. Urbano Lacuna to Capts. Severo and Dionisio de los Santos, 12 August 1900, Taylor, *Philippine Insurrection*, Exhibit 1085, p. 58 GV; Brig. Gen. Urbano Lacuna to Lt. Col. Joaquin Natividad, 22 November 1900, 395/2133, LR 2147; Diary of William C. Brown, 2 January 1901, Brown Papers. Funston's officers reported very few assassinations or assaults in their towns, see correspondence in 395/2133.

22. Brig. Gen. Frederick Funston to AG, DNL, 2 January 1901, 395/2263, Box 4. Brig. Gen. Frederick Funston to AG, DNL, 13 January 1901, 395/2262. For U.S. operations see "Chronological List" in Brig. Gen. Frederick Funston to AG, DNL, 25 May 1901, 395/2262, LS 2759.

23. Brig. Gen. Frederick Funston to AG, DNL, 8 February 1900, 395/2263, Box 4.

24. Quote "devoted all their energies" and statistics on engagements from Brig. Gen. Frederick Funston to AG, DNL, 25 May 1901, 395/2262, LS 2759. For reports on operations, see *WD* 1900 1:7:365–76; "Reports of Operations in Fourth District, Department of Northern Luzon," *WD* 1901 1:5:130–34; Brig. Gen. Frederick Funston to AG, DNL, 25 January and 10 May 1901, 395/2263, Box 4; Capt. John J. Crittenden, "Report of Operations," 16 February 1901, 395/2133, LR 3787; Brig. Gen. Frederick Funston to AG, DNL, 10 March 1901, 395/2133, LR 803; Funston, *Memories of Two Wars*, pp. 381–83. For evidence of Lacuna's having to threaten his subordinates see Brig. Gen. Urbano Lacuna to Capts. Severo and Dionisio de los Santos, 12 August 1900, Exhibit 1085, Taylor, *Philippine Insurrection*, p. 58 GV; Brig.

Gen. Urbano Lacuna to Majors and Captains Commanding Companies of the 1st and 2d Btlns., 7 December 1900, PIR SD 658.4.

25. Capt. Erneste V. Smith to Capt. Robert W. Dowdey, 10 March 1901, 395/2263, Box 4; Brig. Gen. Frederick Funston to AG, DNL, 10 April 1901, 25 April 1901, 29 April 1901, 9 May 1901, all in ibid.; Alejandrino, *Price of Freedom*, pp. 172–74. For accounts of Aguinaldo's capture, see *WD* 1901 1:5:122–30; Funston, *Memories of Two Wars*, pp. 384–426; Lt. James D. Taylor to AG, 4D, DNL, 10 February 1901, 395/2269; Lt. James D. Taylor to Adj., 24th Inf., 8 April 1901, 395/2133, LR 10677; PIR SD 697; Diary of William C. Brown, 10–12 February 1901, Brown Papers; Bain, *Sitting in Darkness*.

26. Diary of William C. Brown, 14 August 1900, Brown Papers.

27. Quote "hard to beat" from Funston, *Memories of Two Wars*, p. 373, also see pp. 344–46. Brig. Gen. Frederick Funston to Col. Charles Keller, 20 April 1900; Brig. Gen. Frederick Funston to AG, DNL, 19 May, 14 and 16 October 1900, and 10 January 1901, all in 395/2263, Box 1; Brig. Gen. Frederick Funston to AG, DNL, 8 May 1900, 395/2262; Brig. Gen. Frederick Funston to Provost Marshal General, 13 December 1900, ibid.; Capt. Frank A. Sullivan to Adj., 34th Inf., 20 May 1900, 395/4047, LR 141. For a later districtwide campaign to spread photographs of prominent revolutionaries, see Capt. Erneste V. Smith to C.O., San Isidro, etc., 18 April 1901, 395/2261, LS 1306.

28. Col. Lyman W. V. Kennon to AG, DNL, 5 June 1900, 395/3248, LS 79.

29. Lt. David Wheeler to Adj., 22d Inf., 3 October 1900, 395/2269, LR 1435.

30. Funston, *Memories of Two Wars*, pp. 315–16; Ganzhorn, *I've Killed Men*, pp. 147–49; Brig. Gen. Frederick Funston to AG, DNL, 25 May 1901, 395/2262, LS 2759; Lt. Col. Charles Keller to AG, 4D, 8 October 1900, 395/2269; Adj. to Col. Lyman W. V. Kennon, 10 October 1900, 395/3248; Lt. David P. Wheeler to Adj. 22d Inf., 22 October 1900, 395/2269, LR 1674; Col. Lyman W. V. Kennon to AG, 4D, DNL, 17 and 31 October 1900, 395/3248, LS 476 and 532; Diary of William C. Brown, 31 October 1900, Brown Papers.

31. Capt. Erneste V. Smith to C.O., San José, 7 January 1900, 395/2263, Box 1. For official policy, see Capt. Erneste V. Smith to Col. Lyman W. V. Kennon, 31 January 1900, ibid.; Capt. Erneste V. Smith to C.O., Cabiao, 5 February 1900, ibid.

32. Brig. Gen. Frederick Funston to AG, DNL, 3 January 1901, ibid., Box 4.

33. Brig. Gen. Frederick Funston to AG, DNL, 29 October 1900 and 8 January 1901, ibid., Box 4; Maj. Thomas Baldwin to AG, 4D, DNL, 4 June 1900, 395/2133, LR 6474; Capt. Erneste V. Smith to AG, DNL, 1 and 2 June 1900, 395/2263, Box 2. Funston was under considerable pressure to retaliate for wire cutting, see Maj. Benjamin Alvord to Brig. Gen. Frederick Funston, 3 January 1901, 395/2270, Hq, 4D, DNL, Telegrams Received, Jan. 1900 to Oct. 1901.

34. Capt. Ernest V. Smith to C.O.'s, 3 June 1900, 395/2263, Box 2.

35. Lt. Henry A. Ripley to AAAG, San Isidro, 15 March 1900, 395/2270. Capt. Erneste V. Smith to Lt. Henry A. Ripley, 15 March 1900, 395/2262.

36. Capt. George C. Gibson to Adj., San Isidro, 31 March 1900, 395/4967. Capt. Erneste V. Smith to AG, DNL, 1 and 2 June 1900, 395/2263, Box 2.

37. Col. Lyman W. V. Kennon to Rosa Cajucon, 24 July 1900, 395/3248, LS 179.

38. Lt. Day to Lt. Frank Jernigan, 30 December 1900, 395/2263, Box 3. For the

incident regarding the summary execution of the guerrillas, see Brig. Gen. Frederick Funston to AG, 2d Div., 27 March 1900, 395/2263, Box 1; Funston, *Memories of Two Wars*, pp. 331–35; Ganzhorn, *I've Killed Men*, pp. 166–69; *ANJ* 37 (14 April 1900).

39. Funston, *Memories of Two Wars*, pp. 355–56.

40. Quote "duress of the strongest kind" from Brig. Gen. Frederick Funston to AG, DNL, 8 July 1901, 395/2262. C. Gonzales to Teodoro Sandico, 3 August 1900, Taylor, *Philippine Insurrection*, Exhibit 1083, p. 57 GV.

41. Brig. Gen. Frederick Funston to AG, DNL, 2 and 8 January 1901, 395/2262. For relations between Tinio and Funston, see Brig. Gen. Frederick Funston to Col. Lyman W. V. Kennon, 27 October 1900, 395/2263, Box 3; Brig. Gen. Frederick Funston to Brig. Gen. J. Franklin Bell, 25 July 1900, 395/2263, Box 2; Capt. Erneste V. Smith to Brig. Gen. Frederick Funston, 15 March 1901, ibid., Box 4; Col. Casmirio Tinio to Brig. Gen. Frederick Funston, 29 July and 26 September 1900, PIR SD 480.8–9.

42. Funston, *Memories of Two Wars*, p. 433. Brig. Gen. Frederick Funston to AG, DNL, 9 and 19 May 1901, 395/2263, Box 4; "Translation of Surrender Terms for Urbano Lacuna," 18 May 1901, PIR SD 658.6. For other negotiations, see Brig. Gen. Frederick Funston to AG, DNL, 28 June 1900; Brig. Gen. Frederick Funston to Maj. Joseph Wheeler, 9 July 1900; Capt. Erneste V. Smith to C.O.'s, Gapan and Peñaranda, 10 July 1900; Brig. Gen. Frederick Funston to Lt. Col. Wilbur E. Wilder, 12 July 1900, all in 395/2263, Box 2; William H. Taft to Elihu Root, 14 July 1900, Taft Papers, series 21; Brig. Gen. Frederick Funston to AG, DNL, 10 March 1901, 395/2133, LR 803; Lt. Burton J. Mitchel to AG, DNL, 7 April 1901, 395/2263, Box 4; Brig. Gen. Frederick Funston to AG, DNL, 10 April 1901, ibid.; Col. Henry B. Freeman to AG, DNL, 8 October 1900, 395/2129, LS 670; Maj. Gen. Loyd Wheaton to Col. Henry B. Freeman, 8 October 1900, ibid., LS 670; Capt. Frank A. Sullivan to AAG, 4D, DNL, 30 December 1900, 395/2788, LS 55; Brig. Gen. Frederick Funston to AG, DNL, 5 and 6 January 1901, 395/2263, Box 4; Maj. Benjamin Alvord, AAG, DNL, to Brig. Gen. Frederick Funston, 7 January 1900, 395/2270, Box 5.

43. Col. Lyman W. V. Kennon to AG, 7 July 1900, 395/3248, LS 148. Brig. Gen. Frederick Funston to AG, DNL, 10 and 30 December 1900, 395/2263, Box 3; "The General Situation," in Col. Lyman W. V. Kennon to Secretary Proctor, 17 January 1902, Kennon Papers; Col. Lyman W. V. Kennon to AG, DNL, 7 June 1900, LS 83; Col. Lyman W. V. Kennon to AG, DNL, 8 June 1900, LS 94; Col. Lyman W. V. Kennon to Lt. Col. Robert L. Howze, 13 June 1900, LS 114; Col. Lyman W. V. Kennon to AG, 4D, DNL, 30 June 1900, LS 142, all in 395/3248; Maj. Edwin B. Bolton to AG, 4D, 16 December 1900, 395/2269. For Americans serving with the Ilocano Scouts, see Capt. Erneste V. Smith to C.O.'s, Co's A and B, Ilocano Scouts, 16 January 1901, 395/2262.

44. Col. Lyman W. V. Kennon to C.O., Bayombong, 8 March 1900, 94/117, 34th Inf., LS Bk 1, LS 328. Col. Lyman W. V. Kennon to AAG, San Isidro, 29 March 1900, ibid., LS 427. For correspondence on the use of Ilocanos, see Col. Lyman W. V. Kennon to CS, 10 December 1899, LS 187; Col. Lyman W. V. Kennon to Brig. Gen. Loyd Wheaton, 12 December 1899, LS 197; Col. Lyman W. V. Kennon to Maj. Benjamin Alvord, AG, 28 December 1899, LS 255; Col. Lyman W. V. Kennon to AG,

3d Brig., 6 March 1900, LS 318, all in 94/117, 34th Inf., LS Bk 1; Brig. Gen. Frederick Funston to AG, 2d Div., 15 January 1900, 395/2263, Box 1; Col. Lyman W. V. Kennon to Capt. William Dame, 13 January 1900, LS 97; Lt. Col. Charles Keller to AG, 3d Brig., 27 March 1900, all in 395/2270.

45. Col. Lyman W. V. Kennon to AG, 3d Brig., 2d Div., 8th A.C., 8 March 1900, 94/117, 34th Inf., LS Bk 2, LS 443. For recruitment of Ilocano Scouts, see Col. Lyman W. V. Kennon to AG, 4D, DNL, 29 May 1900, 395/3248, TS 50; Col. Lyman W. V. Kennon to C.O., San José, 5 June 1900, 395/3248, LS 76; Col. Lyman W. V. Kennon to Chief Ordnance Officer, DivPhil, 29 May 1900, 94/117, 34th Inf., LS Bk 2, LS 560; Col. Lyman W. V. Kennon to Lt. Col. Robert L. Howze, 13 June 1900, 395/3248, LS 114; Maj. Gen. Ewell S. Otis to Col. Lyman W. V. Kennon, 24 April 1900, 94/117, 34th Inf., LS Bk 2, LS 443.

46. Adj., 34th Inf., to Capt. Frank A. Sullivan, 14 April 1900, 395/2070. For Ilocano operations, see "Miller" to Col. Lyman W. V. Kennon, 2 September 1900, 395/3248, LS 340; Col. Lyman W. V. Kennon to AG, DivPhil, 8 October 1900, 395/2133, LR 848; Brig. Gen. Frederick Funston to AG, DNL, 25 May 1901, 395/2262, LS 2759; Brig. Gen. Frederick Funston to AG, DNL, 5 December 1900, 395/2263, Box 3; Funston, *Memories of Two Wars*, pp. 344–46; Brig. Gen. Frederick Funston to Col. Charles Keller, 20 April 1900, 395/2263, Box 1; Col. Lyman W. V. Kennon to Capt. Frank A. Sullivan, 12 June 1900, 395/3248, LS 110; Col. Lyman W. V. Kennon to Military Governor, San Isidro, 7 and 9 November 1900, 395/3248, LS 566 and 572.

47. Col. Lyman W. V. Kennon to AG, DNL, 7, 8, and 30 June 1900, 395/3248, LS 83, 94, and 142; Capt. Frank A. Sullivan to AG, 4D, DNL, 23 December 1900, 395/2788, LS 49.

48. Maj. Gen. Loyd Wheaton to AG, DNL, 26 September 1900, 94/369141; Brig. Gen. Frederick Funston to AG, DNL, 10 and 30 December 1900, 395/2263, Box 3; Brig. Gen. Frederick Funston to Maj. Benjamin Alvord, 26 August 1900, ibid., Box 2; Capt. Erneste V. Smith to Col. Lyman W. V. Kennon, 8 September 1900, ibid., Box 3; William H. Taft to Elihu Root, 13 September 1900, Taft Papers, series 21; "The General Situation," Kennon Papers. Funston felt that the shortage of U.S. officers was so critical that he would have to disband some native units, see Brig. Gen. Frederick Funston to AG, DNL, 6 February 1901, 395/2263, Box 4. For the episode of the payment for the Ilocano rifles see Capt. Charles A. Green to AG, 13 June 1900, 395/2133, LR 8933; Lt. Col. Samuel D. Sturgis to C.G., DNL, 6 October 1900, 395/2130, LS 767; Col. Lyman W. V. Kennon to C.O., Aliaga, 31 October 1900, 395/3248, LS 521.

49. Lt. Col. Alfred C. Markley to AG, 4D, 22 January 1901, 395/2270, Box 5; Pantaleon Aliciano y Dias to U.S. Colonel, Cabanatuan, 16 July 1900, 395/4047, LR 371; Col. Lyman W. V. Kennon to Capt. Frank A. Sullivan, 17 and 19 August 1900, 395/3248, LS 320–21; Col. Teodoro Sandico to Maj. Gen. Arthur MacArthur, 20 November 1900, PIR SD 567.4; Col. Teodoro Sandico to Col. Lyman W. V. Kennon, 1900, 395/2269, LR 630; Brig. Gen. Frederick Funston to Col. French, 16 January 1900, 395/2263, Box 1.

50. Lt. Ivers W. Leonard to C.O., San Antonio, 15 December 1900, 395/2264, Box 2. Maj. William C. Brown to Grace [sister], 16 December 1900, Brown Papers,

Box 1; Maj. William C. Brown to AG, 4D, DNL, 24 December 1900, 395/2269, Box 2.

51. Quote "enforce discipline" from Maj. Benjamin Alvord to Brig. Gen. Frederick Funston, 2 January 1901, 395/2270. For Funston's comments, see Brig. Gen. Frederick Funston to Lt. Henry A. Ripley, 31 December 1900, 395/2261, LS Bk 4, LS 2924.

52. Brig. Gen. Frederick Funston to AG, DNL, 10 December 1900, 395/2262. Diary of William C. Brown, 25 June 1900, Brown Papers. For correspondence on civil government, see Maj. James A. Baldwin to Military Governor, 17 May 1900, 395/2133, LR 4022; Col. Lyman W. V. Kennon to Judge Advocate, Manila, 19 March 1900, 94/117, 34th Inf., LS Bk 1, LS 381; Col. Lyman W. V. Kennon to AG, 4D, DNL, 13 May 1900, 395/3248, LS 44; Col. Henry B. Freeman to AG, 2d Div., 11 April 1900, 395/2269; Lt. Col. Alfred L. Markley to AG, DNL, 22 January 1901, 395/2133, LR 3622. For Funston's attempt to organize civil government in July, see Brig. Gen. Frederick Funston to AG, DNL, 9 May 1900, 395/2262, LS 224; Brig. Gen. Frederick Funston, G.O. 1, 28 July 1900, 395/3198, Bongabon, Nueva Ecija, Miscellaneous Letters, Telegrams, Orders, and Reports, 1900–1903; Brig. Gen. Frederick Funston to AG, DNL, 20 September 1900, 395/2262, LS 1692; Brig. Gen. Frederick Funston to AG, DNL, 14 October 1900, 395/2261, LS Bk 3, LS 1930. For the results in local areas, see the following entries in 395/3248: Col. Lyman W. V. Kennon to C.O., Bongabon, 9 August 1900, LS 274; Col. Lyman W. V. Kennon to AG, 4D, DNL, 19 September 1900, LS 379; Col. Lyman W. V. Kennon to C.O., Santa Rosa, 19 September 1900, LS 378; "Number of Qualified Electors-Bongabon-Sept. 20 1900," all in 395/3198.

53. Brig. Gen. Frederick Funston to AG, DNL, 12 December 1900, 395/2262, LS 2374; Col. Lyman W. V. Kennon to AG, 4D, 30 September 1900, 395/3248, LS 1929; Brig. Gen. Frederick Funston to AG, DNL, 4 October 1900, 395/2261, LS 1929; Capt. Erneste V. Smith to AG, DNL, 31 July 1900, 395/2262, LS 1085; Brig. Gen. Frederick Funston to AG, DNL, 13 April 1901, ibid., LS 1290.

54. "Report of the Governor of Nueva Ecija," 15 January 1902, Senate, *Affairs*, p. 502. For Funston's optimistic reports, see Brig. Gen. Frederick Funston to AG, DNL, 13 January 1901, 395/2262; Brig. Gen. Frederick Funston to AG, DNL, 4 March 1901, 395/2261, LS 799. For more pessimistic, and probably more accurate reports, see Capt. Erneste V. Smith to C.O.'s, 11 March 1901, 395/2262; Capt. Erneste V. Smith to AG, DNL, 1 May 1901, 395/2261, LS Bk 5, LS 1633; Capt. M. Black to AG, 4D, 30 June 1901, 395/3248, LS 38; Lt. Col. Alfred C. Markley, "Report for the Month of May 1901 on Native Police in 24th U.S. Infantry Territory," 395/2269.

55. Maj. James A. Baldwin to AG, 3d Brig., 2d Div., 8 March 1900, 395/4965.

56. Maj. James A. Baldwin to Military Governor, 17 April 1900, 395/2133, LR 4022. For other information and views on education, see Col. Lyman W. V. Kennon to AG, 4D, DNL, 13 May 1900, 395/3248; Capt. Jacob F. Kreps to Adj., 22d Inf., 11 May 1900, 395/4965; Lt. Col. Alfred L. Markley to AG, 4D, DNL, 22 January 1901, 395/2133, LR 3622; Lt. Stanley Howland to Adj., 24th Inf., 1 June 1901, 395/5045, San José, Nueva Ecija, LS, Mar. 1900 to May 1902; Capt. Erneste V. Smith to AG, DivPhil, 7 October 1901, 395/2262.

57. Brig. Gen. Frederick Funston to AG, DNL, 13 January 1901, 395/2262.

Chapter Four

1. Col. Walter Howe, "Historical Sketch of the 47th Infantry, U.S.V.," 94/187.
2. Wernstedt and Spencer, *Philippine Island World*, pp. 605–6, 631–32; Galang, *Encyclopedia of the Philippines*, 16:119–20, 162–70.
3. Owen, "Kabikolan in the Nineteenth Century"; Wildman, "Hemp Industry."
4. Owen, "Winding Down the War in Albay," pp. 558–61; Ataviado, *Revolution in the Bicol Region*; Schumacher, *Revolutionary Clergy*, pp. 62–64, 155–60; Zaide, *Philippine Revolution*, pp. 224–25; LeRoy, *Americans in the Philippines*, 1:338–39.
5. Ataviado, *Revolution in the Bicol Region*, esp. pp. 164–67. For background on Belarmino, see "Notes for the History of the Glorious Epopée of the Independence of the Philippines," Taylor, *Philippine Insurrection*, Exhibit 70, p. 70 LY; Maj. Gen. Vito Belarmino to Emilio Aguinaldo, 28 May 1899, PIR SD 1014.2; Vito Belarmino Files, PIR SD 341, 747, and 1070. Manuel, *Dictionary of Philippine Biography*, pp. 297–99; Taylor, *Philippine Insurrection*, p. 43 AJ; "Ignacio Paua File," PIR SD 355.
6. For an organizational breakdown of the Republican forces in Albay, see Ataviado, *Lucha y Libertad*, 2:31–38; Owen, "Winding Down the War in Albay," pp. 560–61; "Presidencia Local de Sagnay," 10 February 1899, PIR SD 1150.2; Estanislas Legaspi to "Ilustre General" [Belarmino?], 8 May 1899, PIR SD 257.8; "Ligeros Apuntes sobre las Provincias del Sur de Luzon," U.S. Navy, ZE Files, "Philippine Islands"; Brig. Gen. Ignacio Paua to Emilio Aguinaldo, 10 November 1898, PIR SD 355.10; Brig. Gen. Vicente Lukban to Emilio Aguinaldo, 25 October 1898, PIR SD 844.3; Maj. Gen. Vito Belarmino to Emilio Aguinaldo, 28 May 1899, PIR SD 1014.1.
7. *WD* 1900 1:7:15.
8. Maj. Gen. Henry C. Corbin to Maj. Gen. Elwell S. Otis, 9 January 1900, *CWS*, 2:1130. For Otis's reply, see Maj. Gen. Elwell S. Otis to AG, Washington, D.C., 10 January 1900, ibid., 2:1131. For a discussion of the "hemp panic," see Owen, "Winding Down the War in Albay," pp. 575–78.
9. For Kobbé's work in civil government, see Gates, *Schoolbooks and Krags*, pp. 88–89; Kobbé Papers.
10. *WD* 1900 1:7:19–28; Ataviado, *Lucha y Libertad*, 2:43–50; Howe, "Historical Sketch of the 47th," 94/187; Maj. Hugh D. Wise to Adj., 47th Inf., 23 January 1900, 395/3668, Donsol, Sorsogon, LS, Dec. 1899 to Mar. 1902, LS 19; Maj. Hugh D. Wise, "Information on Philippine Islands Questionnaire—Donsol," 1901, 395/2421, Hq, 3D, DSL, LR Relating to Civil Affairs, 1900–1901; Maj. Gen. Vito Belarmino to Lt. Gen. Mariano Trías, 28 February 1900, PIR SD 1070.2.
11. Brig. Gen. William A. Kobbé to AG, D.P., 24 January 1900, 395/893, D.P. and 8th A.C., Letters, Telegrams, Reports, and Memoranda Sent, Jan. to Apr. 1900, no. 6; Brig. Gen. William A. Kobbé to SMG, 14 March 1900, ibid., no. 42; *WD* 1900 1:7:10–11; Ataviado, *Lucha y Libertad*, 2:51–70; Howe, "Historical Sketch of the 47th," 94/187; Linninger, *Best War at the Time*, pp. 122–27.
12. Brig. Gen. William A. Kobbé to C.O., Donsol, 22 January 1900, 395/893, LS 3. For Kobbé's rules on trade, see OMG, G.O. 15 and 22, 27 January and 10 February 1900, 395/2420; *WD* 1900 1:7:18–19.
13. Maj. Hugh D. Wise to Adj., 47th Inf., 23 January 1900, 395/3668, LS 19.
14. Maj. James A. Shipton to Col. Walter Howe, 29 January 1900, 395/5371,

Tabaco, Albay, LS, Oct. 1899 to Apr. 1900, LS 8; Ataviado, *Lucha y Libertad*, 2:71–79.

15. Brig. Gen. William A. Kobbé to SMG, 14 March 1900, 395/893. For accounts of the battles, see Ataviado, *Lucha y Libertad*, 2:80–89; *WD* 1900 1:7:32–34; Howe, "Historical Sketch of the 47th," 94/187; Col. Walter Howe to AG, P.B., 8th A.C., 2 and 11 February 1900, 94/117, 47th Inf., LS Bk 1, LS 354 and 377.

16. Howe, "Historical Sketch of the 47th," 94/187; Brig. Gen. William A. Kobbé to SMG, 14 March 1900, 395/893, no. 4; Col. Walter Howe to AAG, D.P., 10, 16, and 27 February 1900, 94/117, 47th Inf., LS Bk 1, LS 364, 378, and 413; Ataviado, *Lucha y Libertad*, 2:89–91. Indicative of either revolutionary optimism or propaganda is Belarmino's claim that the Americans had more than 150 killed while the Filipinos had lost only 10 men, see Maj. Gen. Vito Belarmino to Lt. Gen. Mariano Trías, 28 February 1900, PIR SD 1070.2.

17. Col. Joseph H. Dorst to AG, U.S. Army, 3 June 1901, Col. Joseph H. Dorst, "Historical Sketch of the 45th Infantry, U.S.V.," 94/187; *WD* 1900 1:4:400–403, 1:6:660–65; Col. Edward A. Godwin to AAAG, 25 February 1900, 395/2427, DSL, 3D, Reports of Military Operations, 1900–1901; Lt. Col. James Parker to AAG, 24 February 1900, ibid.; Brig. Gen. James M. Bell to AAG, 1st Div., 8th A.C., 1 March 1900, 395/2418, 3D, DSL, Letters and Telegrams Sent, Feb. 1900 to Oct. 1901, LS Bk 1; Col. Joseph H. Dorst to AAG, Bell's Expeditionary Brigade [BEB], 1 March 1900, 395/2420; Maj. Michael M. McNamee to AG, BEB, 6 March 1900 ibid.; Lt. Samuel P. Lyon to Mary P. Lyon, 3 March 1900, Lyon Papers. For U.S. efforts to avoid unnecessary casualties, see Parker, *Old Army*, pp. 310–12; Capt. Tom Rogers to Adj., BEB, 24 February 1900, 395/2420. Belarmino was very worried about his rice supplies and accurately predicted that the Army might land in the Camarines, see Maj. Gen. Vito Belarmino to Lt. Gen. Mariano Trías, 28 February 1900, PIR SD 1070.2.

18. Quote "the Americans cannot reach us" from Maj. Hugh D. Wise to Adj., 47th Inf., 5 May 1900, *WD* 1901 1:5:340–42. For reprisals, see "El Montero" to Lt. Col. Raymond Sanz, n.d., 1900, PIR SD 2007.1. For reports on anti-American propaganda, see Brig. Gen. James M. Bell to AAG, 1st Div., 8th A.C., 3 March 1900, 395/2418, LS Bk 1; Capt. Tom Rogers to Adj., BEB, 24 February 1900, 395/2420; Capt. Leslie McGinn to Maj. Michael M. McNamee, 7 March 1900, ibid. For the depopulation of towns, see Ataviado, *Lucha y Libertad*, 2:103–7; Maj. Hugh D. Wise to AG, P.B., 8 A.C., 1 February 1900, 395/3668, LS Bk 1, LS 23; Col. Walter Howe to AAG, D.P., 12 February 1900, 94/117, 47th Inf., LS Bk 1, LS 373; Maj. Hugh D. Wise to Adj., 47th Inf., 14 February 1900, 395/3668, LS Bk 1, LS 26; Anon., 21 June 1900, 395/4082, LS 4; Capt. John W. Gulick to AG, 3D, DSL, 23 February 1901, 395/3801, Gubat, Sorsogon, LS Nov. 1900 to May 1902, LS 68; "Circular no. 21," Col. Ramon Santos to Military Central and Zone Commanders of the National Militia, Ligao, 24 August 1900, Taylor, *Philippine Insurrection*, Exhibit 1086, p. 58 GV; Col. Ramon Santos to Esteban Nieves, 6 November 1900, ibid., Exhibit 1111, p. 66 GV; Col. Ramon Santos to Exequiel Quinto, 19 December 1900, ibid., Exhibit 1135, p. 74 GV; Owen, "Winding Down the War in Albay," pp. 562–64.

19. Maj. Gen. Vito Belarmino, "Proclamation," 3 April 1900, PIR SD 1198.3; Maj. Gen. Vito Belarmino to Anon., 7 November 1900, Taylor, *Philippine Insurrection*,

Exhibit 1112, p. 67 GV; Maj. Gen. Vito Belarmino to Sr. Patricio Alcala, 13 October 1900, PIR SD 341.9; Lt. W. H. Haskell, "Descriptive Card of Inhabitants—Gen. Bito [*sic*] Belarmino," 26 February 1902, 395/3399, Camalig, Albay, Letters and Reports Received by the Intelligence Officer; Ataviado, *Lucha y Libertad*, pp. 222–27; Owen, "Winding Down the War in Albay," p. 567. For Belarmino's early pessimism and surrender attempt, see Howe, "Historical Sketch of the 47th," 94/187; Maj. Gen. Vito Belarmino to Lt. Gen. Mariano Trías, 28 February 1900, PIR SD 1070.2.

20. Lt. Col. James Parker to AAG, D.P., 18 May 1900, 395/4577, Nueva Caceres, Camarines, LS, Apr. 1900 to Aug. 1902, LS 43; Col. Joseph H. Dorst to AAG, BEB, 28 February 1900, 395/2427; Col. Joseph H. Dorst to Capt. Peter Murray, AAG, BEB, 7 March 1900, 94/117, 45th Inf., LS Bk 2, LS 227; "Relacion de Jefes Officials que no se han presentado," n.d., PIR SD 1180.3; "Statement of Daniel Imperial, Col.," n.d., PIR SD 2011.2; Owen, "Kabikolan," p. 365; Owen, "Winding Down the War in Albay," pp. 565–68. For information on Lt. Col. Ludovicio Aréjola, see Dorst, "Historical Sketch of the 45th Infantry, U.S.V.," 94/187; Col. James Lockett to AG, DSL, 31 July 1900, 395/2418, LS Bk 2; Maj. Dennis M. Nolan to AG, 3D, DSL, 21 September 1900, 395/4577, LS 135; Maj. William H. Johnson to AG, 3D, DSL, 26 December 1900, Roosevelt Papers, reel 8; Claude E. Harris Questionnaire.

21. Dorst, "Historical Sketch of the 45th Infantry, U.S.V.," 94/187. Brig. Gen. James M. Bell to AAG, 1st Div., 8th A.C., 11 April 1900, 395/2418, LS Bk 1.

22. Quote "bamboo tomtoms" from Capt. C. P. Lee to Adj., 45th Inf., 18 April 1900, 395/2428. Quote "I cannot send" from Col. Walter Howe to AG, IB, 1st Div., 8th A.C., 15 April 1900, 94/117, 47th Inf., LS Bk 1, LS 539; Col. James Lockett to AG, DSL, 31 July 1900, 395/2418, LS Bk 2; Maj. William C. Forbush to AAG, 3D, DSL, 21 October 1900, 395/3835, Guinobatan, Albay, LS, Oct. 1900 to Mar. 1902, LS 1; Lt. S. Adams to Adj., 14 January 1901, 395/4082, Ligao, Albay, Letters and Telegrams Sent, Sept. 1899 to Jan. 1902, LS 87; Maj. Hugh D. Wise to Adj., 47th Inf., 14 February and 1 October 1900, 395/3668, LS Bk 1, LS 26 and 205; Maj. Gen. Vito Belarmino, "Proclamation," 3 April 1900, PIR SD 1198.3; Lt. Col. Charles G. Starr to AG, DSL, 4 September 1900, 395/4830, Regan Barracks [Legaspi], Albay, LS, July 1900 to Aug. 1906, LS Bk 1, LS 56; Maj. Gen. Vito Belarmino to Patricio Alcala, 15 October 1900, PIR SD 341.9; Maj. Gen. Vito Belarmino to Col. Ramon Santos, 15 March 1901, Taylor, *Philippine Insurrection*, Exhibit 1149, p. 79 GV.

23. Maj. Hugh J. Sime to AG, 3D, DSL, 12 May 1900, 395/2420, LR 7. Col. Walter Howe to AG, 3D, DSL, 28 April and 19 June 1900, 94/117, 47th Inf., LS Bk 2, LS 595 and 749; Maj. Hugh D. Wise to Adj., 47th Inf., 16 June 1900, 395/3668, LS Bk 1, LS 112.

24. Quote "tin-can ammunition," from Col. Walter Howe to AG, 3D, DSL, 21 June 1900, 94/117, 47th Inf., LS Bk 2, LS 755. For information on guerrilla weapons, see Howe, "Historical Sketch of the 47th," 94/187; Lt. Col. Charles G. Starr to AG, 3D, DSL, 17 September 1900, 395/4830, LS Bk 1, LS 76; Col. Walter Howe to AG, 3D, DSL, 27 April 1900, 395/2330, Box 1, LR 522; Lt. Lanning Parsons to C.O., Camalig, 19 November 1900, *WD* 1901 1:5:363; Ataviado, *Lucha y Libertad*, pp. 165–66. For the guerrillas' emphasis on the importance of arms, see Col. José Natera to Anon., 17 June 1900, Taylor, *Philippine Insurrection*, Exhibit 1068,

pp. 51–52 GV. For veterans' disparaging views on guerrilla marksmanship and weapons, see Charles F. Anderson, George R. Clements, Frank R. Schallert, Purl A. Mulkey, Jesse A. Jackson, Richard Mason, Lewis A. Wheeler, and Edward Johnson Questionnaires.

25. Quote "strange sort of warfare" from Brig. Gen. James M. Bell to AAG, DSL, 7 May 1900, 395/2418, LS Bk 1. Col. Orense to Col. José Natera, 26 May 1900, PIR SD 1198.5; Col. Ramon Santos to Maj. Eleuteria Reveta, 14 October 1900, Taylor, *Philippine Insurrection*, Exhibit 1104, pp. 63–64 GV; Lt. Col. James Parker to AAG, BEB, 9 April 1900, 395/4577, LS Bk 1, LS 5. According to Howe's "Historical Sketch of the 47th," 94/187, only one soldier in that regiment was injured by falling into a mantrap. Norman Owen correctly notes the reluctance of the *principalia* who led the guerrilla forces to sanction destructive tactics, see Owen, "Winding Down the War in Albay," p. 567. However, on several occasions the guerrillas did destroy property in an attempt to drive both Americans and Filipinos from the towns or to retaliate against *americanistas*, see Howe, "Historical Sketch of the 47th," 94/187; Brig. Gen. James M. Bell to AAG, 1st Div., 8th A.C., 1 March 1900, 395/2418, LS Bk 1; Col. Joseph H. Dorst to AAG, BEB, 1 March 1900, 395/2420; "Statement of Sutorio Salinas," 4 January 1901, PIR SD 2011.2; Lt. Jens E. Stedge to Adj., 47th Inf., 29 March 1900, 395/2420, LR 2; "Report of Operations for the Garrison of Gubat, Sorsogon Province, P.I. for the Month of August, 1900," 395/3808, Gubat, Sorsogon, Monthly Report of Garrison Operations, 1900–1901; Lt. Col. Charles G. Starr to AG, 3D, DSL, 17 September 1900, 395/4830, LS Bk 1, LS 76; Col. Joseph H. Dorst to AAG, BEB, 28 February 1900, 395/2427; Capt. Charles Monroe, "Report of a Trip to Irocin," 12 March 1900, 395/2420; Col. Walter Howe to AAG, 3D, DSL, 20 and 28 April 1901, 94/117, 47th Inf., LS Bk 3, LS 590 and 595.

26. Lt. Col. Charles G. Starr to AG, DSL, 4 September 1900, 395/4830, LS Bk 1, LS 56; Col. Walter Howe to AG, IB, 1st Div., 8th A.C., 15 April 1900, 94/117, 47th Inf., LS Bk 2, LS 539; Col. Ramon Santos, "Letter," 19 April 1900, PIR SD 2006.1; Col. Ramon Santos to Luis Romano, 27 September 1900, Taylor, *Philippine Insurrection*, Exhibit 1099, p. 62 GV; Col. Ramon Santos to Torino Poblete, 12 December 1900, ibid., Exhibit 1132, pp. 73–74 GV; Col. Ramon Santos, "Circular," 7 January 1901, ibid., Exhibit 1141, p. 76 GV; Capt. J. T. Nance to C.O., Sorsogon, 30 June 1901, 395/2442, LS 22.

27. Brig. Gen. James M. Bell to AAG, DSL, 15 November 1900, 395/2420.

28. Maj. Gen. Arthur MacArthur to AG, Washington, D.C., 9 January 1901, *CWS*, 2:1244, see also correspondence, pp. 1241–42, 1249–52; Owen, "Winding Down the War in Albay," pp. 577–78. For evidence of ties between Manila firms and the guerrillas, see Capt. Ralph Van Deman to AG, DSL, 19 October 1901, 395/2424; Capt. Ralph Van Deman, "Appendix K," 5 December 1901, 395/2635, Box 1, LR 256. For reports on smuggling, see Maj. Hugh D. Wise to AG, P.B., 8th A.C., 5 April 1900, 395/2420; LS 4: Maj. William C. Forbush to Adj., S-D Albay, 31 January 1901, 395/3835, LS 72; Maj. William C. Forbush to AAG, DSL, 19 March 1901, 395/3835, LS 90; Maj. Lorenzo W. Cooke to C.O., Daet, 24 June 1901, 395/2420.

29. Ataviado, *Lucha y Libertad*, 2:107.

30. LeRoy, *Americans in the Philippines*, 2:171.

31. Quote "breaking up" from Lt. Samuel P. Lyon to Mary P. Lyon, 1 June 1900,

Lyon Papers. For administration, see G.O. 1, OMG, DSL, 28 March 1900; Hq, DSL, G.O. 1, 1 April 1900; Hq, 3D, DSL, G.O. 1, 1 May 1900, all in 395/2424; *ANJ* 37 (5 May 1900). For Bell's retirement, see *WD* 1901 1:7:416.

32. Howe, "Historical Sketch of the 47th," 94/187; Dorst, "Historical Sketch of the 45th Infantry, U.S.V.," 94/187; Col. Walter Howe to AAG, P.B., 2 and 17 March 1900, 94/117, 47th Inf., LS Bk 1, LS 413 and 447; Betts, "Memoirs," pp. 22–23. For Paua's surrender, see Ataviado, *Lucha y Libertad*, pp. 190–98; Brig. Gen. James M. Bell to AG, Albay and Guinobatan, 27 March 1900, 94/117, 47th Inf., LS Bk 2, LS 467; Brig. Gen. James M. Bell to AAG, 1st Div., 8th A.C., 1 April 1900, 395/2418; Col. Walter Howe to AG, 1st Div., 8th A.C., 1 April 1900, 94/117, 47th Inf., LS Bk 2, LS 495; *ANJ* 37 (14 April 1900).

33. Brig. Gen. James M. Bell to AAG, 1st Div., 8th A.C., 11 April 1900, 395/2418.

34. Lt. Samuel P. Lyon to Mary P. Lyon, 12 April 1900, Lyon Papers. Col. Walter Howe to AAG, D.P., 12 February 1900, 94/117, 47th Inf., LS Bk 1, LS 373; Col. Walter Howe to AG, IB, 1st Div., 8th A.C., 6 April 1900, 395/2420, LR 6.

35. Brig. Gen. James M. Bell to AAG, 1st Div., 8th A.C., 26 March and 1 April 1900, 395/2418, LS Bk 1; Brig. Gen. James M. Bell to AAG, DSL, 19 May 1900, 395/2330, Box 1, LR 522; Brig. Gen. James M. Bell to AAG, DSL, 27 May 1900, 395/2418; Howe, "Historical Sketch of the 47th," 94/187. Otis believed Bell's reports on the desperate lack of men were "rather pessimistic," see Maj. Gen. Elwell S. Otis to Elihu Root, 10 April 1900, *CWS*, 2:1159; Elihu Root to Maj. Gen. Elwell S. Otis, 9 April 1900, ibid., 2:1158. For Kobbé's report, see Brig. Gen. William A. Kobbé to AG, D.P., and 8th A.C., 28 March 1900, 395/893, LS 54.

36. Hq, DSL to C.G., 3D, DSL, 1 September 1900, 395/4077, Libmanan, Camarines, Miscellaneous Letters, Orders, and Reports Received, 1900–1902; George A. McCarter to Theodore Roosevelt, 24 November 1900, Roosevelt Papers, reel 7; Col. Walter Howe to AG, 3D, DSL, 29 July 1900, 94/117, 47th Inf., LS Bk 1; Col. Joseph H. Dorst to AAG, 3D, DSL, 28 and 29 May 1900, 94/117, 45th Inf., LS Bk 2, LS 668 and 675; Lt. Col. Charles G. Starr to Col. Walter Howe, 18 June 1900, 395/4082, LS 3; Col. James Lockett to AG, DSL, 31 July 1900, 395/2418, LS Bk 2.

37. Dorst, "Historical Sketch of the 45th Infantry, U.S.V.," 94/187; Howe, "Historical Sketch of the 47th," 94/187; Col. Walter Howe to AG, DSL, 27 April 1900, 94/117, 47th Inf., LS Bk 2, LS 582; Col. Joseph H. Dorst to Lt. Col. James Parker, 27 July 1900, 395/5035, San José de Lagonoy, Camarines, Letters and Telegrams Received, 1900–1901; Lt. Col. James Parker to AAG, DSL, 23 August 1900, 395/5032, San José de Lagonoy, Camarines, Letters and Telegrams Sent, June 1900 to Mar. 1902, LS Bk 1, LS 56; Capt. Arlington U. Betts to AG, DSL, 24 October 1900, 395/5379, Tabaco, Albay, Miscellaneous Letters, Telegrams, Orders, Circulars, and Reports Received, 1900–1902; Gen. James M. Bell to Anon., 4 January 1901, 395/2418, LS Bk 3, LS 1544; Maj. Samuel E. Armstrong, "Special Report of the Sanitary Condition and Medical Equipment of the Post of Nueva Caceres," 3 October 1900, 395/2330, Box 16, C235; Col. Joseph H. Dorst to AG, Nueva Caceres, 17 July and 21 October 1900, 395/3929, Iriga, Camarines, LS, July 1900 to Mar. 1902, LS Bk 1, LS 38 and 740; Col. Joseph H. Dorst to Lt. McCormick, 10 September 1900, 395/3929, LS Bk 1, LS 434. For intradepartmental transport problems, see Dorst, "Historical Sketch of the 45th Infantry, U.S.V.," 94/187; Howe, "Historical Sketch of

the 47th," 94/187; Col. Joseph H. Dorst to Capt. Peter Murray, 15 May 1900, 395/2420; Col. James Lockett to AG, DSL, 31 July and 1 September 1900, 395/2418, LS Bk 2; Capt. F. N. Simpson to AG, 3D, DSL, 24 July 1900, 395/2330, Box 6, M1374. For an ingenious solution to the problem posed by lack of pay, see Betts, "Memoirs," pp. 35–36. For the accounts of veterans, most of whom dwelt with great detail on the horrors of food and medical supplies, see George R. Clements, Frank R. Schallert, Purl A. Mulkey, Lewis A. Wheeler, and Richard Mason Questionnaires.

38. Maj. Hugh D. Wise to AG, DSL, 12 December 1900, 395/2330, Box 4, C3099.

39. Howe, "Historical Sketch of the 47th," 94/187; Maj. Hugh D. Wise to Adj., 47th Inf., 16 June 1900, 395/3668, LS Bk 1, LS 112; Col. Joseph H. Dorst to AAG, 3D, DSL, 28 and 29 May 1900, 94/117, 45th Inf., LS Bk 2, LS 668 and 675; Col. Joseph H. Dorst to Chief Surgeon, DSL, 30 September 1900, 94/117, 45th Inf., LS Bk 3, LS 1470.

40. Quote "at times American officers" from Owen, "Winding Down the War in Albay," p. 566. Quote "it is my earnest" from Lt. Col. James Parker to AAG, DivPhil, 3 July 1901, 395/3929, LS Bk 3, LS 518. For officers who distrusted the entire population, see Capt. Charles Young to DMI, November 1901, 395/5379; Lt. Col. Charles G. Starr to AG, 3D, DSL, 17 September 1900, 395/4830, LS Bk 1, LS 76. For the official policy, see Brig. Gen. William A. Kobbé to C.O., Donsol, 22 January 1900, 395/893, LS 3; Brig. Gen. James M. Bell to all C.O.'s [3D], 28 June 1900, 395/2418. For examples of the belief that the guerrillas won support only by intimidation or through popular ignorance, see Lt. Samuel P. Lyon to Mary P. Lyon, 17 March 1900, Lyon Papers; Lt. Col. James Parker to AG, 3D, DSL, 30 June 1900, 395/5032, LS Bk 1, LS 6; *ANJ* 38 (1 September 1900); Maj. William H. Johnson to AG, 3D, DSL, 25 December 1900, Roosevelt Papers, series 1, reel 8; Capt. S. E. Smiley to Brig. Gen. James M. Bell, 17 April 1900, 395/2420; Maj. Hugh D. Wise to Adj., 47th Inf., 12 February 1900, 395/3668, LS Bk 1, LS 57; Maj. Hugh D. Wise to AG, P.B., 8th A.C., 14 February 1900, ibid., LS 26.

41. Col. Joseph H. Dorst to AAG, BEB, 28 February 1900, 395/2427. Col. Joseph H. Dorst to Capt. Peter Murray, AAG, BEB, 7 March 1900, 94/117, 45th Inf., LS Bk 2, LS 227; Maj. William C. Forbush to AAG, 3D, DSL, 30 November 1900, *WD 1901* 1:5:369–71.

42. Lt. Col. Charles C. Starr to AG, 3D, DSL, 17 September 1900, 395/4830, LS Bk 1, LS 76.

43. Lt. Col. James Parker to AAG, D.P., 18 May 1900, 395/4577, LS 43.

44. G.O. 7, 27 April 1900, 395/5379; Col. Joseph H. Dorst to Maj. Edwin T. Cole, 13 May 1900, 94/117, 45th Inf., LS Bk 2, LS 543; Maj. James A. Shipton to AG, 1st Div., 8th A.C., 1 June 1900, 395/5371, LS 53; Col. Joseph H. Dorst to AG, 21 September 1900, 395/3929, LS Bk 1, LS 514. For earlier attempts at government, see G.O. 3, Brig. Gen. James M. Bell, 2 April 1900, 395/2441; Col. Joseph H. Dorst to AG, Nueva Caceres, 25 April 1900, 94/117, 45th Inf., LS Bk 2, LS 380; Lewis A. Wheeler to Editor, *Indiana Progress*, 17 April 1900.

45. Capt. B. Patrick, Adj. to Maj. Theodore K. Birkhaeuser, 2 and 15 March 1900, 94/117, 45th Inf., LS Bk 2; Juan de los Herras to Sr. Preboste, 13 March 1900, PIR SD 2007.3; Col. Joseph H. Dorst to Capt. Peter Murray, 1 June 1900, 395/2420;

Maximo Noble to Col. Joseph H. Dorst, 16 June 1900, 395/2420; Col. Joseph H. Dorst to AG, Nueva Caceres, 4 July 1900, 94/117, 45th Inf., LS Bk 3, LS 1064; Col. Walter Howe to AG, 3D, DSL, 10 July 1900, 94/117, 47th Inf., LS Bk 2, LS 798; Col. Joseph H. Dorst to AG, Nueva Caceres, 22 July and 18 September 1900, 395/3929, LS Bk 1, LS 87 and 481; Maj. Hugh D. Wise to Adj., 47th Inf., 1 July 1900, 395/3668, LS Bk 1, LS 129; Maj. Frank Taylor to Adj., S-D Albay, 2 May 1901, 395/5376, Tabaco, Albay, Letters and Telegrams Received, 1900–1902; Lt. C. E. Stodter to Governor of Albay, 2 November 1901, 395/4082, LS 178; Parker, *Old Army*, p. 352.

46. Brig. Gen. James M. Bell to SMG, 4 March 1901, 395/2440, LS 55. Capt. B. Patrick to Maj. Theodore K. Birkhaeuser, 2 March 1900; Col. Joseph H. Dorst to AAG, BEB, 15 March 1900, LS 232; Col. Joseph H. Dorst to AG, Nueva Caceres, 5 May 1900, LS 465, all in 94/117, 45th Inf., LS Bk 2; Capt. Edwin Cole to AG, 3D, DSL, 24 May 1900, 395/2420; Col. Joseph H. Dorst to AG, 3D, DSL, 28 June 1900, 94/117, 45th Inf., LS Bk 3, LS 982; Col. Joseph H. Dorst to AG, Nueva Caceres, 16 July 1900, 395/3929, LS Bk 1, LS 31; Maj. Hugh D. Wise to Adj., 47th Inf., 1 July 1900, *WD* 1901 1:5:346–48; Esteban Delgado to Col. Ramon Santos, 4 and 28 July 1900, PIR SD 1014.3; Eusebio San José to Cmdte. Gregorio Mascate, 19 December 1900, PIR SD 1198.8; E. Villareal to Col. Ramon Santos, 13 February 1901, PIR SD 1014.7; Capt. John W. Gulick to Hipolito Freola, 9 March 1901, 395/3801, LS 87; Gen. Antonino Guevara to Maj. Gen. Vito Belarmino, 15 March 1901, Taylor, *Philippine Insurrection*, Exhibit 1149, p. 80 GV.

47. Lt. E. J. Balsh to AG, BEB, 3 March 1900, 395/2420. Col. Walter Howe to AG, 3D, DSL, 10 July 1900, 94/117, 47th Inf., LS Bk 2, LS 798; Lt. Col. James Parker to AAG, 3D, DSL, 11 July 1900, 395/5032, LS Bk 1, LS 21; Col. Joseph H. Dorst to AAG, BEB, 2 March 1900, 94/117, 45th Inf., LS Bk 2, LS 232; Lt. Col. Charles G. Starr to AG, 3D, DSL, n.d., 395/4082, LS 4; Lt. Albert O'Dell to Lt. Col. James Parker, 16 July 1900, 395/5040. For Bell's policies, see Brig. Gen. James M. Bell to SMG, 26 December 1900, 395/2440, LS 9.

48. Maj. Hugh D. Wise to Vicario de Sorsogon, 7 May 1900, 395/3668, LS Bk 1, LS 74.

49. Betts, "Memoirs," pp. 15–18. Quote "nowhere else was there" from Schumacher, *Revolutionary Clergy*, p. 174, also pp. 157–75. For priests serving with the revolutionaries, see Maj. Hugh D. Wise to Adj., 47th Inf., 23 January and 1 July 1900, LS 19 and 129; Maj. Hugh D. Wise to AG, P.B., 8th A.C., 1 February 1900, LS 33; Maj. Hugh D. Wise to AG, DSL, 29 April 1900, LS 68; Maj. Hugh D. Wise to Vicario de Sorsogon, 7 May 1900, LS 74, all in 395/3668, LS Bk 1; Lt. Brice P. Disque to C.O., Bulan, 6 October 1900, *WD* 1901 1:5:358–59; Col. Ramon Santos to Maj. Gen. Vito Belarmino, 14 November 1900, Taylor, *Philippine Insurrection*, Exhibit 1113, p. 67 GV; "Guerrilla Warfare," 27 October 1900, PIR SD 1014.8; Lt. Col. Charles G. Starr to AG, 3D, DSL, n.d., 395/4082, LS 4.

50. Gen. Antonino Guevara to Maj. Gen. Vito Belarmino, 15 March 1901, PIR SD 1014.9. Col. Joseph H. Dorst to AG, Nueva Caceres, 30 April and 6 June 1900, 94/117, 45th Inf., LS Bk 2, LS 414 and 736; Col. Walter Howe to AG, 3D, DSL, 21 May and 24 July 1900, 94/117, 47th Inf., LS Bk 2, LS 654 and 853; Lt. Col. James Parker to AAG, 3D, DSL, 6 July 1900, 395/5032, LS Bk 1, LS 14; Capt. George W.

Winterburne to AG, 3D, DSL, 9 July 1900, 395/2420; Father Mauricio Barrameda to C.O., Donsol, 11 November 1900 and 24 January 1901, 395/3671, LR 180; Maj. Hugh D. Wise to Father Mauricio Barrameda, 24 January 1901, 395/3669, LS Bk 2, LS 30; Capt. Charles C. McLain to Adj., 47th Inf., 4 February 1901, *WD* 1901 1:5:421–22; Parker, *Old Army*, p. 328.

51. Brig. Gen. James M. Bell to AAG, DSL, 27 May 1900, 395/2418, LS Bk 1; Maj. William H. Johnson to AG, 3D, DSL, 25 November 1900, 395/2420, LR 204; "Requisition for Ordnance Stores for 3rd District, DSL," 27 May 1900, 395/2420; Col. James Lockett to AG, DSL, 31 July 1900, 395/2418, LS Bk 2; Col. Thomas MacGregor to AG, DSL, 12 October 1900, 395/2330, Box 2, LR B2344. For *presidentes'* demands for armed police, see Capt. Edwin Cole to AG, 3D, DSL, 24 May 1900, 395/2420; Col. Joseph H. Dorst to AG, Nueva Caceres, 16 July 1900, 395/3929, LS Bk 1, LS 31; Brig. Gen. James M. Bell to AAG, DSL, 8 June 1900, 395/2418, LS Bk 1.

52. Col. Joseph H. Dorst to AG, Nueva Caceres, 3 August 1900, 395/3929, LS Bk 1, LS 195. Lt. Col. James Parker to AAG, DivPhil, 18 May 1900, 395/4577, LS Bk 1, LS 43; "Avisio," 10 June 1900, PIR SD 1068.4; Maj. Hugh D. Wise to Maj. Keller Anderson, 24 July 1900, 395/3668, LS Bk 1, LS 148; Lt. Col. James Parker to AAG, 3D, DSL, 31 July 1900, 395/5032, LS Bk 1, LS 35; Brig. Gen. James M. Bell to AAG, 3D, DSL, 22 January 1901, 395/2418; Lt. William S. Chamberlain to AG, S-D, Camarines Norte, 20 July 1900, 395/4673, Paracale, Camarines, LS, July 1901, LS 30; Charles F. Anderson and Lewis A. Wheeler Questionnaires.

53. Maj. Hugh D. Wise to AG, 14 January 1900, 395/3668, LS Bk 1, LS 26. Maj. Hugh D. Wise to Adj., 47th Inf., 23 January and 12 February 1900, ibid., LS 19 and 57; Capt. Tom Rogers to Adj., BEB, 24 February 1900, 395/2420, Box 1, LR 1; Parker, *Old Army*, pp. 310–11. For Bell's orders, see G.O. 3, 16 February 1900, 395/2427.

54. Col. Joseph H. Dorst to AG, 3D, DSL, n.d. [1900], 395/3929, LS 687.

55. Quote "the enemy was the insurrecto" from Linninger, *Best War at the Time*, p. 236. Owen, "Winding Down the War in Albay," pp. 574–75, 578. James Parker credited the U.S. Volunteers who served in the Third District with far better relations with the Filipinos than the regulars who followed them, see Parker, *Old Army*, p. 315. For social relations between officers and Filipinos, see Col. Joseph H. Dorst to AG, 28 April 1900, 94/117, 45th Inf., LS Bk 2, LS 406; Col. Joseph H. Dorst to AG, Nueva Caceres, 4 July 1900, ibid., LS Bk 3, LS 1064. For generally favorable views of the Bicol populace among officers and enlisted men, see Howe, "Historical Sketch of the 47th," 94/187; Lt. William McKinley to SMG, 26 January 1901, 395/2420; William L. Bliss to Aunt, 30 April 1900, Harry W. Bliss Letters; Charles E. Brossman Questionnaire. For instances of torture, see Claude E. Harris MS. For looting, see Lt. Col. Charles G. Starr to Maj. William C. Forbush, 26 November 1900, 295/4830, LS Bk 1, LS 195; Joseph H. Dorst to AG, Nueva Caceres, 14 October 1900, 395/3929, LS Bk 1, LS 676; Lt. Col. James Parker to AAG, 3D, DSL, 22 September 1900, 395/5032, LS Bk 1, LS 72; Lt. Lewis Forrester to AAG, 3D, DSL, 8 September 1900, 395/2428. Of the six veterans who replied to questions about looting, only one claimed he had seen any while the rest denied any knowledge of it, see Purl A. Mulkey, Charles F. Anderson, George R. Clements, Claude E. Harris, Frank R. Schallert, Joseph W. Ford, Richard Mason Questionnaires.

56. Betts, "Memoirs," pp. 18–19.

57. Quote "received early and constant attention" from Brig. Gen. James M. Bell to SMG, 4 March 1901, 395/2440, LS 55. Bell also proposed a land tax on the *principalía* which would be used for education, see Brig. Gen. James M. Bell to AG, DSL, 3 July 1900, 395/2418. For the work of officers in garrison towns, see Lt. Col. Charles G. Starr to AG, 3D, DSL, 8 October 1900, 395/4830, LS 114; Maj. William C. Forbush to C.O., Legaspi, 23 December 1900, 395/3835, LS 49; Maj. William C. Forbush to C.O., Legaspi, 1 January 1901, 395/3835, LS 14; Capt. Edwin T. Cole to AG, 3D, DSL, 24 May 1900, 395/2420; Lt. Col. James Parker to Officer in Charge of Public Instruction, 17 August 1900, 395/5032, LS Bk 1, LS 49; Col. Thomas MacGregor to AG, DSL, 31 October 1900, 395/2418, LS Bk 3, LS 1162; Capt. Walter L. Findley to AG, 3D, DSL, 9 February 1901, 395/4072, LS 31 and 32; Maj. Hugh D. Wise to General Superintendent of Education, 16 November 1900, 395/3668, LS Bk 1, LS 269; Lt. Col. William Quinton to AG, 17 April 1901, 395/3929, LS Bk 3, LS 795; Maj. James A. Shipton to SMG, 22 February and 14 April 1901, 395/5032, LS Bk 1, LS 29 and 114; Betts, "Memoirs," pp. 38–41; Parker, *Old Army*, p. 351.

58. Capt. Augustus C. Hart to Adj., 47th Inf., 1 September 1900, 395/3668, LS Bk 1, LS 179. Ramon Gonzalez, Vicar General, to Lt. Col. James Lockett, 18 September 1900, 395/2420; Maj. Hugh D. Wise to Father Mauricio Barraneda, 11 November 1900, 395/3668, LS Bk 1, LS 267; Col. Edward Moale to AG, 3D, DSL, 24 February 1901, 395/4830, LS Bk 1, LS 120; Acting Surgeon Edwin P. Hayward to Adj., 1 March 1901, 395/5376, LR 288; Parker, *Old Army*, p. 335; Brig. Gen. James M. Bell to Capt. Chas Wilcox, Ast. Surgeon, 17 January 1901, 395/2418, LS 1683; Col. Joseph H. Dorst to AG, 3D, DSL, n.d., 395/3929, LS 687.

59. Col. Joseph H. Dorst to AG, 28 April 1900, 94/117, 45th Inf., LS Bk 2, LS 406; Col. Joseph H. Dorst to AG, Nueva Caceres, 14 September 1900, 395/3929, LS Bk 1, LS 457; Lt. Col. James Parker to AAG, Nueva Caceres, 19 March 1901, 395/3929, LS Bk 3, LS 595; Lt. Col. William Quinton to AG, Nueva Caceres, 4 May 1901, 395/3929, LS Bk 3, LS 886–87; Special Orders, 25 June 1901, 395/2420; Capt. H. H. McMaster to AG, S-D Camarines Norte, Daet, 24 July 1901, 395/2420; Parker, *Old Army*, pp. 357–58; Gatewood, *Smoked Yankees*, pp. 301–3.

60. Capt. Augustus C. Hart to Adj. 47th Inf., 1 September 1900, *WD* 1901 1:5:352–53. For the entire correspondence, see *WD* 1901 1:5:346–54.

61. Owen, "Winding Down the War in Albay," pp. 566, 564–68, 574; Descriptive Cards of Inhabitants—Anacleto Solano, Domingo Sampson, Macario Sampson, 18 March 1902, 395/3399; Maj. Hugh D. Wise to Maj. Keller Anderson, 24 July 1900, 395/3668, LS Bk 1, LS 148; *WD* 1900 1:6:666–69, 674–76; "El Montero" to Lt. Col. Raymond Sanz, 1900, PIR SD 2007.1. For good relations between the *principalía* and Army personnel, see Betts, "Memoirs," p. 20; Linninger, *Best War at the Time*, p. 233; Parker, *Old Army*, pp. 331–33, 339; Samuel P. Lyon to Mary P. Lyon, 27 February and 6 July 1900, Lyon Papers; Lt. Col. James Parker to AAG, 3D, DSL, 11 July 1900, 395/5032, LS Bk 1, LS 21.

62. Col. James Lockett to AG, DSL, 31 July 1900, 395/2418.

63. Linninger, *Best War at the Time*, p. 189. Lt. Col. Charles G. Starr to AG, 3D, DSL, 12 October 1900, 395/4830, LS 123; Lt. George M. Wray, "Record of Troop D, 11th Cavalry, U.S.V. for the month of May 1900," 395/4085, Libmanan, Albay,

LR, 1900, LR 37; Maj. Hugh T. Sime to Hq, 2d Squadron, 11th Cavalry, 24 May 1900, 395/4085, LS 710; Lt. Col. Charles G. Starr to Col. Walter Howe, 18 June 1900, 395/4082, LS 3; Lt. Col. Charles G. Starr to AG, DSL, 4 September 1900, 395/4830, LS Bk 1, LS 56; Lt. George M. Wray to AG, DSL, 1 October 1900, 395/2033, Box 2, A916. Brig. Gen. James M. Bell to AAG, 1st Div., 8th A.C., 5 March 1900, 395/2418; Col. Walter Howe to AG, IB, 20 March 1900, 94/117, 47th Inf., LS Bk 1, LS 549; Col. James Lockett to AG, DSL, 1 September 1900, 395/2418, LS 578; Col. Thomas MacGregor to AG, DSL, 30 October 1900, 395/2418, LS Bk 3, LS 1157; Capt. John G. Livingston to Adj., 47th Inf., 14 January 1901, 395/2420.

64. Maj. William C. Forbush to AAG, 3D, DSL, 30 November 1900, 395/3835, LS 16. Col. Joseph H. Dorst to AAAG, BEB, 15 March 1900, 94/117, 45th Inf., LS Bk 2, LS 232; Brig. Gen. James M. Bell to AAG, DSL, 3 February 1901, 395/2418, LS Bk 3, LS 1957. For Third District policy on rice restrictions, see Hq, DSL to C.G., 3D, 25 July 1900, 395/2402; AG, 3D, DSL, to C.O., Legaspi, 10 August 1900, 395/4833; Hq, 3D to C.O., Libmanan, 20 October 1900, 395/4077.

65. Maj. Hugh D. Wise to C.O., Sorsogon, 6 April 1900, 395/3668, LS Bk 1, LS 46; Maj. Hugh D. Wise to Ynchausti and Co., Sorsogon, 5 May 1900, 395/3668, LS 45; Maj. Hugh D. Wise to AG, P.B., 8th A.C., 6 May 1900, 395/3668, LS Bk 1, LS 53; Dorst, "Historical Sketch of the 45th Infantry, U.S.V.," 94/187; Col. Joseph H. Dorst to AG, Nueva Caceres, 30 April 1900, 94/117, 45th Inf., LS Bk 2, LS 414; Col. Joseph H. Dorst to AG, Nueva Caceres, 9 May 1900, 94/117, 45th Inf., LS Bk 2, LS 505; Col. Walter Howe to Maj. James A. Shipton, C.O., Tabaco, 28 April 1900, LS 583; Col. Walter Howe to AG, 3D, DSL, 28 April, 21 May, and 5 August 1900, LS 584, 654, and 870, all in 94/117, 47th Inf., LS Bk 2.

66. Col. Joseph H. Dorst to AG, Nueva Caceres, 12 August 1900, 395/3929, LS Bk 1, LS 277; P.L. of Nabua to C.O., Iriga, 22 August 1900, 395/3931, Iriga, Camarines, Register of LR, July 1900 to Mar. 1902; Col. Joseph H. Dorst to AG, Nueva Caceres, 27 August 1900, 395/3929, LS Bk 1, LS 358; Adj., 45th Inf., to C.O., Iriga, 23 November 1900, 395/3929, LS Bk 2, LS 1082; Maj. William C. Forbush to AAG, 3D, DSL, 30 November 1900, 395/3835, LS 16.

67. Edward Johnson Questionnaire; Claude E. Harris MS; Col. Joseph H. Dorst to AG, Nueva Caceres, 23 August 1900, 395/3929, LS Bk 1, LS 344; Col. Joseph H. Dorst to AG, Nueva Caceres, 30 April 1900, 94/117, 45th Inf., LS Bk 2, LS 414; Col. Joseph H. Dorst to AG, Nueva Caceres, 11 July 1900, ibid., LS Bk 3, LS 1114; *WD* 1901 1:5:349–67, 402. For operational orders, see Maj. Hugh D. Wise to AG, DSL, 12 December 1900, 395/2330, Box 4, C3099.

68. Maj. Gen. Vito Belarmino to Lt. Gen. Mariano Trías, 28 February 1900, PIR SD 1070.2; Col. Joseph H. Dorst to AG, Nueva Caceres, 10 July 1900, 94/117, 45th Inf., LS Bk 3, LS 1109; Hq General Staff, "Decree," 14 November 1900, PIR SD 1068.10; Capt. Edward E. Terry to Adj., 47th Inf., 29 January 1901, *WD* 1901 1:5:415–16; Col. Ramon F. Santos to Lt. Col. Rufino Nieves, 10 and 18 February 1901, PIR SD 1068.10; Dorst, "Historical Sketch of the 45th Infantry, U.S.V.," 94/187.

69. "Statement of Patricio Alcala after Surrendering to the Commanding Officer at Guinobatan, P.I., 5th of December 1900," PIR SD 389.2. For an overview of these

operations, see "Report of Operations in the Third District, Department of Southern Luzon," *WD* 1901 1:5:321–453; Dorst, "Historical Sketch of the 45th Infantry, U.S.V.," 94/187; Howe, "Historical Sketch of the 47th," 94/187.

70. Capt. Peter Murray to Lt. Col. James Parker, 23 July 1900, 395/5040, San José de Lagonoy, Camarines, Correspondence, Reports, and Descriptive List of Native Scouts, 1900–1901. Col. Joseph H. Dorst to AG, Nueva Caceres, 28 May 1900, 94/117, 45th Inf., LS Bk 2, LS 668; Col. Joseph H. Dorst to AG, Nueva Caceres, 14 and 21 July 1900, 395/3929, LS Bk 1, LS 22 and 84; Brig. Gen. James M. Bell to AAG, DSL, 3 December 1900, 395/2418, LS Bk 3, LS 1319; "Report of the Intelligence Officer, Nueva Caceres, P.I.," 6 January 1902, 395/4587, Nueva Caceres, Camarines, Miscellaneous Correspondence, Reports, Orders, and Circulars, 1901–3. For area reports on the effect of the rinderpest epidemic throughout the Third District, see the "Information on the Philippine Islands," correspondence in 395/2421.

71. Col. Joseph H. Dorst to AG, Nueva Caceres, 20 July 1900, 395/3929, LS Bk 1, LS 72; Lt. Col. James Parker to Smith Bell and Co., Tabaco, 17 August 1900; Parker, *Old Army*, pp. 336–37; Maj. Gen. Vito Belarmino, "Proclamation," 3 April 1900, Taylor, *Philippine Insurrection*, Exhibit 1053, p. 48 GV.

72. Lt. Col. Charles G. Starr to AG, 3D, DSL, 4 December 1900, 395/4830, LS Bk 1, LS 223. For similar sentiments, see Maj. William C. Forbush to AAG, 3D, DSL, 1 December 1900, 395/3835, LS 19; Lt. Col. Charles G. Starr to AG, 3D, DSL, 7 December 1900, 395/4830, LS Bk 1, LS 239; Maj. William C. Forbush to AAG, 3D, DSL, 1 February 1901, 395/3835, LS 77. For operational accounts of this expedition, see *WD* 1901 1:5:371–82.

73. Maj. Hugh D. Wise to AG, DSL, 5 February 1901, 395/3668, LS Bk 2, LS 42; Maj. Hugh D. Wise to AG, DSL, 21 February 1901, 395/2421; Maj. Hugh D. Wise to AG, U.S. Army, 7 February 1901, *WD* 1901 1:5:425–26; Howe, "Historical Sketch of the 47th," 94/187; Capt. Oscar Brown to AAG, 3D, DSL, 10 April 1901, 395/5606, Virac, Catanduanes, LS, Feb. 1900 to Jan. 1902; Capt. Harry Walsh to Adj., 47th Inf., 31 March 1901, 395/3668, LS Bk 2, LS 124.

74. Howe, "Historical Sketch of the 47th," 94/187. For reports on operations, see Brig. Gen. James M. Bell to Anon. [AG, DSL], 27 December 1900, 395/2418, LS Bk 3, LS 1462; Lt. Col. James Parker to C.O.'s, 1 March 1901, 395/3929, LS Bk 3, LS 463; Dorst, "Historical Sketch of the 45th Infantry, U.S.V.," 94/187.

75. Capt. Charles F. McLain to Adj., 47th Inf., 4 February 1901, *WD* 1901 1:5:421–22. For the clergy's acceptance of American rule, see Schumacher, *Revolutionary Clergy*, pp. 172–75.

76. Brig. Gen. Antonio Guevara to Maj. Gen. Vito Belarmino, 15 March 1901, PIR SD 1014.9; Maj. William H. Johnson to AG, 3D, DSL, 26 December 1900, Roosevelt Papers, series 1, reel 8; Moseley, "One Soldier's Journey," Moseley Papers.

77. E. Villareal to Col. Ramon Santos, 13 February 1901, PIR SD 1014.7.

78. Brig. Gen. Antonino Guevara to Maj. Gen. Vito Belarmino, 15 March 1901, PIR SD 1014.9.

79. Lt. Lucien G. Berry to Adj., 2 March 1901, 395/5376, LS 285; Maj. William C. Forbush to AAG, 3D, DSL, 10 February 1901, 395/2835, LS 79; Col. James Lockett to AG, 3D, DSL, 30 December 1900, 395/5032, LS Bk 1, LS 117; Col.

James Lockett to AG, 3D, DSL., 13 January 1901, 395/5032, LS Bk 1, LS 2; Maj. James A. Shipton to Officer in Charge of Civil Affairs, 3D, DSL, 30 March 1901, 395/5032, LS 83; Lt. Sterling Adams to AG, 3D, DSL, 31 May 1901, 395/4082, LS 121.

80. Quote "actively engaged" from Capt. John W. Gulick to AG, Provost Guard, 5 March 1901, 395/3801. Brig. Gen. James M. Bell to AAG, DSL, 5 March 1901, 395/2418, LS Bk 3, LS 2135. For operations in Sorsogon, see Howe, "Historical Sketch of the 47th," 94/187; *WD* 1901 1:5:345–67.

81. Col. Walter Howe to AG, 3D, DSL, 14 March 1901, 94/117, 47th Inf., LS Bk 3, LS 195. Capt. John W. Gulick to Maj. Esteban Fulay, 27 February 1901, 395/3801, LS 91; Capt. John W. Gulick to Adj., 47th Inf., 4 March 1901, 395/2420.

82. *WD* 1901 1:5:323; Moseley, "One Soldier's Journey," Moseley Papers. For operations against Aréjola, see *WD* 1901 1:5:394–99, 440–42; "Reservada," 20 March 1901, PIR SD 1230.2.

83. Capt. Henry H. Benham to C.O. Guinobatan, 5 June 1901, 395/3668, LS Bk 2, LS 174. For accounts of the attack, see Capt. John M. Cotter to AG, DSL, 26 May 1901, LS 165; Capt. Henry H. Benham to AG, 3D, DSL, 31 May 1901, LS 166; Capt. John M. Cotter to AG, 3D, DSL, 30 May 1900, LS 167, all in ibid. For an overly optimistic view of the level of pacification in Sorsogon, see Col. William Howe to AG, 3D, 8 April 1901, 395/5311, Sorsogon, Sorsogon, Letters and Telegrams Sent, LS Bk 1, LS 37.

84. "Report of Operations in the Fourth Separate Brigade," *WD* 1902 1:7:336–64; Col. Constant Williams to Col. Theodore Wint, 14 June 1901, 395/2424; Capt. Dana E. Kilbourne to Adj., 26th Inf., 3 August 1901, 395/2420; Lt. Leo M. Cutts, "Report of Wray's Scouts," 19 July 1901, 395/2424; Maj. Gen. Vito Belarmino to Lt. Gen. Mariano Trías, 7 July 1901, PIR SD 747.1. There was some controversy over Col. Theodore J. Wint's attempts to appropriate all the credit for Belarmino's surrender to himself and the Sixth Cavalry, see Col. Theodore J. Wint to AG, DSL, 13 August 1901, *WD* 1902 1:9:345–47, and endorsement by Col. Constant Williams, 3 October 1901, ibid., pp. 347–48.

85. *WD* 1902 1:9:338–82; Lt. R. B. Parrot to AG, 3D, DSL, 11 September 1901, 395/4449, Matnog, Sorsogon, LS, May 1900 to July 1902, LS 68; Capt. Edmund Wittenmyer to C.O., Sorsogon, 12 September 1901, 395/5314, Sorsogon, Sorsogon, LR, 1901–4; Lt. Col. Leon A. Matilde to AG, 3D, DSL, 1 October 1901, 395/5311, LS Bk 1, LS 228; "List of Natives in 'Anting-Anting' and Similar Organizations in Albay and Sorsogon," PIR SD 673.12; "Report of the Governor of Sorsogon," Senate, *Affairs*, pp. 458–59; Coats, "Philippine Constabulary," pp. 54–64, 80–106; Owen, "Winding Down the War in Albay," pp. 569–72. For a pessimistic view of the state of pacification, see the reports of intelligence officers, esp. Capt. Charles Young to DMI, November 1901, 395/5379; Lt. T. Bruce Esty to DMI, 6 January 1902, 395/4587.

86. Owen, "Winding Down the War in Albay," p. 578.

Chapter Five

1. "Report of Brig. Gen. J. F. Wade, U.S.A., Commanding Department of Southern Luzon," *WD* 1901 1:7:290.

2. Ibid., p. 289.

3. Wernstedt and Spencer, *Philippine Island World*, pp. 392–407; "Province of Tayabas: Press Abstract to be released September 11, 1901," 350/2760, "Tayabas File"; Millett, *The General*, pp. 137–38; May, "Filipino Resistance," p. 533; U.S. War Department, *Pronouncing Gazetteer*, pp. 344, 570, 882.

4. May, "Resistance and Collaboration," p. 71; May, "Filipino Resistance," pp. 533–36; "Santa Cruz, Laguna," PIR SD 631.10; Sturtevant, *Popular Uprisings*, pp. 83–95; Ileto, *Payson and Revolution*, pp. 37–91; Guerrero, "Luzon at War," pp. 213–17; May, "150,000 Missing Filipinos," pp. 215–43.

5. Col. Juan Cailles to Lt. Gen. Secretary of War, 13 April 1899, PIR SD 1195.3; LeRoy, *Americans in the Philippines*, 2:34–35; Gleeck, *Laguna in American Times*, pp. 3–4; *ANJ* 38 (16 December 1899); Sexton, *Soldiers in the Sun*, pp. 149–61.

6. LeRoy, *Americans in the Philippines*, 2:164. *WD* 1900 1:4:368–95, 1:5:387–564; Sexton, *Soldiers in the Sun*, pp. 224–31; Holli, "A View of the American Campaign," pp. 97–111; "Diario de Operaciones realizadas por las fuerzas de Batallón de Banahao," PIR SD 942.3; Parker, *Old Army*, pp. 299–303.

7. William H. Taft to Elihu Root, 23 October 1900, Taft Papers, series 21; Maj. Gen. John C. Bates to AG, DivPhil, 15 June 1900, 395/2412, 2D, DSL, Correspondence and Reports Relating to the District, Oct. 1900 to Apr. 1901; "Annual Report of Maj. Gen. John C. Bates, U.S.V., Commanding Department of Southern Luzon," *WD* 1900 1:5:227.

8. Quote "cold blooded" from Diary of Robert L. Bullard, 2 May 1900, Bullard Papers; "a damned old nasal-toned fool" from Maj. Matthew F. Steele to Stella [wife], 29 April 1900, Steele Papers, Box 7; C. Van Ness Radcliffe, "Personal Sketch of Wm. E. Birkhimer," Harry M. Moot File; Turnbull, "Reminiscences," p. 44.

9. Quote "we must take care" from Col. William E. Birkhimer to AAG, 2d Brig., 1st Div., 8th A.C., 31 March 1900, 94/117, 28th Inf., LS Bk 1, LS 437. Col. William E. Birkhimer to AG, DSL, 2 May 1900, 395/2408, Box 1.

10. Col. William E. Birkhimer to AG, DSL, 30 June 1900, 395/2330, LR 898. Col. William E. Birkhimer to Col. Cornelius Gardener, 1 June 1900, 395/2408, Box 1, LR 902; Col. William E. Birkhimer to AG, DSL, 2 May 1900, ibid.

11. Col. William E. Birkhimer to AAG, 2d Brig., 1st Div., 8th A.C., 6 March 1900, 94/117, 28th. Inf., LS Bk 1, LS 446.

12. "Report of Brig. Gen. Robert H. Hall, U.S.A., Commanding District," *WD* 1901 1:5:267–315. The available source material for Hall's correspondence can be found in 395/2403, 2D, DSL, Letters, Telegrams, and Endorsements Sent.

13. *WD* 1900 1:5:208; Millett, *The General*, pp. 111–19.

14. Capt. John L. Jordan to Mother, 5 and 28 February 1900, Jordan Papers; Diary of Robert L. Bullard, 21 and 31 January 1900, Bullard Papers; Maj. Charles T. Boyd to CS, D.P. and 8th A.C., 16 February 1900, 94/117, 37th Inf., LS Bk 1, LS 35; Col. Benjamin F. Cheatham to AG, Calamba, 4 May 1900, ibid., LS 109; Col. Robert L. Bullard to AAG, 1st Div., 8th A.C., 2 March 1900, 94/117, 39th Inf., LS Bk 1; Col.

Robert L. Bullard to AG, Wheaton's Brig., 12 March 1900, ibid., LS 499; Diary of William C. Brown, March to May 1900, Brown Papers; Eustacio Maloles to P.L., Mauban and Capt. Mateo Almorsara, 24 March 1900, PIR SD 1219.7.

15. Col. Cornelius Gardener to Hazen S. Pingree, 21 February 1900, quoted in Holli, "A View of the American Campaign," p. 105.

16. Col. George S. Anderson to AG, DSL, 11 May 1900, 94/117, 38th Inf., LS Bk 1, LS 664. Maj. William C. Brown to AG, DSL, 9 May 1900, 395/2408, Box 1; Lt. Col. William H. Beacom to AG, DSL, 30 April 1900, 395/2330, LR 333; Col. William E. Birkhimer to AG, DSL, 8 May 1900, ibid., LR 257; Col. Benjamin F. Cheatham to AG, 2D, 9 May and 5 June 1900, 94/117, 37th Inf., LS Bk 1, LS 115 and 211; Maj. Lewis E. Goodier to Adj., 38th Inf., 13 May 1900, 395/2408, Box 1; "Reports from Station Commanders in 39th Inf.," 20 May 1900, ibid.

17. Orton, "Memoirs."

18. Col. Cornelius Gardener to Hazen S. Pingree, 21 February 1900, quoted in Holli, "A View of the American Campaign," pp. 100–111. Quote "considerable latitude" from Col. Cornelius Gardener to C.O., Tiaong, 10 June 1900, 395/5488, Tiaong, Tayabas, Letters and Telegrams Received, May–Dec. 1900 and May 1902, LR 7.

19. Col. Cornelius Gardener to AG, DSL, 8 February 1901, 350/2670. Holli, "A View of the American Campaign," pp. 97–111; Col. Cornelius Gardener, "To the Inhabitants of the Province of Tayabas," February 1900, 395/5473, Tayabas, Tayabas, General and Special Orders, June 1900 to May 1902; Col. Cornelius Gardener to C.O., Lucban, 29 April 1900, 395/4165, Lucban, Tayabas, Letters and Telegrams Received, 1900–1902, LR 84; Col. Cornelius Gardener to AG, DSL, 8 May and 25 July 1900, 395/2408, Box 1.

20. Maj. Matthew F. Steele to Stella, 19 and 29 April 1900, Steele Papers; Maj. Matthew F. Steele to Col. Cornelius Gardener, 4 April 1900, 395/4162, Lucban, Tayabas, LS, Feb. 1900 to June 1900, LS Bk 2, LS 51; Maj. Matthew F. Steele to Adj., 30th Inf., 8 May 1900, ibid., LS 149.

21. Maj. Matthew F. Steele to Stella, 29 August 1900, Steele Papers.

22. Hq, DSL to C.O., Lucban, 5 December 1900, 395/4165, LR 704. Col. Cornelius Gardener to AG, DSL, 10 September 1900, 395/2133, CA100; Col. Cornelius Gardener to AG, DSL, 7 May 1900, 395/2408, Box 1. Capt. F. D. Buckingham to C.O., Lucena, 29 November 1900, LS Bk 3, LS 767; Maj. Matthew F. Steele to AG, DSL, 25 June 1900, LS Bk 2, LS 263; Maj. Matthew F. Steele to AG, DSL, 11 August 1900, LS Bk 3, LS 421, all in 395/4162; Maj. Matthew F. Steele to Stella, 7 January 1901, Box 7, Steele Papers; "Testimony of Maj. Matthew F. Steele," 94/421607, encl. 2, "Proceedings of a Board of Officers to Inquire into Allegations made by Maj. Cornelius Gardener, 13th U.S. Infantry in His Report of December 16, 1901," pp. 762–66 (hereafter cited as *Gardener Board*).

23. Maj. Matthew F. Steele to Col. Cornelius Gardener, 20 December 1900, 395/4162, LS Bk 3, LS 814.

24. Maj. Gen. James C. Bates to SMG, 11 October 1900, 94/386152; Brig. Gen. Robert H. Hall to AG, DSL, 2 February 1901, 395/2133, CA208; Capt. Charles Humphreys to AG, 1D, DSL, 13 July 1901, ibid., CA102; Col. Benjamin F. Cheatham to AG, DSL, 9 May 1900, 94/117, 37th Inf., LS Bk 1, LS 115.

25. Maj. Gen. John C. Bates to AG, DivPhil, 15 June 1900, 395/2412. Col. William E. Birkhimer to AG, DSL, 10 June 1900; Maj. John H. Parker to Adj., 39th Inf., 28 June 1900, "Reports of Native Police" Packet, ibid.; Lt. Col. Robert W. Leonard to AAG, Calamba, 26 May 1900, 94/117, 28th Inf., LS Bk 1, LS 503. For the initial instructions to organize police, see Lt. Col. Enoch Crowder to C.G., DSL, 21 June 1900, 395/2412, LS M806.

26. Col. Cornelius Gardener to AG, DSL, 21 June 1900, 94/117, 30th Inf., LS Bk 2, LS 1190; Col. Cornelius Gardener to Col. Arthur Wagner, 24 July 1900, 295/2412, LS 1484; Col. Cornelius Gardener to AG, DivPhil, 15 January 1901, 395/2133, CA18; Col. Cornelius Gardener to AG, DSL, 7 June 1900, 395/2412; Col. Cornelius Gardener to AG, DSL, 21 June 1900, LS 1190; Col. Cornelius Gardener to C.O.'s Atimonan, Lopez, Guinyañgan, 11 July 1900, LS 1322; Col. Cornelius Gardener to C.O.'s, Lucena, Sariaya, Lucban, 31 July 1900, LS 1557, all in 94/117, 30th Inf., LS Bk 2; Capt. Harrison Kerrick to AG, DivPhil, 14 July 1900, 395/5254, Sariaya, Tayabas, LS, Apr. 1900 to Apr. 1902, LS 84; Capt. Lawrence J. Hearn to Adj., 21st Inf., 18 January 1901, ibid., LS 19; Maj. Matthew F. Steele to Col. Cornelius Gardener, 30 August 1900, 395/4162, LS Bk 3, LS 501; Col. Cornelius Gardener to AG, DSL, 16 June 1901, 395/5721, Lucena, Tayabas, Letters and Telegrams Sent, Mar. 1900 to Sept. 1902, LS Bk 1, LS 13.

27. "Report of Native Police for December 1900," 395/2412; "Report of Native Police for February 1901," 395/3287, Calamba, Laguna, LR, 1901–6, LR 81.

28. Quote "emergency work" from Hq, DivPhil to C.G., DSL, 29 December 1900, 395/5726, Lucena, Tayabas, Letters and Telegrams Received, 1901 to Aug. 1902; Capt. Charles J. Sterrett to Adj., 8th Inf., 23 January 1901, 395/3284, Calamba, Laguna, Letters and Telegrams Sent, Nov. 1900 to Sept. 1906, LS Bk 1, LS 15; Col. Jacob Kline to AG, 2D, DSL, 8 February 1901, 395/4134, Lipa, Batangas, LS, Nov. 1900 to Jan. 1905, LS Bk 1, LS 33; Capt. William G. Haan to Maj. Cornelius Gardener, 22 May 1901, 395/2133, CA819; Hq, DSL to C.G., 2D, DSL, 18 February 1901, 395/3092, LR 79; Lt. Traber Norman to AG, DSL, 5 February 1901, 395/4255, Majayjay, Laguna, LS, Jan. 1901 to June 1902, LS 8; Capt. Alexis R. Paxton to AG, DSL, 25 March 1901, 395/4638, Paete, Laguna, Letters, Telegrams, and Endorsements Sent, Oct. 1900 to July 1902, LS 31.

29. Brig. Gen. Robert H. Hall to AG, DSL, 2 February 1901, 395/2133, CA209.

30. Lt. Col. Charles J. Crane to Adj., 38th Inf., 13 May 1900, 395/2412; Col. George S. Anderson to SMG, 17 May 1900, 94/117, 38th Inf., LS Bk 1, LS 679; Col. Benjamin F. Cheatham to AG, DSL, 10 May 1900, 94/117, 37th Inf., LS Bk 1, LS 126. For reports on schools, see file on "Public Schools—2nd District," 395/2412.

31. *ANJ* 38 (23 March 1901).

32. Capt. John L. Jordan to Mother, 29 August 1900, Jordan Papers; Col. Cornelius Gardener to Secretary, Philippine Commission, 18 December 1900, 94/117, 30th Inf., LS Bk 3, LS 304; Maj. Leonard A. Lovering to SMG, 26 June 1900, 395/5721, LS 103; Maj. George T. Langhorne to AG, DSL, 30 September 1900, 395/2133, LR B2227; Maj. George T. Langhorne to AG, DivPhil, 14 March 1901, 94/117, 39th Inf., LS Bk 2, LS 47; Anon., "The Soldier Teacher in the Philippines," p. 74.

33. Maj. Frederick K. Ward to AG, 2D, DSL, 12 February 1901, 395/3089, Bauan, Batangas, Letters and Telegrams Sent, Dec. 1900 to July 1903, LS 20; District Commander, 2D to C.O., Calamba, 11 February 1901, 395/3287, LR 49.

34. Capt. William P. Burnham to AAG, 1D, DSL, 30 September 1901, 395/2355, 1D, DSL, LR, 1901; Col. Cornelius Gardener to AG, DSL, 21 June 1900, 94/117, 30th Inf., LS Bk 2, LS 1190; Col. Robert L. Bullard to AG, Wheaton's Expeditionary Brig., 21 March 1900, 94/117, 39th Inf., LS Bk 1; Maj. George T. Langhorne to P.L., Balayan, 5 November 1900, 395/4564, Nasugbu, Batangas, Letters and Telegrams Sent, Oct. 1900 to Sept. 1906, LS 9; *ANJ* 37 (3 March 1900); *Manila Times* (29 January 1900).

35. Col. Cornelius Gardener to C.O. Tayabas, n.d. [1901], 395/5472, Tayabas, Tayabas, Miscellaneous Letters, Telegrams, Orders, and Reports Received, 1900–1902. Surgeon to Chief Surgeon, DSL, 30 June 1901, 395/3287; Capt. Harrison Kerrick to AG, DSL, 1 September 1900, 395/5254, LS 38.

36. Quote "true loyalty and contentment" from Col. Cornelius Gardener to Civil Governor of the Philippine Islands, 16 December 1901, Senate, *Affairs,* p. 885. Quote "This business of fighting" from Capt. John L. Jordan to Mother, 29 October 1900, Jordan Papers.

37. Bullard, "Autobiography," Box 9, Bullard Papers.

38. For casualty statistics for the Twenty-eighth Infantry, see Lt. G. M. Genity to Chief Surgeon, 10 August 1900, 94/117, 28th Inf., LS Bk 1, LS 668; Col. William E. Birkhimer to AG, Calamba, 28 September 1900, 94/117, 28th Inf., LS Bk 1, LS 837. For statistics on the Thirtieth Infantry see Col. Cornelius Gardener to AG, DSL, 21 June, 20 July, 11 August, 10 September 1900, LS 1190, LS 1427, LS 1657, LS 1992, all in 94/117, 30th Inf., LS Bk 2; Col. Cornelius Gardener to AG, DSL, 20 October, 20 November, 20 December 1900, LS 2546, LS 2866, LS 3427, all in ibid., LS Bk 3. For a bitter criticism of Gardener's attempts to prevent the evacuation of his sick, see Maj. William F. de Niedman to Chief Surgeon, 27 September 1900, 395/2330, LR A1575. For statistics on the Thirty-seventh Infantry see Col. Benjamin F. Cheatham to AG, DSL, 8 August 1900, 94/117, 37th Inf., LS Bk 2, LS 452. For statistics on the Thirty-eighth Infantry, see Col. George S. Anderson to Chief Surgeon, DSL, 30 July, 30 August, 30 September 1900, LS 90, LS 1050, LS 1229; Lt. Col. Charles J. Crane to Chief Surgeon, 10 October 1900, LS 1318, all in 94/117, 38th Inf., LS Bk 3. For statistics on the Thirty-ninth Infantry, see, "Report of Chief Surgeon on Sanitary Conditions at San Pablo and San Tomas," 14 May 1900, 395/2408, Box 1; Col. Robert L. Bullard to AG, DSL, 16 May, 31 August, and 10 October 1900, all in 94/117, 39th Inf., LS Bk 1; Diary of Robert L. Bullard, 31 August 1900, Bullard Papers.

39. Maj. William C. Brown to AG, DSL, 22 May 1900, 395/2408, Box 1; "Report of First Lt. and Ast. Surg. Leis A. Griffith," 23 May 1900, 395/2408, Box 1; Col. Cornelius Gardener to AG, DSL, 13 August 1900, 94/117, 30th Inf., LS Bk 2, LS 1680; Col. Cornelius Gardener to C.O., Tiaong, 14 August 1900, ibid., LS 1689; "Report of Chief Surgeon on Sanitary Conditions at San Pablo and San Tomas," 14 May 1900, 395/2408, Box 1.

40. Col. Cornelius Gardener to AAG, DSL, 28 July 1900, 94/117, 30th Inf., LS Bk 2, LS 149; Col. Cornelius Gardener to Capt. Albert D. Nisken, 17 September

1900, ibid., LS 2103; Col. George S. Anderson to Maj. George B. Davis, Chief Commissary, 24 June 1900, 94/117, 38th Inf., LS Bk 1, LS 762; James F. Edwards Questionnaire.

41. Maj. Matthew F. Steele to Stella, 4 August 1900, Steele Papers; Brig. Gen. Juan Cailles to Col. Pablo Astilla, 6 August 1900, PIR SD 941.3. For statistics on engagements, see *WD* 1900 1:5:5–43, 1901 1:5:266–78.

42. Col. Benjamin F. Cheatham to AG, DSL, 8 June 1900, 94/117, 37th Inf., LS Bk 1, LS 222. Diary of Robert L. Bullard, 10 April 1900, Bullard Papers; Col. George S. Anderson to AG, DSL, 5 June and 5 July 1900, 395/2408, Box 2, LS 728 and 798.

43. Lt. Col. Charles J. Crane to Adj., 38th Inf., 4 July 1900, 94/117, 38th Inf., LS Bk 2, LS 517. Lt. Col. Charles J. Crane to Sr. Valirio Callao, 4 July 1900, ibid., LS 522.

44. Quote "Hostilities almost resumed," from Diary of Robert L. Bullard, 3 July 1900, Bullard Papers. Quote "we control within the line" from Col. William E. Birkhimer to AG, DSL, 15 July 1900, 94/117, 28th Inf., LS Bk 1, LS 516.

45. Majul, *Mabini*, pp. 271–73; Zaide, *Philippine Revolution*, pp. 351–52; May, "Resistance and Collaboration" pp. 71–75; May, "Filipino Resistance," pp. 534–35, 540–41; "Notes for the History of the Glorious Epopeé of the Independence of the Philippines," Taylor, *Philippine Insurrection*, Exhibit 70, pp. 70–71 LY. Malvar was criticized for his willingness to subordinate civil authority to the military; see Col. Manuel Arguelles to Emilio Aguinaldo, 22 September 1898, PIR SD 1246.3. For information on Malvar, see PIR SD 692, 772, 779, 902, 1132.

46. Quote "War, war, is what we want," from Col. Juan Cailles to Secretary of War, 10 January 1899, Taylor, *Philippine Insurrection*, Exhibit 374, p. 10 KU. Col. Juan Cailles to P.L., Cavinti, Luisiana, Majayjay, 27 May 1899, PIR SD 294.1; Col. Juan Cailles to Lt. Gen. Secretary of War, 13 April 1899, PIR SD 1195.3; Col. Juan Cailles, "Proclamation," 21 June 1899, PIR SD 339.1; Col. Juan Cailles to Local Chiefs, 21 July 1899, PIR SD 602.1; Col. Juan Cailles to Local Chiefs, 22 July 1899, PIR SD 294.2; Ambriosio Flores to Secretary de Hacienda, 9 August 1899, PIR SD 1195.2; Pedro A. Paterno to Secretary of War, 25 August 1899, PIR SD 294.3; Emilio Aguinaldo, "Proclamation," 20 June 1898, Taylor, *Philippine Insurrection*, Exhibit 37, pp. 29–30 MG; Hq, DSL to C.O., Bauan, 11 March 1901, 395/3092, LR 122B. For information on Cailles, see PIR SD 294, 602, 653, 712, 716, 1195.

47. "Testimony of Miguel Malvar," *Gardener Board*, p. 650. Leonardo Miguel [pseud.] to Brig. Gen. Juan Cailles, 12 March 1900, PIR SD 294.6; Brig. Gen. Juan Cailles to Vicente Zotomeyer, 24 April 1900, PIR SD 294.10; Maj. John H. Parker to Col. Robert L. Bullard, 17 May 1900, 395/2408, Box 1; Brig. Gen. Juan Cailles to Col. Pablo Astilla, 6 August 1900, Taylor, *Philippine Insurrection*, Exhibit 1084, p. 57 GV; Maj. Gen. Miguel Malvar, "Provisions and Instructions Issued by the Superior Commander of Southern Luzon for Observation in this Department," 28 April 1901, ibid., Exhibit 1156, pp. 82–83 GV; Brig. Gen. Mariano Noriel, "Resumé of the General Orders and Instructions Given and Issued by these Superior Headquarters of the Departmental Government from the 29th of August to Date," 9 September 1901, ibid., Exhibit 1169, pp. 88–89 GV; Col. Julio Herrera to Maj. Domingo Ramos, 14 November 1900, PIR SD 605.2.50.

48. May, "Resistance and Collaboration," p. 76, also pp. 75, 79–81; Hq, DSL to C.O., Bauan, 18 March 1901, 395/3092, LR 122A; "Statement of Martin Apelo before Lieut. W. T. Vaughn, 37th Infantry U.S.V., Manila, May 14, 1901," PIR SD 631.8; May, "Private Presher," pp. 50–52.

49. Maj. Gen. Miguel Malvar, "Copy of a Reply to General Trías," 19 April 1901, Taylor, *Philippine Insurrection*, Exhibit 1155, p. 82 GV. For evidence of the connections between the revolutionary officer corps and local landowners, see May, "Filipino Resistance," pp. 536–37; May, "Resistance and Collaboration," pp. 75–76, 79–81; Ileto, "Tiaong, Tayabas," p. 74.

50. Col. Buenaventura Dimaguila to Lt. Gen. Mariano Trías, 30 November 1900, Taylor, *Philippine Insurrection*, Exhibit 1125, pp. 70–72 GV; Capt. John D. Hartman to Adj., Batangas, 16 November 1901, 395/3089, LS 218.

51. "Testimony of Col. Eustacio Maloles," *Gardener Board*, pp. 97–100.

52. Maj. Gen. Miguel Malvar, "Guerrilla Warfare. Instructions," 27 October 1900, PIR SD 1132.4. "Instructions of Letter found on the Adjutant of Martin Cabrera," 5 August 1901, PIR SD 692.10.

53. José Maghirang, Lieutenant of Barrio, Miguel Pasco, Anselmo Brinas to the Lieutenant of Barrios and to the Chief, n.d., PIR SD 719.2. See also "illegible" to Maj. Luciana Atienza, 7 September 1901, ibid.; "Relaciones de los soldados revolucionarios," n.d., PIR SD 712.8; "Testimony of Col. Eustacio Maloles," *Gardener Board*, pp. 97–100; "Testimony of Peotacio Silvala," ibid., pp. 170–71. The term *regulares* as distinct forces is used in Florencio Trinidad to Brig. Gen. Juan Cailles, 23 March 1901, PIR SD 712.1.

54. May, "Private Presher," p. 53. This overview of the guerrilla forces is taken from the following sources: *WD* 1900 1:5:227; Diary of Robert L. Bullard, 3 February 1900, Bullard Papers; Brig. Gen. Juan Cailles to Col. Pedro Caballes, 14 February 1901, PIR SD 753.1; Col. Cornelius Gardener to SMG, 17 October 1900, 94/117, 30th Inf., LS Bk 2, LS 2506; Col. Robert L. Bullard to AG, DSL, 19 May 1900, 94/117, 39th Inf., LS Bk 1, LS 679; Maj. George T. Langhorne to AG, DSL, 9 February and 4 March 1901, ibid., LS Bk 2, LS 25 and 42; Col. Robert L. Bullard to AG, DSL, 10 January 1901, ibid., LS Bk 2, LS 6; Maj. Lewis E. Goodier to AG, DSL 12 October 1901, 395/5007, San José, Batangas, LS, Feb. 1900 to Feb. 1903, LS 88; "Statement of Cecilio Rosal," 25 January 1901, 395/3092; Col. George S. Anderson to Provost Marshall General, 23 May 1900, 94/117, 38th Inf., LS Bk 1, LS 692; "Descriptive List," n.d., 395/3289, Calamba, Laguna, LR Relating to Insurgents, 1902; Capt. Charles M. McLester to AG, DSL, 22 November 1901, 395/2330, LS C2621; Brig. Gen. Samuel S. Sumner to AG, DSL, 2 August 1901, 395/5101, San Pablo, Laguna, Miscellaneous Correspondence, 1901–2; "Reorganización de la Laguna," August–September 1901, ibid.; Brig. Gen. Juan Cailles to Anon. [P.L.'s?], 1899, PIR SD 602.6; Capt. Charles D. Rhodes, "Military History of Lieutenant Colonel Eustaguio Castelltor," 1901, PIR SD 805.1; Capt. Ralph Van Deman, "Report," 21 December 1901, PIR SD 796.1; May, "Resistance and Collaboration," pp. 81–82; May, "Filipino Resistance," p. 539; Zaide, *Philippine Revolution*, pp. 278–79.

55. Diary of Frederick Presher, 13 January 1902, Presher Papers. Diary of Charles D. Rhodes, 11 February 1902, Rhodes Papers; Col. Benjamin F. Cheatham to AG,

DSL, 8 June 1900, 94/117, 37th Inf., LS Bk 1, LS 222; Lt. Arthur L. Bump to Adj., 29 August 1901, *WD* 1902 1:9:294; Brig. Gen. Samuel S. Sumner to AG, DSL, 28 September 1901, 395/2349, 1D, DSL, Press Copies of LS, Dec. 1900 to Dec. 1902; "Memorandum of Arms Secured," 30 September 1901, ibid.; Col. Almond B. Wells to AG, 3SB, 19 November 1901, 395/2408, LS 251; Maj. Gen. Miguel Malvar to Brig. Gen. Juan Cailles, 4 April 1901, PIR SD 692.4; Brig. Gen. J. Franklin Bell, "Report of Operations in the Third Separate Brigade," *WD* 1902 1:7:267. Malvar, for example, stated that any guerrilla who surrendered his weapon would be fined 250 pesos. See Maj. Gen. Miguel Malvar, "Orders and General Observances Dictated by Superior Headquarters of Southern Luzon," 28 August 1901, in "Appendix F," 395/2635, Box 1, no. 256; Brig. Gen. Mariano Noriel, "Resumé of the General Orders and Instructions Given and Issued by these Superior Headquarters of the Departmental Government from the 29th of August to Date," 9 September 1901, Taylor, *Philippine Insurrection*, Exhibit 1169, pp. 88–89 GV. Maj. Peotacio Silvala had a force of 100 men but only 5 rifles. Not surprisingly, he only assembled his forces four times in 1900, "Testimony of Peotacio Silvala," *Gardener Board*, pp. 170–71.

56. Diary of Frederick Presher, 10 May 1901, Presher Papers. Maj. Gen. Miguel Malvar, "Proclamation," 11 November 1901, PIR SD 902.10; Capt. John L. Jordan to Mother, 28 April 1900, Jordan Papers; Capt. Charles J. Sterrett to AAG, 2D, DSL, 15 and 21 December 1900, 395/3284, LS Bk 1, LS 8 and 13; Col. Robert L. Bullard to AG, DSL, 31 October 1900, 94/117, 39th Inf., LS Bk 1, LS 886; Brig. Gen. Juan Cailles to E. Riego Dios, 21 November 1900, PIR SD 653.4; Brig. Gen. Juan Cailles to P.L., Paete, Pangil, etc., PIR SD 941.9; Maj. Frederick K. Ward to AG, DSL, 7 January 1901, 395/2408, Box 3, LR 250; Lt. John W. Craig to AG, 2D, DSL, 29 January 1901, 395/5052, San Juan de Bocboc, Batangas, Letters and Telegrams Sent, July 1900 to Mar. 1903.

57. Capt. John L. Jordan to Mother, 11 July 1900, Jordan Papers.

58. Lt. Col. Mariano Cabrera to Eliseo Claudio, 14 January 1900, PIR SD 936.7.

59. Maj. Gen. Miguel Malvar, "Provisions and Instructions Issued by the Superior Commander of Southern Luzon for Observation in this Department," 28 April 1901, Taylor, *Philippine Insurrection*, Exhibit 1156, pp. 82–83 GV; Maj. Gen. Miguel Malvar, "To the Public and Army of the Department of the South," 19 April 1901, ibid., Exhibit 1158, pp. 83–84 GV; "Testimony of Miguel Malvar," *Gardener Board*, p. 650.

60. Lt. Col. Charles J. Crane to AG, 2D, DSL, 14 November 1900, 395/4134, LS Bk 1, LS 1084.

61. The guerrilla treatment of American prisoners of war varied greatly. Juan Cailles sent prisoners back to the American lines, but in Tayabas captured prisoners were tortured and dead soldiers were mutilated. See Frank L. Rose and Bernard Lichtig Questionnaires; *ANJ* 38 (22 September 1900).

62. Taylor, *Philippine Insurrection*, p. 44 HS; Capt. William N. Blow to AG, DSL, 1 June 1901, 395/2355, 1D, DSL, LR, 1901; Capt. John L. Jordan to Mother, 18 February 1900, Jordan Papers; Lt. Col. Pedro Caballes to Brig. Gen. Juan Cailles, March 1901, PIR SD 712.2; Brig. Gen. Juan Cailles to P.L., 18 November 1900, 395/2408, Box 3, LR 896.

63. Brig. Gen. Juan Cailles to P.L.'s, 22 March 1900, PIR SD 706.14; Maj. Pedro Caballes to P.L., Cavinti, Laguna, 15 July 1900, PIR SD 510.1; Col. Julio Herrera to

Brig. Gen. Juan Cailles, 30 April 1900, encl. in Hq, 1D, DSL to C.O., Bay, 5 March 1901, 395/3116, Bay, Laguna, Memorandums, Circulars, Copies of Telegrams, and Miscellaneous Papers, Dec. 1900 to Feb. 1902, LR 215; "Proclamation of Lt. Col. Emilio Zurbano, Military Governor of Tayabas, to his Fellow Citizens," 23 April 1901, Taylor, *Philippine Insurrection*, Exhibit 1154, p. 81 GV; Col. Pedro Caballes, "Articles," 26 July 1901, ibid., Exhibit 1167, pp. 87–88 GV; Manuel Quiroque to Brig. Gen. Juan Cailles, 31 March 1900, ibid., Exhibit 1132, p. 81 GV; Leonardo Miguel to Brig. Gen. Juan Cailles, 12 March 1900, PIR SD 294.7; Col. Julio Herrera to P.L., Nagcarlan, Rizal, etc., 30 April 1900, PIR SD 220.4; Capt. Henry A. Hutchings to AG, Wheaton's Expeditionary Brig., 19 March 1900, 94/117, 37th Inf., LS Bk 1, LS 60; "Extracts for Letters Sent Book of Cailles, pages 45, 46," PIR SD 716.5; Brig. Gen. Juan Cailles to Vicente Zotomayer, 24 April 1900, PIR SD 294.10; Brig. Gen. Juan Cailles to P.L., 20 March 1901, PIR SD 712.3; Julio Infante to Brig. Gen. Juan Cailles, 18 November 1900, PIR SD 653.10.

64. "Copy of charges against Hermano Marquiz and Nemencio Ylagan," and "Assassins of Tomas Diocampo," 28 September 1901, 395/3092, LR 333 A and B; Homer V. Cook MS; Capt. John L. Jordan to Mother, 10 March 1900, Jordan Papers; Col. George S. Anderson to AG, Wheaton's Expeditionary Brig., 8 March 1900, 94/117, 38th Inf., LS Bk 1, LR 486–87; Capt. Edward N. Jones to AG, Calamba, 16 February 1901, 395/3106, Bay, Laguna, TS, Dec. 1900 to Aug. 1902, TS 103, 125, 137, 138, 139; *ANJ* 38 (27 April 1901); May, "Private Presher," p. 42; Lt. Col. Charles J. Crane to P.L., Lipa, 19 July, 94/117, 38th Inf., LS Bk 2, LS 609; Crane, *Experiences*, pp. 351, 358; Capt. Charles A. Humphreys to AG, 1D, DSL, 25 February 1901, 395/2330, C1495; Capt. John Morrison to AG, 3SB, 27 November 1901, 395/2354, 1D, DSL, LR, Nov. 1901–2; Diary of Charles D. Rhodes, 26 February 1902, Rhodes Papers; Worcester, *Philippines Past and Present*, pp. 235–36; Taylor, *Philippine Insurrection*, p. 53 HS.

65. Lt. Traber Norman to AG, DSL, 3 April 1901, 395/2408, Box 3, LR 1186; Capt. Charles J. Sterrett to Adj., 8th U.S. Inf., 23 January 1901, 395/3284, LS 16; Maj. Henry B. Mulford to AG, DSL, 25 May 1900, 395/2408, LR 826; Alejandro Sancho to Brig. Gen. Juan Cailles, 13 January 1901, PIR SD 653.5; Maj. Matthew F. Steele to Stella, 13 and 26 August 1900, Steele Papers.

66. Col. Buenaventura Dimaguila to Lt. Gen. Mariano Trías, 20 November 1900, Taylor, *Philippine Insurrection*, Exhibit 1125, pp. 70–72 GV. See also Brig. Gen. Samuel S. Sumner to AG, DSL, 28 September 1901, 305/2349; Maj. Frederick K. Ward to AG, 1D, DSL, 22 October 1901, 395/2355.

67. "List of Men Executed or Ordered to be Executed by Order of General Juan Cailles as shown by his letter and order book 24 August 1900 to 25 April 1901," PIR SD 716.2; "List of Men Ordered Captured or Arrested by Order of General Juan Cailles," PIR SD 716.1; *U.S. v. Andres Pax* and *U.S. v. Gabrial Macahia*, 13 June 1902, 395/2635, Case no. 13224 and 13251. Simeon A. Villa to Chiefs of the Philippine Guerrillas, 15 November 1900, Taylor, *Philippine Insurrection*, Exhibit 1115, p. 68 GV; ibid., p. 63 HS.

68. One of the most hideous crimes, for example, was the torturing and murder of the family of Maj. Antonio Maximo by a group of what were supposed to be *ladrones*. However, because the military commander in the area, Col. Cornelius Gardener,

viewed all armed men in his area as *ladrones*, when in fact many were guerrillas, it is possible the murderers were guerrillas acting under orders. Certainly the fact that they attacked Maximo's family immediately after he surrendered and began to collaborate is indicative of some revolutionary sympathies, see Col. Cornelius Gardener to AAG, DSL, 23 June 1900, 94/117, 30th Inf., LS Bk 2, LS 1104; Col. Cornelius Gardener to AG, DSL, 6 July 1900, ibid., LS 1252; "Testimony of Charles P. Newberry," *Gardener Board*, pp. 734–35, 747–51; *ANJ* 38 (23 February 1901).

69. Senate, *Affairs*, p. 1000; Capt. Charles J. Sterrett to Adj., 8th Inf., 23 January 1901, 395/3284, LS 16; Maj. Frederick K. Ward to AG, DSL, 31 December 1900, 395/3089, LS 8; Col. Cornelius Gardener to President, U.S. Philippine Commission, 18 December 1900, 94/117, 30th Inf., LS Bk 4, LS 3571; Col. Robert L. Bullard to AG, 1D, DSL, 22 December 1900, 94/117, 39th Inf., LS Bk 2, LS 949.

70. Col. George S. Anderson to AG, 2d Brig., 30 March 1900, 94/117, 38th Inf., LS Bk 1, LS 532. For other guerrilla attempts to burn Batangas, see Capt. John L. Jordan to Mother, 18 February 1900, Jordan Papers.

71. Maj. Frederick K. Ward to AG, 1D, DSL, 22 October 1901, 395/2355. Maj. William C. Brown to AG, DSL, 9 May 1900, 395/2408, Box 1.

72. "Statement of Cecilio Rosal," 25 January 1901, 395/3092; "Testimony of Lt. Col. Ladislao Magcansay," *Gardener Board*, pp. 400–407; "Testimony of Major Peotacio Silva," ibid., pp. 170–71; 395/2093, Hq, DivPhil, Register of Persons Charged with Making Collections for Insurgents, Dec. 1901 to Jan. 1902; Maj. George T. Langhorne to AG, 1D, DSL, 9 February 1901, 94/117, 39th Inf., LS Bk 1, LS 25; Brig. Gen. Juan Cailles to P.L., Lumban, etc., 19 November 1900, 395/2408, Box 3, LR 896; Brig. Gen. Juan Cailles to P.L., Siniloan, 8 November 1900, ibid., LR 986; Maj. Elmore F. Taggart to AAG, DSL, 23 May 1900, 395/2330; "Manifesto of Major Julio Infante, Chief of the 6th Column of the Province of La Laguna to the Residents of the Town of San Pablo," September 1900, Taylor, *Philippine Insurrection*, Exhibit 1087, p. 58 GV; Brig. Gen. Juan Cailles to P.L., 18 November 1900, PIR SD 941.9.

73. "Testimony of Miguel Malvar," *Gardener Board*, pp. 659–60; Brig. Gen. Juan Cailles to Vicente Reyes, 12 July 1900, PIR SD 631.2; Gregorio Alvarez, presidente San Pedro Tunasan to Brig. Gen. Juan Cailles, 27 May 1900, PIR SD 631.7; "Statement of Cecilio Rosal," 25 January 1901, 395/3092; Col. Robert L. Bullard to AG, 1D, DSL, 2 and 10 January 1901, 94/117, 39th Inf., LS Bk 2, LS 3 and 6; Maj. Gen. Miguel Malvar, "Copy of a Reply to General Trías," 19 April 1901, Taylor, *Philippine Insurrection*, Exhibit 1155, p. 82 GV; Brig. Gen. Samuel S. Sumner to C.O., Magdalena, 3 April 1901; Brig. Gen. Samuel S. Sumner to Capt. Traber Norman, 30 May 1901; Brig. Gen. Samuel S. Sumner to Lt. Col. Allen Smith, 30 April 1901, all in 395/5155, Santa Cruz, Laguna, TS by Brig. Gen. Sumner while in the field, Apr. to May 1901; Lt. Peter Traub to C.G., 2D, 22 December 1900, 395/2408, Box 3, LR 5; Capt. Sancho Calbelo to Brig. Gen. Juan Cailles, 22 December 1900, PIR SD 653.2; Capt. William F. Hase to AG, 24 November 1901, 395/5052; Col. Benjamin F. Cheatham to AG, DSL, 17 July 1900, 94/117, 37th Inf., LS Bk 1, LS 337; "Testimony of Luciano Alabastro," 94/421607; *WD* 1902 1:9:285–88; Ileto, "Tiaong, Tayabas" pp. 73–75.

74. "Testimony of Miguel Malvar," *Gardener Board*, pp. 647–48, 654; Declarations of Eleneo de Gala, Raymundo Gonzales, Padre Gregorio Alma, "Candalaria. Tayabas

P.: Statements of Insurgent Prisoners to U.S. Provost Marshal of said town outlining the methods of insurrection in Tayabas in 1901 + 1902," PIR SD 942.1; Ileto, "Tiaong, Tayabas," p. 73; Schumacher, *Revolutionary Clergy*, p. 127, "Report of Maj. Gen. Loyd Wheaton, U.S. Army, Commanding Department of North Philippines," *WD* 1902 1:9:230–31; Capt. William T. Johnston to AG, 3SB, 10 March 1902, ibid., 1:9:285–88. For evidence of guerrillas being consulted or notified of town appointments, see Gregorio Alvarez, P.L., San Pedro Tunasan to Brig. Gen. Juan Cailles, 27 May 1900, PIR SD 631.7; "Extracts from Correspondence Appertaining to Tayabas Province Captured by Captain Wilson Chase, 21st Infantry, in Cailles Camp, April 26, 1901," PIR SD 719.1; J.[uan?] de la Cruz to Brig. Gen. Juan Cailles, 20 April 1901, PIR SD 712.9; Romuldo Vila to Brig. Gen. Juan Cailles, 15 July 1900, PIR SD 706.3. Much of the correspondence for Tiaong is in 94/421607, encl. 4; 395/5493, Tiaong, Tayabas, Charges and Specifications for Cases Tried by the Judge Advocate of the Summary Court, 1900–1902; 395/5494, Tiaong, Tayabas, Register of Charges and Disposition of Native Prisoners, Feb. to Apr. 1902; 395/5495, Tiaong, Tayabas, Testimonies of Natives Suspected of Aiding Insurgents, Feb. to Apr. 1902.

75. Maj. Gen. Miguel Malvar, "Provisions and Instructions Issued by the Superior Commander of Southern Luzon for Observation in this Department," 28 April 1901, Taylor, *Philippine Insurrection*, Exhibit 1156, pp. 82–83 GV; Brig. Gen. Mariano Noriel, "Resumé of the General Orders and Instructions Given and Issued by these Superior Headquarters of the Departmental Government from the 29th of August to Date," 9 September 1901, ibid., Exhibit 1169, pp. 88–89 GV; Juan Gabella to Brig. Gen. Juan Cailles, 11 July 1900, PIR SD 706.5; Capt. Traber Norman to AG, DSL, 14 September 1901, 395/4255, LS 88; Capt. William Hase to AG, 3SB, 6 November 1901, 395/5052; "Proceedings of a Military Commission . . . Case 7—Manuel Caag," 2 October 1901, 395/5349, Taal, Batangas, Charges and Specifications for Cases Tried by the Judge Advocate of the Summary Court, 1901; Col. Jacob Kline to AG, 1D, DSL, 27 August 1901, 395/4134, LS Bk 1, LS 273; Sicuando Belen to Tenientes of Barrio, San Gregorio, etc., encl. in Capt. Ralph Van Deman to I.O., Pila, 28 December 1901, 395/4749, Pila, Laguna, Letters and Telegrams Received, 1902; Col. Pedro Caballes, "Orders," 19 December 1901, PIR SD 914.8; Lt. Col. Charles J. Crane to AG, DSL, 21 July 1900, 94/117, 38th Inf., LS Bk 2, LS 623; Ileto, "Tiaong, Tayabas," pp. 75–76.

76. The best indication of the guerrillas' difficulty in assessing taxes is in *Gardener Board*, PIR SD 942.1, and 395/2093. For American views of the effectiveness of the guerrilla tax structure, see White, "Pacification of Batangas," pp. 431–44.

77. May, "Filipino Resistance," p. 539. See also May, "Resistance and Collaboration," pp. 79–81. For Army views on the revolutionary sympathies of the *principales*, see Maj. George H. Morgan, "Proclamation," 9 April 1900, 395/2408; Col. Benjamin F. Cheatham to AG, DSL, 29 June 1900, 94/117, 37th Inf., LS Bk 1, LS 281; Lt. Col. Charles J. Crane to P.L., Lipa, 19 July 1900, 94/117, 38th Inf., LS BK 2, LS 609; Lt. Col. Charles J. Crane, "Report of Operations of the Garrison of Lipa, Luzon, P.I. for the Month of October 1900," 15 November 1900, 395/2408; "Statement of William H. Taft," Senate, *Affairs*, p. 105; Capt. Edward N. Jones to AG, Calamba, 18 May 1901, 395/3106, LS 246; Lt. A. C. Allen to Editor, *ANJ* 38 (16 March 1901); Brig. Gen. Samuel S. Sumner to Capt. Peter Traub, 30 April 1901, 395/5155; Brig. Gen. Samuel S. Sumner to Lt. Col. Allen Smith, 30 April 1901,

ibid.; Capt. Charles R. Howland, "Notes in Reference to the Province of Batangas," 12 December 1901, 395/2635, no. 275; Diary of Charles D. Rhodes, 26 February 1902, Rhodes Papers; Capt. Daniel H. Boughton to AG, 3SB, 18 June 1902, 94/450476; "Testimony of Miguel Malvar," *Gardener Board*, p. 669; Capt. Daniel H. Boughton's remarks in *U.S. v. Capt. Edwin H. Hickman*, 153/3423, G.C.M. no. 33367; Capt. Henry T. Allen to Sen. Jeremiah Beveridge, 12 February 1902, Allen Papers, Correspondence, Box 7; Taylor, *Philippine Insurrection*, p. 54 HS.

78. Schumacher, *Revolutionary Clergy*, p. 129, see also pp. 124–28.

79. Quote "monied mainstays" from Capt. William Y. Stamper to AG, DSL, 24 January 1901, PIR SD 834.1. Quote "It is to the interest" from Lt. Col. Charles J. Crane, "Report of Operations of the Garrison of Lipa, Luzon, P.I. for the Month of October 1900," 15 November 1900, 395/2408, Box 3. For similar sentiments tying the clergy to the landholding elite, see "Testimony of an Army Officer," *ANJ* 38 (29 September 1900).

80. Maj. George E. Morgan to AG, DSL, 15 September 1900, 395/2033, Box 6, M1914; "Statement of Cecilio Rosal," 25 January 1901, 395/3092; Schumacher, *Revolutionary Clergy*, pp. 129–30; Col. Robert L. Bullard to AG, DSL, 4 June 1900, 94/117, 39th Inf., LS Bk 1; "Declaration of Padre Gregorio Alma," PIR SD 942.1; "Information in General of 2nd Lt. Floyd L. Frisbee, stationed at Tiaon," 30 January 1902, 395/5486, Tiaong, Tayabas, Letters and Telegrams Sent, May to Aug. 1900; 395/3094, List and Descriptions of Prisoners Received at Bauan, July 1901 to May 1902; "Record of Native Prisoners in Confinement at Taal, P.I., 1902," 395/5361, Taal, Batangas, Descriptive Book of Native Prisoners, Jan. to Apr. 1902; Lt. Edgar T. Collins to C.O., Cavinti, 20 December 1901, 395/3488, Cavinti, Laguna, Miscellaneous Orders and Circulars Received, Jan. to June 1902; Diary of Frederick Presher, 6 December 1901, Presher Papers.

81. Col. Cornelius Gardener to C.O., Sariaya, 28 July 1900, 94/117, 30th Inf., LS Bk 2, LS 1529; Maj. Gen. Miguel Malvar to Curate in Sariaya, 1 November 1900, PIR SD 692.2. For other evidence of priests' volunteering intelligence information to Americans, see Maj. Matthew F. Steele to Stella, 6 September 1900, Steele Papers.

82. Capt. John L. Jordan to Mother, 28 February 1900, Jordan Papers; Lt. Col. Rufino Relova to Brig. Gen. Juan Cailles, 19 March 1901, PIR SD 1240.2; Maj. Willard A. Holbrook to AG, DSL, 14 July 1900, 395/5052, LS 1; Capt. Merrell E. Webb to Col. William E. Birkhimer, 2 June 1900, 395/2408, Box 1; Capt. Edward A. Kreger and Maj. George T. Langhorne to AG, DSL, 30 September 1900, 395/2330, Box 2, LR B2227; Bert McPhail to Anon., 6 October 1900, Nelson E. Bishop Letters; Marselo Javier to C.O., San Juan de Bocboc, 30 December 1902, 395/5055, San Juan de Bocboc, Batangas, Letters and Telegrams Received, July 1900 to Apr. 1903; Capt. Frank D. Buckingham to C.O., Lucena, 19 November 1900, 395/4162, LS Bk 3, LS 745; Col. Cornelius Gardener to AG, DSL, 22 November 1900, 94/117, 30th Inf., LS Bk 3, LS 2908; Col. Cornelius Gardener to Secretary of the Philippine Commission, 8 December 1900, ibid., LS Bk 4, LS 3572; Maj. Daniel Cornman to AG, DSL, 16 October 1901, 395/3284, LR 383; Capt. John Cotter to AG, DSL, 17 March 1901, 395/5295, Siniloan, Laguna, Letters, Telegrams, and Endorsements Sent, Sept. 1900 to Apr. 1901; Maj. Matthew F. Steele to Stella, 22 August 1900, Steele Papers; Taylor, *Philippine Insurrection*, 14 HS.

83. Quote "bare-foot, shirt-tail" from "Autobiography," Bullard Papers. Quote "I

owe it" from Col. William E. Birkhimer to AG, 2D, DSL, 15 July 1900, 94/117, 28th Inf., LS Bk 1, LS 516.

84. "Report of an Engagement near Taal, Province of Batangas, Luzon, P.I., July 17, 1900, by Col. William E. Birkhimer, Twenty-eighth U.S. Volunteer Infantry, Commanding," *WD* 1900 1:7:315–18; "Report of an Attack on Taal, Province of Batangas, Luzon, P.I., July 6, 1900, by Lt. Col. Robert W. Leonard, Twenty-eighth U.S.V. Infantry, Commanding," ibid., pp. 296–97; Col. William E. Birkhimer to AG, Calamba, 6 July 1900, 94/117, 28th Inf., LS Bk 1, LS 513.

85. Col. Benjamin F. Cheatham to AG, DSL, 29 May 1900, LS 192; Col. Benjamin F. Cheatham to AG, DSL, 8 June 1900, LS 222; Col. Benjamin F. Cheatham to AG, DSL, 2 August 1900, LS 418; Col. Benjamin F. Cheatham to AG, DSL, 8 August 1900, LS 452, all in 94/117, 37th Inf., LS Bk 1; Maj. Matthew F. Steele to Stella, 4 August 1900, Steele Papers.

86. Maj. Gen. Arthur MacArthur to AG, Washington, D.C., 19 September 1900, *CWS*, 2:1211; Lt. Thomas R. Harker to AG, DSL, 19 September 1900, *WD* 1901 1:5:287–89; Faustino Pautua to Miguel Estrada, 21 September 1900, PIR SD 631.4; *ANJ* 38 (22 September and 17 November 1900); Col. Benjamin F. Cheatham to AG, DSL, 17 and 18 September 1900, 94/117, 37th Inf., LS Bk 2, LS 572 and 575; Lt. Horace M. Reeves to Maj. Gen. James C. Bates, 20 September 1900, 395/2330, LR B2436; William H. Taft to Elihu Root, 18 September 1900, Taft Papers, series 21.

87. Col. William E. Birkhimer to AG, DSL, 15 July 1900, 94/117, 28th Inf., LS Bk 2, LS 516. For similar sentiments, see Brig. Gen. Samuel S. Sumner to Lt. Col. Allen Smith, 10 May 1901, 153/3423, G.C.M. no. 33367.

88. Col. William E. Birkhimer to AG, DSL, 18 July 1900, 94/117, 28th Inf., LS Bk 1, LS 517. For descriptions of "roundups," see "Report of Operations on San Luis Road Against Ladrones," Maj. John H. Parker to AG, DSL, 26 April 1900, 395/2408, Box 1; Capt. John L. Jordan to Mother, 11 July 1900, Jordan Papers; Capt. David E. W. Lyle to AG, Wheaton's Expeditionary Brig., 18 February 1900, 395/2330, LR 213; Col. William E. Birkhimer to AG, DSL, 15 July 1900, 94/117, 28th Inf., LS Bk 1, LS 516; "Captured Report of Lt. Col. Julio Herrera," 12 July 1900, 395/2408, LR 2192; Col. Robert L. Bullard to AG, DSL, 27 September 1900, 94/117, 39th Inf., LS Bk 1, LS 857; Capt. John Cotter to AG, DSL, 3 January 1901, 395/5295; Capt. Edward T. Jones to AG, DSL, 27 February 1901, 395/2408, Box 3, LR 1028; Diary of Charles D. Rhodes, 23 January 1902, Rhodes Papers.

89. Col. William E. Birkhimer to AG, DSL, 18 July 1900, 94/117, 28th Inf., LS Bk 1, LS 517. Col. Cornelius Gardener to Capt. E. H. Fitzgerald, 27 May 1900, 395/5488; Col. William E. Birkhimer to AG, DSL, 19 June 1900, 395/2033, Box 6, M877; Capt. Beverly Read to C.O., Lipa, 23 April 1900, 94/117, 38th Inf., LS Bk 1, LS 624; Diary of William C. Brown, 1 and 2 June 1900, Brown Papers; Maj. Willard A. Holbrook to Adj., 38th Inf., 23 September 1900, 395/5052, LS 44; Col. William E. Birkhimer to AAG, 2d Brig., 1st Div., 8th A.C., 6 March 1900, 94/117, 28th Inf., LS Bk 1, LS 446; Capt. Harrison J. Kerrick to AG, 2D, DSL, 13 May 1900, 395/5254, LS 4; 2d endorsement, Col. William E. Birkhimer to Col. Cornelius Gardener, 1 June 1900, on Col. Cornelius Gardener to AAG, DSL, 25 May 1900, 395/2408, Box 1, LR 902.

90. Col. Benjamin F. Cheatham to AG, DSL, 29 May 1900, 94/117, 37th Inf., LS

Bk 1, LS 192. Sixto Reyes to General and Politico-Military Commander [Cailles], 2 June 1900, Taylor, *Philippine Insurrection*, Exhibit 1064, p. 51 GV; "Acta," Brig. Gen. Juan Cailles to Vicente Reyes, 12 July 1900, PIR SD 631.2; "Letter from General Malvar," 4 July 1901, PIR SD 1132.8.

91. Maj. George T. Langhorne to AG, DSL, 8 March 1901, 94/117, 39th Inf., LS Bk 2, LS 43; Col. Robert L. Bullard to AG, DSL, 12 June 1900, 94/117, 39th Inf., LS Bk 1, LS 722; Col. Robert L. Bullard to Chief Quartermaster, DSL, 15 May 1900, ibid., LS 666; Col. Benjamin F. Cheatham to AG, DivPhil, 29 September 1900, 94/117, 37th Inf., LS Bk 2, LS 606. For gunboat operations, see Lt. George S. Simonds to AG, DSL, 1 June 1900, 395/2033, Box 6, M703; Lt. Charles M. McLester to AG, DSL, 3 September 1900, 395/2330, LR 1921; Capt. Charles M. McLester to AG, DSL, 22 November 1901, ibid., LR C2621; *ANJ* 38 (23 March 1901). For Gardener's operations see Col. Cornelius Gardener to AG, Calamba, 3 July 1900, LS 1230; Col. Cornelius Gardener to Lt. Wheat, 27 July 1900, LS 1527; Col. Cornelius Gardener to C.O., Sariaya, 28 July 1900, LS 1529; Col. Cornelius Gardener to C.O., Tiaong, 28 July 1900, LS 1537; Col. Cornelius Gardener to AG, DSL, 3 October 1900, LS 2305; Col. Cornelius Gardener to Capt. Charles Newberry, 26 October 1900, LS 2620, all in 94/117, 30th Inf., LS Bk 2; Maj. Matthew F. Steele to Stella, 21 September 1900, Steele Papers.

92. Col. George S. Anderson to AG, DSL, 13 July 1900, 94/117, 38th Inf., LS Bk 1, LS 815. See also the objection to this policy, Lt. Col. Robert W. Leonard to AAG, DSL, 1 July 1900, 94/117, 28th Inf., LS Bk 1, LS 511.

93. Col. Cornelius Gardener to C.O., Lucban, 9 May 1900, 395/4164, LR 95; Col. Cornelius Gardener to C.O., Tiaong, 26 May 1900, 395/5488, LR 16; Maj. Matthew F. Steele to Col. Cornelius Gardener, 11 June 1900, 395/4162, LS Bk 2, LS 209.

94. Capt. Beverly A. Read to C.O.'s, Lipa, San José, Bauan, 22 March 1900, 94/117, 38th Inf., LS Bk 1, LR 519; Maj. Gen. John C. Bates, endorsement on Col. William E. Birkhimer to AG, DSL, 20 April 1900, 395/2408, Box 1; Maj. George T. Langhorne to AG, 2D, DSL, 21 January 1901, 395/2330, CA167.

95. "Autobiography," Bullard Papers; Col. Robert L. Bullard to AG, 1st Div., 8th A.C., 2 March 1900, 94/117, 39th Inf., LS Bk 1; Capt. Beverly A. Read to C.O., Lipa and San José, 11 March 1900, 94/117, 38th Inf., LS Bk 1, LR 497; Capt. Charles H. Hilton to AG, DSL, 16 March 1900, 395/2330, LR 1900; Col. William E. Birkhimer to AAG, Wheaton's Expeditionary Brig., 16 March 1900, 94/117, 28th Inf., LS Bk 1, LS 369; Capt. John L. Jordan to Mother, 15 April 1900, Jordan Papers; *WD* 1900 1:7:296–97; Col. Benjamin F. Cheatham to AG, Calamba, 3 August 1900, 94/117, 37th Inf., LS Bk 1, LS 425; Col. Cornelius Gardener to C.O., Lucban, 17 August 1900, 94/117, 30th Inf., LS Bk 2, LS 1717; Col. Cornelius Gardener to Capt. Gilmore G. Scranton, 26 November 1900, ibid., LS 2955; Maj. Gen. John C. Bates to C.G., 2D, endorsement on Brig. Gen. Robert H. Hall to AG, DSL, 16 January 1901, 395/2408, Box 3, LR 493; Crane, *Experiences*, pp. 359–60.

96. Capt. John L. Jordan to Mother, 11 July 1900, Jordan Papers.

97. Col. Robert L. Bullard, endorsement on Maj. John H. Parker to AG, DSL, 10 May 1900, 395/2408, Box 1. See also Maj. George T. Langhorne to AG, DSL, 19 May 1900, ibid.; Col. William E. Birkhimer to AAG, Wheaton's Expeditionary Brig.,

16 March 1900, 94/117, 28th Inf., LS Bk 1, LS 369; Col. William E. Birkhimer to AAG, DSL, 26 September 1900, 94/117, 28th Inf., LS Bk 3, LS 1407.

98. Capt. Sancho Calbelo to Brig. Gen. Juan Cailles, 22 December 1900, PIR SD 653.3; P. P. Wenrigerr [pseud.] to Brig. Gen. Juan Cailles, 6 December 1900, 395/2408, Box 3, LR 694.

99. Lt. Col. Charles J. Crane to Adj., 38th Inf., 8 August 1900, 94/117, 38th Inf., LS Bk 1, LS 690. Capt. Charles J. Sterrett to Adj., 8th Inf., 23 January 1901, 395/3284, LS 15.

100. Lt. Col. Charles J. Crane to P.L., Lipa, 19 July 1900, 94/117, 38th Inf., LS Bk 2, LS 609. For similar sentiments see Maj. George H. Morgan, "Proclamation," 9 April 1900, 395/2408; Col. Benjamin F. Cheatham to AG, DSL, 29 June 1900, 94/117, 37th Inf., LS Bk 1, LS 28; Lt. A. C. Allen to Editor, *ANJ* 38 (16 March 1901); "Report of Operations of the Garrison of Lipa, Luzon, P.I. for the Month of October 1900," 15 November 1900, 395/2408, Box 3; Capt. Daniel H. Boughton in 153/3423, G.C.M. no. 33367.

101. Col. Benjamin F. Cheatham to AG, DSL, 29 June 1900, 94/117, 37th Inf., LS Bk 1, LS 281.

102. Col. Benjamin F. Cheatham to AG, DSL, 15 August and 1 September 1900, 94/117, 37th Inf., LS Bk 2, LS 483 and 532; Col. Robert L. Bullard to AG, DSL, 9 October 1900, 94/117, 39th Inf., LS Bk 1, LS 870.

103. *WD* 1901 1:7:388, 422, 1:5:5–7.

104. Governor Felix M. Roxas, "Manifesto," 10 May 1901, PIR SD 936.4; "An Act Extending the Provisions of 'The Provincial Government Act' to the province of Tayabas," 12 March 1901, 350/2760.

105. Col. Robert L. Bullard to AG, DSL, 27 September 1900, 94/117, 39th Inf., LS Bk 1, LS 857; Col. Robert L. Bullard to AG, DSL, 28 November and 20 December 1900, 94/117, 39th Inf., LS Bk 2. For a survey of American operations in late 1900, see *WD* 1901 1:5:284–315.

106. Brig. Gen. Samuel S. Sumner to AG, DSL, 13 August 1901, 395/2349; Brig. Gen. Samuel S. Sumner to AG, DSL, 2 August 1901, 395/5101; Capt. Edward N. Jones to AG, DSL, 6 February 1901, 395/2408, Box 3, LR 1028; Capt. John Cotter to AG, DSL, 13 March 1901, 394/5295; Diary of Robert L. Bullard, 10 March 1901, Bullard Papers.

107. Crane, *Experiences*, p. 362; quote "prominent families" from *WD* 1901 1:4:93–94. "Why Has the Philippine War Lasted So Long," Bullard Papers.

108. Brig. Gen. Samuel S. Sumner to Col. William S. McCaskey, 19 July 1901, 395/2349.

109. Brig. Gen. Samuel S. Sumner to All Station Commanders, 15 September 1901, 395/3112, Bay, Laguna, Register of Telegrams Received, Dec. 1900 to Aug. 1902, no. 155. Col. Joseph Kline to AG, 1D, DSL, 12 August 1901, 395/4134, LS Bk 1, LS 259; Lt. Emory S. West to AG, DSL, 1 April 1901, 395/2330, C2174.

110. "Written Record of Instructions Received by Major F. K. Ward from General Sumner," 28 September 1901, 395/3092; "Copies of Charges Against Hermano Marquiz and Nemencio Ylagan," and "Assassins of Tomas Diocampo," 28 September 1901, ibid., LR 333 A and B; Diary of Frederick Presher, 28 September 1901, Presher Papers; May, "Private Presher," p. 42.

111. Diary of Robert L. Bullard, 17 August 1900, Bullard Papers (Bullard's emphasis).

112. Maj. Matthew F. Steele to Stella, 15 August 1900, Steele Papers. For indications of earlier relative U.S. humanity, see James F. Edwards Questionnaire; Col. William E. Birkhimer to AAG, Wheaton's Expeditionary Brig., 27 March 1900, 395/2408, Box 2; Col. William E. Birkhimer to AG, DSL, 3 October 1900, 395/2330, LS 1605; Col. Robert L. Bullard to C.O., Tanauan, n.d., 94/117, 39th Inf., LS Bk 1, LS 698; Maj. Frederick K. Ward to AG, DSL, 7 February 1901, 395/3089, LS 18. For Filipino accusations of U.S. brutality, see Brig. Gen. Juan Cailles to Commandante, encl. in Brig. Gen. Juan Cailles to Vicente Reyes, July 1900, PIR SD 941.7; "La Digna Provencia Laguna y su Valiente General," 12 July 1900, PIR SD 941.6.

113. Col. Morris C. Foote, "Report of an Investigation of Outrages by American Soldiers in Batangas Province, P.I.," February 1902, 94/476653.

114. Edmund Block to Hon. H. L. Wilfrey, 18 July 1902, 350/2760; "Letter from General Malvar," 4 July 1901, PIR SD 1132.8; "Testimony of Macario Losi and Sufio Serano," *Gardener Board*, pp. 290–99.

115. Welch, "American Atrocities," p. 237.

116. Diary of Charles D. Rhodes, 19 and 20 January 1901, Rhodes Papers; "Testimony of Lt. Henry R. Richmond," *Gardener Board*, pp. 90–93; "Testimony of Lt. Edward A. Hickman," ibid., pp. 76–79; 153/3423, G.C.M. no. 33367; Homer V. Cook MS; Diary of Frederick D. Presher, 8 October 1901, Presher Papers.

117. Brig. Gen. Samuel S. Sumner, "Narrative of Events. First District from July 1, 1900 to May 31, 1901," 395/2355.

118. Maj. Frederick K. Ward to AG, 1D, DSL, 22 October 1901, 395/2355.

119. AAG, DSL to C.G., 2D, 3 November 1900, 395/2408, Box 2, LR 2957; Hq, DSL to C.O., Calamba, 13 March 1901, 395/3287, LR 144; Lt. A. M. Reeve to C.O.'s, 11 March 1901, 395/2408, Box 3, LR 1264; Hq, DSL to C.O., Bauan, 18 March 1901, 395/3092, LR 122A; Capt. Ralph Van Deman to C.G., 3SB, 8 January 1902, 395/2354, Box 3.

120. Brig. Gen. Samuel S. Sumner to Lt. Col. Allen Smith, 30 April 1901, 395/5155; Brig. Gen. Samuel S. Sumner to Capt. Traber Norman, 30 April 1901, 395/5155; Hq, DSL to C.O., Bauan, 25 February 1901, 395/3092, LR 103; Capt. John Cotter to AG, DSL, 26 January 1901, 395/5295; "Names of Insurgent Officials and Agents Taken from the Papers of Juan Cailles . . . ," PIR SD 712.7; *ANJ* 38 (4 May 1901); "Information Relating to Insurgent Officials, Military and Civil, Who Lived and Operated in Laguna Province, 1901," 395/3117.

121. Capt. Charles Crawford to AG, 1D, 5 October 1901, 395/4638, LS 100; Lt. Traber Norman to AG, 1D, DSL, 1 May 1901, 395/4255, LS 59; C.O., Magdalena to AG, DSL, 4 April 1901, 395/2408, Box 3, LR 1647; Col. Robert L. Bullard to AG, DSL, 3 November 1900, 94/117, 39th Inf., LS Bk 1, LS 892; Lt. Arthur L. Bump to Adj., 19 August 1902, *WD* 1902 1:9:294; "Trial of Ricardo Aquirre, presidente of Lemeri," 395/5359, Taal, Batangas, Charges and Specifications for Cases Tried by the Judge Advocate of the Summary Court, 1901; Capt. Edward N. Jones to AG, 1D, DSL, 1 August 1901, 395/3105, Bay, Laguna, LS, June 1900 to Aug. 1902, LS 13; Capt. Charles P. Sterrett to Post Adj., Calamba, 24 March 1901, 395/2408, Box 3,

LR 1434; Sotero Batallones to C.O., Calamba, 4 October 1901, 395/3287, LR 377; Maj. Daniel Cornman to AG, DSL, 16 October 1901, 395/3284, LR 383; Sgt. Arthur G. Smith to Post Adj., Calamba, 16 November 1901, 395/3287.

122. Hq, DivPhil to C.G., 2D, 29 December 1900, 395/5726; Hq, DSL to C.G., 2D, 18 February 1901, 395/3092, LR 78; Hq, 1D, DSL to C.O., San José, 15 May 1901, 395/5009.

123. Capt. William G. Haan to Maj. Cornelius Gardener, 22 May 1901, 395/2330, CA819; Maj. Gen. Adna R. Chaffee to Maj. Gen. Henry C. Corbin, 2 September 1901, Corbin Papers; Lt. Traber Norman to AG, 2D, 5 February 1901, 395/4255, LS 8; Lt. Traber Norman to AG, 1D, 1 May 1901, 395/4255, LS 59; Capt. Alexis R. Paxton to AG, DSL, 25 March 1901, 395/4638, LS 31; Lt. Henry B. Clark to AG, 1D, 2 May 1901, 395/4638; Capt. Charles J. Sterrett to Adj., 8th Inf., 23 January 1901, 395/3284, LS 15; Col. Cornelius Gardener to AG, 2D, DSL, 16 June 1901, 395/5721, LS Bk 1, LS 13; Maj. John H. Parker to AG, 1D, DSL, 11 January 1901, 395/2330, CA18; Capt. Joseph B. Caughey to AG, 1D, DSL, 28 February 1901, 395/4654, LS 75; Col. Jacob Kline to AG, 2D, DSL, 8 February 1901, 395/4134, LS 33; "List and Description of Native Prisoners, Bauan," Bauan, Batangas, July 1901 to May 1902, 395/3094; Lt. Charles R. Russell to AG, 1D, DSL, 10 October 1901, 295/3106, TS 575.

124. *WD* 1901 1:7:389.

125. Lt. John C. Craig to AG, 1D, DSL, 1 June 1901, 395/5052; Capt. Traber Norman to AG, DSL, 17 October 1901, 395/4255, LS 103 and 104; Lt. Charles R. Russell to AG, 3SB, 1 November 1901, 395/3110, LR 87; Lt. Patrick A. Connolly to AG, 3SB, 1 December 1901, 395/5007, LS 236.

126. Col. Jacob Kline to AG, 1D, DSL, 28 April 1901, 395/4134, LS 125; Maj. Frederick K. Ward to AG, DSL, 21 March 1901, 395/3089, LS 56; Juan de le Cruz to Brig. Gen. Juan Cailles, 20 April 1901, PIR SD 712.9; Maj. Frederick K. Ward to Sr. Alfonso Panopio, 20 March 1901, 395/3089, LS 55; Capt. Arthur L. Parmeter to C.O., Bauan, 19 March 1901, 395/3092, LR 1205; Pablo Astilla to Brig. Gen. Juan Cailles, 20 March 1901, PIR SD 1230.2.

127. Hq, DSL to C.O., Siniloan, 20 February 1901, 395/5295. For threats, see Lt. Col. Pedro Caballes to Brig. Gen. Juan Cailles, 4 March 1901, PIR SD 1230.1; Lt. Col. Pedro Caballes to Brig. Gen. Juan Cailles, March 1901, Taylor, *Philippine Insurrection,*, Exhibit 1147, pp. 78–79 GV; "Proclamation of Lt. Col. Emilio Zurbano, Military Governor of Tayabas, to his Fellow Citizens," 23 April 1901, ibid., Exhibit 1154, p. 81 GV; Col. Emilio Zurbano, "Bando," 22 March 1901, PIR SD 867.10.

128. Brig. Gen. Juan Cailles, "Proclamation," 4 April 1901, PIR SD 706.1; Brig. Gen. Juan Cailles, "Manifesto of Juan Cailles, Political and Military Commander of Laguna Province," 30 December 1900, PIR SD 602.8; Lt. Col. Pedro Caballes to Brig. Gen. Juan Cailles, 29 March 1901, PIR SD 1240.1; Lt. Col. Rufino Relova to Brig. Gen. Juan Cailles, 19 March 1901, PIR SD 1240.2; Brig. Gen. Juan Cailles to Emiliano Riego de Dios, 21 November 1900, 395/2408, Box 3, LR 694; Col. Buenaventura Dimaguila to Lt. Gen. Mariano Trías, 20 November 1900, Taylor, *Philippine Insurrection*, Exhibit 1125, pp. 70–72 GV; Col. Julio Herrera to Anon., 14 November 1900, PIR SD 605.2; P. P. Wenrigerr [pseud.] to Brig. Gen. Juan Cailles, 8

November 1900, PIR SD 653.1; "Mete miedo y Engaña-tontos," Brig. Gen. Juan Cailles, 22 December 1900, PIR SD 712.5.1; Diary of Robert L. Bullard, 27 April 1901, Bullard Papers; Capt. John Cotter to AG, DSL, 7 March 1901, 395/5295; Brig. Gen. Juan Cailles to P.L., Pagsanjan, 12 May 1900, PIR SD 1195.

129. Lt. Gen. Mariano Trías to "My Dear Comrade" [Malvar], 13 April 1901, Taylor, *Philippine Insurrection*, Exhibit 1155, pp. 81–82 GV; Emilio Aguinaldo, "To the Filipino People," *WD* 1901 1:4:100–01; Juan de la Cruz to Brig. Gen. Juan Cailles, 20 April 1901, PIR SD 712.9. For the negotiations behind Trías' surrender, see Lt. Col. Frank C. Baldwin to AG, DSL, 3 July 1901, 395/2330, C4034.

130. "Testimony of Lt. Col. Noberto Mayo," *Gardener Board*, p. 132. Quote "esta guerra interminable" from Maj. Gen. Miguel Malvar to Brig. Gen. Juan Cailles, 4 April 1901, PIR SD 692.3.

131. Maj. Gen. Miguel Malvar, "Brothers and Companions in the Strife," 12 April 1900, PIR SD 692.7. Maj. Gen. Miguel Malvar, "To the Filipino People and its Army," Taylor, *Philippine Insurrection*, Exhibit 1166, pp. 86–87 GV. For an interesting interpretation of these proclamations, see Ileto, *Payson and Revolution*, pp. 197–205.

132. Maj. Gen. Miguel Malvar to C.O., Albay, 23 April 1901, PIR SD 772.2; Maj. Gen. Miguel Malvar to General Anadio Maxilon, 14 May 1901, PIR SD 1246.3; Maj. Gen. Miguel Malvar to Brig. Gen. Vicente Lukban, 15 May 1901, Taylor, *Philippine Insurrection*, Exhibit 1161, p. 85 GV.

133. Maj. Gen. Miguel Malvar, "Copy of a Private Letter Addressed to Señor Emilio Aguinaldo," 19 April 1901, PIR SD 902.7; Maj. Gen. Miguel Malvar, "Copy of a Reply to General Trías," 19 April 1901, Taylor, *Philippine Insurrection*, Exhibit 1155, p. 82 GV; Maj. Gen. Miguel Malvar, "Provisions and Instructions Issued by the Superior Commander of Southern Luzon for Observation in this Department," 28 April 1901, ibid., Exhibit 1156, pp. 82–83 GV; "Testimony of Maj. Gen. Miguel Malvar," *Gardener Board*, pp. 664–65.

134. Brig. Gen. Mariano Noriel, "Resumé of the General Orders and Instructions Given and Issued by these Superior Headquarters of the Departmental Government from the 29th of August to Date," 9 September 1901, Taylor, *Philippine Insurrection*, Exhibit 1169, pp. 88–89 GV; "General Instructions and Dispositions Issued by these Superior Headquarters Since the 26th of last June Until the Present Date," 28 August 1901, PIR SD 772.9; "General Orders and Instructions Issued from these Superior Headquarters Since the date of October 1901," 11 November 1901, PIR SD 799.2; "Testimony of Maj. Gen. Miguel Malvar," *Gardener Board*, pp. 656–57, 677–81; Capt. Charles Crawford to Adj., Santa Cruz, 21 November 1901, 395/4638, LS 116.

135. Col. Emilio Zurbano, "Fellow Citizens," 23 April 1901, PIR SD 867.8; Col. Emilio Zurbano to P.L.'s, 28 April 1901, PIR SD 867.8; Brig. Gen. Juan Cailles, "Citizens of the Province of Tayabas," 23 April 1901, PIR SD 867.8; Col. Euseibio Malolos, "Bando," 31 December 1899, PIR SD 332.13; "Testimony of Bonifacio Obnamia," *Gardener Board*, pp. 498–99; "Testimony of Maj. Gen. Miguel Malvar," ibid., pp. 645–46, 654, 659–60.

136. "Testimony of Lt. Col. Bernardo Marques," ibid., p. 153; "List of surrenders, Filipino troops, Division of the Philippine; [May 5, 1900 to June 10, 1901]," *WD* 1901 1:4:127–29.

137. "Testimony of Maj. Gen. Miguel Malvar," *Gardener Board*, pp. 671–72. For correspondence on surrender of Zurbano see Sgt. Etterberg to C.O., Lucena, 10 July 1901, LR 417; Lt. Edwin A. Hickman to C.O., Lucena, 11 July 1901, LR 476; Brig. Gen. James F. Wade to C. O., Lucena, 11 July 1901, LR 479; Hq, DSL to Capt. Harry H. Bandholtz, 12 July 1901, LR 782, all in 395/5726.

138. Maj. Gen. Arthur MacArthur to AG, Washington, D.C., 24 June 1901, *CWS*, 2:1288; Brig. Gen. Juan Cailles to "Countryman," 15 April 1901, PIR SD 706.2; Brig. Gen. Samuel S. Sumner to Capt. Peter Traub, 29 April 1901, 395/5155; *ANJ 38* (25 May 1901); Brig. Gen. Samuel S. Sumner to Capt. Peter Traub, 14 and 16 June 1901, 395/3112, Telegrams Received 230 and 237; Col. Arthur L. Wagner to Capt. Edward N. Jones, 25 June 1901, 395/3110, LR 38. For the importance of Cailles's papers, see PIR SD 716 and 719.

139. Lt. Col. Martin Cabrera, "Extract," 31 July 1901, PIR SD 755.1; Capt. Edward N. Jones to AG, 1D, DSL, 1 July 1901, 395/2355. For conditions in Tayabas, see the testimony in the *Gardener Board*.

140. Brig. Gen. Samuel S. Sumner to AG, DSL, 2 August 1901, 395/5101. Brig. Gen. Samuel S. Sumner to AG, DSL, 13 August and 4 September 1901, 395/2349; Capt. Henry T. Allen to Brig. Gen. Samuel S. Sumner, 28 September 1901, 395/2355; Capt. Charles Crawford to Adj., Santa Cruz, 21 November 1901, 395/4638, LS 116; Capt. Charles R. Howland to AG, Department of North Philippines (DNP), 30 November 1901, 395/2354; *ANJ* 39 (14 December 1901); Maj. Gen. Adna R. Chaffee to Maj. Gen. Henry C. Corbin, 2 September and 5 November 1901, Corbin Papers; "Testimony of Maj. Gen. Miguel Malvar," *Gardener Board*, p. 650.

141. Brig. Gen. Samuel S. Sumner to AG, DSL, 28 September 1901, 395/2349.

142. William H. Taft to Elihu Root, 14 October 1901, Root Papers; Maj. Gen. Adna R. Chaffee to Maj. Gen. Henry C. Corbin, 25 October, 30 September, 5 November 1901, Corbin Papers; Capt. Ralph Van Deman, "Confidential. For the Information of the Division Commander," 4 November 1901, PIR SD 1303.2; Capt. Ralph Van Deman to I.O., 23 October 1901, 395/5304; Maj. Gen. Adna R. Chaffee to AG, Washington, D.C., 7 November 1901, *CWS*, 2:1301; *WD* 1901 1:9:263–65. For the effect of the "Balangiga massacre," see Schott, *Ordeal of Samar*, pp. 61–65. The criticism directed at Sumner seems somewhat unfair; according to Col. Arthur L. Wagner, Sumner complained "he was seriously handicapped by his instructions that were given him from department headquarters [Wade]," see "Statement of Col. Arthur L. Wagner, Assistant Adjutant-General, U.S. Army," Senate, *Affairs*, p. 2854.

143. For organization into Separate Brigades, see *WD* 1902 1:9:187; Maj. Gen. Henry C. Corbin to AG, Washington, D.C., 17 July 1901, *CWS*, 2:1289; Maj. Gen. Henry C. Corbin to Elihu Root, 28 September 1901, Corbin Papers. For troop strength and staff, see *WD* 1902 1:9:268, 75.

144. Telegraphic Circular no. 3, 9 December 1901, Senate, *Affairs*, pp. 1607–11.

145. Telegraphic Circular no. 19, 22 December 1901, ibid., pp. 1623–25. See also Telegraphic Circular no. 22, 24 December 1901, ibid., p. 1628.

146. Telegraphic Circular no. 21, 24 December 1901, pp. 1626–27; Telegraphic Circular no. 34, 12 February 1902, pp. 1236–37, both in ibid.

147. Telegraphic Circular no. 3, 9 December 1901, ibid., p. 1610.

148. Ibid., pp. 1607–11; Telegraphic Circular no. 18, 23 December 1901, pp.

1622–32; Telegraphic Circular no. 20, 24 December 1901, pp. 1625–26; Telegraphic Circular no. 24, 28 December 1901, p. 1629, all in ibid. For another example of Bell's early ideas on the complicity of the rich in the continuation of the war, see "Report of General A. E. Bates, 1902," 94/443764; "Diary of Events, Dec. 29, 1901 to Jan. 12, 1902," 22 December 1901, 94/338335.

149. The quote "want peace" is from Telegraphic Circular no. 3, 9 December 1901, Senate, *Affairs*, p. 1607. The information on Bell's policies can be found in Telegraphic Circular no. 4, 11 December 1901, p. 1611; Telegraphic Circular no. 5, 13 December 1901, pp. 1612–14; Telegraphic Circular no. 14, 20 December 1901, pp. 1619–20; Telegraphic Circular no. 15, 23 December 1901, p. 1620; Telegraphic Circular no. 19, 24 December 1901, pp. 1623–24; Telegraphic Circular no. 21, 24 December 1901, pp. 1626–27, all in ibid.; G.O. 372, Hq, D.P., 31 December 1901, 395/5101.

150. Brig. Gen. Samuel S. Sumner to AG, DSL, 4 September 1901, 395/2349. For Bauan, see *WD* 1901 1:9:232. For Marinduque, see Capt. William M. Wright to Maj. Gen. John C. Bates, 10 December 1900, 395/2330, C3011; Maj. Gen. Henry C. Corbin to Maj. Gen. Arthur MacArthur, 19 March 1901, *CWS*, 2:1260; Maj. Gen. Arthur MacArthur to AG, Washington, D.C., 22 March 1901, ibid., p. 1261. For Gardener's attempt to force inhabitants to store food in towns and impose a form of concentration, see Col. Cornelius Gardener to C.O., Lucban, 9 May 1900, 395/4163, LR 95. For an early proposal for population concentration in southwestern Luzon, see Col. Jacob Kline to AG, 1D, DSL, 27 August 1901, 395/4134, LS 273.

151. Telegraphic Circular no. 2, 8 December 1901, Senate, *Affairs*, pp. 1606–7.

152. Capt. Charles Miller to P.L., Lucban, 9 February 1902, 395/4162, LS Bk 4, LS 39. Unsigned [Capt. Charles Crawford] to AG, 3SB, 30 January 1902, 395/4638; Brig. Gen. J. Franklin Bell to Col. William E. Dougherty, 25 February 1902, 395/2354; Sotero Batallones to General of the Armies of United States in Philippines, 15 January 1902, 395/3287, LR 35. For other accounts of concentration, see Diary of Charles D. Rhodes, 11 December 1901, Rhodes Papers; Lt. Patrick A. Connolly to AG, 3SB, 20 December 1901, 395/5007, LS 253; Brig. Gen. J. Franklin Bell to C.O., U.S.S. *Napindan*, 16 December 1901, 395/2349; 395/3121, Bay, Laguna, Monthly and Trimonthly Reports Relating to the Capture of Insurgents, Arms, and Native Prisoners, Sept. 1901 to Apr. 1902.

153. May, "'Zones' of Batangas," pp. 90, 103; Welch, *Response to Imperialism*, pp. 138–39; Col. Arthur L. Wagner to Maj. Gen. Loyd Wheaton, 22 March 1902, 395/2635, Box 6, no. 7788; Senate, *Affairs*, pp. 2847–52, 2871–75. For Bell's efforts to insure food and health measures, see Telegraphic Circular no. 7, 15 December 1901, pp. 1514–15; Telegraphic Circular no. 10, 20 December 1901, pp. 1616–17; Telegraphic Circular no. 16, 23 December 1901, p. 1621; Telegraphic Circular no. 17, 23 December 1901, pp. 1621–22, all in ibid.; Brig. Gen. J. Franklin Bell to All Station Commanders, 16 January 1902, 395/3287; Maj. Louis Breckman to AG, DNP, 30 June 1902, 395/2635, Box 10, 11535; "Report of General A. E. Bates. 1902," 94/443764; Maj. Gen. Adna R. Chaffee to AG, Washington, 11 September 1902, 94/415839. There has been much scholarly debate over the number of casualties in the reconcentrated zones, see Gates, "War-Related Deaths," pp. 372–73; May, "150,000 Missing Filipinos."

154. Capt. Ralph Van Deman to C.G., 3SB, 8 January 1902, 395/2354, Box 3; Diary of Charles D. Rhodes, 14 January 1902, Rhodes Papers; Capt. Henry H. Bandholtz to Officer in Charge, DMI, 4 January 1902, 395/5751, Tayabas, Tayabas, Press Copies of Letters and Endorsements Sent by the I.O., Oct. 1901 to July 1902; 'Unsigned' [Brig. Gen. Samuel S. Sumner] to AG, DSL, 3 August 1901, 395/5101. For Bureau of Information, see Brig. Gen. Samuel S. Sumner to AG, DSL, 4 September 1901, 395/2349; Hq, 1D, to C.O., Calamba, 23 September 1901, 395/3117, Bay, Laguna, Information Relating to Insurgent Officials, Military and Civil, Who Lived or Operated in Laguna Province, 1901; Brig. Gen. Samuel S. Sumner to C.O.'s, 23 September 1901, 395/2349. For the operation of the Bureau of Information, see 395/2392, 1D, DSL, Letters and Endorsements Sent by the I.O., Oct. 1901 to Aug. 1902; 395/2393, 1D, DSL, Register of LR by the I.O., Sept. 1901 to Aug. 1902. For local intelligence officers see G.O. 294, Hq, DivPhil, 28 September 1901, 395/2393; "Sheet No. 1, Secret Service," Capt. John W. Furlong to C.O., Troop M, 6th Cavalry, 19 December 1901 and "Sheet No. 2, List of Band of Emeterio Bries," 395/5101; "Papers of Lt. McLaughlin, I.O.," 395/3289. For Bell's instructions on intelligence see Telegraphic Circular no. 21, 24 December 1901, pp. 1626–27; Telegraphic Circular no. 28, 9 January 1902, p. 1631; Telegraphic Circular no. 36, 15 February 1902, pp. 1637–38, all in Senate, *Affairs*.

155. G.O. 1, Hq, 3SB, 3 December 1901, Senate, *Affairs*, pp. 1642–43; G.O. 1, Hq, 3SB, 13 January 1902, ibid., p. 1644.

156. The quotes and description of the Lipa cleanup are taken from Johnston, "Brief Record," 94/ACP 4625. See also "Interview. Commanding Officer with Principales. Lipa, Batangas, P.I., February 16, 1902," 395/2354, Box 2; "Al General Bell de la Tercera Brigada de las Fuerzas Americanas," 16 February 1902, 395/3287, LS 186. For the Tiaong cleanup, see the descriptive lists and statements of revolutionaries in 395/5486, 395/5494, 395/5495, 395/5496; *WD* 1902, 1:9:285–88; Schumacher, *Revolutionary Clergy*, p. 127; Ileto, "Tiaong, Tayabas," p. 78. For similar cleanups, see "Investigation in the Pueblo of Tayabas," Lt. Grant T. Trent, Exhibit 52, 153/3423, G.C.M. no. 33367; "Report of an Inspection of Civil Conditions at Tayabas, Tayabas Province, P.I. by 2nd Lieut. E. A. Hickman, 1st Cavalry on June 28th 1901," 395/5472; PIR SD 942.1.

157. Carmen Chavarri to Capt. Louis Bash, 16 February 1902, 395/2635, Box 4, no. 5850. For similar policies, see Lt. Col. Daniel Cornman to AG, 3SB, 1 January 1902, 395/2354, Box 2; Brig. Gen. J. Franklin Bell to Lt. Daniel Van Voorhis, 5 March 1902, 395/2349; Testimony of Lt. Edwin A. Hickman, 153/3423, G.C.M. no. 33367; Capt. Charles Miller to P.L., Lucban, 9 February 1902, 395/4162, LS Bk 4, LS 39; "Testimony of Lt. Floyd L. Frisbee," *Gardener Board*, p. 602.

158. Col. Arthur L. Wagner to Maj. Gen. Loyd Wheaton, 22 March 1902, 395/2636, Box 6, no. 7788. For Army sentiment on the benefits of arresting the *principalia*, see Capt. Lawrence Hearn to AG, Batangas, 13 March 1902, 395/5254; "Report of General A. E. Bates, 1902," 94/443763; Senate, *Affairs*, pp. 2851–52. For the alleged sufferings of the rich, see Eyot, *Lopez Family*.

159. [Maj. Gen. George W.?] Davis to All Station Commanders, 3SB, 24 February 1902, 395/3287, LR 168; [Maj. Gen. George W.?] Davis to C.O.'s, All Stations, 11 March 1902, 395/3287; Capt. John C. MacArthur to AG, 3SB, 15 February 1902,

395/4271, Malagi Island Prison and Post, Letters and Endorsements Sent, Jan. 1902 to Jan. 1906; Capt. John C. MacArthur to AG, DNP, 29 March 1902, ibid., LS 131; Capt. John C. MacArthur to Capt. James Lindsey, 11 April 1902, ibid., LS 183; Post G.O. 7, By Order of the Commanding Officer of Malagi Prison, 2 April 1902, 395/2354, Box 3.

160. Brig. Gen. Samuel S. Sumner to AG, DSL, 13 August 1901, 395/2349. For early operations in this area, see Col. Robert L. Bullard to AG, DSL, 10 January 1901, 94/117, 39th Inf., LS Bk 2, LS 6; Capt. John Craig to AG, 1D, DSL, 14 June 1901, 395/5052; Lt. Col. Charles J. Crane to Adj., 38th Inf., 31 August 1900, 94/117, 38th Inf., LS Bk 2, LS 740; Lt. Col. Thomas C. Lebo to AG, 1D, DSL, 6 June 1901, 395/4208, Batangas, Batangas, LS, Sept. 1900 to Feb. 1904, LS 47; Capt. William Hase to AG, 3SB, 14 November 1901, 395/5052; Capt. William Hase to AG, Batangas, 22 November 1901, ibid.; Crane, *Experiences*, p. 348.

161. Brig. Gen. J. Franklin Bell to C.O., San Juan de Bocboc, 11 January 1902, 395/5055. For an account of this operation, see Capt. William Hase to AG, Batangas, 28 January 1902, 395/5052; Col. Theodore J. Wint to AG, 3SB, 8 February 1902, 395/2379; Capt. George Van Horn Moseley to Adj., Batangas, 7 February 1902, 395/2354, Box 2. For earlier operations, see Col. Almond B. Wells to AG, 3SB, 8 January 1902, 395/2354, Box 2; Col. Almond B. Wells to C.O., Lipa, San José, etc., 28 December 1901, 395/4208, LS 297; Lt. Roger S. Fitch to Anon., 28 December 1901, 395/3092, LR 472; Lt. Edgar Conley to C.O.'s, Ibaan and San José, 11 December 1901, 395/4208, LS 272.

162. Capt. William Hase to AG, 10 March 1902, 395/5052; Lt. Roger S. Fitch to AG, 3SB, 24 April 1901, 395/2354, Box 2. A summary of Army operations can be found in "Telegraphic Record of Events Occurring in Third Separate Brigade, D.P., Commanded by Brig. Gen. J. F. Bell, U.S.A. From the Fourth of July 1901," Senate, *Affairs*, pp. 1653–1726; *WD* 1902 1:9:263–323.

163. Diary of Frederick Presher, 2 December 1901, Presher Papers; see also entries for 5 and 13 December 1902. Col. Almond B. Wells to AG, 3SB, 4 April 1902, 395/2354, Box 3; Lt. Ferdinand W. Kobbé to AG, 3SB, 1 January 1902, 395/4564, LS 183; Lt. Halsey E. Yates to Adj., San Pablo, 27 December 1901, 395/5099, San Pablo, Laguna, LR, 1901–2; Lt. Boss Reese to Adj., 19 February 1902, 395/2354, Box 2.

164. Lt. Samuel W. Widdifield to AG, 3SB, 15 January 1902, 395/2635, Box 2, no. 4179.

165. Telegraphic Circular no. 21, 24 December 1901, Senate, *Affairs*, pp. 1626–27; Lt. Samuel Van Leer to Col. Dougherty, 8 February 1902, 395/5295; "Report of Operations of the Garrison of Paete, Laguna, for the Month of December 1901," 395/2379, 1D, DSL, Reports of Operations.

166. Diary of Frederick Presher, 26 and 28 December 1902, Presher Papers.

167. Maj. Gen. Miguel Malvar, "The Reasons for My Change of Attitude," 16 April 1901, Taylor, *Philippine Insurrection*, Exhibit 1172, p. 89 GV. For other guerrilla testimony of the demoralization due to popular hostility, see "Testimony of Ladislao Magcansay," *Gardener Board*, pp. 412–13; Capt. Charles D. Rhodes to AG, 3SB, 4 March 1902, 395/2354, Box 2. For the work of volunteers, see Brig. Gen. Juan Cailles to P.L., San Pablo, 27 February 1902, 395/5101; Brig. Gen. J. Franklin Bell to

C.O.'s, Pueblos of Laguna, 27 February 1902, ibid.; Brig. Gen. J. Franklin Bell to C.O., Calamba, 6 April 1902, 395/3287; Capt. William T. Johnston and Capt. Charles D. Rhodes to Brig. Gen. J. Franklin Bell, 16 April 1902, 395/2635, Box 8, no. 9396; Maj. Gen. Adna R. Chaffee to Maj. Gen. Henry C. Corbin, 20 March 1902, Corbin Papers; Lt. William M. Fasset to Adj., Batangas, 16 April 1902, 395/2354, Box 3; Lt. Frank Skievaski to AG, 3SB, 13 February 1902, 391/2082, 11th Company, Native Scouts (Macabebes), LS Bk 1, LS 18.

168. Brig. Gen. J. Franklin Bell to Maj. Gen. Adna R. Chaffee, encl. in Maj. Gen. Adna R. Chaffee to Maj. Gen. Henry C. Corbin, 17 March 1902, Corbin Papers; Capt. Henry T. Allen to William H. Taft, 24 January 1902, Allen Papers, Box 7.

169. Capt. Charles D. Rhodes to AG, 3SB, 4 March 1902, 395/2354, Box 2; Maj. Gen. Adna R. Chaffee to AG, Washington, D.C., 14 January 1901, *CWS*, 2:1310.

170. Col. Jacob Kline to AG, 3SB, 19 February 1902, 395/3284, LS 71.

171. Ileto, *Payson and Revolution*, p. 209.

172. May, "Filipino Resistance," p. 551.

173. "Testimony of Maj. Gen. Miguel Malvar," *Gardener Board*, pp. 651–52. See also Maj. Gen. Miguel Malvar, "The Reasons for My Change of Attitude," 16 April 1901, Taylor, *Philippine Insurrection*, Exhibit 1172, p. 89 GV.

174. *WD* 1902 1:9:284–85.

175. Col. Cornelius Gardener to the Civil Governor of the Philippine Islands, 16 December 1901, Senate, *Affairs*, p. 884.

176. Schumacher, *Revolutionary Clergy*, p. 134. Wolff, *Little Brown Brother*, pp. 358–59; Roth, *Muddy Glory*, pp. 81–95; Miller, *"Benevolent Assimilation,"* pp. 207–9.

177. Gates, *Schoolbooks and Krags*, p. 263; White, "Pacification," p. 444; Senate, *Affairs*, p. 2855.

178. May, "Private Presher," p. 56.

179. For American civil and military views on the necessity of the campaign, see Capt. Henry T. Allen to Maj. Gen. Adna R. Chaffee, 1 February 1902 and Capt. Henry T. Allen to Sen. Jeremiah Beveridge, 13 February 1902, in Allen Papers, Box 7; Luke Wright to William H. Taft, 19 April 1902, Root Papers, Box 164; "Report of General A. E. Bates. 1902," 94/443763; Senate, *Affairs*, p. 2861. For the guerrilla testimonials as to the necessity of the campaign, see "Testimony of Eustacio Maloles," p. 105; "Testimony of Lt. Col. Noberto Mayo," p. 127; "Testimony of Lt. Col. Bernardo Marques," p. 148; "Testimony of Col. Ladislao Magcansay," pp. 412–13; "Testimony of Genero Brillante," p. 482; "Testimony of Maj. Gen. Miguel Malvar," pp. 651–52, all in *Gardener Board*.

180. Senate, *Affairs*, p. 2850.

181. Gates, *Schoolbooks and Krags*, p. 288.

Bibliography

U.S. Government Record Groups

National Archives
    Suitland, Md.
        Record Group 153. Records of the Judge Advocate General's Office.
    Washington, D.C.
        Record Group 94. Records of the Adjutant General's Office.
        Record Group 159. Records of the Office of the Inspector General.
        Record Group 350. Records of the Bureau of Insular Affairs.
        Record Group 391. Records of U.S. Army Mobile Units, 1821–1942.
        Record Group 395. Records of U.S. Army Overseas Operations and Commands, 1898–1942.

U.S. Government Records on Microfilm

National Archives
    Washington, D.C.
        Microcopy 254. Philippine Insurgent Records. This includes the galley proofs of John R. M. Taylor's *History of the Philippine Insurrection Against the United States, 1898–1903: A Compilation of Documents and Introduction*. Washington, D.C., 1906.
        Microcopy 665. Returns from Regular Army Infantry Regiments, June 1821–December 1916.
        Microcopy 774. Returns from Regular Army Cavalry Regiments, 1833–1916.

Manuscript Collections

Carlisle Barracks, Pa.
    U.S. Army Military History Institute
        Matthew A. Batson Papers
        William C. Brown Papers

Delphey T. E. Casteel Papers
John L. Jordan Papers (photocopies of originals at Tennessee State Library and
    Archives, Nashville)
William A. Kobbé Papers
Samuel Lyon Papers
Frederick Presher Papers
Matthew F. Steele Papers
Samuel B. M. Young Papers
Cincinnati, Ohio
  Cincinnati Historical Society
    Arthur Valentine Papers
Durham, N.C.
  Duke University
    Lyman W. V. Kennon Papers
Topeka, Kans.
  Kansas State Historical Society
    Frederick Funston Papers
Washington, D.C.
  Library of Congress
    Henry T. Allen Papers
    Robert L. Bullard Papers
    Henry C. Corbin Papers
    George V. H. Mosely Papers
    Charles D. Rhodes Papers
    Theodore Roosevelt Papers
    Elihu Root Papers
    William H. Taft Papers

Letters, Diaries, Interviews, Histories, Manuscripts

Austin, Tex.
  Texas State Archives
    Frank A. Musgrove, "A Brief History of the 33rd U.S.V.I."
Carlisle Barracks, Pa.
  U.S. Army Military History Institute
    Frederick Arnold Diary. 4th U.S. Cavalry Box.
    Nelson E. Bishop Letters. 39th U.S.V. Infantry Box.
    Harry W. Bliss Letters. 11th U.S.V. Cavalry Box.
    Howard I. Caster Manuscript. 47th U.S.V. Infantry Box.
    Homer V. Cook Manuscript. 1st U.S. Cavalry Box.
    Matthew E. Cook Typescript. 30th U.S.V. Infantry Box.
    Frank A. Francois Diary. 45th U.S.V. Infantry Box.
    Claude E. Harris Manuscript. 11th U.S.V. Cavalry Box.
    "Personal Sketch of Wm. E. Birkhimer." Harry M. Moot File. 28th U.S.V. In-
        fantry Box.

Milton Nixon Letters. 33d U.S.V. Infantry Box.

Arthur W. Orton, "Memoirs." Joseph H. Schurr File. 39th U.S.V. Infantry Box.

Arthur W. Orton, Fred Shadell, and C. Duffy Lewis, "An Up to Date History of the 39th Vol. Inf. (Bullard's Indians)." Joseph H. Schurr File. 39th U.S.V. Infantry Box.

Charles E. Portenier Diary. 28th U.S.V. Infantry Box.

Frank R. Schallert Manuscript. 45th U.S.V. Infantry Box.

Oliver Tafton Manuscript. 33d U.S.V. Infantry Box.

Lewis A. Wheeler Diary and Letters. 47th U.S.V. Infantry Box.

Washington, D.C.

  U.S. Navy Historical Center

  U.S. Navy, ZE Files, "Philippine Islands."

Veterans' Questionnaires

Carlisle Barracks, Pa.

  U.S. Army Military History Institute

    Charles F. Anderson Questionnaire. 45th U.S.V. Infantry Box.

    Lawrence Benton Questionnaire. 33d U.S.V. Infantry Box.

    Charles E. Brossman Questionnaire. 47th U.S.V. Infantry Box.

    George O. Burwell Questionnaire. 5th U.S. Infantry Box.

    George R. Clements Questionnaire. 47th U.S.V. Infantry Box.

    James F. Edwards Questionnaire. 38th U.S.V. Infantry Box.

    Joseph W. Ford Questionnaire. 11th U.S.V. Cavalry Box.

    Claude E. Harris Questionnaire. 11th U.S.V. Cavalry Box.

    Jesse Ives Questionnaire. 38th U.S.V. Infantry Box.

    Jesse A. Jackson Questionnaire. 45th U.S.V. Infantry Box.

    Edward Johnson Questionnaire. 11th U.S.V. Cavalry Box.

    Soloman O. Kenyon Questionnaire. 38th U.S.V. Infantry Box.

    Peter Konrad Questionnaire. 5th U.S. Infantry Box.

    Bernard Lichtig Questionnaire. 30th U.S.V. Infantry Box.

    Robert L. McNair Questionnaire. 39th U.S.V. Infantry Box.

    Richard Mason Questionnaire. 45th U.S.V. Infantry Box.

    James A. Miller Questionnaire. 34th U.S.V. Infantry Box.

    Elston Mitchell Questionnaire. 5th U.S. Infantry Box.

    Purl A. Mulkey Questionnaire. 45th U.S.V. Infantry Box.

    Myron Murgatroyd Questionnaire. 30th U.S.V. Infantry Box.

    Peder Pederson Questionnaire. 34th U.S.V. Infantry Box.

    Frank L. Rose Questionnaire. 30th U.S.V. Infantry Box.

    Frank R. Schallert Questionnaire. 45th U.S.V. Infantry Box.

    William Weintz Questionnaire. 28th U.S.V. Infantry Box.

    Lewis A. Wheeler Questionnaire. 47th U.S.V. Infantry Box.

Government Publications and Documents

U.S. Army. Adjutant General's Office.
  *Correspondence Relating to the War with Spain and Conditions Growing out of the Same
    Including the Insurrection in the Philippine Islands and the China Relief Expedition,
    Between the Adjutant-General of the Army and Military Commanders in the United
    States, Cuba, Porto Rico, China, and the Philippine Islands from April 15, 1898 to
    July 30, 1902.* Washington, D.C.: Government Printing Office, 1902.
U.S. Congress. House.
  Annual Reports of the War Department for the Fiscal Year Ending June 30, 1898.
    House Doc. 4073, 55th Congress, 3d Session, 1898.
  Annual Reports of the Navy Department for the Fiscal Year Ending June 30, 1898.
    House Doc. 3754, 55th Congress, 3d Session, 1898.
  Annual Reports of the War Department for the Fiscal Year Ending June 30, 1899.
    House Doc. 3902, 56th Congress, 1st Session, 1899.
  Annual Reports of the War Department for the Fiscal Year Ending June 30, 1900.
    House Doc. 2, 56th Congress, 2d Session, 1900.
U.S. Congress. Senate.
  *Affairs in the Philippine Islands. Hearing before the Committee on the Philippines of the
    United States Senate.* S. Doc. 331, 57th Congress, 1st Session, 1902.
  Charges of Cruelty, Etc. to the Natives of the Philippines. S. Doc. 205, 57th Congress,
    1st Session, 1902.
  Report of the Philippine Commission. S. Doc. 112, 56th Congress, 2d Session, 1901.
U.S. Special Mission on Investigation to the Philippine Islands.
  Report of U.S. Special Mission on Investigation to the Philippine Islands. Washington,
    D.C.: Government Printing Office, 1921.
U.S. War Department.
  Annual Reports of the War Department for the Fiscal Year Ending June 30, 1899. Vol. 1
    part 1. Washington, D.C.: Government Printing Office, 1899.
  Annual Reports of the War Department for the Fiscal Year Ending June 30, 1899. Vol. 1
    part 4. Washington, D.C.: Government Printing Office, 1899.
  Annual Reports of the War Department for the Fiscal Year Ending June 30, 1899. Vol. 1
    part 5. Washington, D.C.: Government Printing Office, 1899.
  Annual Reports of the War Department for the Fiscal Year Ending June 30, 1900. Vol. 1
    part 2. Washington, D.C.: Government Printing Office, 1900.
  Annual Reports of the War Department for the Fiscal Year Ending June 30, 1900. Vol. 1
    part 4. Washington, D.C.: Government Printing Office, 1900.
  Annual Reports of the War Department for the Fiscal Year Ending June 30, 1900. Vol. 1
    part 5. Washington, D.C.: Government Printing Office, 1900.
  Annual Reports of the War Department for the Fiscal Year Ending June 30, 1900. Vol. 1
    part 6. Washington, D.C.: Government Printing Office, 1900.
  Annual Reports of the War Department for the Fiscal Year Ending June 30, 1900. Vol. 1
    part 7. Washington, D.C.: Government Printing Office, 1900.
  Annual Reports of the War Department for the Fiscal Year Ending June 30, 1900. Vol. 1
    part 8. Washington, D.C.: Government Printing Office, 1900.
  Annual Reports of the War Department for the Fiscal Year Ending June 30, 1901. Vol. 1
    part 4. Washington, D.C.: Government Printing Office, 1901.

Annual Reports of the War Department for the Fiscal Year Ending June 30, 1901. Vol. 1 part 5. Washington, D.C.: Government Printing Office, 1901.

Annual Reports of the War Department for the Fiscal Year Ending June 30, 1901. Vol. 1 part 7. Washington, D.C.: Government Printing Office, 1901.

Annual Reports of the War Department for the Fiscal Year Ending June 30, 1901. Vol. 1 part 8. Washington, D.C.: Government Printing Office, 1901.

Annual Reports of the War Department for the Fiscal Year Ending June 30, 1902. Vol. 1 part 9. Washington, D.C.: Government Printing Office, 1902.

A Pronouncing Gazetteer and Geographical Dictionary of the Philippine Islands, United States of America, with Maps, Charts, and Illustrations. Also the Law of Civil Government in the Philippine Islands Passed by Congress and Approved by the President July 1, 1902, with a Complete Index. Washington, D.C.: Government Printing Office, 1902.

Newspapers

Army and Navy Journal
Chicago Tribune
Columbus Dispatch
Indiana Progress
Jawbone
Manila Times
New York Times

Books

Achútegui, Pedro S., and Bernad, Miguel A. *Aguinaldo and the Revolution of 1896: A Documentary History.* Manila: Ateneo de Manila Press, 1972.

Agoncillo, Teodoro A. *Malolos: The Crisis of the Republic.* Quezon City, P.I.: University of the Philippines Press, 1960.

_____. *The Revolt of the Masses: The Story of Bonifacio and the Katipunan.* Manila: University of the Philippines Press, 1956.

Aguinaldo, Emilio, and Pacis, Victor A. *A Second Look at America.* New York: Robert Speller and Sons, 1957.

Alejandrino, José. *The Price of Freedom.* Manila: M. Colocol, 1949.

Andrews, William R. *The Village War: Vietnamese Communist Revolutionary Activities in Dinh Tuong.* Columbia: University of Missouri Press, 1973.

Ataviado, Elias. *Lucha y Libertad (Conmonitorio de la Revolución Filipina en las Tierras Albayanas), vol. 2: De febrero de 1899 a abril de 1900.* Manila: Commonwealth Press, 1941.

_____. *The Philippine Revolution in the Bicol Region, vol. 1: From August 1896 to January 1899.* Trans. by Juan T. Ataviado. Manila: Encal Press, 1953.

Baclagon, Uldarico. *Philippine Campaigns.* Manila: Liwayway Publishers, 1952.

Bain, David H. *Sitting in Darkness: Americans in the Philippines.* Boston: Houghton Mifflin, 1984.

Baker, Charles F. *A History of the Thirtieth Infantry, U.S. Volunteers in the Philippine Insurrection, 1899–1901*. N.d., n.p.

Barrows, David P. *History of the Philippines*. New York: World Book Company, 1926.

Beisner, Robert L. *Twelve Against Empire: The Anti-Imperialists, 1898–1900*. New York: McGraw-Hill, 1968.

Berman, Paul. *Revolutionary Organization: Institution-Building Within the People's Liberation Armed Forces*. Lexington, Mass.: Lexington Books, 1974.

Bisbee, William H. *Through Four American Wars*. Boston: Meadow, 1931.

Blount, James H. *The American Occupation of the Philippines, 1898–1912*. New York: G. P. Putnam's Sons, 1912.

Booth, Ewing E. *My Observations and Experiences in the United States Army*. N.p., 1944.

Braisted, William R. *The United States Navy in the Pacific, 1897–1909*. Austin: University of Texas Press, 1958.

Brown, John C. *Diary of a Soldier in the Philippines*. Portland, Maine: n.p., 1901.

Buck, Beaumont B. *Memories of Peace and War*. San Antonio, Tex.: Naylor, 1935.

Callwell, Charles E. *Small Wars: Their Principles and Practice*. 2d ed. London: Harrison and Sons, 1906.

Carter, William H. *The Life of Lt. General Chaffee*. Chicago: University of Chicago Press, 1917.

Chailiand, Gerard, ed. *Guerrilla Strategies: An Historical Anthology from the Long March to Afghanistan*. Berkeley: University of California Press, 1982.

Coffman, Edward M. *The Hilt of the Sword: The Career of Peyton C. March*. Madison: University of Wisconsin Press, 1966.

Constantino, Renato. *A History of the Philippines*. New York: Monthly Review Press, 1975.

Cosmas, Graham. *An Army for Empire: The United States Army and the Spanish-American War*. Columbia: University of Missouri Press, 1971.

Crane, Charles J. *The Experiences of a Colonel of Infantry*. New York: Knickerbocker Press, 1923.

Crouch, Thomas W. *A Yankee Guerrillero: Frederick Funston and the Cuban Insurrection, 1896–1897*. Memphis: Memphis State University Press, 1975.

Cullum, George W. *Biographical Registrar of the Officers and Graduates of the U.S. Military Academy*. Cambridge, Mass.: Riverside Press, 1901.

Cushner, Nicholas. *Spain in the Philippines from Conquest to Revolution*. Manila: Ateneo de Manila University Press, 1975.

———. *Landed Estates in the Colonial Philippines*. New Haven: Yale University Press, 1976.

Dunley, Thomas W. *Wolves for the Blue Soldiers: Indian Scouts and Auxiliaries with the United States Army, 1860–90*. Lincoln: University of Nebraska Press, 1982.

Eckstein, Harry, ed. *Internal War: Problems and Approaches*. London: Free Press of Glencoe, 1964.

Elliott, Charles B. *The Philippines to the End of the Military Regime*. Indianapolis: Bobbs-Merrill, 1917.

Eyot, Canning, ed. *The Story of the Lopez Family: A Page from the History of the War in the Philippines*. Boston: James H. West, 1904.

Fernandez, Leandro H. *The Philippine Republic.* New York: Columbia University Press, 1926.

Forbes, W. Cameron. *The Philippine Islands.* Cambridge, Mass.: Riverside Press, 1928.

Freedham, Needom N. *A Soldier in the Philippines.* New York: F. Tennyson, 1901.

Funston, Frederick. *Memories of Two Wars.* London: Constable, 1912.

Galang, Zolio, ed. *The Encyclopedia of the Philippines, vol. 16: History.* Manila: Exequiel Floro, 1957.

Ganoe, William A. *The History of the United States Army.* New York: Appleton-Century, 1942.

Ganzhorn, Jack. *I've Killed Men: An Epic of Early Arizona.* London: Robert Hale, 1940.

Gates, John M. *Schoolbooks and Krags: The United States Army in the Philippines, 1899–1902.* Westport, Conn.: Greenwood Press, 1975.

Gatewood, Willard B., Jr. *Black Americans and the White Man's Burden, 1898–1903.* Urbana: University of Illinois Press, 1975.

_____. *Smoked Yankees and the Struggle for Empire: Letters from Negro Soldiers, 1898–1902.* Urbana: University of Illinois Press, 1971.

Gleeck, Lewis E. *Laguna in American Times: Coconuts and Revolutionarios.* Manila: Historical Conservation Society, 1981.

_____. *Nueva Ecija in American Times: Homesteaders, Hacendros, and Politicos.* Manila: Historical Conservation Society, 1981.

Gould, Lewis L. *The Spanish–American War and President McKinley.* Lawrence, Kans.: University Press of Kansas, 1980.

Graff, Henry F. *American Imperialism and the Philippine Insurrection.* Boston: Little Brown, 1969.

Hartigan, Richard S. *Lieber's Code and the Law of War.* Chicago: Precedent Press, 1983.

Herrinton, Stuart A. *Silence Was a Weapon: The Vietnam War in the Villages.* Novalito, Calif.: Presidio Press, 1982.

Ileto, Renaldo C. *Payson and Revolution: Popular Movements in the Philippines, 1840–1910.* Manila: Ateneo de Manila University Press, 1979.

Jessup, Philip C. *Elihu Root.* New York: Dodd, Mead, 1938.

Kalaw, Maximo. *The Development of Philippine Politics.* Manila: Escolta Publishers, 1927.

Kalaw, Teodoro M. *An Acceptable Holocaust: Life and Death of a Boy-General.* Trans. by M. A. Foronda. Manila: National Historical Commission, 1974.

Kerkvliet, Benedict. *The Huk Rebellion: A Study of Peasant Revolt in the Philippines.* Berkeley: University of California Press, 1977.

Kitson, Frank. *Low Intensity Operations.* London: Faber and Faber, 1971.

Kohr, Herbert O. *Around the World With Uncle Sam or Six Years in the United States Army.* Ulrichsville, Ohio: n.p., 1907.

LaFeber, Walter. *The New Empire: An Interpretation of American Expansion, 1860–1898.* Ithaca, N.Y.: Cornell University Press, 1963.

Laquer, Walter. *Guerrilla: A Historical and Critical Study.* London: Weidenfeld and Nicholson, 1977.

Larkin, John A. *The Pampangans: Colonial Society in a Philippine Province.* Berkeley: University of California Press, 1972.

Leckie, Robert. *The Wars of America.* Rev. ed. New York: Harper and Row, 1981.

Leech, Margaret. *In the Days of McKinley.* New York: Harper and Brothers, 1959.

LeRoy, James A. *The Americans in the Philippines.* 2 vols. Boston: Houghton Mifflin, 1915.

Linninger, Clarence. *The Best War at the Time.* New York: Robert Speller and Sons, 1964.

McCuen, John J. *The Art of Counter-Revolutionary War: The Strategy of Counter-insurgency.* London: Faber and Faber, 1966.

McCutcheon, John T. *Drawn from Memory.* Indianapolis: Bobbs-Merrill, 1950.

Majul, Cesar. *Mabini and the Philippine Revolution.* Quezon City, P.I.: University of the Philippines Press, 1960.

————. *Muslims in the Philippines.* Quezon City, P.I.: University of the Philippines Press, 1973.

Manuel, E. Arsenio. *Dictionary of Philippine Biography.* 2 vols. Quezon City, P.I.: Filipiana Productions, 1970.

May, Ernest R. *Imperial Democracy: The Emergence of America as a Great Power.* New York: Harcourt, Brace and World, 1961.

Mayo, Katherine. *The Isles of Fear: The Truth About the Philippines.* New York: Harcourt, Brace and Co., 1924.

Miller, Stuart C. *"Benevolent Assimilation": The American Conquest of the Philippines, 1899–1903.* New Haven: Yale University Press, 1983.

Millett, Allan R. *The General: Robert L. Bullard and Officership in the United States Army, 1881–1925.* Westport, Conn.: Greenwood Press, 1975.

Morgan, H. Wayne. *William McKinley and His America.* Syracuse, N.Y.: Syracuse University Press, 1963.

Palmer, Frederick. *With My Own Eyes: A Personal Study of Battle Years.* Indianapolis: Bobbs-Merrill, 1932.

Parker, James. *The Old Army: Memories, 1872–1918.* Philadelphia: Dorrance, 1929.

Phelan, John L. *The Hispanization of the Philippines.* Madison: University of Wisconsin Press, 1959.

Pike, Douglas. *Viet Cong: The Organization and Techniques of the National Liberation Front of South Vietnam.* Cambridge, Mass.: M. I. T. Press, 1966.

Robinson, Albert G. *The Philippines: The War and the People.* New York: McClure, Phillips, 1901.

Rodney, George B. *As A Cavalryman Remembers.* Caldwell, Idaho: Caxton Printers, 1944.

Roth, Dennis M. *The Friar Estates of the Philippines.* Albuquerque: University of New Mexico Press, 1977.

Roth, Russell. *Muddy Glory: America's 'Indian Wars' in the Philippines.* West Hanover, Mass.: Christopher Publishing House, 1981.

Salamanca, Bonifacio S. *The Filipino Reaction to American Rule, 1901–1913.* Quezon City, P.I.: New Day Publishers, 1984.

Sawyer, Frederick. *Sons of Gunboats.* Annapolis, Md.: Naval Institute Press, 1946.

Schott, Joseph. *The Ordeal of Samar.* Indianapolis: Bobbs-Merrill, 1964.

Schumacher, John N. *Revolutionary Clergy: The Filipino Clergy and the Nationalist Movement, 1850–1903.* Manila: Ateneo de Manila University Press, 1981.

Sefton, James E. *The United States Army and Reconstruction, 1865–1877.* Baton Rouge: Louisiana State University Press, 1967.

Sexton, William T. *Soldiers in the Sun: An Adventure in Imperialism.* Harrisburg, Pa.: Military Service Publishing, 1939.

Shirmer, Daniel B. *Republic or Empire: American Resistance to Philippine War.* Cambridge, Mass.: Schenkman, 1972.

Spector, Ronald. *Admiral of the New Empire: The Life and Career of George Dewey.* Baton Rouge: Louisiana State University Press, 1974.

Stanley, Peter, ed. *Reappraising an Empire: New Perspectives of Philippine-American History.* Cambridge: Harvard University Press, 1984.

Steinberg, David J. *The Philippines: A Singular and a Plural Place.* Boulder, Colo.: Westview Press, 1982.

_____. *Philippine Collaboration in World War II.* Ann Arbor: University of Michigan Press, 1967.

Storey, Moorfield, and Lichauco, Marcial. *The Conquest of the Philippines by the United States, 1898–1925.* New York: Knickerbocker Press, 1926.

Sturtevant, David R. *Popular Uprisings in the Philippines, 1840–1940.* Ithaca, N.Y.: Cornell University Press, 1976.

Thompson, Robert. *Defeating Communist Insurgency: The Lessons of Malaya and Vietnam.* New York: Frederick A. Praeger, 1966.

Trask, David F. *The War with Spain in 1898.* New York: Macmillan, 1981.

Twichell, Heath Jr. *Allen: The Biography of an Army Officer 1859–1930.* New Brunswick: Rutgers University Press, 1974.

Villamor, Juan. *Inedita Cronica de la Guerra Americano-Filipina en el Norte de Luzon, 1899–1901.* Manila: Juan Fajardo, 1924.

Walton, John. *Reluctant Rebels: Comparative Studies of Revolution and Underdevelopment.* New York: Columbia University Press, 1984.

Welch, Richard C. *Response to Imperialism: The United States and the Philippine-American War, 1899–1902.* Chapel Hill: University of North Carolina Press, 1979.

Wernstedt, Frederick L., and Spencer, J. E. *The Philippine Island World: A Physical, Cultural, and Regional Geography.* Berkeley: University of California Press, 1967.

Wickberg, Edgar. *The Chinese in Philippine Life, 1850–1900.* New Haven: Yale University Press, 1965.

Wilcox, Marion, ed. *Harper's History of the War in the Philippines.* New York: Harper Bros., 1900.

Wilcox, Willis B. *Through Luzon on Highways and Byways.* Philadelphia: Franklin, 1901.

Williams, T. Harry. *The History of American Wars from 1745 to 1918.* New York: Alfred A. Knopf, 1981.

Wolff, Leon. *Little Brown Brother: How the United States Purchased and Pacified the Philippine Islands at the Century's Turn.* Garden City, N.Y.: Doubleday, 1961.

Worcester, Dean. *The Philippines Past and Present.* New York: Macmillan, 1930.

Yap-Diangco. *The Philippine Guerrilla Tradition.* Manila: MCS Enterprises, 1971.

Zaide, Gregorio F. *The Philippine Revolution.* Manila: Modern Book Co., 1968.

Articles

Anon. "The Soldier Teacher in the Philippines." *Harpers Weekly* 46 (18 January 1902): 74.

Betts, Arlington U. "The Memoirs of Arlington Betts." In Arlington Betts, Elmer Madsen, and Victor Buencamino. *Recollections of the American Regime*. Manila: Historical Conservation Society, 1973.

Bolton, Grania. "Military Diplomacy and National Liberation." *Military Affairs* 36 (1972): 99–104.

Boughton, Donald H. "How Soldiers Have Rule in the Philippines." *International Quarterly* (December–March 1902): 222–23.

Burdett, Thomas F. "A New Evaluation of General Otis' Leadership in the Philippines." *Military Review* 55 (January 1975): 79–87.

Chaput, Donald. "Founding of the Leyte Scouts." *Leyte-Samar Studies* 9 (1975): 5–10.

————. "Leyte Leadership in the Revolution: The Moxica-Lukban Issue." *Leyte-Samar Studies* 9 (1975): 3–12.

Coffman, Edward M. "Batson of the Philippine Scouts." *Parameters* 7 (1977): 68–72.

Cohran, William B. "The Wanderings of Emilio Aguinaldo." *Journal of the Military Service Institution* 34 (May–June 1904): 454–66.

Crane, Charles J. "The Fighting Tactics of Filipinos." *Journal of the Military Service Institution* 30 (July 1902): 499–507.

Farrell, John T. "An Abandoned Approach to Philippine History: John R. M. Taylor and the Philippine Insurgent Records." *Catholic Historical Review* 39 (January 1954): 385–407.

Fritz, David L. "Before the 'Howling Wilderness': The Military Career of Jacob Hurd Smith, 1862–1902." *Military Affairs* 43 (December 1979): 186–90.

Ganley, Eugene F. "Mountain Chase." *Military Affairs* 34 (February 1961): 203–21.

Gates, John M. "Indians and Insurrectos: The U.S. Army's Experience with Insurgency." *Parameters* 13 (March 1983): 59–68.

————. "The Pacification of the Philippines." *Proceedings of the 9th Military History Symposium*. U.S. Air Force Academy. Washington, D.C.: Government Printing Office, 1980, pp. 79–91.

————. "The Philippines and Vietnam: Another False Analogy." *Asian Studies* 10 (1972): 64–76.

————. "War-Related Deaths in the Philippines." *Pacific Historical Review* 53 (November 1983): 367–78.

Guerrero, Milagros C. "Understanding Philippine Revolutionary Mentality." *Philippine Studies* 29 (1981): 240–56.

Holli, Melvin G. "A View of the American Campaign Against the 'Filipino Insurgents': 1900." *Philippine Studies* 17 (1969): 97–111.

Hunt, Michael H. "Resistance and Collaboration in the American Empire, 1898–1903: An Overview." *Pacific Historical Review* 48 (November 1979): 467–71.

Ileto, Reynaldo C. "Toward a Local History of the Philippine-American War: The

Case of Tiaong, Tayabas (Quezon) Province, 1901–1902." *Journal of History* 27 (January–December 1982): 67–79.

Kennon, Lyman W. V. "The Katipunan of the Philippines." *North American Review* 173 (1901): 208–20.

Landor, A. Henry. "The American Soldier as He Is." *North American Review* 178 (1904): 897–903.

Larkin, John A. "Philippine History Reconsidered: A Socioeconomic Perspective." *American Historical Review* 87 (June 1982): 613–24.

Lear, Elmer W. "The Western Leyte Guerrilla Warfare Forces: A Case Study in the Non-Legitimation of a Guerrilla Organization." *Journal of Southeast Asian History* 9 (March 1968): 69–94.

Linn, Brian M. "Guerrilla Fighter: Frederick Funston in the Philippines, 1900–1901." *Kansas History* 10 (Spring 1987): 2–16.

_____. "Pacification in Northwestern Luzon: An American Regiment in the Philippine-American War, 1899–1901." *Pilipinas* 3 (December 1982): 14–25.

_____. "Provincial Pacification in the Philippines, 1900–1901: The First District, Department of Northern Luzon." *Military Affairs* 51 (April 1987): 62–66.

Majul, Cesar A. "Social Background of Revolution." *Asian Studies* 9 (April 1971): 1–23.

May, Glenn A. "Filipino Resistance to American Occupation: Batangas, 1899–1902." *Pacific Historical Review* 48 (November 1979): 531–56.

_____. "150,000 Missing Filipinos: A Demographic Crisis in Batangas, 1897–1903." *Annales de Démographie Historique* (1985): 215–43.

_____. "Private Presher and Sergeant Vergara: The Underside of the Philippine-American War." In Peter Stanley, ed., *Reappraising an Empire: New Perspectives on Philippine-American History*. Cambridge, Mass.: Committee on East-Asian Relations, 1984.

_____. "Resistance and Collaboration in the Philippine-American War: The Case of Batangas." *Journal of Southeast Asian Studies* 15 (March 1983): 69–90.

_____. "Why the United States Won the Philippine-American War, 1899–1902." *Pacific Historical Review* 52 (November 1982): 353–77.

_____. "The 'Zones' of Batangas." *Philippine Studies* 29 (1981): 89–103.

Owen, Norman G. "Winding Down the War in Albay, 1900–1903." *Pacific Historical Review* 48 (November 1979): 557–89.

Palmer, Frederick. "White Man and Brown Man in the Philippines." *Scribners Magazine* 27 (January–June 1900): 73–86.

Raines, Edgar F. "Major General Franklin Bell, U.S.A.: The Education of A Soldier." *Register of the Kentucky Historical Society* 83 (Autumn 1985): 315–46.

Robinson, Michael C., and Schubert, Frank N. "David Fagen: An Afro-American Rebel in the Philippines." *Pacific Historical Review* 44 (February 1975): 68–83.

Sand-30 [pseud.] "Trench, Parapet, or 'the Open.'" *Journal of the Military Service Institution* 30 (July 1902): 471–87.

Schumacher, John N. "Recent Perspectives on the Revolution." *Philippine Studies* 30 (1982): 445–92.

Scott, William S. "Struggle for Independence in Candon." *Cracks in the Parchment*

Curtain and Other Essays in Philippine History. Quezon City, P.I.: New Day Publishers, 1982.

Schreurs, Peter. "Surigao, from General Aguinaldo to General Bates, 1898–1900." *Philippine Quarterly of Culture and Society* 11 (1983): 57–68.

Steinberg, David J. "An Ambiguous Legacy: Years at War in the Philippines." *Pacific Affairs* 45 (1972): 167–79.

Turnbull, Wilfrid. "Reminiscences of an Army Surgeon in Cuba and the Philippines." *Bulletin of the American Historical Collection* 2 (April 1974): 31–49.

Ward, John A. "The Use of Native Troops in Our New Possessions." *Journal of the Military Service Institution* 31 (November 1902): 793–805.

Welch, Richard E. "American Atrocities in the Philippines: The Challenge and the Response." *Pacific Historical Review* 43 (May 1974): 233–53.

———. "The Philippine Insurrection and the American Press." *Historian* 36 (November 1973): 34–51.

White, Herbert A. "The Pacification of Batangas." *International Quarterly* 7 (June–September 1903): 431–44.

Wildman, Edwin. "The Hemp Industry of the Philippines." *Harpers* 44 (1 September 1900): 819.

Dissertations

Borromeo, Soledad M. "El Cadiz Filipino: Colonial Cavite, 1571–1896." Ph.D. dissertation, University of California at Berkeley, 1973.

Coats, George Y. "The Philippine Constabulary: 1901–1917." Ph.D. dissertation, Ohio State University, 1968.

Crouch, Thomas W. "The Making of a Soldier: The Career of Frederick Funston, 1865–1902." Ph.D. dissertation, University of Texas at Austin, 1969.

Delgado, Octavio A. "The Spanish Army in Cuba, 1868–1898: An Institutional Study." Ph.D. dissertation, Columbia University, 1981.

Donovan, Consorcia L. "The Philippine Revolution: A 'Decolonized' Version." Ph.D. dissertation, Claremont Graduate School, 1976.

Edgerton, Ronald K. "The Politics of Reconstruction in the Philippines, 1945–1948." Ph.D. dissertation, University of Michigan, 1977.

Figuracion, Melanio S. "The Background and Development of Philippine Nationalism, 1872–1899." Ph.D. dissertation, University of Pittsburgh, 1958.

Fritz, David L. "The Philippine Question: American Civil/Military Policy in the Philippines, 1893–1905." Ph.D. dissertation, University of Texas at Austin, 1977.

Guerrero, Milagros C. "Luzon at War: Contradictions in Philippine Society, 1898–1902," Ph.D. dissertation, University of Michigan, 1977.

Mulrooney, Virginia F. "No Victor, No Vanquished: United States Military Government in the Philippine Islands, 1898–1901." Ph.D. dissertation, University of California at Los Angeles, 1975.

Oades, Rizalino. "The Social and Economic Background of Philippine Nationalism, 1830–1892." Ph.D. dissertation, University of Hawaii at Manoa, 1974.

Owen, Norman G. "Kabikolan in the Nineteenth Century: Socio-economic Change in the Provincial Philippines." Ph.D. dissertation, University of Michigan, 1976.

Ragsdale, Jane S. "Coping with the Yankees: The Filipino Elite, 1898–1903." Ph.D. dissertation, University of Wisconsin at Madison, 1974.

Raines, Edgar F. "Major General J. Franklin Bell and Military Reform: The Chief of Staff Years, 1906–1910." Ph.D. dissertation, University of Wisconsin at Madison, 1977.

Williams, Vernon L. "The U.S. Navy in the Philippine Insurrection and Subsequent Native Unrest, 1898–1906." Ph.D. dissertation, Texas A & M University, 1985.

Woolard, James R. "The Philippine Scouts: The Development of America's Colonial Army." Ph.D. dissertation, Ohio State University, 1975.

Index

Printed in the United States
29770LVS00005B/55-75